WORLD WHITEWATER
A Global Guide for River Runners

MAPS 88
83
66
Key Map 5 3

Jim Cassady and Dan Dunlap

RAGGED MOUNTAIN PRESS/MCGRAW-HILL
Camden, Maine • New York • San Francisco • Washington, D.C. •
Auckland • Bogotá • Caracas • Lisbon • London • Madrid • Mexico City •
Milan • Montreal • New Delhi • San Juan • Singapore • Sydney •
Tokyo • Toronto

Dedication

To Gerard Aglioni, Brian Judd,

Michael Ghiglieri, Bill McGinnis, Martha Dunlap,

our parents, and to the memory of Melissa Toben and John Foss

Ragged Mountain Press

A Division of The McGraw-Hill Companies

Portions of "Tale of Two Kayaks" and "People" are reprinted with permission from *White Water Nepal.* "Journeys" is reprinted with permission by Lonely Planet Publications, copyright 1996.

10 9 8 7 6 5 4 3 2

Copyright © 1999 Ragged Mountain Press

Library of Congress Cataloging-in-Publication Data
Cassady, Jim
     World whitewater : a global guide for river runners / Jim Cassady and Dan Dunlap.
          p.   cm.
     Includes bibliographical references (p.   ) and index.
     ISBN 0-07-011962-7 (alk. paper)
     1. Boats and boating—Guidebooks.
2. Rivers—Recreational use—Guidebooks.
I. Dunlap, Dan.   II. Title.   III. Title: World whitewater.
GV775.C335   1999
797.1'22—dc1   98-53524
                                                     CIP

Questions regarding the content of this book should be addressed to
     Ragged Mountain Press
     P.O. Box 220
     Camden, ME 04843
     www.raggedmountainpress.com
Questions regarding the ordering of this book should be addressed to
     The McGraw-Hill Companies
     Customer Service Department
     P.O. Box 547
     Blacklick, OH 43004
     Retail customers: 1-800-262-4729
     Bookstores: 1-800-722-4726

This book is printed on 70# Citation, an acid-free paper.

Printed by Quebecor Printing Co., Fairfield, PA
Design by Patrice Rossi Calkin
Production by PD & PS, Sagamore Beach, MA
Project management by Janet Robbins
Production assistance by Shannon Thomas
Edited by Jeff Serena, Jon Eaton, Kate Mallien, and Jane Crosen

Photos courtesy the authors unless otherwise noted, see page 334.
Maps by Audre W. Newman, Ph.D. except for the following from *Western Whitewater;* pages 56, 66, 72, 78, 83 and 88.

TABLE OF CONTENTS

Preface

Why a guidebook to the whitewater rivers of the world? We must have asked ourselves that question more than a few times during the time it took to complete this project. What it really comes down to is that we feel it's important for more people to think about river running on more than a local or regional basis—to paint a "big picture" of the sport. Whitewater is a finite resource, and more of it disappears every year. We need a global community of river runners to protect the resource, to keep wild rivers and wild places for this and future generations. Besides, the world continues to shrink. We've all spent too much time listening to experienced travelers and guides talk about their far-off whitewater adventures. Now there's a convenient reference work to help us appreciate and join in the discussion, and to use in planning our own adventures on the world's greatest rivers.

We didn't run all the rivers listed in this book, but we gave it our best effort. We traveled to every continent except Antarctica and boated, or at least inspected, as many of the featured rivers as we could. But alas, we haven't even seen them all, and it's hard to imagine that any one person ever will. For that matter, running a river once, in one type of craft and in one set of conditions, doesn't make anybody an expert on that stretch of water. So to meet the challenge of writing a guidebook covering over 250 rivers on six continents, we turned to the real experts—the folks who regularly run and guide on them.

We combined our own first-hand information with an exhaustive review of all available printed sources and extensive interviews with local boaters. We circulated the drafts of every chapter to folks who are knowledgeable about the area, other guidebook authors, private boaters, commercial outfitters, and managing agencies. Where possible, we got in touch with river preservation groups for information on conservation issues. We used the mail, telephone, telefax, e-mail—everything but smoke signals—to locate readers and exchange information, but in the final analysis, this work would have been impossible without the Internet and the great number of boaters and outfitters connected together by computer.

Unfortunately, because of the scope of this work, it is necessarily selective; it is not a comprehensive review of all whitewater destinations. In many areas excellent local and regional guidebooks can be found which cover additional runs and often provide more detail. We encourage boaters to obtain and use these books (such as those listed under "Selected Sources" at the back of the book) in exploring areas new to them.

Certain criteria also governed our choice of rivers: the overall quality of the run; the popularity of usage of the run; geographical political balance to cover as many areas or countries as possible; and anticipated future importance of the run. It was not necessarily our intention to describe the top 250 or so whitewater rivers in the world. Rivers in areas such as the midwestern United States or the British Isles are included to convey the flavor of these regions, although even their local adherents would not compare them to the great runs of the Rocky Mountains or Alps.

Unfortunately, the extent of coverage of some areas does not match the quality of the rivers. Politics, lack of access, lack of good information or maps, and language translation problems combine to limit coverage in some areas such as China, Japan, and the republics of the former Soviet Union. We hope you and other readers will help us overcome these shortcomings and help us fill in information for future editions.

—*Dan Dunlap and Jim Cassady*

Acknowledgments

We extend our special thanks for the considerable time and effort contributed by Graeme Addison, David Allardice of Ultimate Descents, Jeff Bennett, Joe Dengler, Fryar Calhoun, Andrew Embick, John Foss, Richard L. Hopley, Peter Knowles, Dave Manby of Coruh River Trips, Paul Mason, Cam and Kate McLeay of Adrift, Paul Schelp, Stuart Smith, and Chris Speilus.

For providing or verifying information we would also like to thank Corran Addison, Alaska Discovery Expeditions, Jerry Albright, Bachti Ailsjahbana, Grant Ameral, Jeff Ansley, Lee Arbach, John Armstrong, Landis Arnold, Stephane Aubree, Chris Ault, Leo Azucena, Alex Bailey, Ajeet Bajaj, Art Balajthy, Richard Bangs, Rick Batts, Ken Bauer, Jeffrey R. Behan, Barend Bezuidenhout, Mike Birch, Tom Boise, David Bolling, Bob Booncock, Stan Boor, John Booth, Roger Boutel, Peik Borud, British Canoe Union, David Brown, David Browne, Ruse Brown of Chilliwack River Rafting, Chris Burrows, Bob Carlson, Bill Carrier, Lluis Rabamelda Casellas, Paulo Castillo, Jim Cavo, Loysha Cherepanov, Javier Chung of Tsanza Adventures, Brian Cooke, Genner Coronel, Bill Cross, Steve Currey, Steven H. Daniel, Leland Davis, Scott Davis of Ceiba Adventures, Scott Davis and David Laird at Sunwolf, Tim Delaney, Steve Dillick, Phillip "Tune" Doex, Tony Dorr, Jean-Francois Dreux, Bill Dvorak, Johm Eames of Rangitikei River Adventures, Jib Ellison, Steve Fairchild, Tatiana Feeka, Roberto Fernandez of Adventuras Naturales, Richard Fisher, Richard Flasher, Rafael Gallo, Casey Garland, Vladimir Gavrilov, Doug Geiger, Steve Givant, Bob Goodman, Rory Gotham, Janice Graham, Dan Grant, Mike Grant, Marco Gressi, Erika Grodzki, Dave Hammond, Diana Hanna, Caren Hansch, Tony Hansen, Mike Hartly, Roger Hardman, Hayak Rafting, Dave Heckman, Rob Heinemann, Gunter Hemmerbach, Bart Henderson of Chilkat Guides, Eric Hertz, Ken and Julie Kastoff, Mike Higgenson, Ed Hill RCMP, Conrad Hirsch, Jeff Hoffinberger, Lars Holbek, Ollie Hopwood at Kumsheen Rafting, Gudmund Host, Sean Hughes at Wedge Rafting, Hungry at Safaris Par Excellence, Jon Imhoff, Yerko Ivelicof Cascada Expediciones, Mark Joffe of Shearwater, Sean Jesson, Mark Joffe, Ken Johnson, Steve Jones, Bill Kallner of Whitewater Specialty, Jimmy Katz, Jerry Kauffman, Norman Kagen, Larry Kendall, Claudia Kerckhoff Van Wijk at the Madawaska Canoe Centre, Cliff Kingston, Peter Knowles, Leland Koll, Andy Kravitz, Yutaka Kyribara, Ann Labonte of North Country Rivers, Lane Larson, Ken Leonty of Ken's Kayak School, Clinton Lewis, Glenn Lewman, Melissa LiCon, Andy Linham, Tony Loro, Emmet Lucey, Ricardo Lugo, Mike Martell, Michael McColl, Bryan McCutchen of Rivers and Oceans, Tom McEwan, Bill McGinnis, Ray McLain, Orial Miribel, Mauricio Morales, Martin Moreno, Jack Morison, Manfred Moser, T. J. Mueller, Julie Munger, the fine folks at Nantahala Outdoor Center, Johannes Adriaan Neuwoudt, Audre and Roger Newman, Tom Nofsinger, Dick Norgaard, Malika Normandine, Richard Garth Oakden, Laura Ogden, Ken Olmsted, Conner O'Neill, Tim Palmer, Marcos Paredes, Bill Parks, Ken Panton, Tim Paton, Dan Patterson, Frazer Pearce, Greg Pearson of Adventure Canoeing, Mark Rainsley, Adrian J. Pullim, Tammy Ridenour, River Run Rafting Paddling Centre, Tom Robey, Perry Robertson, Mark Robbins, Beth Rundquist, Beth Rypins, Mike Sadan, Dennis Sammut, Toby Seiders, Kim Sexton, Lucretia Shroat, Paul Skoczylas, Harold and Sarah Skramstad, Jim Slade, Curt Smith, Monte Smith, Mowry Smith, Andy Sninsky, Peter

Spiers, Jacek Starzynski, Volker Stein, Cliff Stevens, Rebecca Strohmuller, Hanna Swazey of Endless River Adventures, Dr. Tim Tandrow, Beth Thomas, Jeff Thuot, Melissa Toben, Doug Trotter of Interior Expeditions, Diego Valsecchi, Steve van Beek, Wilko van den Bergh, John Volkman, Brad Voorman of New Wave Water Works, Spencer Waddell, Charlie Walbridge, Lawrence Walter, Gabi Kerwald Wanheimer, Whistler River Adventures, Dave Wilson, Jennifer Wilson, Les Wilson, Ethan Winston, Stuart Woodward, Chris Wrazej, David Wood, Dr. Jon Zamora, Roger Zbel, and Ulrich Zoelch.

Introduction

Because of the broad scope of this book, information for some of the regions and rivers is not as reliable as for others. Boaters should always make it a habit to verify published information locally.

Our selection of rivers was designed to appeal to all tastes and levels of boating expertise. We've included beginner to expert water, urban playspots and howling wilderness, one-hour lunchtime paddles and expeditionary runs. Kayakers, canoeists, and rafters will all find runs of special interest.

Locating and Hiring an Outfitter

Nearly all the rivers in this book can be run on tours arranged by professional outfitters who will provide guides, rafts or other craft, and support for kayak trips. In some areas, such as the United States, Canada, Europe, New Zealand, and Australia, or popular rivers in other areas, the adventure traveler has his or her own choice of outfitters on nearly every river. In other areas, such as Latin America or Africa, a few local outfitters may be found to take you on many of the runs. International companies such as U.S.–based Earth River Expedition, Mountain Travel–Sobek, and Ultimate Descents, and New Zealand–based Adrift Expeditions offer a variety of exotic trips, usually in remote areas.

Locating outfitters in heavily boated areas such as the United States, Canada, Europe, New Zealand, and Australia can be as simple as checking a phone book, tourist information agency, or travel agent. *American Outdoors* offers a list of outfitters in the United States, and managing agencies for state and national forests and parks often keep a list of licensed or authorized outfitters. The Internet is another good source, as many outfitters will maintain a home page on the World Wide Web, and a list of outfitters in most areas can be found by revving up the search engines and following links from page to page. Another valuable resource is the USnet newsgroup rec.boats.paddle and its diminutive European cousin, uk.rec.boats.paddle. Specific inquiries as to certain regions, rivers, or outfitters will generate useful responses but unfiltered feedback. These newsgroups are among the most civil on the Internet, but use good judgment and ask follow-up questions.

The quality of outfitting services varies from region to region and company to company. Here are some tips to consider in making a choice:

- Give the most weight to recommendations from disinterested persons.
- The outfitter's promotional materials should be informative and address safety. Paid sales agents who do not have a full knowledge of these services may indicate impersonal service on the river as well.
- Larger adventure travel companies tend to be more reliable but may not offer the individualized service provided by some smaller companies.
- The quality of equipment used and provided by a company is a good indicator of quality of service. Better companies will furnish newer, state-of-the-art boats and, where appropriate, wetsuits and booties or other specialized river gear. Poorly maintained boats and equipment reflect poorly on the company.
- The outfitter or company should be able to address any customer's safety inquiries. An inquiry regarding an outfitter's safety record is appropriate, and better outfitters volunteer information about safety and

are frank regarding the risks customers may assume and encounter. On difficult rivers, an inquiry regarding optimal and/or safe river levels is appropriate, as is an inquiry into the company's policy on refunds should the customer not be comfortable with the river level. On difficult rivers it may be good to inquire whether the outfitter is providing safety kayakers or undertaking other safety measures.

In more remote areas such as Latin America, Africa, and most of Asia, the number of outfitters and the information available may be limited. Travel agents are a better choice in these areas to provide the names and qualifications of outfitters. The quality of outfitters and equipment used may be quite varied unless the outfitter is part of an established international company. In such distant areas the exercise of judgment is even more important.

On Your Own

The descriptions and maps in this book are not intended to be as detailed as those in the region-specific guidebooks available for many areas. The information provided here should enable qualified boaters to get to the put-in and approach the river with a reasonable assessment as to what to expect and what to watch for. We have listed the regional whitewater guidebooks in the bibliography and encourage paddlers interested in a certain area to buy and use these books in conjunction with *World Whitewater*. Some rivers, to our knowledge, are only described in this guidebook.

A few rivers in this book are so remote and exacting that few private boaters should attempt them. However, all of them have been run, and those who have gone before were provided with even less information than what's given here. For these rivers, and on any difficult or extended trip in a remote area, expedition travel and boating skills are a prerequisite.

Maps

We have provided maps for the most important rivers in each area; however, a serious boater may wish to find more detailed maps. The better maps will have a scale of 1:100,000 or smaller. A good source for maps is the map room of any major public or university library. Another source is Map Link (see the Resources chapter, page 323). Many of these runs are in remote areas, and maps are often either unavailable or at too large a scale to be useful. Highly detailed satellite maps of even the most remote reaches of the globe, paid for by the United States taxpayers will hopefully be declassified and made available to river runners.

International Travel

We have not attempted to write *World Whitewater* as a guidebook for international travel. However, a good travel guidebook can prove invaluable for a safe, successful, and rewarding trip. Guidebooks vary widely in quality and intended audience, so do some comparison shopping, and remember to look for the most recent editions. We have found the Lonely Planet publications to be comprehensive and geared well to the concerns of the adventure traveler.

Traveling with Whitewater Gear

Kayaks

If you are planning a trip in a remote area, you have probably already mastered putting a boat and gear on a car or bus. Flying with whitewater gear can be a challenge, especially if you take your hard-shelled kayak with you. Kayaks are usually considered oversized by airlines, and are often just too large to put on a bush plane when flying into remote areas; folding kayaks, however, can be well-suited for air travel. It is essential to check with airlines in advance for their policy on transporting kayaks. Some carriers have friendly policies regarding surfboards, and it may be helpful to portray your boat in the same category, perhaps as a "surf kayak." Get the full name and whereabouts of the airline representative you speak with, and make notes including the date and time. Always arrive at the airport much earlier, as the issue will probably resurface at check-in. If all goes poorly, you may consider parcel carriers traveling the same route.

To avoid problems you may want to consider renting a kayak at your destination, especially if you are already used to paddling a plastic fossil and not too attached to your late-model boat. Rental boats in some areas tend to be older, sturdier models, and even then what you are promised is not what you get. Honing your skills in a Prijon Taifun or a Perception Mirage before you depart can be helpful. Bring your own spray deck, float bags, flotation vest, and paddle (breakdown type preferred), as these can be harder to find and expensive.

We have never attempted to fly with an open canoe and can impart little information to those who paddle them, aside from the information for other craft. As open-canoeists are by nature both stubborn and resourceful, it must be assumed they will solve any problems themselves.

Inflatable Kayaks, Rafts, and Catarafts

Inflatable Kayaks. In general, all inflatables are more suited to air travel than rigid boats. Inflatable kayaks, especially the high-performance type with non-rigid floors, are ideal "jet boats," sometimes small enough to use as carry-on with your breakdown paddle. These specialized boats are great for smaller rivers, but lack some of the performance qualities of hard-shells and will be overmatched in big water.

Rafts. Most decent-sized self-bailing rafts usually exceed the air carrier's weight limits. Removing the floor and thwarts (assuming they are designed to removed) is a possibility but a lot of work. It is a good idea to practice taking the boat apart and putting it together first before you leave. It may be possible to rent rafts in certain areas.

Catarafts. A small cataraft with a breakdown frame may pass air carrier size and weight limitations and make a great support boat on kayak trips.

Respecting Locals and Other River Users

In many regions, local villagers, ranchers, and farmers make their homes along the banks of these rivers. Rivers also attract a wide variety of visitors: boaters, anglers, campers, hikers, swimmers, and others. River dwellers and visitors alike have the right to privacy, quiet, and solitude; please respect that right.

Treat the local people as you would expect to be treated, and respect their customs, property, and privacy. Although in some undeveloped countries their homes may appear to be modest and their means of living disadvantaged, they neither expect nor deserve to be treated in a condescending way by foreigners. While token or actual tribute may be required in a handful of circumstances, hand-outs only serve to perpetuate dependence on future visitors. If you wish to make a contribution to better the lives of the locals, a donation to a nearby hospital or other worthy facility will probably do much more good than a handout.

As for fellow boaters, make room for others at heavily used river access points. At busy put-ins and take-outs, load and unload right away and move your boats and vehicles out of the way as quickly as possible. At river access points, do not park in campsites. Walk around, not through, occupied campsites.

On the river, choose campsites and lunch spots well away from where others have stopped. Friendly discussion of upcoming campsites with other boating parties can avoid conflicts later in the day.

When your group is following another party, give them plenty of room when they head into rapids; this is a matter of safety as well as courtesy.

When approaching an angler, try to hold back and ask where to pass. Use and look for hand signals rather than talking. If in doubt, stay to the far side of the channel and move through as smoothly and quietly as possible. Quiet can be important to the art of fishing.

River Safety

Considering the powerful natural forces with which river runners contend, whitewater boating enjoys a very good safety record. Nevertheless, every year there are injuries and deaths on the river. Beginners and experts alike are represented in the statistics. The danger can't be eliminated, but you can minimize it by being prepared and taking appropriate precautions.

This is a guide to the world's great rivers, not an instruction manual on how to run them. *On the river, you are responsible for your own safety*. The keys to safe boating are adequate skills, proper equipment, and, above all, good judgment—none of which this book can provide. It's up to you.

Be prudent. Don't run a whitewater river without knowing precisely what you are doing. Seek competent advice and qualified instruction first, and make sure your equipment is appropriate for the river and the conditions. Be sure your skills and experience are equal to the situation. Be realistic about your skills and limitations. And don't boat beyond your abilities.

When you're learning, move up the white-water difficulty scale very gradually. Before attempting Class 4, for example, you should be able to handle Class 3 water easily, not just survive it. Proper learning takes time and patience. There are plenty of less difficult runs suitable for honing your skills.

For a comprehensive guide to whitewater safety and rescue techniques, we recommend *Whitewater Rescue Manual*, by Charlie Walbridge and Wayne Sundmacher.

The following is a list of essential skills and precautions for whitewater safety:

- Boating alone is not recommended.
- Wear a snugly fitted life jacket at all times when you are on or near the river. Crotch straps can help prevent the life jacket from coming off over your head.
- Wear your helmet when appropriate: in kayaks, in most all whitewater; in canoes and rafts, in challenging whitewater.
- Be a good swimmer. Know how to float in a whitewater river: feet first and elevated, in the deepest channel, and never just in front of a boat. Know when and how to swim aggressively for an eddy or boat.
- Learn self-rescue techniques, including swimming a rapid, escaping from a capsized boat, and, for you hard-shell boaters, Eskimo rolling.
- Know how to avoid hypothermia and how to deal with it. Hypothermia is a serious risk any time water and air temperatures add up to less than 120°F (49°C). Wear a wetsuit or drysuit when conditions warrant.
- Beware of high water. Most rivers undergo a profound and dangerous change when their flows rise. Never run a river at or near flood stage.
- Know how to recognize and react to river hazards, such as holes, snags, wrap rocks, undercuts, and rock sieves.
- Never run a rapid unless you can see a clear path through it.
- When in doubt, stop and scout. Still in doubt? Portage.
- Know the risks of pins and entrapments and how to avoid them. Pins kill more kayakers than any other kind of mishap.

Foot entrapments are another leading cause of death.

- Know the dangers of brush and trees in the river, usually called "strainers" and "sweepers." These are deadly hazards. Stay clear. Be especially alert for snags during and after high water.
- Know the dangers of man-made obstacles: bridge abutments, fences, and especially weirs and low dams. Boaters can be recycled endlessly even in small "keeper" reversals below weirs.
- Beware of entrapment in loose lines.
- Use sturdy equipment in good repair. Carry personal and group safety gear: knife, carabiners, pulleys, toss bags, safety lines, spare paddles or oars, repair kit, etc.
- Carry a first aid kit and know how to use it. Learn or review first aid and CPR. Know how to recognize and deal with hazards in the locale, including severe weather, venomous or dangerous animals, toxic plants, pollution, and potentially hostile inhabitants. Know how to deal with emergencies if someone is unlucky.
- Mixing alcohol or other drugs with whitewater can be deadly.
- Use caution on shore and on the road. Many injuries and deaths occur off the river—on side hikes, on shuttle roads, in camp—when boaters let their guard down.
- Tell someone where you are going, when you expect to return, and what to do (including where to call) if you don't.

Using This Book

In the regional maps in this book, asterisked numbers indicate areas for which local maps are provided; the legend for each regional map gives page numbers for local maps. Local maps are provided to show access points and are not to be relied on to locate rapids or obstacles on the river. Arrows pointing to the river show put-ins and those pointing away take-outs; double-headed arrows indicate both a put-in and take-out point. Daggers alongside river names indicate direction of flow. Rivers in this guide are rated on the international scale of 1 to 6. We rate rivers, or portions of rivers, according to their most difficult typical rapids. For example, the Futaleafu in Chile is rated Class 5, although it has numerous rapids that by themselves are rated Class 2, 3, or 4.

When there are one or two uncharacteristically tough rapids, we indicate this by a subscript number. For example, one section of Toby Creek in Western Canada is rated Class 3_5, reflecting the presence of a big Class 5 drop in an otherwise intermediate run.

A p indicates one or more portages, as in the case of Cahabon in Guatemala, rated 4_p. A plus or minus sign is roughly equivalent to "low" or "high"; thus, a Class 3– is a "low Class 3," while a Class 3+ is a "high Class 3."

The ratings are intended to be realistic judgments of difficulty at moderate flows. This means, among other things, that we don't overrate rapids to protect boaters. But we also don't downgrade rapids simply because more people are running them these days.

Bear in mind that difficulty changes with the flow; the degree of change depends on the river and the rapid. Most rivers become more difficult at higher flows—in general, Class 3 rivers require Class 4 skills at high flows, and so on—but there are definitely exceptions.

Rating the difficulty of a river, or even of a specific rapid, is a tricky and subjective business and a source of endless debate. Experienced boaters looking at the stretch on the same river may well perceive different challenges and hazards, especially if they are in different kinds of boats, or even if they hail from different countries or regions. Moreover, whitewater equipment and techniques are always evolving, and the rivers themselves are constantly changing.

The truth is that no simple code can fully convey a river's unique combination of potential difficulties—especially when you consider complicating factors, such as degree of risk, possibility for recovery, and variations in flow, season, weather, and water temperature. *The rating system is a rough approximation.* With that in mind, here are the definitions that we use to rate the runs in this book:

Class 1 is merely moving water with a few riffles. There are small waves and no obstacles.

Class 2 rapids have bigger waves but no major obstructions in the channel.

Class 3 rapids are longer and rougher than Class 2, and they have considerably bigger hydraulics (waves, holes, and currents). Route-finding is sometimes necessary, although Class 3 rapids generally require only a few maneuvers. Advanced and expert boaters can usually "read and run" them, but less experienced river runners should scout. Class 3 rapids may seem easy to passengers who are guided by experts, as on a commercial rafting trip, but intermediate and even advanced boaters sometimes run into trouble on Class 3 rapids.

Class 4 rapids are generally steeper, longer, and more heavily obstructed than Class 3 rapids. They are often "technical" runs requiring a number of turns and lateral moves. Preliminary scouting of all Class 4 rapids is definitely recommended unless the boater is highly skilled and knows the river intimately. Few want to try it, but when they must, boaters can usually "swim" Class 4 rapids without high risk of major injury.

Class 5 rapids look different—and bigger—even to the uninitiated. In addition to strong currents, big waves, boulders, and holes powerful enough to hold or flip boats, Class 5 rapids usually have one or more major vertical drops. Everyone scouts Class 5 rapids, even experts. Many are routinely portaged, even if they are runnable at certain water levels. An accident in a Class 5 rapid risks injury to boaters as well as damaged or lost equipment.

Class 6 rapids are magnified versions of Class 5, with additional problems and hazards. They are usually considered unrunnable, and for most boaters they are. But at certain water levels, teams of experts taking all precautions can and have run Class 6 rapids. Nevertheless, even in the best of circumstances, risks include not only injury but loss of life. Definitely not recommended.

Class U or p rapids or falls (unrunnable or portage) should probably never be attempted. This judgment, like any classification of rapids, is subjective to a degree. In fact, a few places that we label *p* have been run. Nevertheless, we consider them unsafe at any flow.

Significant rapids are often mentioned by name, rating, and/or location, and for many we provide a brief description. In some cases we include information on landmarks to help boaters recognize when they are approaching a big drop. Our descriptions are not intended as instructions for running a rapid. That judgment is always left to the boater, who should keep in mind that rapids change, water levels fluctuate, and opinions often differ as to the best and safest approach. We sometimes point out rapids that boaters may want to scout or portage; however, the decision to scout or portage is always the boater's responsibility. Remember the rule: *If in doubt, stop and scout. Still in doubt? Portage.*

We do not pretend to have included anything like a comprehensive list of rapids in our river descriptions. Better-known rivers are described in more detail than those where only a few have ventured. Boaters running more difficult rivers should be prepared for plenty of scouting and portaging.

The location of rapids and other important features is always approximate. The point is to give boaters some idea of how far one thing is from another. Readers are urged to take distances as only a rough indication.

Don't blunder into a big rapid just because you expect it to be farther downstream.

Finally, all the measurements in this book are given in the English system, followed by the approximate metric equivalent in parentheses. The terms "right" and "left" are always used assuming the observer is facing downstream.

Abbreviations Used in This Book

m	meter(s)
km	kilometer(s)
fpm	feet per mile
mpk	meters per kilometer
cfs	cubic feet per second
cumecs	cubic meters per second (approximately 35 cfs = 1 cumecs)

Conversions

gradient		
5 mpk	=	26 fpm
distance		
1 mile	=	1.6 km
1 km	=	0.62 miles
volume		
1,000 cfs	=	28.3 cumecs
100 cumecs	=	3,530 cfs

Minimum-Impact River Running

Pride in caring for the river should be one of the real pleasures of a float trip. Even if it means a little extra effort, every boater should help to maintain the river environment in as pristine a condition as possible. Here are some guidelines:

Leave nothing behind. Pack out all garbage. If fires are permitted in the river corridor, papers and burnables (*not* plastic) can be burned, but the ashes should be packed out (see the following tips on campfires). Before leaving, make a sweep through your entire camp.

Minimize the use of campfires, and exercise care. Most river cooking can be done on camping or expedition-style stoves. If you build a campfire, use a fire pan. Don't build fire rings. Preferred is a fire pan with legs, so the pan itself doesn't touch the ground.

If collecting firewood is permitted, be sure to gather only driftwood and "dead and down" wood. Standing dead wood, snags, and dead limbs are part of the river canyon setting; leave them alone.

Keep a close eye on your fire, and have sand, shovel, and water nearby. Make sure the fire is completely extinguished. Carry out charcoal and partially burned wood as you would garbage.

Dispose of human waste properly. If possible—and it usually is—carry all solid human waste out of the river canyon. This is a requirement on some rivers, and it is highly desirable on most, whether it is required or not.

For many years, river runners carried human waste in watertight ammo cans lined with plastic and doused with lime or some other deodorant. However, legally disposing of these bags is now more or less impossible in many areas. As requirements grow more stringent, new technologies are coming into play on some rivers.

Be careful with soap. Use minimal amounts of biodegradable, phosphate-free soap to wash yourself and your dishes at least 100 feet from the river and any side streams.

Keep wildlife in mind. Dozen of species dwell in the critical riparian zones along most rivers, and others come to the river to drink, hunt, and/or breed. Making noise or approaching too closely to observe wildlife or snap a photo can disturb nesting birds and other animals. Some nesting birds will even abandon their nests if frightened. A pair of binoculars or a telephoto lens will give you a front-row view from a respectful distance. Please respect closures of sensitive sites, and keep your noise down when you pass them.

Maintain a secure and clean camp kitchen. Food and garbage attract animals, which will thereafter associate people with food, hang around the campsites, and become "repeat offenders." Animals that become dependent on people for food may starve in winter when boaters no longer come by.

Respect historical and archaeological sites. Pictographs, petroglyphs, artifacts, and dwellings of earlier inhabitants are an irreplaceable part of the river's history. Please be careful when you explore these sites. Leave everything in its place.

Limit groups to a moderate size. Small groups have less impact—both on the environment and on the wilderness experience of other boaters.

Use extra care at fragile or heavily used sites. River access points, popular campsites, favorite side hikes, legendary hot springs—all of these get intensive use, so more effort is necessary to keep them clean and unspoiled.

For a better understanding of Leave No Trace camping, boaters may want to read some of the many current books on the subject.

Talk to Us!

Do you have new or better information you would like to share about any of the rivers in this book or others you feel should be included? Did we leave information out of a description or include information that you feel is not accurate? Please tell us so we can get it right in future editions of *World Whitewater,* so you and your fellow river runners will have the best information available before they put in.

Contact information

Jim Cassady/Dan Dunlap
World Whitewater
c/o Ragged Mountain Press
P.O. Box 220
Camden, ME 04843-0220

Jim Cassady
Pacific River Supply
3675 San Pablo Dam Rd
El Sobrante, CA 94803
E-mail: pacriver@aol.com

Dan Dunlap
115 Judy Court
Martinez, CA 94553
E-mail: wwh2o@kfogmail.com

NORTH AMERICA

Northeastern United States

The Appalachian Mountains provide the focus of river running in the eastern United States. Formed over 100 million years ago, they were at one time as large as the Himalayas; they have since eroded to their present profile. In the Northeast the Appalachians consist of numerous separate subranges, including the White Mountains in New Hampshire, the Longfellow Mountains in Maine, the Green Mountains in Vermont, the Berkshires in Massachusetts, the Catskills and Adirondacks in New York, the Poconos in Pennsylvania, and others. The range stretches from Maine to Georgia. In this section we only cover the Appalachians down to the Mason-Dixon line at the Pennsylvania-Maryland border. For purposes of organizing the rivers in this book, it serves as the arbitrary border between the Northeast and Southeast regions.

Historically, the canoe was the pioneering craft for river exploration in the eastern United States, and for many whitewater river runners it is still the craft of choice. Native Americans were paddling sleek canoes up and down the river corridors of the Northeast long before Europeans came on the scene, although they were hardly seeking whitewater adventure. They rarely ran rapids and became adept at portaging.

Today, weekend warriors flee the metropolitan centers of New York, Philadelphia, and Boston for the rivers of the Northeast. Although the region is the most urbanized and populated in the United States, beautiful mountain scenery and fine whitewater can still be found in the backcountry. The river canyons serve as a place of repose and renewal for those weary of urban congestion.

Easterners continue to utilize the canoe, learning to paddle as a rite of passage along with learning to bicycle. The canoe became a regional favorite for running whitewater, with greater paddling skills overcoming the craft's shortcomings. It wasn't until the 1960s and 1970s that the kayak began to supplant the canoe in Eastern river-running circles, though purists still prefer open boats. Historically, inflatables have been strictly a vehicle for taking paid customers on commercial river trips. Innovation brings change, however, and in the mid-1990s boat designers in the East redesigned the clumsy inflatable kayak into a sleek, high-performance boat with characteristics similar to those of a plastic or fiberglass playboat. The new inflatable kayak is now a cutting-edge whitewater craft.

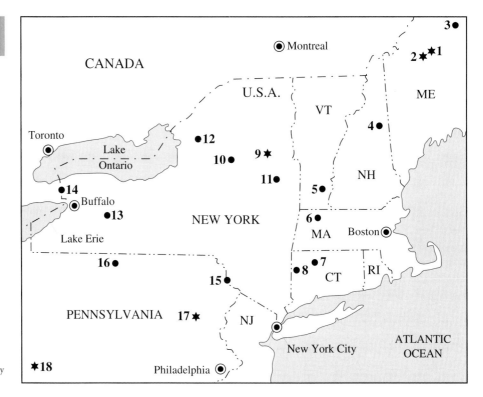

Mount Katahdin, at 5,267 feet (1,843 m), is usually considered the northern end of the Appalachians, rising above the northernmost river described in this section, the West Branch of the Penobscot River in Maine. The mountains of Maine resemble those of the remote, highly glaciated, north-country region of eastern Canada; however, Maine's mountains are higher and more extensive. The combination leads to excellent river running, perhaps the best in the eastern United States. The Appalachians shrink as they approach the Mason-Dixon line, only to rise again as they get closer to the great mountains and rivers of the Southeast. Pennsylvania's mountains are smaller, and the area, which is more urbanized and industrialized, supports fewer good whitewater rivers. The outstanding canyons of the Lehigh and Youghiogheny rivers are exceptions.

Precipitation levels are fairly constant in the Northeast, ranging from 25 to 40 inches a year. Temperatures decrease and snow levels increase as one moves north, but snow runoff here is not nearly as important as it is in the western United States.

◄ Kennebec River (Maine)

INDIAN POND TO CARRY BROOK
(GORGE RUN)
Difficulty: Class 4–
Length: 4 miles (6.4 km)

(continued on following page)

From its headwaters at Moosehead Lake, Maine's largest inland body of water, the Kennebec runs free until it is impounded briefly behind Harris Dam at Indian Pond Reservoir. From there it pours into a deep, steep-walled gorge as one of the best big-volume whitewater runs in the country, tumbling through an isolated north-country forest of spruce and cedar. In spite of its remoteness, the Kennebec has good road access near Interstate 95.

The Kennebec was only recently tamed. Colonial explorers found the river perilous and the area of little economic potential. In 1775, as told in Kenneth Roberts's historical novel *Arundel*, Benedict Arnold and an army of some 1,100 troops undertook an ascent of the Kennebec and its tributary, the Dead River, planning to surprise the British at Quebec. The surprise, however, was on them. Unprepared for the difficulty of the river and its environs and hampered with clumsy, heavily laden craft, Arnold's soldiers lost most of their craft and provisions and struggled to return alive. The corpses of those who did not return gave the name to the nearby Dead River.

Locals long considered the Kennebec too dangerous to run, and it was not until the 1970s that it began to draw interest as a whitewater run. Even at that time, initial descents in non-self-bailing rafts were madcap adventures. Nowadays commercial and private boaters with modern equipment run the big-water rapids, huge waves, and holes with modern techniques and playful abandon. This is the best big-water kayaking run in the Northeast, with fine surf waves and playspots along the length of the gorge.

The gorge and downstream sections are usually combined. Boaters can put in downstream of Harris Dam and Indian Pond Reservoir. Typical dam-releases are around 5,000 cfs (141.5 cumecs), but flows vary, so be sure to check locally before launching. The big-water action takes little time to develop, as the first 4 miles are through the gorge. The first major rapid is about 1 mile (1.6 km) downstream of the put-in and consists of

CARRY BROOK TO THE FORKS
Difficulty: Class 2+
Length: 9 miles (14.4 km)

Season: Dam-releases, May through September
Character: Large flows, remote

Kennebec and Dead Rivers (Maine)

three huge waves known as the Three Sisters. It is followed by Alleyway and Z Turn. At about mile 2½ (4 km) is Magic Falls, the biggest rapid on the run, named for the tendency of kayaks and rafts to submerge before reappearing downstream "as if by magic." A mile downstream, a waterfall on river right marks the entrance of Dead Stream. After one more rapid, Carry Brook enters on the left, and a rough road provides access at this point and marks a division between the difficult gorge and the easier downstream reach. Downstream of Carry Brook the river opens up, the gradient decreases, and the rapids are easier. The fine scenery continues with possible sightings of deer, otters, eagles, and loons. The Kennebec also supports a large landlocked salmon fishery, providing impetus for its preservation. The gradient averages 40 fpm (7.6 mpk) upstream of Carry Brook, 17 fpm (3.2 mpk) downstream.

Moxie Stream enters on the left 2 miles before you reenter civilization at the town of The Forks. A spectacular 90-foot (27.5 m) waterfall is well worth the ½-mile (0.8 km) hike upstream. The usual take-out is at Crusher Pool near the confluence with the Dead River.

From Interstate 95 take Route 201 to the town of The Forks, staging area for both the Kennebec and Dead rivers. To get to the put-in, take Moxie Road east out of The Forks. At Moxie Pond go north on Indian Pond Road to the outlet of Indian Pond. Downstream access is possible at the bottom of Kennebec Gorge via a rough road off Indian Pond Road.

An upstream stretch that gets some usage is from the east outlet of Moosehead Lake to Indian Pond. This run is a mild, 3-mile (4.8 km), Class 2 run with a gradient of 12 fpm (2.3 mpk) and runnable flows of around 1,000 to 1,500 cfs (28.3 to 42.45 cumecs). The area is very isolated, and road access is poor. Some boaters run this stretch the first day, camp on Indian Pond, then portage the dam and run the gorge on the second day.

SPENCER STREAM TO ROUTE 201
Difficulty: Class 3–
Length: 15 miles (24 km)

Season: Dam releases, May through September
Character: Remote north-country river

◁ Dead River (Maine)

This is a secluded run with fine Maine backcountry scenery and few signs of civilization along the way. Typical summertime flows from Flagstaff Dam upstream of the put-in are 900 to 1,200 cfs (25.47 to 33.96 cumecs). Kennebec Water controls the flows and publishes its schedule of releases. Several times a year the operators up the flow to 5,000 to 7,000 cfs (141.5 to 198.1 cumecs), increasing the degree of difficulty by about one full class. At normal flows the rapids of the Dead River are mostly Class 3–.

The stretch downstream of the put-in is an easy warmup until the river reaches a gravel pit on the left, after which the gradient steepens and the rapids become more continuous. Midstream rocks and pourovers are a major hazard. Popular Falls near the end is the biggest rapid on the run. Grand Falls, a 30-foot (9.15 m) waterfall, is a short distance upstream from the put-in at Spencer Stream. The view is worth the hike or paddle upstream, particularly at higher water. Another way to see the falls is to extend the run by putting in upstream just below Flagstaff Dam and portaging Grand Falls.

Most of the land surrounding the run is privately owned by a paper company which may charge a nominal fee ($3 to $6 per person) to use the shuttle roads on busy weekends. The put-in is on a dirt road off Route 201, north of West Forks; multiple logging roads and generally poor road conditions make finding it confusing. The Webb Store, 207-663-2214, in West Forks offers a shuttle service or will at least help you find the put-in. Take out where the Dead River joins Route 201 at the base of Durgin Hill in West Forks, just before the Dead meets the Kennebec. Central Maine Power maintains a fee parking area at the take-out which boaters should utilize. Other possible take-outs are the Webb Store or campgrounds run by rafting companies nearby.

The Dead River's name refers to the corpses of many of Benedict Arnold's men who died along these banks during the disastrous campaign to capture Quebec in 1775 (see previous description). Arnold was not accustomed to failure. Prior to his execution for treason, he was one of the young Continental Army's ablest and most celebrated leaders.

Penobscot River, West Branch (Maine) ➤

Some of the Northeast's best-known rapids, steady flows throughout the summer, and spectacular views of Mount Katahdin, Maine's highest peak at 5,267 feet (1,607 m), combine to make the West Branch of the Penobscot one of the region's the most popular summertime runs. The area is also popular with campers, hikers, and anglers.

Steady flows of 2,000 to 3,000 cfs (56.6 to 84.9 cumecs) result from hydropower releases fueling local mills around the clock. This is a welcome change from the fluctuating flows created by peaking power generation on rivers like the Kennebec. Numerous access points dot this 17-mile (27.2 km) run, as it parallels the Golden Road.

Hardy river runners will want to put in at the top, just below Ripogenus Dam ("Rip" for short). This involves lowering boats on ropes to a pool 80 feet (24.4 m) below and then entering the 2-mile-long Ripogenus Gorge. The gorge features 100-foot (30.5 m) granite walls on either side of the river and some of Maine's most notorious rapids. The biggies include Exterminator, Staircase, Big Heater, and the toughest, the Cribwork, takes its name from an old wooden wall constructed here by loggers.

RIPOGENUS DAM TO BIG EDDY
Difficulty: Class 4+
Length: 2 miles (3.2 km)

BIG EDDY TO DEBSCONEAG FALLS
Difficulty: Class 3+
Length: 15 miles (24 km)

Season: Dam-releases, May through September
Character: Pool-and-drop, remote

Crystal, Bottom Moose, New York. *(Matt Muir)*

Boaters can skip the tough upstream rapids and the tricky put-in by launching downstream at Big Eddy. From here down, rapids alternate with long stretches of flatwater (locally called "deadwater") for the next 15 miles (24 km). This stretch allows the opportunity to spot moose, deer, ospreys, and bald eagles. Learning to spell or pronounce the names of the rapids here can be more of a challenge than learning to run them. Significant rapids include Big Amberjackmockamus Falls, Nesowadnehunk Falls, Pockwockamus Falls, and Debsconeag Falls. Pockwockamus Falls after mile 12 is a popular take-out. Downstream the river is very secluded but is mostly deadwater and requires a difficult shuttle.

The West Branch of the Penobscot is reached by taking the Golden Road northwest from Millinocket. Conserving the character of the river corridor and maintaining the salmon fishery are currently important issues here.

Upstream from Rip Dam lies the 2½-mile (4 km) section from Seboomook Dam to Roll Dam. A maze of logging roads makes finding the put-in here confusing. The run features a few big Class 3 drops, with a fair amount of flatwater. The gradient is 12 fpm (2.3 mpk), and flows are inconsistent.

◁ Swift River (New Hampshire)

LOWER FALLS TO UPSTREAM OF SACO RIVER
Difficulty: Class 4
Length: 9 miles (14.4 km)

Season: Rain or snow runoff, March through May
Character: Mountain runoff river

The aptly named Swift River is regarded by many as New England's premier spring-runoff whitewater river. The Swift flows out of the White Mountains in east-central New Hampshire. It remains undammed and depends on recent rains or snowmelt. Still, it has a longer season than most runoff rivers in the region, usually runnable for several months in the spring. The river runs through a richly forested area, and its boulder-strewn waters are normally pristine, cold, and clear. The Kancamagus Highway, Route 112, follows the river, so, depending on the run, expect either cheers or catcalls from roadside observers.

The rapids on the Swift consist mainly of boulders, ledges, and pourovers that are considerably more difficult at higher flows. The standard put-in is just downstream of Lower Falls. The first 3 miles (4.8 km) are the hardest and include Swift Gorge and Staircase Rapids. Thereafter, the gradient eases from 80 fpm (15.3 mpk) down to 30 fpm (5.6 mpk) and the scenery opens up. Numerous access points are available before the Swift joins the Saco River at Conway, New Hampshire.

◁ West River (Vermont)

BALL MOUNTAIN DAM TO JAMAICA STATE PARK (UPPER RUN)
Difficulty: Class 3+
Length: 3 miles (4.8 km)

JAMAICA STATE PARK TO TOWNSHEND RESERVOIR (LOWER RUN)
Difficulty: Class 2+
Length: 7 miles (11.2 km)

Season: Several dam-releases, usually in the spring and fall
Character: Dam-controlled, popular mountain river when runnable

The West River was once known by its Indian name, Wanrastigeset. Flowing out of the Green Mountains in southern Vermont, it is now a dam-controlled river with two commonly run sections, each with its own distinct character. The upper stretch, from Ball Mountain Reservoir to Jamaica State Park, is isolated and more difficult, with technical rapids formed of boulders and ledges. The swift water of the West can make for good surfs in places. The biggest rapid, Dumpling, is a row of smooth, dumpling-shaped boulders blocking the river, followed by a large recovery pool called Salmon Hole. The easier lower section, from the state park to Townshend Reservoir, parallels Route 30. The surrounding area offers excellent hiking and sightseeing, especially during the changing colors of late autumn. Boaters can take out at the Townshend Reservoir or upstream at the Route 100 bridge. Gradient varies from 40 fpm (7.5 mpk) on the upper section to 20 fpm (3.8 mpk) on the lower section.

Dam-releases usually range from 1,300 to 2,200 cfs (36.79 to 62.26 cumecs), with fall releases coinciding with the best of the fall colors. The Jamaica State Park rangers offer a shuttle service but often close the easiest access road to other vehicles. Large crowds on release days can make the river itself a little crowded, but the influx of river runners makes it a great place to renew friendships. The West is often the site of the National Slalom Championships.

Deerfield River (Massachusetts) ➤

With its headwaters in Vermont and coursing south through the Berkshire Mountains in the northwest corner of Massachusetts, the Deerfield River was overlooked for years due to inconsistent flows from the Sherman, Harriman, and Somerset reservoirs which impounded nearly all its flow. It now enjoys newfound popularity as a result of newly negotiated regular dam-releases from the upstream reservoirs. New England Power Company (NEPCO) and various recreational interest groups, including the American Whitewater (AWA) and the regional Friends for the Liberation of Whitewater (FLOW), negotiated the flows as part of the FERC license renewal of the upstream dams. The AWA has also assisted in the acquisition of adjacent lands as part of the Deerfield River Basin Environmental Enhancement Trust.

The Dryway run, from Sherman Reservoir to Bear Swamp Reservoir (also known as the Monroe Bridge run), is upstream from the much easier Zoar Gap run. The Dryway derives its name from the extensive dewatering undertaken by NEPCO to power downstream turbines. With the renewed flows it may now shed its appellation, at least for part of the time. Recreationalists have negotiated thirty-two release days each summer. The most challenging rapids, Dragons Tooth and Labyrinth, are near the end. On low-flow days, the river is reserved for anglers.

The Zoar Gap run (also known as the Fife Brook run) presently has 105 reliable release days spanning nearly all of the summer, including all weekends. The run is from Fife Brook to Route 2 (Mohawk Trail). A technical boulder dash in a narrowing called Zoar Gap Rapids is the toughest section, but the rapids tend to wash out at higher levels. It is popular with kayakers and features a slalom course. A road follows the river on both sections. It is rarely visible from the river but does allow a car scout of Zoar Gap Rapids. The river offers excellent Berkshire scenery, with birch and pine forests covering the slopes along the river.

SHERMAN RESERVOIR TO BEAR
    SWAMP RESERVOIR
    (DRYWAY RUN)
Difficulty: Class 4–
Length: 4 miles (6.4 km)

FIFE BROOK TO ROUTE 2 (ZOAR
    GAP RUN)
Difficulty: Class 2
Length: 10 miles (16 km)

Season: April through
    October
Character: Dam-controlled,
    regular releases

Farmington River (Connecticut) ➤

The Farmington is a large river that drains a part of southwestern Massachusetts and then flows southward into Connecticut, where it cuts through Talcott Mountain. This stretch, the Tariffville Gorge, holds good whitewater and gets plenty of use in the summertime.

Tariffville Gorge (called "T-Ville" by the locals) is a short but classic run with pushy water and powerful hydraulics at higher flows and playspots at lower flows. River runners can expect good, constant dam-releases year-round from upstream Hogsback Dam. The stretch is popular with paddling clubs and competitors who practice on the racecourse about halfway down.

Put in near the Route 189 bridge or farther upstream near Tariffville on the dirt road on river right toward the sewage treatment plant. Some of the best rapids, including

TARIFFVILLE GORGE
Difficulty: Class 2+
Length: 1 mile (1.6 km)

Season: Spring through fall
    and mild winter days
Character: Short, dam-
    controlled, close to
    population centers

Cathy's Wave, are near road access. It's possible to park right next to Cathy's, a wide, glassy surf wave that forms at higher flows, play the waves and holes, and carry back to your vehicle. Downstream of the pilings of an old bridge is a race course, and below that is good action at Top, Upper, and Lower holes. Near the bottom of the run is a broken dam with a 25-foot (7.63 m) breach on the left. New debris constantly changes the drop, so scout it each time. The runnable chute leads into Car Rock, which is neither a car nor a rock but rather a concrete slab from the dam which is to be avoided, especially at high flows when it becomes an ugly hydraulic. Another chunk just downstream is called Aircraft Carrier. Take out near the Route 187 bridge on Tunxis Road. Boaters may run the gorge over and over to get their fill.

Upstream in Massachusetts is the Upper Farmington, a popular Class 3 run. This run is scenic, but runnable flows are less reliable.

◁ Housatonic River (Connecticut)

Housatonic means "River Beyond the Mountains" in the local Indian dialect, a fitting name for a river with headwaters in the distant Berkshires of western Massachusetts. Throughout these two runs, the Housatonic flows southward through the Litchfield Hills in northwestern Connecticut. The region is rich in Colonial history, and covered bridges span the river on both runs.

The Falls Village Hydro (also known as Covered Bridge) run is the milder of the two runs, with a gradient of 12 fpm (2.3 mpk). Shorter runs are possible, with various access points available off nearby Route 7. The run from Falls Village Hydro to Swift Bridge offers 14 miles (22.4 km) of Class 2 action. At all but high flows, this is a good run for beginners. The biggest rapids are near the covered bridge at West Cornwall. A difficult 2-mile (3.2 km) alternate reach known as Rattlesnake opens up in peak runoff in the spring and during the fall when repairs to the Falls Village Hydro plant require diversions.

Downstream lurks the significantly more difficult Bulls Bridge run. This section runs in the spring naturally and again in the summer when hydroelectric releases reach the run late in the day. Evening paddles before sunset are popular. The run begins in the town of Kent at Bulls Bridge near Henry Kissinger's home and the covered bridge near the Bulls Bridge Inn and goes 2½ miles (4 km) south of the put-in along Route 7 to the turnout just upstream of Gaylordsville Bridge. The biggest rapids include a series of boulder-strewn drops near the beginning called Staircase, followed by The Funnel, where the pushy flow from Dead Horse Gulch complicates the entry and setup for the big drop. After a paddle through a mini-gorge, boaters try to avoid a big hole on the right in the rapid called S-Turn. Pencil Sharpener is a long, hole-filled rapid that narrows progressively. Powerhouse and George's Hole follow. The overall gradient is 40 fpm (7.5 mpk).

In 1988, a proposal for yet another hydroelectric project by Connecticut Light and Power, which would have reduced the boatable days to about thirty per year, was shelved because of its questionable economic benefits and opposition by river runners and others.

FALLS VILLAGE HYDRO TO SWIFT BRIDGE (FALLS VILLAGE HYDRO run)
Difficulty: Class 2
Length: 14 miles (22.4 km)

BULLS BRIDGE TO ROUTE 7 turnout just upstream of Gaylordsville Bridge (Bulls Bridge run)
Difficulty: Class 4
Length: 2½ miles (4 km)

Season: March through June, sometimes further into the summer
Character: Good whitewater 80 miles (128 km) from New York City

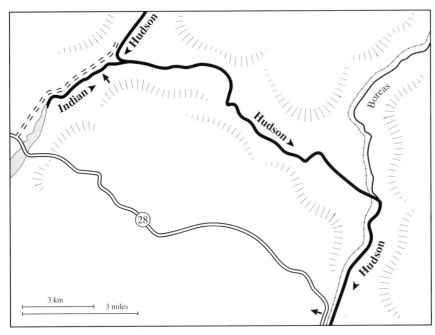

Hudson River (New York)

Hudson River (New York) ➢

Explorer Henry Hudson set sail upstream from the mouth of the Hudson in 1620 on what he believed was the route to the fabled Northwest Passage. His visions of Far East riches faded quickly, however, as the river that would bear his name changed from saltwater to fresh. In fact, the headwaters of the Hudson drain the 5,344-foot (1,630 m) Mount Marcy, New York's highest peak.

The Hudson today is a study in contrasts. Far upstream from the turbid, polluted Hudson River of New York City, whitewater boaters flock to this run for springtime adrenaline fixes and to escape urbanization. Here the Hudson usually runs crystal clear, and there is nary a road within miles of most of the run. This region is scenic, and plenty of wildlife can be found including hawks, herons, and ospreys. With an overall gradient of 40 fpm (7.5 mpk), the river has big, sticky holes, midstream rocks, and some good surf waves. The water is very cold and can run high during springtime, when this is no place for a swim. This is New York's favorite stretch of whitewater, so expect to share the river with other paddlers, especially on spring weekends.

Boaters will want to check the North Creek gauge before they commit to run the gorge. Recommended flows are 7 or less on the gauge. Flows between 8 and 9 are very tough. The put-in is on the Indian River and is reached by turning north off Route 28 on Chain Lakes Road. Launch just below Otter Slide, a 10-foot (3 m) waterfall. The Indian River provides 3 miles of active warm-up before merging with the much larger Hudson. If upstream dams are releasing into the Indian River, the warm-up can be as wild a ride as the Hudson itself. Two miles (3.2 km) downstream from the confluence is the Hudson River Gorge, announced by the imposing 200-foot (61 m) Blue Ledge. The gorge holds

INDIAN RIVER TO NORTH RIVER
Difficulty: Class 3+ at 3 feet, Class 4– at 5 feet, Class 4+ at 7 feet
Length: 15 miles (24 km)

Season: March through May, after heavy rains, plus additional periodic dam-releases
Character: Wilderness gorge, big water during spring runoff

more than thirty rapids. The biggest are The Narrows, Soup Strainer, Slip Rapid, Harris Rift Rapid, and Greyhound Bus Stopper. At Slip Rapids, a half-hour hike up Slip Brook on river right leads to the highest waterfall in New York, higher even than Niagara Falls.

The river meets civilization near the end of the run, first flowing under a railroad bridge, then rejoining Route 28 a couple of miles downstream and before the take-out at the town of North River.

Gung-ho springtime boaters can almost double the length of this run by putting in at Route 28 North on the Hudson River farther upstream. Another springtime favorite in the area is an expert run on the Boreas. The Boreas River enters the Hudson from river left near the end of the Hudson River Gorge run, at mile 11 (17.6 km), just downstream of the railroad bridge.

◁ Moose River (New York)

OLD IRON BRIDGE TO
FOWLERSVILLE ROAD BRIDGE
(LOWER RUN)
Difficulty: Class 4+
Length: 10 miles (16 km)

FOWLERSVILLE ROAD BRIDGE TO
LYONS FALLS (BOTTOM RUN)
Difficulty: Class 5
Length: 4 miles (6.4 km)

Season: Springtime (late March to mid-May); a little longer season on the bottom section, plus several scheduled dam-releases
Character: Small, technical mountain river

Those looking for a bigger challenge than the Hudson River Gorge can go for a wild ride on the Moose River. The Moose River drains the southwestern part of the Adirondacks. The season is short, and the degree of difficulty rises considerably with higher flows. The gradient on the lower run is 38 fpm (7.1 mpk) and 80 fpm (15.1 mpk) on the bottom run.

The put-in for the lower run is 2 miles (3.2 km) downstream of the Route 28 bridge, about 10 miles (16 km) from Old Forge. The run is sometimes called the Old Iron Bridge run after a bridge about a quarter-mile downstream of the put-in. The toughest rapids on this run are Tannery, Rooster Tail, Froth Hole, Mixmaster, and Larry's Drop. An old road on the left provides access near Froth Hole for those with second thoughts. Don't miss the take-out at Fowlersville Road Bridge, as a 40-foot (12 m) drop lurks just downstream. This run is away from the road and offers some fine southwestern Adirondacks scenery. For much of the year the Moose draws anglers to its blue-ribbon trout fishery.

The bottom run is 4 miles (6.4 km) of serious Class 5 drops between Fowlersville Road Bridge and Lyon Bridge. The aforementioned 40-foot (12 m) slide is not the toughest rapid on the run. The drops are technical, and all the big ones should be scouted. Just downstream near an island is an 8-foot (2.5 m) drop followed by Crucible and Knife-Edge. Double-Drop is comprised of two 8-foot (2.5 m) falls in quick succession. After a brisk carry around a paper mill comes Agers Falls. At 18 feet (5.5 m), this is one of the biggest but not the toughest drop on the run, mostly due to the relatively clean landing. Scout and watch out for the left side. Just below is a tricky 10-foot (3 m) sloping drop. Farther downstream are Surform, Powerline, and Crystal rapids, the last a major rapid including a 15-foot (4.5 m) drop. Below this is a carry around a 40-foot (12 m) waterfall. Take out at the next downstream dam.

Local raft outfitters take on the Lower Moose, with flips and swims to be expected. They use different names for some rapids. The scenery in the bottom run is not as good as on the lower run, but who comes here for the scenery? The bottom section is usually run at low flows; generally 2.6 feet on the gauge at McKeever Dam is the minimum flow needed.

Sacandaga River (New York) ➢

This southeastern Adirondacks river is very popular during the summer when warm-water dam-releases provide lots of roller-coaster wave trains on forgiving rapids. It is an excellent river for beginners to hone their skills. Commercial rafting companies cater to guests interested in an easy float. The gradient averages a mild 15 fpm (2.8 mpk). Flows on Saturdays are good, but Sunday flows are less dependable. Sacandaga means "cedar in water-drowned lands."

Put in just below the Stewarts Dam reservoir, and take out where the Sacandaga empties into the Hudson. The legal put-in, parking lot, and changing area are the result of negotiations between American Whitewater and the dam operator, Niagara-Mohawk.

During spring runoff, runs on the Middle, West, and East branches of the Sacandaga upstream of the reservoir offer more challenging whitewater.

STEWARTS DAM TO HUDSON RIVER
Difficulty: Class 2+
Length: 3 miles (4.8 km)

Season: Dam-releases all summer but not on all Sundays; call 518-494-7478
Character: Dam-controlled, crowded on summer Saturdays

Black River (New York) ➢

The Black River, after leaving its headwaters in the Adirondacks and meandering across the northwestern New York state countryside, passes through the mill town of Watertown. Its present name tracks the Indian name "Kamargo," from the dark color of tannins imparted by upstream vegetation. The tannins were eventually replaced by pollution from paper mills, but recent conservation efforts have improved the water quality dramatically—great news for boaters, as this stretch of the Black holds some excellent, big-water, pool-and-drop rapids. The river has other charms as well. Although the run begins in downtown Watertown, about halfway down it drops into a sheer-walled mini-gorge and the scenery changes abruptly. Wildlife sightings in the gorge, including blue herons and bald eagles, are not uncommon. Local outfitters and the American Whitewater Affiliation have negotiated regular releases from newly constructed upstream dams. The agreement assures good flows through most of the summer and fall, and reduces unpredictable flow fluctuations.

River runners can put in at the Adirondack River Outfitters headquarters on Newell Street in Watertown or ¼ mile (0.4 km) downstream at Hudson River Rafting. The action begins in town with a series of rapids known as The First Three Sets. The last of the three, just downstream of Court Street Bridge and the Hudson River Rafting put-in, is Hole Brothers, a popular spot with the surfing set. Just downstream of the Interstate 81 bridge is a long, difficult rapid known as Knife Edge.

About halfway through the run, Glen Park Falls announces the beginning of the gorge. This is usually portaged on the right. If flows permit (up to 2,500 cfs, 70.75 cumecs), thrill-seekers can go right and run two smaller ledges followed by a 12-foot (3.7 m) waterfall.

Downstream, boaters encounter Three Rocks, Zig-Zag, and Cruncher, followed by a 10-foot (3 m) dam called Hadrian's Wall, which can be run either on the left at higher flows (called the Rocket Ride), or over the much more difficult Poopchute on the right. If in doubt, portage left. One rapid of note just below Rocket Ride is Wailing Wall, named for the cries of commercial rafting customers momentarily caught in the undercut limestone walls lining the gorge.

Take out after paddling flatwater to the public boat access in Dexter unless access is allowed at the more convenient Rexum Paper Company lot in Brownsville. The gradient on this run is 28 fpm (5.3 mpk). Soon after the take-out, the Black flows into Lake Ontario.

WATERTOWN TO DEXTER
Difficulty: Class 4-p
Length: 8 miles (12.8 km)

Season: April through October
Character: Large-volume, pool-and-drop urban river

Black River, New York. *(Whitewater Challengers)*

◁ Genesee River (New York)

LETCHWORTH STATE PARK, LEE'S
LANDING TO ST. HELENA
Difficulty: Class 2–
Length: 6 miles (9.6 km)

Season: Mid-April through
October
Character: Small, tight
gorge in western New
York state

The Genesee flows through a 600-foot-deep (183 m) gorge of shale and sandstone in Letchworth State Park in western New York, well away from the Appalachian mountain ranges. The whitewater here is mild. The scenery, however, is tough to beat, with dramatic canyon walls, nearby waterfalls, and turkey vultures and red-tailed hawks often soaring overhead. A rich array of wildflowers appear along the banks in the spring. This stretch is heavily regulated; check with local authorities for permit requirements. The authorities may close the river at higher levels. Access requires a short hike to the river at both put-in and take-out. Wolf Creek Falls, located upstream on Wolf Creek on river left, is a popular side hike. The gradient averages 20 fpm (3.8 mpk).

◁ Niagara Gorge (New York)

MAID OF THE MIST POOL TO
LEWISTON PARK
Difficulty: Class 5+
Length: 3 miles (4.8 km)

Season: April through
October
Character: Huge volume,
currently illegal to run

Set between two nations and just downstream of the most visited waterfalls on the planet, the Niagara Gorge holds perhaps the biggest whitewater in the continental United States or Canada. Here the massive flows of the Niagara River between Lakes Erie and Ontario drop off the continental fall line at Niagara Falls. They continue to surge over a huge pile of debris left by the falls as it eroded upstream. Sadly, these huge waves, holes, whirlpools, and eddylines are off limits to legal boating. It is hoped that park officials' good judgment will someday allow reasonable use to qualified boaters.

The history of whitewater boating in the gorge goes back to the 1970s, when a few daring souls learned the tricks of running this classic. A drowning in 1976 caused officials to close the river. In 1986 ABC Television, with generous gifts to local authorities on both shores, was able to gain permission to film a descent. In 1987 a loophole created by a jurisdictional transfer resulted in a court order requiring the park service to allow limited runs after tourist season. In September and October of that year at least three descents were made without incident. The participants hailed the tremendous attributes of the run. However, park officials reimposed the ban, and it remains in place to this day.

Flows are usually in excess of 100,000 cfs (2,830 cumecs), with a total vertical drop of 60 feet (18 m). The river features an enormous hole in the center near the top that grows and produces a massive exploding wave at lower flows. There are several ledge holes on the right. Whirlpool Eddy is a monster boil-eddy on the left near the end. This feature has a dramatic reverse gradient of several feet and is almost a quarter of a mile long. Paddlers beware: strange hydraulics in the eddy suck water from the surface, leaving flotsam to collect inside. Boats and boaters in the eddy get pulled down as well, reappearing mysteriously yards away. The flows and the eddy fence are powerful enough that failing to catch Whirlpool Eddy is also a possibility. Should the gorge reopen, it's best not to come to learn to run big water. Exercise all precautions to avoid involvement of rescue personnel, which could retrigger the ban.

Delaware River (Pennsylvania, New York) ➢

The clear, free-flowing Delaware is a National Scenic and Recreational River managed as part of the National Park System. It defines the border between New York state on the left and Pennsylvania on the right and downstream between Pennsylvania and New Jersey. It also supplies water to New York City and other cities. In spite of all this, the scarcity of urban or industrial centers upstream assure excellent water quality. Proximity to New York and Philadelphia guarantees that the river will never be lonely for boaters. As rivers go, the Delaware is a workhorse providing recreation, repose, and river scenery to city dwellers in the hot summer months.

Logistics are easy here. The Delaware has frequent river access, and lots of restaurants, inns, and campgrounds catering to all. Canoe liveries put thousands of canoes to the river during the summer months. The easy stretches are popular with innertubers. Canoe camping is possible along the entire run, but most of the surrounding land is privately owned and most landowners have lost their appreciation for trespassers. Those interested should check for available public camping. The described section is the most popular and holds the most rapids, although the gradient is a scant 6 fpm (1.2 mpk). Long stretches of boatable flatwater extend both upstream and downstream.

Boating the Delaware is also a spectator sport. Crowds gather on summer weekends to watch a demolition derby of inexperienced boaters butting heads with the run's few significant rapids. About 5 miles downstream of the put-in at Damascus is Skinners Falls (Class 2−), a prime site of human carnage often drawing a crowd on the shore. Boaters are free to carry up on the left for endless reruns of what is probably the toughest rapid on the river. Near the bottom of the run is Mongaup Rapids, another place where accidents wait to happen and gear waits to be lost. On a more serious note, fatalities are not uncommon on the Delaware as inexperience, cold springtime flows, and alcohol often play a part.

DAMASCUS TO MILL RIFT
Difficulty: Class 1+
Length: 40 miles (64 km)

Season: April through October
Character: Heavily used canoeing river

All this is not to say the Delaware doesn't have much to offer for those who want to get away. The scenery varies along the different reaches and the river regularly wanders away from the road, providing some isolation. Small mammals, waterfowl, and birds of prey appear along the banks and in the river. About halfway down the run stands the oldest surviving suspension bridge in the country. It was originally designed by John A. Roebling to carry traffic on the Delaware and Hudson Canal and over the river, thereby avoiding collisions with timber floating down the river. Roebling would later demonstrate his talents in downtown Brooklyn.

Upstream of Damascus is flatwater all the way up to the beginning of the protected river corridor where the East Fork and West Fork join to form the Delaware proper just downstream of Hancock. The most popular stretches downstream of the featured run are from Dingman's Ferry to Tock's Island and from Tock's Island to Martins Creek. These runs are in the Delaware Water Gap where the river cuts through the mountains. Unfortunately, there is no whitewater to be found here, either.

◁ Pine Creek (Pennsylvania)

ANSONIA TO BLACKWELL
Difficulty: Class 1+
Length: 17 miles (27.2 km)

Season: Rain-fed, April to June and after heavy rains
Character: Easy, undammed gorge

Pine Creek runs through a spectacular gorge known as the Little Grand Canyon of Pennsylvania. Although a private road follows the river on the right and railroad tracks follow on the left, the run is still near wilderness. The only rapid of consequence is Class 2—Owassee Rapid. Primitive camping is allowed at mile 9 (14.4 km) on the left at Tiadaghton (which means "lost" or "bewildered" in Native American tongue). The banks along the lower part of this run are a little more developed but still quite scenic. Most of the land is state park or state forest land. The river has an average gradient of 16 fpm (3 mpk).

Downstream, the gorge continues until Pine Creek joins the Susquehanna, but civilization is close in this section.

◁ Lehigh River (Pennsylvania)

LEHIGH GORGE, WHITE HAVEN TO JIM THORPE
Difficulty: Class 2+
Length: 24 miles (38.4 km)

Season: Spring, after heavy rains and periodic dam-releases
Character: Gorge in a mini secluded area in a heavily populated region

The Lehigh River runs through what was once the coal-mining and railroad center in eastern Pennsylvania. Despite a history of heavy use, the Lehigh area retains its lush woods and most of its natural beauty. The best of the Lehigh is the Lehigh Gorge where the river cuts a path approaching 1,000 feet deep (305 m) through the Pocono Mountains. The gorge is roadless and wooded. It is managed by the state as Lehigh Gorge State Park.

Nearby population centers (New York City and Philadelphia) make this a very popular whitewater center, with both commercial and private river traffic heavy on summer weekends. The upper stretches are popular with hikers and anglers, and a bike trail follows on the right on parts of the river. Railroad tracks also follow the river. The run holds numerous Class 2 and 2+ rapids such as No Way, Staircase, Kayak Play Spot (a good place for enders, depending on the flow), Beaver Hole, and Wilhoyt's Rock. Below Rockport, the action is even better with Pinball, Needle's Eye, Mile-Long, Snaggletooth (also known as Tower), and Hole-in-the-Wall, the latter named for an abandoned railroad tunnel overhead. Most take out at this rapid on the right bank. This is upstream of Jim Thorpe at the state park access at Glen Onoko. An unimproved road to Jim Thorpe crosses on the bridge just downstream. Mid-gorge access can be found at Rockport.

Lehigh River, Pennsylvania. *(Pocono Whitewater Rafting Center)*

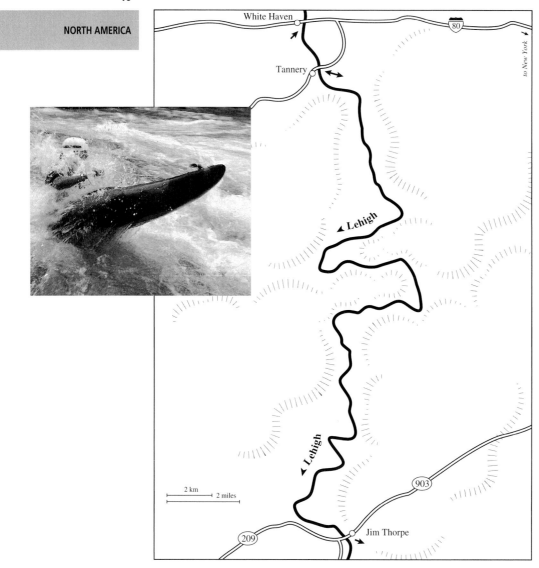

Lehigh River (Pennsylvania)

Flows are regulated by Francis Walter Dam. Although the U.S. Army Corps of Engineers provides flow schedules, they tend to be unreliable, and boaters planning on running the Lehigh should call ahead to local outfitters for current information.

Beginners may want to head for the runs upstream and downstream of the gorge. These include the 8 miles (12.8 km) from Francis Walter Dam to Tannery Bridge (2 miles downstream of White Haven) and the 5 miles (8 km) from Jim Thorpe to Bowmanstown. Check access at Tannery Bridge, which may be restricted, requiring a take-out upstream at White Haven. Both runs are easier and more accessible than the described run, with more frequent access. Boaters can usually scrape down the lower stretch even when the dam is not releasing much water.

The take-out town of Jim Thorpe was originally called Mauch Chunk. In the 1950s, hard economic times caused the town fathers to seek a new direction. That direction came from Oklahoma with the death of legendary athlete Jim Thorpe in 1955. When the governor of Oklahoma vetoed a memorial for Thorpe in his native state, his widow struck a deal with Mauch Chunk. Hoping to give the town an economic boost—and probably weary of the name "Mauch Chunk"—the voters changed the name to Jim Thorpe in 1957. Thorpe's burial site can be seen in town on Route 903, though he probably never set foot in the town that bears his name.

Lower and Middle Youghiogheny Rivers (Pennsylvania) ➢

Located on the western slope of the Appalachians in southwestern Pennsylvania, the Lower Youghiogheny (pronounced "yock-uh-GAY-nee") is synonymous with whitewater boating. In the 1980s the Lower "Yough" was the most heavily used whitewater river in the eastern United States. In the last decade it has slipped to third in the face of the soaring popularity of the Nantahala and the Ocoee. Still, with its reliable flows, fine

CONFLUENCE TO OHIOPYLE (UPSTREAM OF OHIOPYLE FALLS)
Difficulty: Class 1+
Length: 11 miles (17.6 km)

OHIOPYLE (DOWNSTREAM OF OHIOPYLE FALLS) TO BRUNER RUN
Difficulty: Class 3– when under 2 feet on gauge
Length: 7½ miles (12 km)

Season: April through October (year-round when weather and road conditions permit)
Character: Dam-regulated reliable flows, popular

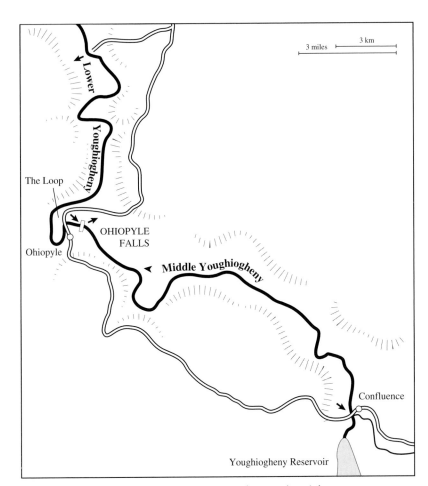

Lower and Middle Youghiogheny Rivers (Pennsylvania)

Eastern mountain scenery, isolation, and a steady diet of challenging rapids, it's easy to see why Eastern whitewater rafting began here.

Much of the action is in the first mile below Ohiopyle Falls, where the river turns south and then almost doubles back on itself. This is The Loop, and boaters can earn a mile of great whitewater reward for the effort of a shuttle of a few hundred yards back across the track bed of the Western Maryland Railroad. The gradient for the entire run averages 27 fpm (5 mpk), and the 1 mile (1.6 km) of The Loop drops 50 feet (15 m). The rapids are numerous and each a subject of river legend. The biggest are Entrance Rapid (just above Sugarloaf Rock), Cucumber (named for a creek entering on the left), and Railroad Rapid at the end of The Loop featuring a big hole called Charlie's Washing Machine on the right. Good rapids downstream make the rest of the run worthwhile.

Boaters wishing to pass on this action can put in below Railroad Rapid and portage the bigger downstream rapids, such as Dimple and River's End, for a Class 2 run at lower flows.

Currently, Ohiopyle State Park runs the shuttle exclusively. More details about the shuttle and updated river regulations are available at the put-in or by contacting the park at 412-329-8591.

The run upstream of Ohiopyle Falls (the Middle Youghiogheny) is also very scenic, with only railroad tracks and a bike path following the river. This stretch has some mild action, but be sure not to miss the take-out above the falls! Daredevils presently flirt with danger and the law to run the falls.

The whitewater of the Yough was not always appreciated. Early explorers, including George Washington, had high hopes for the Youghiogheny River, suspecting it could be part of a water highway to the Ohio Valley. The same rapids that now delight about 100,000 people a year put a damper on the hopes of the original explorers. Eventually a waterway to the Ohio Valley was developed farther north in New York state, with the Erie Canal linking the Hudson River on the eastern slope and the Mohawk River on the western slope.

Southeastern United States

$\mathcal{W}$hile a few diehard souls could be found exploring the rivers of the southeastern United States, they were largely ignored until 1972. That year the heroics of Burt Reynolds and company hit the screen in the whitewater classic *Deliverance*, filmed largely on the Chattooga River in Georgia. Since then, river running in the Southeast has been literally mainstream. Commercial rafting ventures flourished, and thousands were introduced to the sport. Its resulting popularity led to innovation in boat building and design and the publication of many books and other writings on river lore. Several quiet river towns were transformed into well-established paddling centers, providing a basis for the local economy. River running is now a pastime here and embraced as nowhere else. Blessed with heavy rainfall, moderate weather, and a landscape of rugged mountains, the river runners of the Southeast seemingly have whitewater running through their veins.

South of the Mason-Dixon line, excellent whitewater runs drain the Appalachians all the way down to where the mountains peter out in northern Georgia. Compared to

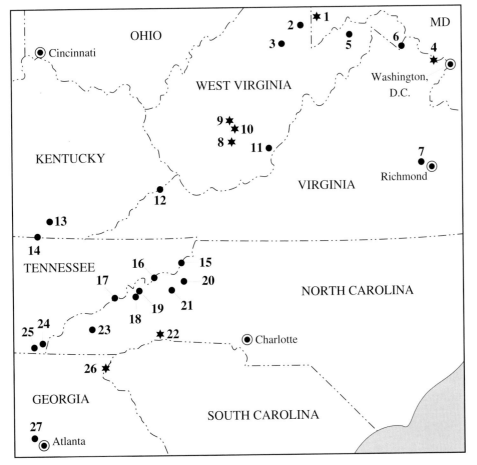

1 Upper Youghiogheny River (see page 21)
2 Cheat River
3 Tygart River
4 Potomac River (see page 27)
5 Potomac River, South Branch
6 Shenandoah River
7 James River
8 New River (see page 30)
9 Gauley River (see page 30)
10 Lower Meadow River (see page 30)
11 Greenbrier River
12 Russell Fork
13 Cumberland North Fork
14 Big South Fork
15 Watauga River
16 Nolichucky River
17 French Broad
18 Big Laurel Creek
19 Pigeon River
20 Wilson Creek
21 Linville Gorge
22 Green River (see page 40)
23 Nantahala River
24 Hiwassee River
25 Ocoee River
26 Chattooga River (see page 43)
27 Chattahoochee River

the Appalachians of the Northeast, those of the Southeast are a little higher, peaking with Mount Mitchell in North Carolina at 6,684 feet (2,039 m).

We begin with the Youghiogheny River. Although the Lower Youghiogheny in southern Pennsylvania is included as part of the Northeast region, the Upper Youghiogheny, with its headwaters in West Virginia and its best whitewater in Maryland, is included in the Southeast section. Farther south, the mountain elevations rise and average annual rainfall increases from around 40 inches to over 50 inches. As the Appalachians reach northern Georgia they taper off and disappear near Atlanta. As in the Northeast, there are many subranges; some of the better-known ones are the Blue Ridge on the east side and the Alleghenies on the west side. Rivers like the North Fork of the Cumberland and the Big South Fork are on the Cumberland Plateau of Kentucky and Tennessee on the west side of the main ranges.

The focus of river running in the eastern United States has gradually shifted from north to south. One reason may be that the more moderate weather allows for a much longer season farther south. At one time the center of Eastern whitewater was the Lower Youghiogheny in Pennsylvania. The first major river guidebook covered mainly the Virginia and West Virginia area. Now the attention is on rivers like the Nantahala and Ocoee, both in the South. The Ocoee hosts over a quarter-million boaters annually as well as the world's best for the whitewater competition of the '96 Olympics. On the other end of the river spectrum, the Chattooga is the consensus choice as the free-flowing classic wilderness river in the region.

The canoe was the pioneering whitewater craft in the Southeast, as it was in the Northeast. More recently, hard-shelled kayaks have dominated the whitewater runs, but the Southeast still produces fine C-1 and open-boat purists who would rather fight than take up the double blade. Historically, inflatables have been the domain of commercial rafting companies, but design pioneers in the region have made high-tech inflatable kayaks the boat of choice for many, especially for the region's steep, low-volume creeks.

◄ Upper Youghiogheny River (Maryland)

SANG RUN TO FRIENDSVILLE
Difficulty: Class 5– at moderate flows; *not boatable at high flows*
Length: 10 miles (116 km)

Season: Rain and snow runoff in the spring and after rains; weekday dam-releases in summer and fall; currently additional dam-releases on the first Saturday of each month
Character: Technical and difficult, very popular for experts

Usually just called the Yough (pronounced "yock"), this is a collection of rocky, technical drops and ledges in a remote, beautiful setting. It is always included among the premier runs of the East. Seasonal flows benefit from snow and rain runoff in the spring, and are extended by releases from upstream Deep Creek Reservoir. The gradient averages 50 fpm (9.5 mpk) on a narrow streambed, but this includes lots of easy stretches. The middle of the run drops well over 100 fpm (19 mpk).

The first 3 miles (4.8 km) to Gap Falls are easy. After Gap Falls it is another mile (1.6 km) before the river gets tough and stays tough for about 4 miles (6.4 km), with big boulders often blocking both the flow and clear views of upcoming rapids. Although there are many drops, the biggest rapids are Bastard and then Triple Drop (which includes the option of running National Falls on the right—an option we do not recommend). Downstream are Heinzerling and Meat Cleaver, followed by a good stretch including an ender hole and good surf waves. This is followed by Lost and Found, where boaters should avoid an undercut rock on the left. The last few miles to the take-out in downtown Friendsville are fairly easy. The shuttle between Friendsville and Sang Run is best done on the roads to the east of the river.

The difficulty of the Upper Yough is very dependent on flows. Boaters should be

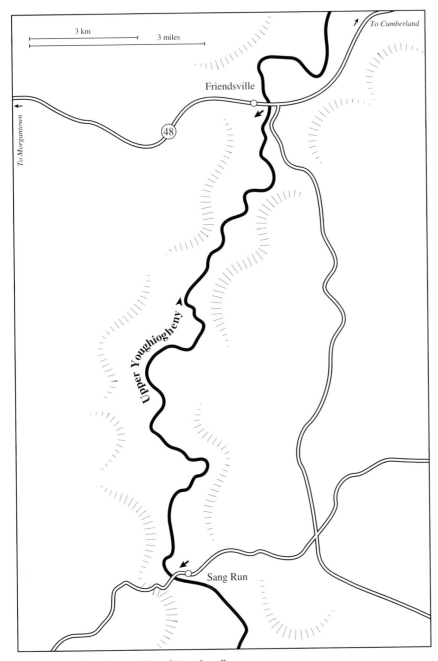

Upper Youghiogheny River (Maryland)

keenly aware of the potential for fluctuations, with higher flows being potentially treacherous. In spring, snow or rain runoff provides good flows, but upstream rainstorms can turn the river into a torrent with little warning. Without rains, boaters run weekday releases. The duration of the releases can be as short as a few hours, so boaters who pussyfoot or dawdle can find themselves high and dry. Be careful; civilization is far away, and the locals have a bit of a reputation for not cottoning to river runners. Get good local flow information before venturing down. Precision Rafting in Friendsville is a good source. Dam-release information is also available from Pennsylvania Electric, 814-533-8911.

Expert boaters can tackle an upstream 6-mile (9.6 km) section from Swallow Falls to Sang Run called the Top Yough, which is usually runnable in the spring when the Upper Yough is often too high. Swallow Falls, a 32-foot (9.8 m), partly sloping falls, is followed by Swallowtail Falls. Both are easily scouted and often portaged. Just downstream on the left is Maryland's highest waterfall at 63 feet (19 m), Muddy Creek Falls. Consistent whitewater continues from here with Suckhole, the most difficult and infamous rapid, awaiting boaters downstream. The rapids ease to flatwater below Hoyas Run, and some boaters take out at the power plant to avoid the less interesting flatwater paddle down to Sang Run. The power plant returns upstream diversions to the river.

In April 1972, after a week of paddling in West Virginia, I stopped by Dave Demaree's place along the Savage River in Bloomington, Maryland, to meet him and his brother Dan. Rivers in the area were running high, so I was surprised when Dave suggested doing the Upper Yough. This Class 5 run had a nasty reputation, and only a handful of people were running it. But I was confident. In the past year I'd run the Gauley, Tygart, and Blackwater rivers, all considered good preparation. I was twenty-four years old, an active racer and river runner, but I had no idea what I was getting into.

We arrived in Sang Run to find the river running at 3 feet. The temperature was in the 40s, with a cold rain that later changed to sleet. Dave and Dan were really excited; they'd run the river often at summer levels of around 2 feet and wanted to see what it looked like. We quickly passed through the 3 miles of flatwater and easy rapids and got to the meat of the run. I back-endered in Gap Falls, a sloping ledge 4 feet high. I was shaken, but Dave was cool, and suggested that I "relax and do a few enders" to get loose. I wasn't interested. After scrambling through some "easy," but pushy, Class 4 below, we arrived at Bastard. I rolled three times and went for a long, long surf in the big holes in this long, steep drop. Below here there were only a few fast rapids before entering the next big drop. I flipped, rolled up, then broached against a huge rock. I pushed off with my hands and ran the next drop backwards. I rolled up, popped my sprayskirt, then scrambled for an eddy. After dumping my boat I was shaking so hard I couldn't get my sprayskirt back on.

I was embarrassed to tell Dave that I was carrying out, but he and Dan were pretty shaken, too. After I settled down, we ferried over to river left and started carrying up along a small stream. An hour later we reached the road. Here we left our boats and walked back to Sang Run. That evening all I could dream of was steep drops and huge holes.

—*Charlie Walbridge*

Cheat River (West Virginia) ➤

The Cheat is the largest undammed river in the East, draining a large watershed and set in a spectacular, scenic canyon. Although this is coal country and pollution from abandoned mines upstream detracts from water quality, the remote, narrow canyon retains its wild beauty, and there is abundant wildlife. The area has a long history of recreational use from nearby cities, including Pittsburgh. The river can be busy on weekends.

The derivation of the name is disputed. Some believe it came from the name of an early trapper. Others say it comes from the predominance of cheat grass along the river's banks. Still others point to a French-English treaty that cheated nearby settlers of their property. The most chilling explanation comes from Native American lore that the river will "cheat" the life from swimmers.

Boaters will not be cheated by the more than thirty rapids along this run's length. Most are technical, often blind drops formed by huge boulders that become wild holes and hydraulics at higher flows. Like the Upper Youghiogheny, the river is very sensitive to flow fluctuations. In the springtime or after heavy rains the river can turn into a real torrent that should be avoided. Low-water runs in late summer are becoming more popular, with suitable small craft such as kayaks, canoes, and inflatable kayaks. The gradient averages 25 fpm (4.7 mpk). Boaters should be aware that once in the canyon, getting out other than by the downriver route can be difficult. The best bet is a trail high above the river on the right.

In November 1985, a flood of catastrophic proportions brought on by Hurricane Juan hit the Cheat and other nearby drainages and destroyed much of the put-in town of Albright. Peak flows estimated in excess of 250,000 cfs rearranged the riverbed, leaving scour marks some 30 feet (9.2 m) up the canyon walls. Two of the biggest rapids, the aptly named Big Nasty and Coliseum, were made more difficult. Big Nasty was replaced with a keeper that boaters now avoid if possible. Coliseum, a series of drops traditionally considered the toughest rapid in the stretch, draws its name from patterns resembling Greek architecture on the nearby limestone cliffs. More recent floods in 1996 have made the upper part of Coliseum easier again, but a swim near the top here may be a long one. Boaters often gauge flows and abilities in the first rapid, Decision. Trouble here means it's time to consider a hike back to Albright.

Just below the take-out, Big Sandy Creek enters on the right. The 5½-mile (8.8 km) reach of Big Sandy Creek just upstream of the confluence is a playground for top experts. It highlights several runnable waterfalls including 18-foot (5.5 m) Big Sandy, with a pool landing, and 15-foot (4.6 m) Big Splat, with the possibility of a rocky landing if the setup move is missed. This is a spring runoff run and usually too low in the summer.

The Cheat has been threatened with several dam proposals, all of which are currently halted, but it is likely the Army Corps of Engineers will offer new projects to the locals under the guise of flood control.

CHEAT RIVER CANYON, ALBRIGHT TO JENKINSBURG

Difficulty: Class 4 at moderate flows; *not boatable at high flows*

Length: 11 miles (17.6 km)

Season: Rain and snow runoff, usually April through June and after rains

Character: Undammed, isolated river canyon

◁ Tygart River (West Virginia)

Season: Gorge run is rainfed, usually March to June; Valley Falls run depends on dam-releases, March through October
Character: Varies; a classic west-slope river

The Tygart River runs down the west slope of the Appalachians and resembles the Cheat River in many respects. Set in a remote, rugged canyon and laced with technical, boulder-enhanced drops, it has several runnable sections, but its whitewater potential was not discovered until after the Cheat was well known. Perhaps because of this it doesn't yet draw the big crowds. The river generates relatively big-volume flows, although upstream coal mining can affect water quality. Boaters should visually check flows, and exercise good judgment by going elsewhere at high flows. A railroad follows the river on the right.

The most popular section is the 12-mile (19.2 km) gorge run from the bridge at Bellington to a mile (1.6 km) below the Buckhannon confluence. Reach the put-in by turning off Route 250 near Ralph's Country Store. This tight, technical run with rapids formed by massive rocks and ledges develops some very pushy hydraulics and big waves at most flows. The gradient is about 37 fpm (7 mpk).

Downstream of the gorge run is an 8-mile (12.8 km) run, the Arden section, sometimes called the Tygart Valley run. This section is more difficult and not as scenic or as popular as the gorge run, but a road along the right allows a pre-run scout of the bigger drops. Like the gorge, the rapids are mostly boulder-strewn with ledges and holes. Two notable big drops are Moat's Falls, a 15-foot (4.6 m) river-wide falls runnable at higher flows, and Wells Falls, one of the toughest rapids in the East, a 12-foot (3.7 m) sloping drop into a powerful hole. The gradient here is 27 fpm (5 mpk).

When late-summer flows are too low for these sections, boaters turn their eyes downstream to the Valley Falls section, many miles downstream of Tygart Reservoir and Grafton Dam. This is a short, action-packed run from Valley Falls State Park to Hammond, with a gradient of about 100 fpm (19 mpk). Boaters will want to scout and possibly portage two big drops in the state park and a downstream behemoth called Hamburger Helper.

◁ Potomac River (Maryland, Virginia)

Season: All year
Character: Adjacent to urban area; wide, big-volume; major falls at fall line

"The navigation of this river is equal, if not superior, to any in the Union."
—*George Washington*

It has been said that every spot on the Potomac is another page in U.S. history. Even more than the mighty Mississippi, the Potomac runs through the core of the American experience. Its banks were chosen as the site of the nation's capital. Many of the great battles of the Civil War took place along its length, as the great Union army of McClellan and Meade took the river's name.

George Washington was an early explorer and advocate of the commercial potential of the Potomac in the mid-1700s. Though hardly by design, Washington helped to forward the cause of modern river running by working to construct a suitable route along the Potomac from the Atlantic Ocean through the Appalachian Mountains to the Ohio Valley. His coordination of efforts to construct a canal around the Great Falls, and his vision of a commercial river highway upstream, set in motion concepts that would lead to the Interstate Commerce Clause of the U.S. Constitution and its protections for the navigability of waterways. Fortunately for modern river runners, this constitutional clause has done more than any other enactment to ensure free recreational access to the nation's rivers. However, George Washington would not be remembered as the father of American river running or even commercial river transport, as others later found a more successful route on the Hudson and Mohawk rivers via the Erie Canal.

The Potomac is bordered on the Maryland shore by the Chesapeake & Ohio Canal National Historic Park. In 1996, the river served as a focal point for the right to river access with the much-publicized arrest of world slalom canoe champion Davey Hearn, who was accused by park officials of disregarding an alleged high-water river closure order, charges that were dismissed by a federal judge at trial.

The majesty of the river itself is equal to its historical significance. The river is a free-flowing, year-round classic passing through an imposing, rock-walled canyon. Although the run is just miles away from the nation's capital, in the midst of suburban sprawl, it is impossible to perceive this from the river, where an almost untouched panorama unfolds and wildlife abounds.

Like many other Eastern Seaboard cities, Washington is situated at the fall-line drop, where the river tumbles off the Piedmont Plateau and into the tidewater region in spectacular fashion. The Great Falls of the Potomac have migrated upstream some 9 miles,

Back in the 1970s, several rafting companies ran self-guided trips down the Cheat Canyon. Groups of eight to ten six-man rafts were accompanied by groups of four guides, two of whom were in kayaks ahead to set safety, direct traffic, and then lead everyone down. Each crew elected a "raft commander," who was usually the person with the biggest mouth. If the raft flipped, the kayakers picked up swimmers and gear. A "grunt guide," bringing up the rear, helped free any boats that got stuck on rocks.

When the water got over 4 feet on the Albright gauge we moved the trips upstream to the Cheat Narrows. This Class 3 roadside run is fast and wild when the water is over 7 feet. The best action is at Calamity Rock, a rounded obstruction 10 feet high and shaped like a giant Volkswagen Beetle. At these high levels it created a pretty impressive hole. One day, when the water was screaming along at 8 or 9 feet, we launched at Rowlesburg and floated the fast-moving flatwater, trying to prepare our group for what lay below.

One raft had a crew of Sikhs from India, wearing turbans. By the time we got to Calamity we knew we were dealing with a serious language barrier. Despite our frantic gestures, they went right over the pourover into a huge exploding wave. The raft, along with its occupants, was thrown end for end. The men were tossed so high and hard that their turbans unraveled. They were all recovered safely, but without their headgear, some distance downstream.

The entire sequence was recorded by another outfitter, who was filming on the site. It was rumored that he intended to use the footage to embarrass his competitor, but instead it became a classic among the guides. Every Memorial Day there was a huge party for all the Cheat guides, and among the films projected on the walls was this particular piece. As it got late the guides would chant, "Swa-mis! Swa-mis!" until the footage was shown. Regrettably, this footage was lost in the '85 flood, which leveled the town of Albright and ravaged the headquarters of three outfitters.

—Charlie Walbridge

leaving behind the canyon and rapids that make up the downstream run. For boating purposes, the river upstream of the Great Falls is flat and uninteresting, although it gets some use by flatwater canoeists.

The Great Falls is the definitive East Coast Class 6 drop. Above the falls is the 5-foot (1.5 m) Great Falls Dam, built around 1850 as part of the drinking water system. The river then bends left, splitting around several islands into a spectacular series of chutes and drops with an overall drop of 77 feet (23.5 m). This is a fine attraction and even more enjoyable if one is a whitewater enthusiast with little else to do but examine the multitude of precipices, chutes, holes, and sieves, looking for the best runnable route. It was not until 1976 that Tom McEwen, Wick Walter, and Dan Schnurrenberger made the first descent of the Great Falls, running the Spout on the Virginia side. Others have since found other routes, including Fishladder on the Maryland shoreline near the C & O Canal, and a route with three drops including Charlie's Hole, a vicious drop that has made swimmers out of many river legends. Streamers is the last drop in the centerline, a route available at higher flows. The most difficult route is the Bridge Channel, the channel dividing Olmsted and Falls islands, where the entire vertical fall of the rapid is focused into a single continuous, twisting maelstrom.

Running the falls has now become almost commonplace. Organizers even stage an annual race over the drops. All this does not mean you should come here to learn. Park rangers allow runs only before 9:00 A.M. and after 6:00 P.M., so as not to encourage anyone. As a disaster or near disaster would probably trigger a complete closure, the locals would ask that you master your waterfall skills elsewhere before coming here.

That summer of 1960, I was a fourteen-year-old in an aluminum rental canoe going hellbent down the rapids of the Potomac River. If there ever was a classic formula that spelled trouble, this was it—a bunch of teenagers with the summer off, craving adventure, and lacking the knowledge or maturity to find it without getting into trouble.

It all started innocently enough. On a blisteringly hot day, we took the bus down to Fletcher's Boathouse and rented a canoe. We paddled on the C & O Canal until we got to a lock and a sign saying something like "No Rental Canoes Beyond This Point." Off to the west, beyond the sign were beautiful woodlands past which one could hear the distant rumble of the Potomac River. Heck, it was summertime, and we were teenagers with too much time on our hands and a big thirst for adventure. What else could we do?

That's right, we carried the canoe through the woods to the Potomac. We started out feeling good, floating along on moving water. The moving water became swiftly moving water, then ripples, then rapids. We were in heaven. The excitement! The exhilaration! It was wonderful. Capsize? Who cared—we were young and immortal. At the end of the rapids we carried the canoe up and ran them again.

I can't remember exactly how many times we shot the Potomac that summer. The last time I do recall losing my glasses and a friend of mine receiving a large bruise on his thigh. That put a stop to our canoe adventures for the season. The next summer my family moved to California and I forgot about the thrill of whitewater, until the movie Deliverance drew me back in—this time for good.

—Jim Cassady

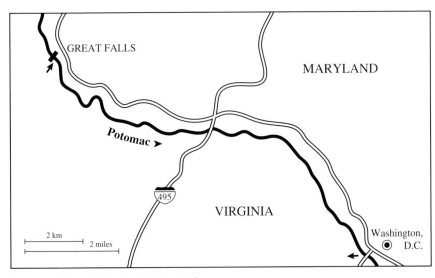

Potomac River (Maryland, Virginia)

After the falls, the Potomac travels through a mild canyon that is sometimes called Mather Gorge. Generally the rapids get more difficult as one continues down the run. Major drops include O-Deck (near the observation stand), S-Turn, Rocky Island, Wet Bottom Chute, Difficult Run, Yellow Falls (to the right of a large island with easier Calico Falls to the left), and Stubblefield Falls. Downstream is a mandatory portage left near a pumping station over the deceptively dangerous Brookmont Dam (also known as Little Falls Dam), another city drinking water project. Farther downstream, the tough Little Falls section awaits boaters. Paralleling the river on the Maryland side is the historic Chesapeake & Ohio Canal, which allows boaters parking, access, and a chance to paddle back in certain sections to rerun rapids. Most of the property on the Virginia side is privately owned.

The Beltway (Interstate 495) crosses the river about halfway down. This is the only bridge across the run but provides no access. The river enters the Washington, D.C., city limits and hits tidewater at the take-out. The gradient averages 14 fpm (2.6 mpk).

Potomac River, South Branch (West Virginia) ➢

The attraction of the South Branch of the Potomac is not only the good whitewater near the top of the Smoke Hole run, but also the beautiful, rugged mountain country through which it passes. This is Appalachian countryside at its best, an area rich in Civil War history and a tradition of independence.

The Smoke Hole run is 25 miles (40 km) from Route 220 to Petersburg. The most difficult whitewater (Class 3) is in the first 5 miles (8 km) to Smoke Hole Campground. Watch for landslides and old dams in this stretch. Downstream is Class 2, but the beauty of this stretch justifies doing the run, often considered the most rugged and beautiful in the Potomac drainage. About 4 miles (6.4 km) downstream of Smoke Hole Campground is Big Bend Campground, a popular place to camp overnight with good vehicle access. Downstream from here, access is very limited. The canyon opens up about

ROUTE 220 TO BIG BEND
    CAMPGROUND (UPPER SMOKE
    HOLE RUN)
Difficulty: Class 3
Length: 9 miles (14.4 km)

BIG BEND CAMPGROUND TO
    PETERSBURG (LOWER SMOKE
    HOLE RUN)
Difficulty: Class 2
Length: 16 miles (25.6 km)

OLD FIELDS TO HARMISON'S
    LANDING (TROUGH RUN)
Difficulty: Class 1+
Length: 11 miles (17.6 km)

Season: Rain-fed, usually
    March into June; longer
    in the Trough
Character: Scenic,
    undammed mountain
    river

Senior Prom

I was still hung up on Arlene. So was Ricky. But it was unrequited love. As the school year wound down, she started dating a Young Republican, and it seemed like a radical act for the Vietnam era. When Ricky and I independently asked her to the senior prom, she turned us both down for her radical right-winger.

We'd been left, as it were, high and dry. Neither of us found other dates for the most socially significant event of a teenager's life. So we turned to one another and said, "Let's go run a river."

We picked the Smoke Hole Canyon section of the South Branch of the Potomac in West Virginia for two reasons: We'd never done it before, and it was as far away from the prom as we could get and still be on our river. It was a section George Washington described as "two ledges of Mountain Impassable running side by side together for above seven or eight miles and ye River down between them." So, as the senior class was slipping into crinoline and tuxedos, we were putting on knee pads and lifejackets; as carnations were being exchanged, we were trading strokes on the Upper Potomac.

—Richard Bangs

5 miles (8 km) from the take-out, and shortly thereafter the North Fork of the South Branch enters on the left. From there it is an easy float down to Petersburg.

The Trough run is from near Old Fields to Harmison's Landing (near hamlets of Globe and Sector). This reach is popular with canoeists and novice groups. Though not a whitewater run, it does pass through a deep canyon with some fine scenery.

◁ Shenandoah River (West Virginia)

MILLVILLE TO SECOND ROUTE 340 BRIDGE, OR WEAVERTON (BULL FALLS AND STAIRCASE RUN)
Difficulty: Class 3–
Length: 6 miles (9.6 km), 7 miles (11.2 km) to Weaverton
Season: March to November; sometimes too low after long, dry spells
Character: Scenic, historical, undammed mountain river

As the Potomac cuts through the Blue Ridge Mountains it is joined by the Shenandoah River near the beautiful and historic town of Harpers Ferry, West Virginia. While most reaches of the Potomac and Shenandoah are flat with barely a few ripples, the Shenandoah offers some fine whitewater just as it passes Harpers Ferry on its way to the Potomac.

The put-in is in West Virginia, about 5 miles (8 km) upstream of the Potomac-Shenandoah River confluence near Millville. The biggest rapid is Bull Falls at mile 3 (4.8 km), a river-wide ledge with several runnable routes depending on water levels. Downstream are Bull Tail's Rapid, Lunch Rock Follies, and the mile-long (1.6 km) Staircase at mile 4 (6.4 km).

There is much more to the Shenandoah than whitewater. The landscape is impressive, as the river is often lined with cliffs and split by islands before passing through a dramatic gap in the Blue Ridge Mountains. Waterfowl are common, and the bass fishing is reportedly excellent.

The status of the take-out access is presently unclear. Boaters have a choice of two legal exits: One is at Potomac Wayside on the Potomac at the second Route 340 bridge, carrying gear from a small upstream creek on the right. The second involves paddling an additional mile (1.6 km) of flatwater to Weaverton and exiting at the creek mouth and trail leading to Keep Tryst Road. Some risk taking out at Harpers Ferry or at a nearby gravel pit, although the legal status of both take-outs is uncertain. Local paddling groups are attempting to establish better access.

It is a good idea to set time aside to take in the sights at Harpers Ferry. Abolitionist John Brown's last stand on the eve of the Civil War is just part of the history in this area. Thomas Jefferson wrote that the panorama here was inspiring enough to justify the trip across the ocean from Europe. Other outdoor opportunities can be found here as well. Harpers Ferry is one of the main waypoints for through-hikes on the Appalachian Trail.

James River (Virginia) ➤

REEDY CREEK TO MAYO ISLAND
Difficulty: Class 4–
Length: 6 miles (9.6 km)

Season: All year
Character: Urban whitewater river at fall line

Like many Eastern towns, the city of Richmond grew up at the fall line, where the rivers tumble off the Piedmont for their final run to the coast. In Richmond, the power of the rapids was used to run mills and other industries. What began as a mill town became a focus of contention during the Revolutionary War. Later it served as the capital of the Confederacy during the Civil War, and its conquest became an obsession with the Union. As a result, it suffered some of the most prolonged and environmentally destructive campaigns of the war. In many respects the river has still to recover from battles fought almost 150 years ago.

Like the Potomac, the biggest whitewater action on the James is at the fall line, though neither the river nor the drop here are as dramatic. Upstream runs are essentially flat through hilly country, and downstream the river enters tidelands. The rapids are located right in downtown Richmond where the town grew up. Most put in at Reedy Creek at River Road, although another possible put-in is Pony Pasture. Take out at the east side of Mayo Island/14th Street. Local boaters have built a wooden ramp here to solve the problem of the muddy carry to the parking lot. A kayak shop here, Old Downtown Adventures, can help with info and a shuttle.

The current run became possible due to breaches in dams beginning in 1969. The conglomeration of the ruins of countless dams and weirs form the chutes and ledges we see today. The rapids probably bear little resemblance to nature's long-lost original, but the location suits city dwellers, for many good playspots can be found just a few hundred yards from their office. Two well-known rapids are Hollywood (across from the Hollywood Cemetery) and a series of drops called Pipeline (named for a huge pipe on the left bank).

First-timers may want to boat with someone familiar with the river. Some rapids hold debris and rebar and are substantially more difficult and dangerous at high flows, when this stretch should probably be avoided.

New River (West Virginia) ➤

SANDSTONE FALLS TO MCCREERY
(UPPER RUN)
Difficulty: Class 2
Length: 15 miles (24 km)

MCCREERY TO THURMOND
(MIDDLE RUN)
Difficulty: Class 2+
Length: 16 miles (25.6 km)

(continued on following page)

The New River cuts a northerly course from its headwaters in North Carolina to the foothills of West Virginia. Its route takes it through several ridges in the Alleghenies, confirming that it was in place since a time when the Appalachians were a much different range. Ironically, the New River may be the oldest river in North America. Some say it's second only to the Nile as the oldest in the world. The river now exposes strata hundreds of millions of years old, so whatever its perch on the pecking order of river seniority, it has indeed been around for a while. In 1978 Congress designated it a National River.

The New River features relative isolation and large volume, generating some big flows as it reaches the 1,400-foot-deep (427 m) New River Gorge. It is one of the few rivers of the East where overnight trips are common. The river is usually divided into three sections: the upper, middle, and gorge runs. All three are within the New River

Difficulty: Class 4–
Length: 14 miles (22.4 km)

Season: March to
November
Character: Big water, big
streambed; railroad
tracks follow river,
secondary roads follow
in some places; isolated
by eastern standards

Gorge National River boundary. The gradients for the different sections are 8 fpm (1.5 mpk), 10 fpm (2 mpk), and 14 fpm (2.6 mpk), respectively.

The upper section is the least run due to its long flat stretches, but it has plenty of good camping and fishing. As in the rest of the canyon, wildflowers in the spring and colorful leaves in the fall provide good scenery. The long pools and easy rapids are formed by a series of ledges and make this stretch popular with open-boaters. Put in just downstream of Sandstone Falls parking area about 8½ miles (13.6 km) downstream of the bridge at Hinton. The take-out (and put-in for the second run) is in McCreery, on the

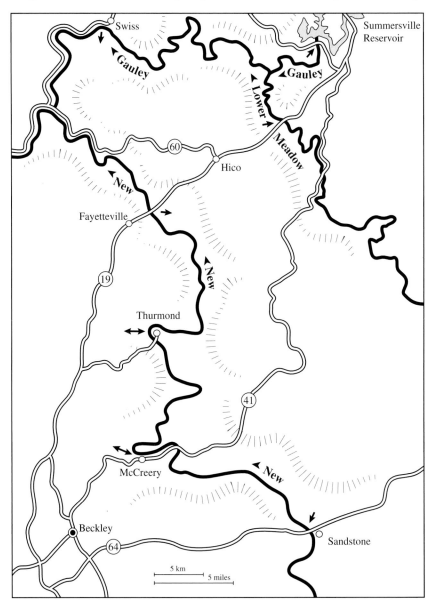

New, Gauley, and Lower Meadow Rivers (West Virginia)

left, about 200 yards (183 m) above the first bridge you see. The public access is across from a country store, or alternate access can be found nearby in Prince.

The middle section is a little more interesting, and open-boaters and novices sometimes combine the first two sections, depending on river conditions. Rafting companies also combine this section with the gorge run for multi-day trips. The take-out (and the put-in for the gorge section) is on the right at the Thurmond Store. Thurmond is what remains of a colorful coal-mining town that had its heyday in 1910 when some 76,541 passengers came or left here via the rail spur. A new access point can be found 1½ miles (2.4 km) downstream of Thurmond at the Dunglen day use area. The first several miles below Thurmond, however, are mostly flatwater. Those with little patience for the flat stuff can put in farther downstream at Canard, just above the Railroad rapids.

In the gorge section, the river cuts through a rugged canyon sometimes divided into Surprise Canyon above the Cunard access and the Lower Gorge below. Of the three sections, the gorge has the best whitewater and is the most popular with big-water devotees and commercial rafting companies. The first rapid, Surprise, culminates in a big, but forgiving, wave hole. A railroad bridge signals Upper, Middle, and Lower Railroad, a series of three ledges with big holes and some popular surfing action. Boaters sometimes scout Lower Railroad on the left. Next is the big action of Upper, Middle, and Lower Keeney, rated Class 4– at moderate levels. These are straightforward, distinct drops with pools or eddies at the bottom. Some great play-holes and surf spots are found here and farther down on Lollygag and Dudley's Dip, followed by Double Z just downstream.

The take-out is down a steep, narrow road under the Route 19 bridge, a single span 876 feet (267 m) above the river. Once a year a crowd gathers as authorities allow BASE jumping (fixed-point parachuting) from the bridge. Summer flows usually range from 1,000 to 5,000 cfs (28.3 to 141.5 cumecs), but flows run higher on a regular basis, raising the difficulty a full class as wicked hydraulics, whirlpools, and huge holes dominate.

Downstream is a challenging section correctly called the Dries, which unfortunately is only runnable on rare occasions when upstream flows are high enough (over 9,000 cfs) to overcome water diversions at Hawk's Nest Dam.

Gauley River (West Virginia) ➤

One of the flagship rivers of the eastern United States, the Gauley (pronounced "golly") is a dam-release classic with reliable flows provided by late-season reservoir drawdowns. It features tough, rocky rapids, stunning canyon walls, and occasional side streams cascading into the river. The source of the excitement is the giant tubes of Summersville Dam as they open up for autumn releases from Summersville Reservoir. The jets literally shake the entire area as boats and boaters launch into the tough rapids. River runners can expect to find plenty of fellow paddlers, both commercial and private, to share in the weekend fun. The Gauley put-in at peak season is a carnival.

The area also has a bit of history to it which can be seen from the river. On September 10, 1861, Union troops forced Confederates under General Floyd to retreat from positions above the Camifex Ferry at the confluence of the Gauley and Meadow rivers. The area is now preserved as a state park. At the beginning of the 1900s a railroad was brought in to transport timber. Old-timers still tell of floating the easy lower reaches on

SUMMERSVILLE DAM TO BELOW
  SWEETS FALLS
Difficulty: Class 5– at
  2,800 cfs (79.24
  cumecs), Class 4 at
  1,000 cfs (28.3 cumecs)
Length: 9 miles (14.4 km)

BELOW SWEET'S FALLS TO PETERS
  CREEK
Difficulty: Class 3 at 2,800
  cfs (79.24 cumecs), Class
  3– at 1,000 cfs (28.3
  cumecs)
Length: 7 miles (11.2 km)

(continued on following page)

PETERS CREEK TO SWISS
Difficulty: Class 4 at 2,800 cfs (79.24 cumecs), Class 4– at 1,000 cfs (28.3 cumecs)
Length: 11 miles (17.6 km)

Season: September and October, plus low-water spring and summer flows
Character: Spectacular canyon, choice whitewater, considered tops in the East during fall drawdown of upstream dam

railroad ties. In 1988 the lower 25 miles (40 km) of the Gauley River were placed in the Gauley River National Recreation Area, operated by the National Park Service.

The Gauley is most famous for its countless rapids. The river has an average overall gradient of 27 fpm (5 mpk), and much of the riverbed is sandstone with many of the midstream boulders undercut. It is usually divided into two or three parts: Summersville Dam to below Sweet's Falls, below Sweet's Falls to Peters Creek, and Peters Creek to Swiss; however, running the middle section is contingent on permission to use private access points. Running just the middle section avoids the tougher rapids above and below. Private access points may be found below Sweet's Falls, at Mason Branch at the end of Richmond Chapel Road, at Koontz Bend, at Panther Creek, and/or at Peters Creek.

The first stretch is the most challenging. The put-in is just below the dam. The first tough rapid is Insignificant. This misnomer is drawn from an entry in the journal of a kayaker of the first descent that any rapid above Pillow Rock was "insignificant." While that has caused more than a little head-scratching over the years, it does give deserved respect to bigger rapids such as Pillow Rock, a house-sized boulder on the left which takes the brunt of the entire river, pushing it to the right where the current is then split by a large chunk of sandstone. A portage on the right is available.

At mile 5 (8 km) the Meadow River enters on the left, near the site of Camifex Ferry Battlefield. The railroad also begins to follow the river here. The demanding upstream run on the Lower Meadow is described in its own section below.

Just downstream is Lost Paddle, a long and difficult series of drops and undercuts with the option of a ½-mile (0.8 km) portage. Next is Iron Ring, where the history of logging on the river is evident. An iron ring left by logging operations in the early 1900s was secured to a rock on the right until it was stolen in 1988. Blasting associated with logging apparently disfigured a submerged midstream rock which now vents its wrath on river runners by generating bizarre hydraulics at lower flows. Sweet's Falls at mile 8½ (13.6 km) offers the choice of a big drop on the right, a tough sneak route through rocks on the left, or a portage farther left.

Easier whitewater lies downstream of Sweet's Falls; access is at Panther Creek Road on the right, with permission of a rafting company on the property. Put in 200 yards (183 m) upstream of Koontz Flume. Access may also be available at Peters Creek on the right at mile 18 (28.8 km). Other big rapids below Koontz Flume include Upper and Lower Mash, Heaven's Gate, Riverwide Stopper, and the last major drop, Pure Screaming Hell, where Hell Hole dominates the right side of the river. Take out at Swiss after a 2-mile (3.2 km) flatwater paddle. The Gauley and New rivers join downstream.

ROUTE 19 TO GAULEY RIVER
Difficulty: Class 5+
Length: 5 miles (8 km)

Season: Rain-fed, usually from April into June
Character: Small, steep, very difficult; paddlers must take out on the Gauley

◁ Lower Meadow River (West Virginia)

While the Gauley River was once regarded as the pinnacle of paddling skills in the East, the steep collection of ledges and drops laced with undercuts and sieves of the Lower Meadow River has replaced it as the regional standard. With an overall gradient of 94 fpm (17.5 mpk) and some stretches over 120 fpm (22.8 mpk), this is a technical, exacting, and potentially perilous stretch of river that becomes even more dangerous above optimum flows of about 1,000 cfs (28.3 cumecs). In 1989 alone, the Lower Meadow claimed the lives of two excellent boaters. For all the anxiety and hazards, many great and almost great boaters accept the challenge and the thrill of the nonstop action. True masters display top form by paddling in solitude, transfixed by the steep, laurel-covered hills set beneath magnificent sandstone bluffs. Most mortals focus on surviving the drops of up to 10 feet (3 m), catching the needle-eye eddies and dealing with the tough hydraulics and dearth of pools or clear lines of vision downstream.

Put in after a steep climb down from the Route 19 bridge. The toughest rapids include Rites of Passage, Brink of Disaster, Home Sweet Jesus (usually portaged), Gateway, Big and Little Down and Out, Island Falls, Sliding Board, and Double Undercut. Railroad tracks follow the river high on the left, providing some measure of comfort. At mile 5 (8 km) the Lower Meadow River meets the Gauley River at the site of the Camifex Ferry Battlefield and just upstream of Lost Paddle rapid. Boaters can hike a steep mile (1.6 km) up to the park or continue on the Gauley 14 miles (22.4 km) to Swiss or upstream private access (see Gauley River description). After the Meadow River, the Gauley may seem flat; however, flows will be high when the Meadow is running. Come summertime, the Meadow is usually too low to run. Easier runs on the Meadow can be found upstream of the Route 19 bridge, with access points at Rainelle and Nallen.

Greenbrier River (West Virginia) ➤

Many an Eastern whitewater devotee first gets his or her feet wet on the Greenbrier in southeastern West Virginia. The Greenbrier features some great campgrounds and good fishing in a near-wilderness setting. Boaters have their options of boatable stretches: the most popular is the 44-mile (70.4 km), Class 2– reach from Durbin to Marlinton with a gradient of up to 15 fpm (2.8 mpk). The midway point on this run is the town of Cass.

Most of the river is quite easy, with only a few decent-sized waves and an occasional midstream rock to avoid. Towards the end of the run the streambed broadens. Downstream of Talcott, near the end of Greenbrier, lurks Bacon Falls (Class 4), on a reach known as the Big Bend.

WILDELL TO NEW RIVER
Difficulty: Class 1 to 2–
Length: 167 miles (267.2 km)

Season: All year
Character: Long, meandering run, popular in the summer and especially with canoeists

Russell Fork (Virginia, Kentucky) ➤

Its proper name is the Russell Fork of the Levisa Fork of the Big Sandy River, understandably shortened to Russell Fork by most. Saving your breath may come in handy when taking on what is considered one of the toughest runs in the East and almost certainly the toughest commercially run stretch of water in the region. In one 2½-mile (4 km) stretch, the river drops 200 fpm (38 mpk), generating some imposing drops, nasty hydraulics, and bad undercuts.

The essence of the Russell Fork is its relentless erosion through Pine Ridge, an area set on two converging faults. The result is an impressive 1,600-foot (488 m) gorge cut from sandstone. The gorge is sometimes called "The Breaks of Pine Ridge" and forms part of the border between Virginia and Kentucky. Breaks Interstate Park is the product of cooperation between the two states. The area is beautiful, especially when autumn colors provide the backdrop during the late-season releases.

Although the run starts out easy for the first 1½ miles (2.4 km) downstream of the put-in at John W. Flannagan Dam and Reservoir on the Pound River, it gradually gets tougher. The toughest section starts shortly after the river turns away from the railroad tracks that cut through the Towers Loop. It's nearly nonstop action until you reach the Kentucky-Virginia border, where Grassy Creek enters on the right. Just downstream a trail comes down from Route 80.

BREAKS INTERSTATE PARK, FLANNAGAN DAM (VIRGINIA) TO ELKHORN CITY (KENTUCKY)
Difficulty: Class 5
Length: 10 miles (16 km)

Season: Dam-releases, usually in October
Character: Steep, very difficult, with limited dam-releases

Russell Fork, Virginia/Kentucky. *(Dave Manby)*

El Horrendo, Russell Fork, Virginia. *(Russell Fork Expeditions, Inc./Southern Exposures)*

The first significant rapid is Tower Falls, a comparatively straightforward drop set next to a mammoth boulder. Farther downstream is Triple Drop, a series of three big drops forming hungry keepers at higher flows. Next is El Horrendo, perhaps the signature rapid of the Russell Fork. The rapid consists of two even bigger drops formed by ledges set between sedimentary slabs. Climax, a boulder-clogged passage beneath red sandstone cliffs, is farther downstream. At lower flows the runnable routes on Climax may disappear entirely beneath the rocks.

Scouting is a must, and those unfamiliar with the gorge should probably run with a Russell Fork veteran or scout the entire run on foot beforehand. Be careful when using the railroad tunnels on the left to get a better view, as train traffic is not uncommon. The run is very sensitive to flows, and boaters should go elsewhere at high water. Scheduled drawdown releases of around 800 cfs (22.64 cumecs) are usually in October and are a little below the optimal level for kayaks—about 1,300 cfs (36.79 cumecs). At lower levels this is a good run for high-performance inflatable kayaks.

Cumberland North Fork (Kentucky) ⮞

This choice scenic gorge run is located just below the spectacular Cumberland Falls and is usually referred to as the Cumberland "Below the Falls" run. The river is remote and enjoys the protection of the State of Kentucky as a wild river. Most of the rapids are formed by boulders, but the river remains runnable even at very low flows. Logs and strainers can be a hazard. The overall gradient is 12 fpm (2.3 mpk).

The run has some drawbacks, including the flatwater paddle at the end that is usually shortest when the reservoir is lowest in fall and spring. Check with local outfitters for levels. It is a steep ¼-mile (0.4 km) carry down to the put-in, and the shuttle is difficult.

At the put-in boaters can paddle back up to get great views of the falls but are advised to stay well clear of the water recirculating upstream under the falls. The best-known rapids include Center Rock, Bradford's Rock, Surfing Rapid, Pinball, Screaming Right Turn, Stairsteps, and Last Drop. Some of the lower rapids may be inundated, depending on the reservoir level. Upstream of Cumberland Falls is over 100 miles (160 km) of easy paddling.

CUMBERLAND FALLS TO CUMBERLAND RESERVOIR (BELOW THE FALLS RUN)
Difficulty: Class 3–
Length: 10 miles (16 km) total, but only 5–8 miles (8–12.8 km) of fast water, depending on the Cumberland Reservoir level at the bottom

Season: Rain-fed, but the river is runnable all year; the most popular months are March through October
Character: Undammed river with widely fluctuating river levels; length of run on river varies with the level of downstream reservoir

Big South Fork (Tennessee, Kentucky) ⮞

Set beneath the eroded sandstone bluffs and hardwood forests of the Cumberland Plateau and Daniel Boone National Forest, this classic run was protected in 1974 as part of the Big South Fork National River. All shuttles are long, and the roads are bad.

The first section to Leatherwood Ford (called the gorge run) has a gradient of 20 fpm (3.8 mpk). Put in on the Clear Fork River at Burnt Mill Bridge. About 4 miles (6.4 km) downstream is the confluence with the New River, which forms the Big South Fork. Most rapids are the result of innumerable boulders in and about the river. The most challenging rapids are about 1 mile (1.6 km) downstream of the New River confluence, including Double Falls, Washing Machine (also known as Slot), and E 1. Downstream, the river passes through Rion's Eddy, the Narrows, Jake's Hole, and O&W Rapid, just upstream of the O&W railroad bridge at mile 9 (14.4 km).

The second section from Leatherwood Ford to Blue Heron is fairly mild except for two drops, Angel Falls at the beginning and Devils Jump near the end. The gradient is 8 fpm (1.5 mpk).

The third section to Yamacraw also has a gradient of 8 fpm (1.5 mpk). Cumberland Reservoir is just downstream.

BURNT MILL BRIDGE TO LEATHERWOOD FORD (GORGE RUN)
Difficulty: Class 3+
Length: 11 miles (17.6 km)

LEATHERWOOD FORD TO BLUE HERON
Difficulty: Class 4–
Length: 24 miles (38.4 km)

BLUE HERON TO YAMACRAW
Difficulty: Class 2
Length: 5 miles (8 km)

Season: Rain-fed; usually November through May, longer on lower runs
Character: Scenic, remote, undammed

◄ Watauga River (North Carolina, Tennessee)

The Watauga River Gorge is one of the finest pieces of whitewater in the East. It cuts through Stone Mountain Ridge, the border between North Carolina and Tennessee. The gorge itself is 5 miles (8 km) long, dropping at 100 fpm (19 mpk). The river enters the gorge just below the put-in at Guys Ford Bridge, and the action starts about half a mile (0.8 km) downstream after the river takes an abrupt right turn. The biggest obstacle is Watauga Falls (also known as State Line Falls) where boaters must decide whether to portage a 16-foot (4.9 m) drop and/or the second, 8-foot (2.5 m) drop. Scout early and often. Boaters often portage some of the other big drops. Watch the flows here, as differences in levels can make a big difference in difficulty. Watauga Reservoir provides about a 1-mile paddle out at the end.

Immediately below Watauga Reservoir, the river is flat and uninteresting, but below Elizabethton the river enters an easy, scenic mini-gorge. There are several road access points, so the length of the run varies.

◄ Nolichucky River (North Carolina, Tennessee)

After leaving its headwaters on Mount Mitchell, at 6,684 feet (2,037 m) the highest point in the eastern United States, the Nolichucky River, like the Watauga, cuts through the ridge that is the border between North Carolina and Tennessee. The Noli's path takes it through Pisgah and Cherokee national forests. The gorge is dramatic, some 900 feet (275 m) deep, with the river some 2,500 feet (763 m) below the tops of the surrounding ridges. Though the two rivers have similar settings, the Nolichucky is a bit easier than the Watauga, with a bigger streambed, better flows, and a longer season. Hard-boaters may consider it more of a play run than the Watauga, which is more of a steep creek.

Put in at the forest service access in Poplar, North Carolina. Most of the big action is at the top. Big rapids include On the Rocks and Quarter-Mile, and a good surfing hole can be found between them. The gradient on the run averages 36 fpm (6.8 mpk) overall but drops at 67 fpm (12.6 mpk) for the first half. The lower half is mellow, with some smaller surf spots for hard-boaters. The river is dangerous at high flows. Flows get low in the summer, but the river can usually still be run in small craft.

A good side hike at Devils Creek on the right at mile 6 (9.6 km) leads to an intimate waterfall and pool.

Upstream mining tends to cloud the water on the Nolichucky. Here as elsewhere, mining areas and strange history go hand in hand. Volume 1 of William Nealy's classic *Whitewater Home Companion* recounts some of the curious historical events that are said to have taken place here, including the arrival of the Conquistadors, the lynching of a circus elephant, and the disappearance of 90 pounds of weapons-grade plutonium. The Clinchfield Railroad follows the river on the left. Be careful when walking along its tracks, as the line still gets regular use.

French Broad River (North Carolina) ➢

The French Broad is a big river that starts in southwestern North Carolina, flows north through Ashville, and then cuts through the Big Bald Mountains of Tennessee. The river offers little of interest to the whitewater enthusiast except for the stretch from Barnard to Hot Springs, close to the North Carolina–Tennessee border where it leaves civilization and carves a jumbled course through the mountains.

Many of the rapids on the French Broad are formed by ledges. Downstream of where Big Laurel Creek enters on the right is Needle Rock, where boaters can run the optional drop at Kayaker's Ledge on the right. The biggest rapid is just downstream, a series of ledge drops with a big bottom hole called Frank Bell's Rapid, sometimes used by skilled hard-boaters as a playspot. The river drops at 25 fpm (4.7 mpk) through Pisgah National Forest and is followed by railroad tracks. There is road access about halfway down on the right at a small building called Stackhouse just after Big Laurel Creek enters on the right. Stackhouse, a former waystation for the underground railroad, offers an interesting history. Big Laurel Creek is a scenic alternative route to paddle to Hot Springs when there is enough water; it is described below.

BARNARD TO HOT SPRINGS
Difficulty: Class 3+
Length: 8 miles (12.8 km)

Season: All year
Character: Large, undammed drainage area downstream of urban area, away from civilization

Big Laurel Creek (North Carolina) ➢

This beautiful tributary of the French Broad is an attractive and challenging alternative to the bigger river when it is runnable. It drops at 50 fpm (9.7 mpk) through a 1,000-foot-deep canyon and is about the same distance to the Hot Springs take-out as the main stem of the French Broad. Another advantage is the easy shuttle, just 5½ miles (8.8 km) on one road, Route 25/70.

Don't be fooled if flows look low at the put-in; things will be better as the stream narrows downstream. The rapids are tough and the streambed at least twice as steep as on the French Broad. Big drops include Stairstep, Suddy Hole, and the Narrows. A railroad bridge announces the confluence with the main stem. Big Laurel Creek is in Pisgah National Forest as well.

ROUTE 25/70 BRIDGE TO HIGHWAY BRIDGE AT HOT SPRINGS ON THE FRENCH BROAD RIVER
Difficulty: Class 4–
Length: 8 miles (12.8 km)

Season: Rain-fed; usually runnable into June and after heavy rains
Character: Small, tight, scenic tributary of the French Broad River

Pigeon River (Tennessee) ➢

The Pigeon River starts in North Carolina and offers its best whitewater as it cuts through the ridge that forms the border between North Carolina and Tennessee. In this run it passes through parts of the Great Smoky Mountains, just northeast of the Great Smoky Mountains National Park and Pisgah National Forest. Interstate 40 follows the river and provides the put-in access, below the power plant at Waterville, and take-out access, where parking may be available at USA Raft. Flows are diverted at an upstream reservoir and returned to the river just above this run. Put in at Waterville, just downstream of the power plant where the water reenters the streambed, and get ready for about a dozen Class 3 rapids and a few Class 4– drops, the biggest of which is Lost Guide.

The Pigeon River received much less attention in the past than it does today, mostly due to pollution from upstream sources and irregular flows from dam-releases. Two events have brought whitewater enthusiasts to the Pigeon. One is the continued im-

WATERVILLE TO HARTFORD
Difficulty: Class 4–
Length: 5 miles (8 km)

Season: Dam-releases, not always predictable but often daily releases
Character: Dam-controlled; interstate highway near

provement of water quality due to modernization of the almost century-old Champion International pulp mill upstream. Improvements were made in both the 1980s and '90s; some feel that further improvements are possible and hopefully will be forthcoming. The second event was the rupture of an upstream dam on May 20, 1996, which ultimately resulted in better flows. Downstream of the take-out at Hartford, the Pigeon drifts calmly through Tennessee.

◁ Wilson Creek (North Carolina)

ABOVE TEN-FOOT FALLS TO
BROWN MOUNTAIN BEACH
(GORGE RUN)
Difficulty: Class 5–
Length: 3 miles (4.8 km)

Season: Rain-fed, usually March through May
Character: Small, technical, rain-fed; avoid at high flows

Steep-creekin' is big in the Southeast, and North Carolina has some fine steep creeks, among them Wilson Creek and the Linville River described below. Wilson Creek drops through a granite gorge at a rate of 60 to 100 fpm (11.58 to 19.3 mpk). Most of the rapids are of the technical, pool-and-drop variety. The biggest drops are Ten-Foot Falls, Boat Buster, Thunder Ball, Stairstep (sometimes portaged over island), and Razorback, an 8-foot (2.4 m) drop. These are just the notables; many lesser, but still challenging, rapids lurk along the way. Some of the big rapids are long, and the big drops don't always have an obvious upstream signature, so frequent scouting is essential. Flows make a big difference here, and the run is significantly more dangerous at high flows (flows that are too low expose hard-boaters to danger). A dirt road follows the river on the right.

Wilson Creek, North Carolina. *(Russell Fork Expeditions, Inc.)*

The put-in is ¼ mile (0.4 km) upstream of the Pisgah National Forest sign (and upstream of Ten-Foot Falls), and the take-out is at Brown Mountain Beach. Please be nice to the folks at Brown Mountain Beach; they have been friendly to boaters in the past and deserve better treatment than they sometimes receive. If you are not allowed to take out here, you will have to continue downstream to the next available spot.

Linville River (North Carolina) ➤

Those who have graduated from the Lower Meadow River and are now ready for one of the very toughest runs in the East might consider the Linville River. Seventeen miles of whitewater laced with Class 5+ drops and several portages await those who are up for it. This pristine classic tumbles and turns at the bottom of Linville Gorge, below canyon rims rising up to 2,000 feet (610 m) in several places. The Cherokee reportedly called the stretch Eeseeoh, meaning "a river of many cliffs." Both sides of the river are protected as part of the 11,000-acre Linville Gorge Wilderness Area. Once inside, access is limited to a network of trails. Although the area is good for hiking, be ready for a long climb out in case of an emergency.

The Linville's headwaters are in the Grandfather Mountain drainage, and there are two upstream dams. Water levels are critical to a successful run; so is avoiding undercuts on many of the drops. The overall gradient of 110 fpm (21.2 mpk) includes a 5-mile (8 km) stretch from Babel Tower to Chimney Branch where the river nose-dives at 208 fpm (40 mpk). The action is continuous and steep until near the bottom. Just below the take-out the Linville flows into a reservoir.

The gorge is not often run, and its inclusion here should not be seen as a green light to "go for it." It should not be attempted by anyone who has not mastered creek-boating skills or is not comfortable with other Class 5 runs such as the Lower Meadow. It has been run in one day, but multi-day trips are more realistic for those not completely familiar with the river. Those up to the task should look for good weather and longer days to provide some extra time.

LINVILLE GORGE, BELOW LINVILLE
FALLS TO ROUTE 126
Difficulty: Class 5+ₚ
Length: 17 miles (27.2 km)

Season: Rain-fed, small drainage; April and May are good times
Character: Small, tight, wilderness, rain-fed

Green River (North Carolina) ➤

Besides sharing the same dam-releases and the same riverbed, Green Narrows and the lower Green (Cove run) have little in common. The lower Green is a pleasing, easily accessible, Class 2 run. The Narrows is a spectacular, experts-only free-fall, with the steepest 1-mile (1.6 km) section of the run dropping at the hair-raising rate of 365 fpm (70.45 mpk). The Narrows section is a relatively recent discovery, considered by many to be the top challenge in the region.

Put in for the Narrows below the Tuxedo Powerhouse downstream of Summit Reservoir. Disputes have arisen recently with local landowners over access and parking, so check locally where to put in and park when planning a trip.

The powerhouse usually releases around 300 cfs (8.5 cumecs) daily. First up is a ½-mile (0.8 km) Class 2 warm-up before the big action starts. The more notable of many tough rapids are Frankenstein, Boof or Consequences, Squeeze, Zwik's Backender, and Chief; beware of pin rocks in Chief. The toughest rapid commonly run is a series of drops called Gorilla (also known as the Flume), supposedly so named by early visitor Woody Callaway who felt the first person to run it would need "gonads the size of a go-

GREEN NARROWS, TUXEDO
POWERHOUSE TO GREEN
COVE ROAD, WHERE IT MEETS
THE RIVER
Difficulty: Class 5+
Length: 6 miles (9.6 km)

GREEN COVE ROAD TO GREEN
COVE (LOWER GREEN, ALSO
KNOWN AS THE COVE RUN)
Difficulty: Class 2
Length: 6 miles (9.6 km)

Season: Year-round, daily dam-releases
Character: The Narrows run is steep, difficult; the Cove run is mild, crowded on summer weekends

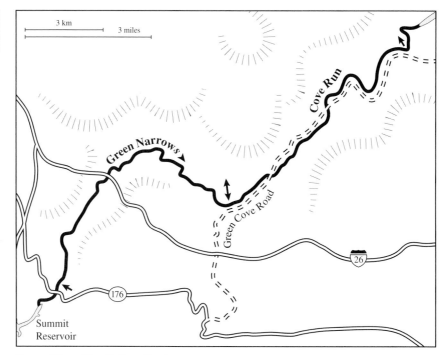

Green River (North Carolina)

rilla." Those not so endowed can portage left, starting above the first 10-foot (3 m) drop. After a few more big drops is Nutcracker, a spectacular rapid that is almost always portaged, followed quickly by Sunshine Falls, a 15-foot (4.6 m) drop into a pile of rocks that most should consider portaging. Things ease up for the last mile until Hammer Factor (also known as Fishtop Falls), just above the take-out. Interstate 26 crosses high above the river.

Boaters must treat this run, and all difficult runs, with utmost respect regardless of perceived skills. Expert boater and author Slim Ray had a serious accident at Sunshine Falls in the summer of 1991 and remains without the use of his legs. Land along the Narrows was recently purchased from Duke Power by the State of North Carolina and is now designated state game land.

As the Green reaches civilization again, boaters can take out from the Narrows run or put in for the Cove run. In this relatively mild stretch the gradient is a manageable 20 fpm (3.8 mpk). Green Cove Road follows the river from here. This float is popular with open canoeists and many others, so it can get crowded on weekends. Just downstream the Green flows into Lake Adger. The reliable dam-releases of 300 cfs (8.5 cumecs) from the Tuxedo Powerhouse usually arrive here at around 1 P.M. Flow information is available from Duke Power, 704-698-2068.

Nantahala River (North Carolina) ➢

The Nantahala River and environs is one of the great paddling areas in the U.S. and home to the high temple of southeastern whitewater, the Nantahala Outdoor Center. The setting is appropriate. The Nantahala Gorge is quite scenic, and the river is a good paddle in its own right.

Of the Nantahala runs clear and very cold from the bottom of Aquone Reservoir and provides a fine training ground. The gorge is so situated that it gets little direct sunlight. Some say the Indian name Nantahala reflects this and translates as "river of the noonday sun." The river runs so cold it sometimes generates its own layer of fog above its waters. The frigid waters give novice kayakers incentive to master that fast roll. The overall gradient is 35 fpm (6.8 mpk).

Most of the rapids are on the upper half of the run, and all are well known to scores of paddlers. The biggest are Patton's Run, Delebar's Rock, and Nantahala Falls (Class 3–). The latter, near the Outdoor Center, was once considered Class 5, but such are the adjustments to be made for progress in equipment and technique. Folks still gather like vultures to watch the carnage, while others toss throw ropes to hapless swimmers for practice. Put in at the public access off Route 19 below the powerhouse. Take out just downstream of Nantahala Falls, and be sure to avoid Wesser Falls (Class 5+), just downstream. Route 19 follows the river on the left and then crosses the river, providing access midway at around mile 3 (4.8 km); it then follows on the right. Railroad tracks follow the river on the left. As you might expect, things can get crowded here on the weekends.

NANTAHALA GORGE, OFF ROUTE 19 BELOW POWERHOUSE TO WESSER
Difficulty: Class 2+
Length: 8 miles (12.8 km)

Season: Dam-releases year-round (except November)
Character: Scenic, dam-controlled; heavily used by rafts, canoes, and kayaks; road close

Hiwassee River (Tennessee) ➢

The Hiwassee is an excellent novice run set beneath the Blue Ridge Mountains in the southeast corner of Tennessee. It offers cold, reliable dam-releases from the Appalachia Dam. This run is the domain of earnest boaters who are learning the basics of paddling as well as those decidedly not so serious who are learning how to get an innertube from the top to the bottom of the run in the most enjoyable manner. Trout also love the cold water, and the Hiwassee is considered a blue-ribbon fishery, drawing anglers to ply their pastime along the many rocks and holes. Fortunately, fishing is best during periods of minimal, unboatable releases, so anglers and river runners happily coexist.

Railroad tracks follow the river on the left, and the highway is nearby most of the way on the right. Put in on the right below the Appalachia Powerhouse. A parking lot at mile 2 (3.2 km) on the right is the last public access. Take out at the small town of Reliance on river left between the railroad bridge and the highway bridge.

APPALACHIA POWERHOUSE TO RELIANCE
Difficulty: Class 2
Length: 6 miles (9.6 km)

Season: Dam-controlled, year-round
Character: Dependable, runnable dam-releases, novice run

Ocoee River (Tennessee) ➢

The Ocoee River has the air of an amusement park ride, and a popular one at that. With about 300,000 annual user-days, it is the second most heavily used whitewater river in the world, surpassed in usage only by the Arkansas River in Colorado. Its location an hour's drive north of Atlanta assures its popularity, and its role in hosting the 1996 Olympic whitewater events brought it notoriety.

Things were once much different. Until 1976, the Ocoee was little more than a dry pile of rocks downhill from a TVA (Tennessee Valley Authority) hydroelectric system.

OCOEE #3 DAM TO OCOEE #2 POWERHOUSE
Difficulty: Class 3+
Length: 4½ miles (7.2 km)

Season: Dependable dam-releases summer through fall
Character: Dam-releases in beautiful setting, continuous rapids, short run

That year a wooden flume used to divert water ruptured, forcing operators to send water down the streambed. Repair efforts were delayed, and, to the chagrin of the TVA, river runners long curious about the reach seized the opportunity. News of the fine whitewater spread, and a campaign began to preserve the inadvertently restored run. The TVA disseminated dubious information and attempted to hinder river traffic as river supporters countered with grass-roots as well as celebrity support. Local outfitters sued the TVA. As the flume was rebuilt, Congress came to the rescue by attaching a rider to the appropriations bill assuring boatable releases as long as commercial rafting companies compensated the TVA for lost revenue. The dam now releases around 1,000 to 1,500 cfs (28.3 to 42.45 cumecs) Thursdays through Mondays during the summer and on weekends in the spring and fall. Schedule changes are always possible, so check ahead before committing.

The action on the Ocoee is somewhere between pool-and-drop and continuous, and is generally more difficult at higher flows. The overall gradient is 57 fpm (11 mpk). The usual put-in below the dam is at an artificial eddy, but some put in below the entrance rapid. The bigger rapids are Gonzo Shoals, Broken Nose, Second Helping, Slice-n-Dice, Moon Chute (named for the resemblance of two rounded boulders to an anatomical backside), Double Suck (watch out for that second hole), and Double Trouble. The river then passes through a flatwater stretch known as the Doldrums. Below the Doldrums are Diamond Splitter, Slingshot, Cat's Pyjamas, Hell Hole, and Powerhouse Ledge.

Goforth Creek near the beginning of the Doldrums provides good mid-run access and/or a lunch spot. Route 64 follows the river, making for an easy shuttle. A new take-out for private boaters is located ¾ mile (1.3 km) downstream of the traditional take-out below the powerhouse on the right. The river has few drawbacks, but it does get busy on weekends. Hard-boaters often tire of dodging commercial rafts and sometimes tend to forget that the companies pay the freight for the water releases. Parking on weekends can be a problem. The water quality is questionable due to the long history of upstream mining.

◁ Chattooga River (Georgia, South Carolina)

The free-running Chattooga offers rapids for most skill levels, excellent water quality, and inspiring wilderness scenery. The watershed gets over 60 feet (18.3 m) of rain annually on average, making it runnable all year. The Chattooga River was accorded Wild and Scenic status in 1974, and many consider it the top river in the East. Along the length of the run it forms part of the border between Georgia, on the left, and South Carolina, on river right.

The runs are usually identified in three numbered sections which roughly coincide with the rapid ratings at moderate flows. The gradients are 12, 30, and 45 fpm (2.32, 5.79, and 8.69 mpk), respectively. Section 2 from Route 28 to Earl's Ford is an easy float through an area rich in Native American history in its upper reaches and fine wilderness scenery farther downstream. The upper area was once a major Indian settlement and trading area, and is now mostly farmland. The best put-in is at Long Bottom Ford, with access off Route 28. Be ready for a ¼-mile (0.4 km) carry at the take-out at Earl's Ford.

Earl's Ford is also the put-in for Section 3, a superb wilderness canyon that may be the most spectacular on the Chattooga. The run has fast-moving water and plenty of action, with more than a dozen rapids in the Class 3 to 4 range. The first is Dicks Creek Ledge (or First Ledge), marked by Dicks Creek Falls on the right. High flows can make

ROUTE 28 TO EARL'S FORD (SECTION 2)
Difficulty: Class 2
Length: 7 miles (11.2 km)

EARL'S FORD TO ROUTE 76 BRIDGE (SECTION 3)
Difficulty: Class 3₄₊
Length: 14 miles (22.4 km)

ROUTE 76 BRIDGE TO TUGALO RESERVOIR (SECTION 4)
Difficulty: Class 4+
Length: 8½ miles (13.6 km)

Season: Rain-fed, year-round
Character: Beautiful, undammed classic with sections suited to all types of boaters and outdoor enthusiasts

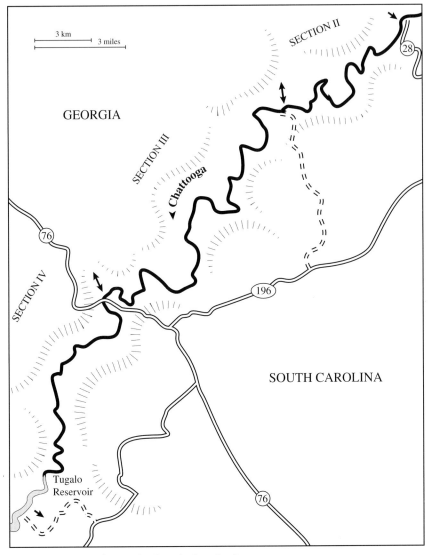

Chattooga River (Georgia, South Carolina)

for a nasty reversal here. Below Dicks is an alternate access at Sandy Ford. Other well-known rapids include the Narrows, with a bad undercut near the bottom on the left, followed quickly by a 6-foot drop called Second Ledge, Eye of the Needle, and Painted Rock. Bull Sluice (Class 4+) at the end is the toughest rapid and is scouted and/or portaged on the right. Just downstream is the Route 76 bridge, the take-out for Section 3 and the put-in for Section 4, although some put in for Section 5, above Bull Sluice. Play-boaters will find a good ender spot just downstream of the bridge.

Section 4 is the best-known section. Although a Class 4+ run at moderate levels, it kicks up to a bona fide and potentially dangerous Class 5 at higher flows. If you never run the Chattooga, you can still enjoy running this stretch vicariously in the 1972 whitewater classic *Deliverance*, as many of the scenes were shot here. If you are actually running it, there are things to look out for. At mile 2 (3.2 km) is Woodall Shoals, a deceptive and dangerous keeper which may make a portage on the left attractive if the sneak route on the right is not available. Just downstream is Seven-Foot Falls, with the big drop on the left and, at higher flows, a sneak route on the right. Just downstream of Long Creek Falls is Deliverance Rock, site of some of the scenes from the movie. One more good drop, Raven's Chute, leads to an ominously long flat section and the toughest stretch on the river, the Five Falls.

The Five Falls, respectively called Entrance (First Falls), Corkscrew, Crack-in-the-Rock, Jawbone, and Sock-'em-Dog, should all be scouted before running. Each is a tight technical drop, and logs and other hazards (including boats jammed in the openings) are not uncommon. Crack-in-the Rock offers a choice of three "cracks" between boulders that block the river. The right crack is usually the easier route, and more so since a log jammed here vertically for more than a decade is now gone; nevertheless, be sure to look carefully as another may have taken its place. The narrower middle crack can be run at low flows, and a cheat route appears to the extreme right at high flows. Stay away from left crack which has fatally entrapped at least three swimmers; the most recent incident in 1997 resulted in a televised plea from the parents of the victim to modify the rapid. Shortly after the Five Falls is the backwater of Tugalo Reservoir and a 2-mile (3.2 km) flatwater paddle to the take-out.

Flows can greatly affect the difficulty of the river. After heavy rains the lower sections are much tougher. One high-water option is to put in at Sandy Ford and take out at Woodall Shoals. Flows can also be very low, usually by midsummer. Undercut rocks are a serious concern, even in the easier upper sections, and entrapments are not uncommon. Be sure to register before running, and take note of river regulations; they are enforced.

◄ Chattahoochee River (Georgia)

While not in the same league as some of the near-wilderness mountain classics of the Southeast, the Chattahoochee is set in a beautiful area and conveniently located near Atlanta.

The upper run, located above Lanier Reservoir, is favored by boaters looking for easy whitewater. Put in at the Route 255 bridge and take out at Duncan Bridge or other possible access points nearby. Midpoint access is at the Route 115 bridge. Flows here can vary greatly. Even easier runs can be found both upstream and downstream. Upstream from Helen is some challenging whitewater, but the small drainage area makes for a short season.

The lower run, located below Buford Dam (Lanier Reservoir) and Morgan Falls Dam (Bull Sluice Reservoir), is an even easier float. The run begins at Morgan Falls Dam and goes to Pace Mill Road, with midway access points at Johnsons Ferry Road at mile 2 (3.2 km) and at Powers Island Landing at mile 6 (9.6 km), just upstream of Interstate 285.

The Chattahoochee can be crowded. Please be courteous to private landowners and other boaters.

ROUTE 255 BRIDGE TO DUNCAN
BRIDGE (UPPER RUN)
Difficulty: Class 2
Length: 10 miles (16 km)

MORGAN FALLS DAM TO PACE
MILL ROAD (LOWER RUN)
Difficulty: Class 1+
Length: 9 miles (14.4 km)

Season: Rain-fed (upper),
dam-releases (lower);
both sections runnable
year-round
Character: Downstream
run after the river has
left the mountains and is
in hill country; rain-fed
(upper), dam-releases
(lower)

Midwestern United States

$\mathcal{B}$etween the Appalachians in the East and the Rockies in the West are the Great Plains and the Mississippi Valley. The Midwest is the "Heartland of America," and boaters here take advantage of the numerous flatwater lakes and rivers for both paddling and camping. For those yearning for whitewater action, there are some possibilities both north and south. The Northwoods area of upper Wisconsin, Minnesota, and Michigan has several fine runs, as do the Ozark Mountains, particularly in northwestern Arkansas and southern Missouri. Both are remnants of larger, older mountain ranges. Ground down by glaciers over the various ice ages, the once mighty mountains of the Northwoods now rise to only about 2,000 feet (610 m). The Ozarks are also heavily eroded, reaching only about 2,500 feet (762.5 m). Both areas feature hardwood forests, fine scenery, and lend some texture to the otherwise level Midwestern landscape.

Like the Native Americans of the Midwest, boaters here favor canoes that are well suited for long flatwater paddles and for carrying gear. Although the native river runners of the Midwest probably carried around any real whitewater, open canoes today provide extra excitement and demand an extra degree of skill of the Midwestern whitewater paddler.

The Northwoods

The Northwoods and Eastern Canada are more than a little bit alike. Both occupy the Canadian Shield, the oldest formation on the continent with some rocks dating from between 3.6 and 2.5 billion years ago. Over the ages, layers of sedimentary rock were so heated and squeezed as to be completely recrystallized into belts of green stones and pockets of rich minerals, especially around Lake Superior. More recently, glaciers decimated the once mighty mountains; the last great glacier retreated some 6,000 years ago, leaving the land scoured down to the bare rock. The glaciers transported huge boulders called "erratics" hundreds of miles, scattering many along Northwoods rivers; the Wolf River is a good example. The glaciers also carved the basins for thousands of lakes, which store water and keep streams flowing even during the driest months. The lakes and rivers provide endless flatwater as well as several whitewater opportunities.

The lakes and rivers also serve as a haven for waterfowl. Emblematic of the area is the loon, with its forlorn warbling cry. Once-rich forests of first-growth hemlock, fir, and spruce were timbered in the nineteenth century, although many areas are still heavily wooded.

The streams of the Northwoods belong to the two watersheds, one flowing toward the St. Lawrence and the North Atlantic via the Great Lakes, the other down to the Mississippi and the Gulf of Mexico. The rivers, especially those of Michigan's Upper Peninsula, or the "U.P." are often overlooked by river runners.

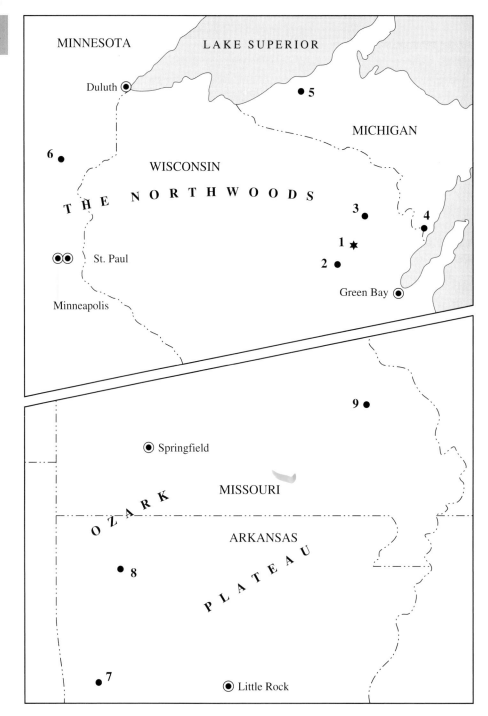

MINNESOTA

LAKE SUPERIOR

Duluth

5

MICHIGAN

6

WISCONSIN

T H E   N O R T H W O O D S

3

4

1

2

Green Bay

St. Paul

Minneapolis

9

Springfield

MISSOURI

O Z A R K

ARKANSAS

P L A T E A U

8

1   Wolf River (see page 48)
2   Red River
3   Peshtigo River (Wisconsin)
4   Piers Gorge, Menominee River
5   Presque Isle River
6   Kettle River
7   Cossatot Shut-ins
8   Buffalo River
9   St. Francis River

7

Little Rock

Wolf River (Wisconsin) ➤

Although the Wolf River is not the most difficult river in the Midwest, its popularity borders on legend. The Wild and Scenic Wolf features some fine technical boulder-filled rapids and good local scenery that gets even better as the foliage changes in autumn. The river provides almost 40 miles of good paddling through peaceful, undeveloped country, much of which is on the Menominee Indian Reservation.

Boating on the Wolf begins as the ice breaks up in mid-March or April, with flows usually peaking in April. At higher flows the rapids become considerably more difficult, and wetsuits are recommended in cool spring weather. Rainfall determines the water levels for the rest of the season, and the river can be quite "bony" at low flows. The water is tinged slightly brown by tannins from leaves.

The above sections are traditionally numbered one through four with gradients of 14, 14, 18, and 12 fpm (2.7, 2.7, 3.5, 2.3 mpk), respectively. The upper sections are easier, with the gradient steepening to 35 fpm (6.8 mpk) in some parts near the end. There is no camping along the river, and local rules prohibit cans or bottles along the river.

Section 1 from Lily to Hollister is easy but not as interesting as the lower sections, and gets little use. The take-out for this section and the put-in for Section 2 is off a dirt road just west of Hollister. Section 2 includes several easy rapids, as boaters must pick routes around boulders and islands. At higher flows some rapids are Class 3, and at these levels wetsuits are a good idea.

Section 3 begins at the take-out for Section 2, the Route 64 bridge at Langlade, at a public parking lot downstream of the bridge. In this section (from Langlade to Gilmore's Mistake) the gradient is 18 fpm (3.5 mpk). The flatwater takes boaters into Crowle, Horserace, and Twenty-Day rapids. Farther downstream is Boy Scouts Rapids, a long passage near Gardner Day Boy Scout Camp, and Gilmore's Mistake where the river is squeezed through a 20-foot channel between rock ledges filled with rollers and holes.

Gilmore was not a paddler but a timber cruiser who advised his employer not to log upstream of this point as the constriction would make it too difficult to transport logs downstream. Others dynamited the rapid and profitably logged the upper section, all to the chagrin of Gilmore and his employer.

The take-out at the bridge in Markton is also the put-in for Section 4. Here the river flows through the Menominee Indian Reservation. The river was reopened for river running in 1988 after being closed by the Menominees for some ten years. The closure was the result of political turmoil and in part in response to a lack of perceived respect for the land by outsiders. Entrepreneurial tribe members purchased a local rafting company and persuaded the tribal legislature to reopen the river for boating. The tribe now charges a nominal "trespass fee" and includes a shuttle service (as of July 1998 the fee was $20). Access to the river on tribal grounds is only allowed at commercial operations. Permits and the mandatory shuttle can be obtained at Big Smoky Falls Rafting, 715-799-3359.

Section 4 holds Wild and Scenic designation and has the most to offer. The most challenging rapids are on this section, and restrictions on development assure that there are no homes or other signs of civilization along the river. Major rapids include Shot Gun, Pismire Falls, and the even tougher Sullivan Falls; the latter is formed by an island and features an 8-foot drop on the left channel, with the right channel often too shallow or blocked with trees. Those intimidated can use the short portage on the left bank. Kayakers enjoy a good playhole on the right below the drop.

LILY TO HOLLISTER (SECTION 1)
Difficulty: Class 1+
Length: 7 miles (11.2 km)

HOLLISTER TO LANGLADE (SECTION 2)
Difficulty: Class 1+
Length: 8 miles (12.8 km)

LANGLADE TO MARKTON (SECTION 3)
Difficulty: Class 2–
Length: 10 miles (16 km)

MARKTON TO ROUTE M BRIDGE (SECTION 4)
Difficulty: Class 3–
Length: 13 miles (20.8 km)

Season: April through October, often low in late summer

Character: Different options of runs, scenic hills, popular; some rapids are considerably more difficult in high water

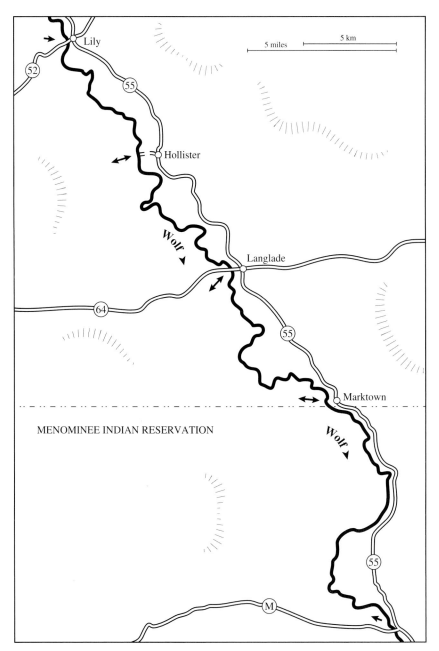

Wolf River (Wisconsin)

Just downstream is Duck Nest Rapids. Farther downstream the river approaches Dalles Gorge (sometimes called Upper Dalles), a popular lunch spot with tables and a concession stand. Below here the river narrows and the whitewater becomes continuous, especially at higher flows. The last drop just before the take-out is Smoky Falls, a narrow channel ending in a 6-foot (1.8 m) drop.

Red River (Wisconsin) ➢

The Red River is a tributary of the Wolf that flows south from the Stockbridge Indian Reservation. Dam-controlled flows make it runnable year-round.

The put-in is 1⅓ miles (2.1 km) southeast of Gresham on a gravel bar just downstream of the power house and dam. This is a pool-and-drop river with several midstream boulders and many ledges. The biggest drop is Monastery Falls (Class 3–), sometimes called Alexian Falls, located next to the Novitiate, an impressive, chateau-like edifice, more reminiscent of the Loire Valley in France than Wisconsin. The historic structure was seized by protesting Menominee Indians in 1975. More recently it was saved from demolition.

Monastery Falls is a two-tiered, 15-foot (4.6 m) drop where the river narrows to about 6 feet (1.8 m). It can be portaged on the right. A mile (1.6 km) downstream is Ziemers Falls where the current divides into two narrow channels. Alternate road access can be found here. Take out on the right downstream of the bridge at Red River.

SOUTHEAST OF GRESHAM TO THE TOWN OF RED RIVER
Difficulty: Class 2+
Length: 4 miles (6.4 km)

Season: All year; best April through October
Character: Pool-and-drop, reliable but limited whitewater

Peshtigo River (Wisconsin) ➢

The Peshtigo River boasts some of the best wilderness woodland scenery in the Midwest and the largest concentration of whitewater in the region, with an average gradient of some 40 fpm (7.72 mpk) in the Roaring Rapids section.

The rapids start just downstream of the dam at Silver Cliff and are especially challenging during big springtime flows. Here the Roaring Rapids earn their name, starting with constant Class 2 action, then building up to the first, second, and third drops. A small island precedes the third drop that in turn immediately precedes the biggest drop on the run, Five-Foot Falls (1.5 m). Horserace and S-Curve rapids round out the ride. In the last mile the river calms and development reappears. Boaters can also warm up with easier runs upstream.

Much of the land along the Peshtigo is privately owned, and development is on the rise. Conflicts between inconsiderate boaters and property owners are not uncommon. Boaters are reminded to avoid excessive noise and to respect the property of others. Carry out trash, and use designated toilets.

SILVERCLIFF TO ROUTE C (ROARING RAPIDS SECTION)
Difficulty: Class 3–; Class 4– at high water
Length: 4 miles (6.4 km)

Season: April through October, though very low at the end of summer
Character: Widely fluctuating flow, excellent whitewater for the Midwest

Menominee River (Wisconsin, Michigan) ➢

The Menominee flows east for much of this run as it etches the border between Wisconsin and Michigan before emptying into Lake Michigan. For Midwesterners this is the closest thing in the region to big water. Ample upstream water-releases from facilities jointly managed by Niagara Wisconsin Paper Corp. and Wisconsin Electric Corp. provide plenty of flow and good play rapids all summer. Recent efforts have helped upgrade the water quality in this developed area.

Boaters can put in right below Little Quinnesec Falls Dam in Niagara, upstream of Piers Gorge where the biggest rapids are found. The most impressive of these is Misicot Falls, just downstream of a blind left turn at the entrance to the gorge. Misicot has been the scene of several tragedies, and boaters may wish to scout and/or portage; a foot trail

PIERS GORGE, BELOW LITTLE QUINNESEC FALLS DAM IN NIAGARA TO ROUTE 8
Difficulty: Class 3+
Length: 4 miles (6.4 km)

Season: April through October
Character: Big-volume, developed area

leads out on the left. Farther down the gorge is a series of rapids, one big enough to earn the name Backroller (also known as Terminal Surfer). Take out upstream of the U.S. Route 8 bridge on the right.

◅ Presque Isle River (Michigan)

M28 BRIDGE TO SOUTH
 BOUNDARY ROAD BRIDGE
Difficulty: Class 4$_p$
Length: 18 miles (28.8 km)

Season: April through October; summer flows are undependable
Character: Isolated pool-and-drop river, possibly the toughest in the Midwest

Located in the sparsely populated Upper Peninsula (the "U.P."), the Presque Isle River is wild, difficult, and no place for beginners. The river is laced with difficult drops as it runs through a tight, narrow canyon in a remote area.

Although the Presque Isle has 18 miles (28.8 km) of whitewater, few attempt the entire run in one day. The midway access is private, and permission must be obtained at Steiger's Bridge (Connersville Bridge). This can be done by politely asking for the gate key from Steiger's Hardwood and Home Center on U.S. Route 2 just east of Bessemer. Steiger's has been friendly to river runners in the past, and deserves their utmost courtesy and patronage.

The upper run begins at the M28 bridge at Wakefield and is fairly easy for the first 2 miles; then short drops appear at the end of several pools. The pools get bigger and the drops more difficult as boaters work their way downstream through wild and rugged terrain. The biggest rapids, Minnewawa Falls and Nimikon Falls, cause most boaters to portage.

Steiger's Bridge is a wooden trestle marking the take-out of the upper run and the put-in for the lower run. The whitewater in the lower run is both challenging and relentless. About a mile (1.6 km) below the bridge is the gorge, where the river plummets 140 feet (42.7 m) through a mile-long, steep-sided, wooded canyon. The faint of heart may carry along an old logging road on the left, portaging Nokomis Falls. The action downstream is nonstop, with another big drop to Porcupine Mountains State Park. Here first-growth pine and hemlock provide a home for abundant wildlife, including bald eagles and black bear. Take out at the South Boundary Road bridge. Although the river continues with good gradient to Lake Superior, three unrunnable falls on the way make driving to the camping area there a better option.

◅ Kettle River (Minnesota)

ROUTE 23 TO SANDSTONE ABOVE
 ROUTE 123 BRIDGE
Difficulty: Class 2
Length: 5 miles (8 km)

Season: April through October, except after extended dry periods
Character: Small canyon in agricultural region

Located between the Minneapolis–St. Paul area and Duluth, the Kettle River flows through a steep-walled gorge consisting of sandstone escarpments and rock cliffs in Banning State Park. The Kettle has a large drainage but can still get too low during extended dry periods.

Boaters can put in at the bridge on Route 23. The whitewater begins about ½ mile (0.8 km) downstream with Blueberry Slide. The next 2 miles (3.2 km) hold most of the rapids including Mother's Delight, Dragon's Tooth, and Hell's Gate, where the river narrows between high sandstone cliffs, churning up some big waves. Wolf Creek enters on the right about a mile (1.6 km) above the take-out, and Wolf Creek Falls makes a nice side hike.

It is an easy float from here to the take-out below the railroad bridge at Sandstone on the right. Although this is an easy one-day float, those set on camping can use any of several primitive campsites along the river. Boaters can also consider an easier Class 1+ section downstream near where the Kettle meets the St. Croix.

The Ozarks

The Ozark Mountains are spread out over parts of Oklahoma, Missouri, and Arkansas. Composed primarily of sedimentary sandstone and limestone, the forces of nature have reshaped and ground down the Ozarks over the ages. Some sections, such as the St. Francis Mountains in Missouri, are primarily igneous and less eroded. Although nearly two hundred years of civilization have had their effect on the area, the hills along most of the river corridor are still covered with lush stands of oak, hickory, and shortleaf pine. Indigenous animals can still be seen, including deer, beaver, and black bear. As for boating, the canoe remains the craft of choice for the whitewater devotees who make the pilgrimage to test their skills here. They are rewarded with the relatively unspoiled wilderness, fine scenery, and good camping.

Because the mountains are modest in comparison to other whitewater centers, some of the best river running in the region is on Class 1 rivers such as the Jack Fork River, Mulberry River, North Fork Bryant Creek, Big Pine Creek, Eleven Point River, and Current River. Three rivers with good whitewater are featured here.

Cossatot Shut-ins (Arkansas) ➤

Route 246 to Route 4
Difficulty: Class 4
Length: 10 miles (16 km)

Season: Rain-fed; best chance of runnable levels is in the spring after heavy rains; upstream clear-cutting probably shortens season

Character: Challenging whitewater, runnable only in springtime or after heavy rain

The rough translation of the river name Cossatot from the original French is "skull crusher," so take the cue and buckle up your helmet for the Shut-ins, the most challenging whitewater run in the Ozark region. Located near the western edge of Arkansas in the Quachita Range below the town of Mena, the Shut-ins section of the Cossatot River drops 80 fpm (15.4 mpk) for the first third of a mile (0.5 km), a gradient unheard of in these parts.

The run begins at the Route 246 bridge and starts with a 6-mile warm-up of easy Class 2–3 rapids including such drops as Zig-Zag and the Esses. This mild character changes dramatically 2 miles after the low-water bridge at Ed Banks. Boaters with second thoughts can use this last take-out opportunity before the big rapids downstream. At the end of 2 miles (3.2 km) of solid Class 3 water, a suspiciously long pool and telltale roar announce the big drops below. The Shut-ins are seven big drops over bedrock ledges, each between 4 and 7 feet (1.2 and 2.1 m), all within the space of about 150 yards (137 m). They include BMF, Washing Machine (a 7-foot, 2.1 m, drop with ugly hole at bottom at high water), Whiplash, and Last One. The drops require expert skills, especially of open-canoeists. The section provides a striking photo opportunity, best enjoyed looking upstream from the bottom. Downstream of the falls stretch are two more rapids of note, Deer Camp Rapids and Devil's Hollow Falls. The latter deserves caution in light of two previous fatalities.

Preservation of the river's character remains an issue. Upstream clear-cutting threatens the area and especially the quality and duration of the water flow. The Nature Conservancy has recently purchased property along the river to perpetuate its undeveloped character.

PONCA TO WHITE RIVER
Difficulty: Class 1+
Length: 128 miles
(204.8 km)

BOXLEY TO PONCA (UPPER RUN)
Difficulty: Class 3
Length: 14 miles (22.4 km)

Season: Rain-fed, but large
watershed allows year-
round boating; upper-
river season is during
spring and after heavy
rains
Character: Long, beautiful
float with some
whitewater in upper
stretches when runnable

◁ Buffalo River (Arkansas)

The Buffalo is a river with such fine scenery, historical significance, and recreational potential that it is now the equivalent of a national park, achieving the status as the nation's first National River in 1972. It is the only free-flowing river left in Arkansas, a distinction rescued from the U.S. Army Corps of Engineers in 1964 by conservationists and river lovers who successfully lobbied to stop a dam proposed that would have wiped out 50 miles of the middle section of the river.

For boaters of the region, the Buffalo is truly a magical place. The minty-green water twists, bends, and tumbles for well over 100 miles (160 km) of good boating along a corridor lined with hardwood forests and painted limestone bluffs. Red-tailed hawks, herons, turtles, snakes, and even imported elk find a home along its banks.

The Buffalo begins as a trickle about ½ mile downslope of Buffalo Knob, the highest point in the Ozarks. Although the mountains here barely top 2,600 feet (793 m), the terrain is difficult and many areas are inaccessible.

The most commonly paddled sections are between Ponca and the White River, a stretch known for its superb backwoods scenery, especially in the autumn. Rapids such as Bucking Shoals, Close Call, Crisis Curves, Wrecking Rock, and Hell's Half Acre are found on this reach, though the names may be a bit overstated to the experienced whitewater boater. Of the many beautiful bluffs along the river, the most spectacular is Big Bluff, which, at 500 feet (153 m), is the tallest cliff face in the Midwest. Boaters can take the time to hike the "goat trail" partway up for some spectacular views. Just below Wrecking Rock is a short side hike that leads to Hemmed-in-Hollow and a spectacular 200-foot (61 m) waterfall, the tallest falls between the Rockies and the Appalachians in a canyon that may once have been an underground cavern. Numerous bluffs, caves, and other sights are found along the river's length. Though the scenery and current slacken somewhat for the last 58 miles (92.8 km), there are still choice campgrounds for camping, swimming, and relaxation. Near the end of the run is the old ghost town of Rush, a turn-of-the-century boomtown that is worth the time to wander around.

An upstream run from Boxley to Ponca has some good Class 3 rapids, but it is only runnable for a few days after rains in the winter and spring months. Willows make it a bit brushy. An added attraction on this stretch is the short side hike to "Lost Valley" in which campers and boaters will find Cobb's Cave, a natural amphitheater dome, and Eden's Cave, which holds an underground waterfall and a natural bridge.

ROUTE 72 TO ROUTE D
Difficulty: Class 3–
Length: 5¼ miles (8.4 km)

Season: Rain-fed, usually
enough water into May
and after heavy rains
Character: Whitewater run,
with easy runs above
and below

◁ St. Francis River (Missouri)

The whitewater of the St. Francis River owes its reputation to the stubborn igneous rocks of the St. Francis Mountains, a subrange of the Ozarks. Despite its geological age, this area refuses to become part of the Great Plains, a trait appreciated by the river runners in the area. The St. Francis has prominent rock formations and good-quality water.

The featured stretch of this river drops 24 fpm (4.6 mpk) and includes the Tiemans Shut-in, a ¾-mile (1.2 km) stretch with the best scenery and the most difficult rapids. A footpath follows the river here. The rapids include Big Drop, Cat's Paw, and Double Drop, the last having a good ender spot near the bottom. Downstream are the ruins of Silver Mines Dam, an obstacle often portaged at higher levels. Take out at the Route D bridge in the Silver Mines recreational area.

Western United States

$\mathcal{T}$he western United States probably has the finest assemblage of whitewater river anywhere on the globe. Nowhere else can river runners find such a remarkable combination of vast wilderness areas, spectacular and diverse landscapes ranging from high mountains to rugged deserts, extensive public lands, and beautiful yet accessible rivers. Here is where whitewater river running got its start with the Powell Expedition in 1869 and where commercial river running began in the 1930s. Among the innovations in whitewater equipment from this region are the plastic kayak and the self-bailing raft.

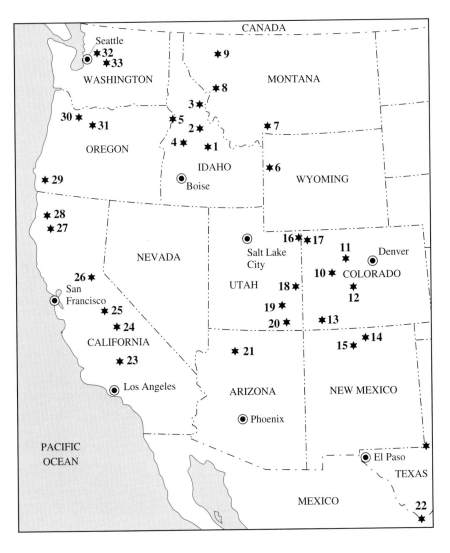

1. Middle Fork Salmon River (see page 56)
2. Salmon River (see page 56)
3. Selway River (see page 56)
4. North Fork Payette River (see page 56)
5. Hells Canyon, Snake River (see page 56)
6. Snake River (see page 56)
7. Yellowstone River (see page 56)
8. Clark Fork River (see page 56)
9. Flathead River (see page 56)
10. Roaring Fork River (see page 66)
11. Upper Colorado River (see page 66)
12. Arkansas River (see page 66)
13. Animas River (see page 66)
14. Rio Grande (see page 66)
15. Rio Chama (see page 66)
16. Green River (see pages 66 and 72)
17. Yampa River (see pages 66 and 72)
18. Colorado River, Westwater Canyon (see page 72)
19. Colorado River, Cataract Canyon (see page 72)
20. San Juan River (see page 72)
21. Colorado River, Grand Canyon (see page 72)
22. Lower Rio Grande (see page 78)
23. Kern River (see page 83)
24. Kings River (see page 83)
25. Tuolumne River (see page 83)
26. South Fork American River (see page 83)
27. Trinity River (see page 83)
28. Klamath River (see pages 83 and 88)
29. Rogue River (see page 88)
30. Clackamas River (see page 88)
31. Deschutes River (see page 88)
32. Skykomish River (see page 88)
33. Wenatchee River (see page 88)

For a more comprehensive look at the rivers of this region we suggest *Western Whitewater* (see Resources chapter).

Below is a brief summary of over thirty outstanding rivers in the western United States. We've also included a locator map along with reprints of six regional maps of the 115 primary rivers covered in *Western Whitewater*.

BOUNDARY CREEK TO SALMON RIVER
Difficulty: Class 3+
Length: 100 miles (160 km)

Season: May through August
Character: Exotic, multi-day, mountain wilderness trip

◁ Middle Fork Salmon River (Idaho)

A trip down the Middle Fork Salmon River is one of the finest wilderness floats in the world. No roads reach the river between the Boundary Creek launch site and the confluence with the main branch Salmon, and the river is narrower, steeper, and more technically demanding than the Salmon itself. Wildlife is abundant here, especially early in the season when the surrounding peaks, some above 9,000 feet (2,743 m), are still covered with snow. Bighorn sheep and bald and golden eagles are among the sights.

The Middle Fork begins at the confluence of Bear Valley Creek and Marsh Creek, only 10 miles upstream from the Boundary Creek put-in. At first the river is narrow, but soon the combined flow of scores of tributaries turns it into a big river.

Most of the rapids are fairly easy, but a few, especially Velvet Falls at mile 5 (8 km) and the big rapids in the final gorge, are more challenging.

A high-water trip on the Middle Fork is no place for the inexperienced. During peak runoff the river changes character. Rapids in the steep upper section become nearly continuous. Less experienced boaters might consider flying in to Indian Creek at mile 25 (40 km). Downstream, in the climatic gorge known as the Impassable Canyon (impassable for horseback parties, not boaters), the swollen river crashes through big waves and holes. Sudden rainstorms can speed up the snowmelt and produce flood conditions in a matter of hours.

Middle Fork, Salmon River, Idaho. *(Larry Harrel/ECHO)*

In 1968 the Middle Fork Salmon River became one of the charter members of the National Wild and Scenic River System. Interest in the Middle Fork probably peaked in 1979, the year President Jimmy Carter and his wife made a well-publicized trip down the river in outfitter Norm Guth's sweep boat. Today, some 10,000 people float the Middle Fork every year under a strict USFS permit system.

Put in at Boundary Creek Boat Ramp. The biggest rapid in the upper reaches is Velvet Falls (Class 4–) at the mouth of Velvet Creek 5 miles (8.2 km) downstream of the put-in. Big rapids are also found in Impassable Canyon, which begins at Bernard Creek and Haystack Rapid at mile 67½ (108 km), including Redside (Class 3+), Weber (Class 3+), and Rubber (Class 3+). The Middle Fork meets the main branch Salmon at mile 96 (154 km). Take out at Cache Bar Boat Ramp on the Salmon.

The Middle Fork is also legendary for its hot springs, which provide a relaxing break from river travel. They include Trail Flat Hot Springs at mile 7 (11.2 km); Sheepeater Hot Springs at mile 13 (20.8 km); Loon Creek Hot Springs at mile 49½ (79.2 km); and Hospital Bar Hot Springs at mile 52 (83.2 km).

Salmon River (Idaho) ➢

The Salmon River is one of the longest undammed rivers in the Lower Forty-Eight states and is the longest river entirely within a single state. From its headwaters in the mountains of south-central Idaho to its confluence with the Snake just below the Washington-Oregon border, the Salmon meanders more than 400 miles (640 km).

The Salmon River Canyon is one of the deepest in North America, measuring over 6,000 feet (1,828 m) from the river bottom to the tops of the tallest surrounding peaks. The rugged mountain scenery gradually changes from pine forest, interrupted by somber black granite gorges, to the drier, more open slopes of the high desert.

CORN CREEK TO CAREY CREEK ("RIVER OF NO RETURN")
Difficulty: Class 3
Length: 82 miles (131.2 km) Carey Creek to White Bird (civilized section)

Difficulty: Class 3
Length: 51 miles (81.6 km)

WHITE BIRD TO HELLERS BAR ON THE SNAKE RIVER (LOWER SECTION)
Difficulty: Class 3
Length: 73 miles (116.8 km)

Season: May through October
Character: Big river with two popular wilderness sections and a section in between followed by a road

Main Salmon. *(Howard Weamer/ECHO)*

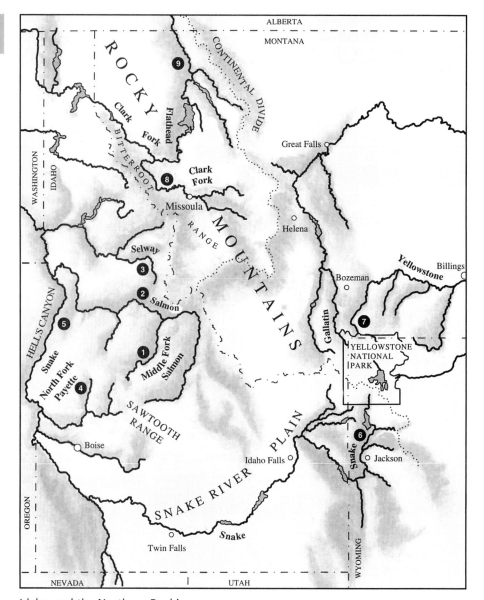

Idaho and the Northern Rockies

The Shoshone called the river Tom-Agit-Pah, or "Big Fish Water." Lewis and Clark later explored the area, and Clark named the river in honor of Lewis, and gave the name "Salmon" to a side creek. Mapmakers mistakenly called the main river the Salmon, in addition to showing it flowing in the wrong direction. They eventually turned the river around, but the name stuck.

The main Salmon is a big river. Rolling rapids alternate with deep, calm pools which grow longer toward the end of the run. During peak runoff standing waves and holes can become huge, and only experienced boaters should attempt the run. Later in the summer, at moderate and lower levels, the Salmon is a perfect long wilderness river trip for intermediate boaters. They will enjoy the big but hardly terrifying rapids, camp on sandy beaches, and perhaps see bighorn sheep on the crags above. With no upstream dams to block the movement of sediment, the main Salmon renews its superb beaches every year. Hot springs, though not as numerous as on the Middle Fork, add a bit of luxury to the Salmon. In the late 1970s the Forest Service instituted a strict minimum-impact camping policy.

For the most popular "River of No Return" section, put in at the Corn Creek boat ramp. Major rapids, mostly Class 3, are well spaced along the river's 82 miles (131.2 km) and include Rainier, Devil's Teeth, Salmon Falls, Bailey, Split Rock, Big Mallard, Elkhorn, Chittam, and Vinegar Creek. Carey Creek boat ramp is the most popular take-out.

There are numerous access points in the 51-mile (81.6 km) middle "civilized" section from Carey Creek to White Bird. The lower Salmon section starts at White Bird where the river again leaves civilization, and ends at Hellers Bar on the Snake River. This lower section is not as isolated as the upstream "River of No Return" section.

Selway River (Idaho) ➢

The Selway bisects the vast Selway-Bitterroot Wilderness, which has protected the river canyon since 1936. The river's headwaters lie within the adjoining Frank Church–River of No Return Wilderness, and the Selway itself is a charter member (1968) of the National Wild and Scenic Rivers System. The run described here remains largely untouched by civilization. The waters teem with fish and wildlife abounds as side creeks join the river. The Selway is lined with beaches of clean white sand.

A trip down Idaho's Selway is one of the rarest river experiences in the West. The Selway is the least often run of the nation's famous wilderness rivers, due to a very strict (and some may argue overzealous) Forest Service policy that permits fewer than 1,300 boaters to float the river each year.

From its 9,000-foot (2,743 m) headwaters in the Bitterroot Range, the Selway flows north and then west to Lowell, Idaho, where it joins the Lochsa to form the Middle Fork Clearwater. Though it begins on a ridge just 7 miles north of the main Salmon's Corn Creek put-in, the Selway has little in common with the Salmon. The Selway's lush, intimate canyon and short, intense season contrast with the main Salmon's more open landscape and summer-long flows. Heavy precipitation in the Selway drainage produces a thick, dark green forest of fir, hemlock, cedar, and pine. The watershed's rich vegetation and clean granite soils filter the heavy runoff, keeping the Selway pristine and clear.

Timing the runnable flows on the Selway is a task. Snowmelt season is usually brief and unpredictable. A sudden hot spell or a warm rain can quickly raise the river to dangerous levels. The river's many large tributaries roughly quadruple or quintuple the flow between put-in and take-out.

In addition to challenging rapids and fluctuating flows, the Selway's potential hazards include logs, icy water, and unpredictable weather that can turn cold and rainy well into June. Early-season trips usually face all these challenges at once (plus possible snow on the road to the put-in). The Selway canyon is extremely remote and lightly traveled, so evacuation in case of mishap can be very difficult.

Floats begin at Paradise Launch Site, just 32 miles from the headwaters. Major rapids include Galloping Gertie and Washer Woman (both Class 3), Ham (Class 4–), Double Drop and Wa-poots (both Class 3–4), and Ladle (Class 4+), probably the toughest rapid

PARADISE TO RACE CREEK
Difficulty: Class 4
Length: 47 miles (75.2 km)

Season: May through July
Character: Exotic, multi-day mountain wilderness trip

on the run. Downstream are Little Niagara (Class 3–4) and Wolf Creek (Class 4), which generates big hydraulics, especially at higher levels, followed by Tee Kem Falls and Crenshaw (both Class 3). Take out on the right just below Race Creek campground. Don't miss the take-out; a little over a mile (1.6 km) downstream is Selway Falls (Class 6).

◄ North Fork Payette River (Idaho)

BELOW SMITHS FERRY TO BANKS
Difficulty: Class 5+
Length: 16 miles (25.6 km)

Season: June through September
Character: Warm water, civilization near

The North Fork Payette is one of Idaho's most dramatic whitewater rivers. Below Smiths Ferry on this featured run, the North Fork is emphatically for experts only. In its final 16 miles (25.6 km) the river crashes some 1,700 vertical feet (518 m)—nearly a third of a mile—through a nonstop cascade of steep, technical Class 5 rapids. It becomes truly unrunnable only at high flows.

This disquieting stretch of North Fork Payette wasn't kayaked until the 1970s and was first rafted in 1987. With a gradient of more than 100 fpm (19 mpk), the river is both powerful and highly technical. The riverbed is further constricted by riprap tumbled into the channel during construction of the highway and railroad that follow the run. Many of the rocks are sharp, and eddies are scarce in some sections.

The water is relatively warm: late-summer irrigation releases from Cascade Reservoir, some 20 miles (32 km) upstream, provide flows near 70°F (21°C) through most of August and September. Most boaters avoid the North Fork when icy snowmelt fills the river in spring. The highway nearby allows an easy exit, short shuttles, and easy scouting of most sections.

Put in at any of several access points on the right bank roughly 2½ miles (4 km) below Smiths Ferry. The biggest, mostly Class 5, rapids include Nutcracker, Disneyland, Bouncer Down the Middle, Pectoralis Major, Jacobs Ladder, Golf Course, Screaming Left Turn, The Jaws, Hounds Tooth (Class 4+), Otters Run (Class 4), Juicer, and Crunch.

Take out on river right opposite the settlement of Banks at the confluence of the North Fork and the South Fork, or continue down the main Payette.

Upstream is the scenic Class 3, 12-mile (19.2 km) Carbarton run between Carbarton Bridge and Smiths Ferry, perfect for boaters with intermediate skills.

◄ Snake River, Hells Canyon (Idaho, Oregon, Washington)

HELLS CANYON DAM TO HELLERS BAR
Difficulty: Class 3₄
Length: 79 miles (126 km)

Season: April into November
Character: Big water, deep canyon, dam-controlled

There is no agreed standard by which canyons are measured, but Hells Canyon is by some measurements the deepest gorge in North America and certainly one of the most imposing canyons in the West. The gorge, roughly 10 miles across, is not as sudden or dramatic as the Grand Canyon, and the rim peaks are rarely visible from the river. But when these heights do come into view, the sense of depth is tremendous. The Snake lies, on the average, 5,500 feet (1,676 m) below the nearby ridges. He Devil Mountain, tallest of the Seven Devils at 9,393 feet (2,863 m), towers some 8,000 feet (2,438 m) above the river near the put-in.

Put in on the left bank, about ¾ mile below the dam. Voyages down Hells Canyon start out with a bang, then ease into a long, lazy float. Boaters have only 5 miles to warm up for Wild Sheep and Granite Creek, the remaining two of the original six big drops. Take out below the confluence with the Grande Ronde on the left at either the Grande Ronde or Hellers Bar boat ramp.

The river itself is on a scale in keeping with this monumental landscape. The total flow averages 35,000 cfs, and is often over 100,000.

Unfortunately, the same characteristics that gave the Snake great whitewater—big volume, good gradient, and a narrow canyon—proved irresistible to hydropower developers. In the 1950s the Idaho Power Company buried over 100 miles of river and all but two of the biggest rapids beneath the slack waters of Brownless, Oxbow, and Hells Canyon reservoirs. Then two utilities and the Department of the Interior proposed still more dams, including the notorious Nez Perce Dam. At its projected site a mile below the Snake-Salmon confluence, this 700-foot-high behemoth would have flooded the lower 60 miles of the Salmon and an equal distance on the Snake. Its reservoir would have extended all the way to the base of Hells Canyon Dam.

In 1967 the U.S. Supreme Court, guided by Justice William O. Douglas, stunned dam builders with a landmark conservation decision. The court ordered the government to consider not just the three competing dam proposals, but also a fourth, then unthinkable alternative: that the public interest might best be served by no dams at all. In the end, none of the dams was built. In 1975 a citizens' movement won National Wild and Scenic River designation for 68 miles (108.8 km) of the Snake, and National Recreation Area status for over 600,000 acres of adjacent land.

Snake River (Wyoming) ➢

The Snake is one of the longest rivers in the western United States, stretching some 1,040 miles (1,664 km) from Yellowstone National Park in Wyoming to the Columbia River in Washington. Although the Upper Snake offers a variety of boatable reaches, it is usually thought of as a calm river with sweeping curves at the feet of the Tetons. Yet other stretches offer good whitewater as well as great vistas.

For the Flagg Canyon run, put in at the Yellowstone park entrance. Just downstream the river cuts through the narrow volcanic gorge of Flagg Canyon. Most of the rapids are concentrated in a single mile of river. Most boaters take out at the highway bridge at Flagg Ranch.

The stretch through Grand Teton National Park is mostly flat, but novices should not be lulled by the easy rating; strainers, log hazards, cold water, braiding, and even the temperamental moose can be encountered below Pacific Creek.

After a straight stretch, boating increases after South Park Bridge boat ramp, where the river enters Bridger-Teton National Forest. This 17-mile reach has easy to moderate water and the highway is nearby. Take out at West Table Creek.

The Snake then drops into Snake River Canyon. Here the river turns west and bisects the rugged Snake River Range. Swollen by upstream tributaries, the Snake becomes a big-water river. Anything above 15,000 cfs (425 cumecs) means huge waves and a Class 4 rating. Lunch Counter, the best-known drop, is a popular surfing spot. This popular run records nearly 100,000 user days a year. Put in at West Table Creek and take out at Sheep Gulch.

FLAGG CANYON, YELLOWSTONE NATIONAL PARK ENTRANCE TO FLAGG RANCH
Difficulty: Class 3–
Length: 3 miles (4.8 km)

GRAND TETON NATIONAL PARK, JACKSON LAKE DAM TO MOOSE
Difficulty: Class 2–
Length: 25 miles (40 km)

SOUTH PARK BRIDGE TO WEST TABLE CREEK (BRIDGER-TETON NATIONAL FOREST RUN)
Difficulty: Class 2–
Length: 17 miles (27.2 km)

SNAKE RIVER CANYON, WEST TABLE CREEK TO SHEEP GULCH
Difficulty: Class 3
Length: 8 miles (12.8 km)

Season: Late April into November, except the first run which normally gets too low by early August
Character: Varied runs, all in scenic mountain setting

Difficulty: Class 3–
Length: 17 miles (27.2 km)

Season: Late April through October
Character: Undammed, road near; river running not allowed in national park upstream

◄ Yellowstone River (Montana)

The 680-mile-long (1,088 km) Yellowstone is the lower Forty-Eights' longest undammed river. The first 60 miles (96 km) from Gardiner to Livingston flow through Paradise Valley, a picturesque high mountain valley between the Gallatin and Absaroka ranges. U.S. Route 89 follows this reach, providing frequent access.

The first 17 miles (27.2 km) downstream of the park contain all of this great river's legal whitewater. The action begins with 3 miles of Class 2+ water (Class 3 at high flows) below Gardiner. Some boaters take out after this short run, while others float through 5 more miles of easy Class 2 to Corwin Springs. Nearly 5 miles of flatwater lead to Yankee Jim Canyon. The difficulty of Yankee Jim's whitewater varies widely with the flow. All the major rapids can easily be scouted from the highway. The Yellowstone below Carbella offers good boating, though it is no longer a whitewater river.

Above Gardiner the Yellowstone flows through the nation's first national park. The National Park Service prohibits river running inside Yellowstone National Park. The forbidden sections begin with 20 miles (32 km) of easy rapids and riffles below Yellowstone Lake. Then the bottom drops out. The river vaults over the Upper and Lower Falls of the Yellowstone—109 and 308 feet (33 and 94 m), respectively. From the foot of the Lower Falls the river plunges into the spectacular, turbulent Grand Canyon of the Yellowstone. Then, below Tower Junction, the river crashes through Black Canyon, another blend of sublime scenery and violent rapids.

Mom always looked forward to my summer visits, which offered her a chance to get out of the house after the long Montana winters. We would take the raft I kept in Montana to float and fish the Yellowstone, Big Hole, and Jefferson Rivers. On one memorable trip on the Yellowstone she caught a 4½-pound brown trout. Over time my interest turned to whitewater. In the summer of 1990 I decided to take Mom, then 75 years old, on the Alberton Gorge with my sister and her friends.

On the way to Missoula, Mom carefully inquired to make sure we were not taking her on a whitewater river. I assured her we weren't, reasoning to myself that at low flows the rapids would be barely Class 2–3. Hardly whitewater at all.

The first part of the trip was easy, but as the river swung south under the highway, my sister and her friends donned their helmets. My mother asked why, and one of my sister's friends explained that it was to "keep our heads warm—it's getting windy and cold." This assurance didn't last for long. Mom was soon seated on the floor of the raft, clutching athwart, barely able to peer over the side tubes. With each bounce of the raft she yelled "Dan'l! . . . Dan'l!"

At the take-out I asked Mom if she had a good time. Her unforgettable reply was, "Children are God's punishment for having sex!" My sister and I stared at each other slack-jawed in disbelief. This was the first time in our lives we had ever heard our Irish-Catholic mother refer to sex.

—Dan Dunlap

These Class 5 and 6 wilderness sections are among the world's most promising and exciting whitewater runs, but the Park Service has placed them strictly off limits. A few experts have occasionally made the descents (apart from the waterfalls, of course), but they have often been caught and fined.

Clark Fork River (Montana) ➤

With its headwaters in the mining area of Butte, the Clark Fork basin, on the west side of the Continental Divide, generates Montana's largest river. It winds its way along Interstate 90 to the west and north until some 30 miles (48 km) downstream of Missoula where the steep, lofty ridges of Alberton Gorge constrict the river into a narrow course, producing 9 miles (14.4 km) of renowned big-water rapids. Montana and Idaho boaters come here to test their skills against such local legends as Tumbleweed, Boat Eater, and Fang.

The difficulty of the whitewater in Alberton Gorge varies widely with the flow. Peak flows of 15,000 to 30,000 cfs (425 to 849 cumecs) in late May and early June produce continuous action. Long swims are likely in these conditions. By contrast, in late summer when flows diminish to a mild 1,500 to 3,000 cfs (42.5 to 84.9 cumecs), most of the rapids ease to Class 2+ or 3–.

Put in at the Saint Johns fishing access on the right bank to run Rest Stop, a rapid that becomes a huge hydraulic at big flows; or put in downstream at the developed put-in at Cyr Bridge on the left side at mile 2½ (4 km).

River egress is possible at Tarkio; however, permission is required, and a four-wheel-drive is recommended. Otherwise, take out at Forest Grove ½ mile (0.8 km) downstream on the right.

Flathead River (Montana) ➤

The Flathead drains the western slope of the Rockies in and near Glacier National Park in northwestern Montana. Glaciers shaped this region during the last ice age, and today the river's three forks flow through three parallel valleys. After the three forks join, the main Flathead leaves the mountains and empties into Flathead Lake, the largest body of fresh water west of the Great Lakes. Below the lake the Lower Flathead rolls through drier canyons toward its confluence with the Clark Fork River.

In 1976, 219 miles (350 km) of the Flathead's three forks were added to the National Wild and Scenic Rivers System. Although the runs vary in difficulty, some things are constant: boaters may encounter grizzlies anywhere, log hazards are common, and hypothermia can be a serious threat.

The river takes its name from the Flathead Indians, who were named by Lewis and Clark in a mistaken reference to a custom actually practiced by some other tribes along the Pacific Coast, of deforming an infant's head by lashing a padded board to its forehead.

The North Fork of the Flathead offers a rare combination of relatively easy water and rugged alpine scenery. Aside from a few rapids near its mouth, the North Fork takes boaters on an easy float past a string of inspiring peaks. For 58 miles (92.8 km), from the Canadian border to the Middle Fork confluence at Blankenship Bridge, the North Fork follows the western boundary of Glacier National Park. The river has a strong wilderness flavor despite a gravel road on the west (right) bank and a rough dirt track along parts of the east bank. These lightly used routes are generally well away from the river. The white-

---

ALBERTON GORGE, SAINT JOHNS TO FOREST GROVE
Difficulty: Class 3
Length: 17 miles (27.2 km)

Season: March through October
Character: Big water during peak runoff, interstate highway near

NORTH FORK FLATHEAD, CANADIAN BORDER TO MIDDLE FORK FLATHEAD CONFLUENCE
Difficulty: Class 1+ to 3–
Length: 58 miles (92.8 km)

MIDDLE FORK FLATHEAD, SCHAFER MEADOWS TO NORTH FORK CONFLUENCE
Difficulty: Class 2 to 4
Length: 72 miles (115.2 km)

SOUTH FORK FLATHEAD, BIG PRAIRIE TO UPPER TWIN CREEK
Difficulty: Class 2 to 4p
Length: 50½ miles (80.8 km)

(continued on following page)

Lower (Main) Flathead, Kerr
Dam to Buffalo Rapids
Difficulty: Class 3
Length: 7 miles (11.2 km)

Season: May to early
October
Character: Many different
runs, varying from total
wilderness to big-water,
dam-controlled releases

water is mostly confined to a 12-mile stretch from Big Creek to Glacier Rim, not far above the river's mouth. Upper Fool Hen (Class 3) is the toughest rapid.

The Middle Fork Flathead is two contrasting rivers. Not far below its Continental Divide headwaters south of Glacier National Park, the upper Middle Fork follows an unforgettable course through one of the West's finest wilderness areas. These 28 miles (44.8 km) from Schafer Meadows to Bear Creek tumble through untouched scenery in a steep, remote canyon. Below Bear Creek lies the other Middle Fork, a milder river followed by a railroad and highway. The lower stretch attracts far more use due to its easy access and popular commercial rafting trips. The Middle Fork is a wildlife haven. Almost anywhere along or in the river, boaters may spot bear, deer, moose, elk, and other large animals.

Access to the wilderness run of the Middle Fork is possible by pack train, but most groups fly in to a remote airstrip at Schafer Meadows. At lower flows, some boaters choose to pack in to Granite Creek, 10 miles (16 km) into the run.

The canyon is composed mostly of ancient sedimentary layers. This soft rock erodes easily, producing steep slopes and a constantly changing riverbed. Boaters must be alert for new or altered rapids as well as log hazards from undercut trees, especially at high or rising water. Particular caution is needed at Three Forks and Spruce Park, two series of very demanding rapids located near the beginning and end of the run. At high flows several rapids rate Class 5 as the whitewater becomes nearly continuous.

U.S. Route 2 and a railroad follow the Middle Fork from Bear Creek to Blankenship Bridge, remaining relatively unobtrusive while offering easy access and short shuttles. The best whitewater lies below Moccasin Creek, where the river produces seven rapids in quick succession. This section gets heavy use from local outfitters.

Below Blankenship Bridge the Middle Fork is a big-volume, low-gradient river. Nine miles below Blankenship Bridge the South Fork enters, marking the beginning of the main Flathead. The first easy take-out is at Teakettle Access, near the U.S. Route 2 bridge east of Columbia Falls.

The South Fork Flathead flows through a gentle, pristine landscape, giving boaters a glimpse of what much of western Montana was once like. Crystalline water, fine camping, abundant wildlife, and wilderness seclusion make the South Flathead one of the finest floats in the northern Rockies. Boating use is generally light, especially on the remote upper river, where access is by trail only.

In 1952 the Army Corps of Engineers built 564-foot-high (172 m) Hungry Horse Dam 5 miles (8 km) above the mouth of the South Fork, drowning nearly 40 miles (64 km) of river and 22,000 acres (8,903 hectares) of lush valley. Fortunately, the remainder of the South Fork is now protected as a National Wild and Scenic River, while the Bob Marshall Wilderness shelters the upper watershed.

From Big Prairie to Big Salmon Creek the river is mostly Class 1; from Big Salmon to Mid Creek, Class 2. Below Mid Creek the gorges begin, and most boaters leave the river and pack out about 3 miles to Meadow Creek Trailhead.

The upper and lower reaches of the South Fork are separated by Meadow Creek Gorge. Here bedrock squeezes the South Fork down to a narrow jet of water rushing through a deep, shadowy chasm. Swift current, sheer walls, difficult rapids, possible portages, and the danger of logjams make Meadow Creek Gorge an experts-only passage. The 15 miles (24 km) below Meadow Creek Gorge offer fine scenery, easy water, and a longer season.

The 7-mile (11.2 km) Buffalo Rapids run below Kerr Dam on the main Flathead offers good intermediate whitewater, culminating with the big waves and holes of Buffalo Rapids itself. Unlike many runs, this section becomes more difficult at moderate and low flows. This popular run is entirely within the Flathead Indian Reservation.

Roaring Fork River (Colorado) ➤

True to its name, the Roaring Fork drains two spectacular wilderness areas on the west side of the Sawatch Range, then roars down to Aspen, America's most famous ski resort. It meanders for several miles through alpine meadows before coming into its own again as it leaves Aspen behind. Swollen by waters rushing down from the Maroon Bells Snowmass Wilderness and in spite of trans-divide diversions, the Roaring Fork careens down a scenic mountain canyon filled with expert whitewater. Farther downstream the river eases, but its lower reaches continue to offer outstanding scenery and inspiring views of the peaks where it was born.

The river is divided here into three runs. The first, Slaughterhouse Bridge to Upper Woody Creek Bridge, is the most difficult. Put in on the right bank at Slaughterhouse Bridge. Some of this run's many difficult rapids include Entrance Exam (Class 4+) and Slaughterhouse Falls (Class 6), which is scouted and portaged on the right.

The second section is Upper Woody Creek Bridge to Basalt. Here the river is still steep, but the channel is not as constricted or boulder choked as it is upstream. Class 2 and 3 rapids continue most of the way to Basalt. Bigger rapids include Toothache (Class 4) and Snowmass (Class 3+). Interim access can be found at Snowmass Bridge and downstream on the right along Route 82.

The third and easiest section is from Basalt to Glenwood Springs. Interim access is available at Carbondale. Take out on the right at Two Rivers Park. Boaters may also continue down the Colorado River.

SLAUGHTERHOUSE BRIDGE TO UPPER WOODY CREEK BRIDGE
Difficulty: Class 4+$_6$
Length: 5 miles (8 km)

UPPER WOODY CREEK BRIDGE TO BASALT
Difficulty: Class 3 sub 4
Length: 12 miles (19.2 km)

BASALT TO GLENWOOD SPRINGS
Difficulty: Class 2
Length: 26 miles (41.6 km)

Season: May through July
Character: Varied runs; civilization is always near

Upper Colorado River (Colorado) ➤

The West's most famous river, the Colorado, is born along the crest of the Continental Divide and flows west-by-southwest across the state of Colorado. This is only the first leg of its 1,440-mile (2,304 km) journey to the Gulf of California, and it hasn't always been called the Colorado this far upriver. Throughout the white settlement of the West in the nineteenth century, it was known as the Grand River—hence, Colorado place names like Grand Junction (at the confluence of the Grand and the Gunnison) and Grand County. The Colorado River proper began at the confluence of the Green and the Grand in eastern Utah. In 1921 the Colorado Legislature renamed the Grand after its state of origin.

After trans-divide diversions and wandering gently across the broad alpine amphitheater of Middle Park and past the mouth of the Blue River, the Colorado runs smack into the Gore Range, a wall of 11,000-foot (3,355 m) peaks standing like an enormous natural dam across the river's path. The river was here before the most recent uplift of these mountains and held to its course as the range rose around it, carving in the process the 5-mile-long, 2,500-foot-deep (763 m) gash known as Gore Canyon where the Colorado drops 340 feet (104 m) with a peak gradient of 120 fpm (23.2 mpk). Added to the mix are huge boulders, left in the river decades ago by blasting for the railway.

GORE CANYON, KREMMLING TO PUMPHOUSE
Difficulty: Class 5+
Length: 11 miles (17.6 km)

PUMPHOUSE TO STATE BRIDGE (PUMPHOUSE RUN)
Difficulty: Class 2+
Length: 15 miles (24 km)

STATE BRIDGE TO DORSERO
Difficulty: Class 2+
Length: 45 miles (72 km)

UPPER GLENWOOD CANYON
Difficulty: Class 1
Length: 8 miles (12.8 km)

(continued on following page)

Gore Canyon should be attempted only at low to moderate flows, and only by teams of experts prepared for scouting and portages. Gore overwhelms many excellent boaters. Above 2,000 cfs (56.6 cumecs) the run is very powerful and treacherous and should be attempted only by the most daring experts.

Put in at the Route 9 bridge south of Kremmling. Five miles of flatwater lead to the dramatic canyon entrance. The first rapid inside the canyon is a rocky 9-foot (2.7 m) drop known as Applesauce (Class 5–), also called Gateway or Pearly Gates. Not far downstream is a difficult passage known as Gore Rapid (Class 5+), a third of a mile (0.5 km) of continuous, constricted whitewater that includes three especially notable drops: the Gore, with a treacherous undercut, followed quickly by Double Pourover or Twin Holes, and finally the 8-foot (2.5 m) drop of Pyrite Falls.

Downstream is a series of three railroad tunnels on the right in the deepest part of the canyon. Beside the second tunnel is a 12-foot (3.7 m) vertical plunge known as Tunnel Falls (Class 5+), which is hard to spot from upstream and can be portaged on the left. Below the falls is Toilet Bowl (Class 5), a very nasty and deceptive river-wide keeper hydraulic. Immediately downstream is the last major rapid, Kisschbaum (Class 5). Easier water leads to the take-out on the left at the Pumphouse access, 11 miles (17.6 km) below the Route 9 put-in.

The Pumphouse run, from Pumphouse to State Bridge, is Colorado's second most popular stretch of river (after Browns Canyon of the Arkansas River). Here, below Gore Canyon, the Colorado reverts to a more mellow character, winding for the most part through a shallow, semiarid valley of sagebrush, juniper, and pinyon pine. Two short mini-canyons—carved from the same dark bedrock as Gore—and the prominence of big waves at high water provide some scenery and excitement.

Below State Bridge, the highway parallels the right bank, after which an unpaved road follows the river much of the way to Dotsero, crossing it several times and providing access. The biggest drop is Rodeo (Class 3), two abrupt drops among sharp rocks. Boaters may wish to take out at the BLM's Pinball Point access to avoid a dangerous railroad bridge just a mile downstream at a left bend. Take out at Dotsero where I-70 crosses the Colorado and the Eagle River enters on the left.

Below Dotsero the river is calm and uninteresting as it parallels the freeway. The action begins again as the river gradually enters Glenwood Canyon and cuts a swath through colorful layers of sandstone, limestone, and granite. Construction of Interstate 70, a railroad, a dam, and a diversion now severely impact what may have been Colorado's finest wilderness canyon. Various problems with access closure and parking restrictions necessitate that boaters check locally for the best put-ins and take-outs. Glenwood Canyon above the dam can still be run, and it provides fine views of the steep rock walls. The rapids here are only Class 1, and boaters are required to navigate flatwater once they reach the reservoir. Boating below the dam is not recommended.

River running resumes at a concrete boat ramp just below Shoshone Powerhouse where the water is returned to the river from Shoshone Dam. The rapids in this stretch are straightforward Class 3 to 3+ at normal flows but develop huge hydraulics at high flows, raising the rating to at least a Class 4. A popular take-out is Grizzly Creek, 2 miles (3.2 km) below the boathouse. A bicycle shuttle on a nearby bike path is a possibility.

The last stretch, Grizzly Creek to New Castle, includes lower Glenwood and South Canyons and provides good Class 2 action for novices. Take out at New Castle or various alternate points upstream.

Arkansas River (Colorado) ➢

The Arkansas is the world's most popular whitewater river. Its fine variety of runs, good to excellent scenery, long season, and easy access provide the attraction. More than 300,000 people float the river annually, mostly with commercial outfitters who operate an enormous flotilla of rafts. Boasting more than 100 boatable miles (160 km) within easy reach of major highways flanking the river, the Arkansas is less than three hours from Denver and one hour from Colorado Springs. It features splendid vistas of the many surrounding peaks more than 14,000 feet (4,270 m) high.

For most of its 1,472-mile (2,355 km) length, the Arkansas is a Great Plains river. It is the second-largest tributary of the Mississippi, after the Missouri. Whitewater boaters know only the uppermost sections of the Arkansas in the mountains west of Colorado Springs.

Much of the Arkansas's fame here is due to its difficult rapids, concentrated at either end of the river: high up in Pine Creek Rapid and the Numbers, and far downstream in spectacular, sheer-walled Royal Gorge. But there is also whitewater for non-daredevils.

Action starts at the little town of Granite where river runners can put in at the bridge. The 11 miles (17.6 km) through Granite Canyon, Pine Creek, and the Numbers make up one of the West's most famous stretches of difficult whitewater. This continuous-gradient mountain torrent is no place for the inexperienced. The opening rapids in Granite Canyon are not hard, but there are hazards and one portage. Then comes Pine Creek, a tough Class 5 at low and moderate flows and Class 6 above 2,500 cfs (70.75 cumecs). Just downstream, the run through the Numbers is only slightly less difficult, rating Class 4 (Class 5 at higher flows) at the bridge in the town of Granite. Take out at

GRANITE TO CANON CITY

Difficulty: Class 2 to 6$_p$, but mostly Class 3

Length: 104 miles (166.4 km)

Season: May through August

Character: Varied runs; the most heavily used whitewater river in the world

---

It was the summer of 1977, and there was a drought in California and across the West. Rivers were down everywhere, and I was desperate for whitewater. Surf kayaking had helped, but it just wasn't the same as a river. There weren't many guidebooks around then, but I heard there was some water in the Rockies, and I had a friend in Canon City, Colorado. As I drove along the Arkansas River on the way to Canon City, I saw some rafts, kayaks, and some river runners. They told me about running the Royal Gorge, which up to then I had considered just a tourist trap, based on the countless bumper stickers on countless Winnebagos.

I couldn't get anyone to join me the next day, so I left Route 50 behind me while boating alone (not a recommended practice). The canyon deepened and narrowed, allowing only a small passage for the frothing whitewater. It was awesome. In the heart of the canyon, the Royal Gorge Suspension Bridge crossed above the vertical walls about 1,500 feet (458 m) overhead. I even did a roll for the tourists who were by the river via the Incline Railroad. Soon the canyon opened and the whitewater slackened. I had made it, but more importantly I had one of my most moving whitewater experiences, in a drought year with few expectations. Now the Arkansas in Colorado has more whitewater use than any river in the world, but on that day in 1977 I felt like John Wesley Powell.

—*Jim Cassady*

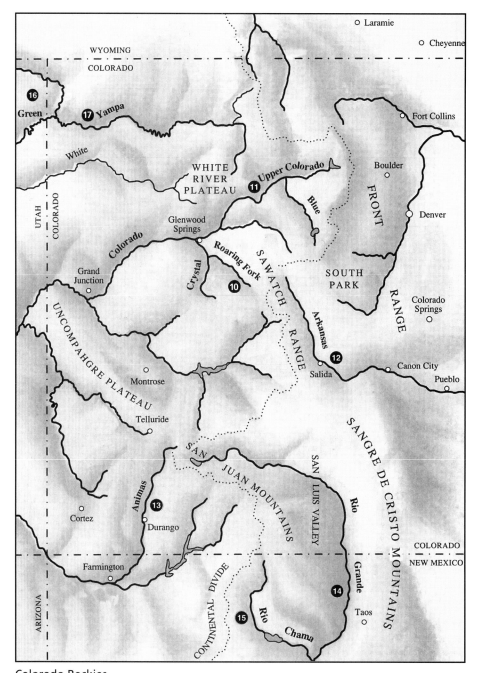

Colorado Rockies

the Railroad Bridge Recreation Site on the left bank, just upstream from the railroad bridge across the river.

The next section, a scenic 15-mile (24 km) stretch between the Numbers and Browns Canyon, is less frequently boated.

For many recreational boaters, the Arkansas means Browns Canyon. It's not hard to see why this exhilarating ride has become one of the most popular whitewater runs in the country. Here the Arkansas pours through a dramatic granite canyon, the highway disappears, and only the railroad follows the river. By this point the Arkansas has become a pool-and-drop river of considerable volume.

At any level, Browns Canyon is laced with boulder gardens and challenging whitewater, especially at higher flows. Unguided novices should stay away.

Below Salida striking views of the Sangre de Cristo Mountains open to the south as the Arkansas flows through Pleasant Valley's aptly named countryside. In this section, sometimes called the Rincon run and recently named Bighorn Sheep Canyon by the Colorado Legislature, long calms are punctuated by Class 3 rapids. (Bighorn sheep can indeed be seen on the canyon walls.)

Downstream from Coaldale, the river turns sharply northeast and enters the Lower Arkansas River Canyon (sometimes called the Parkdale run). Here the rapids are more frequent and a little more difficult. Most should take out at the Parkdale Recreation site, as downstream the river swings to the southeast and plunges into the rapids of the legendary Royal Gorge, site of the world's highest suspension bridge.

The Royal Gorge's continuous whitewater is the toughest on the Arkansas except for Pine Creek and the Numbers. In case of emergency, the only legal way out is by river. (The Denver & Rio Grande Western Railroad, for liability reasons, formally prohibits trespassing on the tracks on the left bank.) Little sunlight reaches the bottom of the narrow canyon, so wetsuits are advised for boaters at any time of year.

The run has easy water for the first 4 miles followed by big rapids including Sunshine Falls (Class 5), also known as Caretaker or Whitehorse, followed by Class 4 rapids including Sledgehammer, Squeeze Box, Bridge Rapid, Corner Pocket, and Soda Fountain Rock. Take out at Centennial Park in Canon City on the right.

Animas River (Colorado) ⯈

The Animas River flows just over 100 miles (160 km) from its headwaters in the San Juan Mountains to the confluence with the San Juan River in the high desert of New Mexico. The river, which is the largest tributary of the San Juan, is most famous for its upper reaches. The put-in for the Upper Animas is above 9,000 feet (2,745 m), the shuttle road climbs above 10,000 feet (3,050 m), surrounded by peaks over 14,000 feet (4,270 m). In the Animas Gorge just below Silverton, continuous Class 5 whitewater defines the term "limits of navigability." Downstream from Durango, the Lower Animas is much milder.

Animas country has a history as rich as any in the Colorado Rockies region. Spanish explorers named the river "El Rio de las Animas Perdidas en Purgatorio," or "The River of the Lost Souls in Purgatory." In later years the name was shortened to "Animas." Gold was discovered here in 1870. To link the mines along the upper river with processing mills downstream, the Denver & Rio Grande Railroad pushed a narrow-gauge spur line upriver through the rugged Animas Gorge. Today the steam locomotive of the Durango & Silverton Railroad carries tourists along the upper river, treating them to some of the most spectacular mountain scenery in America.

Few rivers can match the Upper Animas for intense whitewater action. In the 30-mile-long (48 km) Animas Gorge the river drops 2,450 feet (747 m). With few eddies,

NEAR SILVERTON TO TACOMA
POWERHOUSE
Difficulty: Class 5
Length: 25 miles (40 km)

TRIMBLE BRIDGE TO DURANGO
Difficulty: Class 1+
Length: 11 miles (17.6 km)

DURANGO TO BONDAD BRIDGE
(LOWER ANIMAS RUN)
Difficulty: Class 3–
Length: 20 miles (32 km)

Season: April through August

Character: The Upper Animas is a difficult wilderness run, yet considered one of the world's classic runs; the Lower Animas is relatively tame, with civilization nearby

several Class 5 rapids, and an unrunnable gorge below the take-out, the Animas is a daunting undertaking. Added to the mix are high altitude, cold water, variable flows increasing throughout the run, and isolation. Just before it flattens out above Durango, the Animas crashes through an unrunnable, unportageable, sheer-sided gorge with a gradient of more than 200 fpm (38.6 mpk).

Logistics are a challenge as well. River runners are obliged to leave the canyon via the railroad (downstream is an unrunnable section). An overnight run is possible either by packing very light or by having overnight gear hauled in by the train to Needleton, near the halfway point. River runners can end their trips at the take-out opposite Tacoma Powerhouse at mile 25 (40 km) and take the train back to the put-in.

The three biggest of the many difficult rapids are Garfield Slide (Class 5), No Name Falls (Class 5+), the most difficult rapid on the run, and Broken Bridge Rapid (Class 5).

Below the cataracts of the Lower Box the Animas abruptly changes character for the Lower Animas run as the railroad and the highway rejoin the right bank. The first section of the Lower Animas includes 11 miles (17.6 km) of Class 1 water below the put-in at Trimble Bridge. Most boaters take out at the 32nd Street bridge at the north end of Durango.

Below Durango the Animas offers 20 miles (32 km) of intermediate-to-novice boating through a shallow, semi-arid canyon. Commercial outfitters run frequent trips on portions of this reach. The most popular put-in for intermediate boaters is Schneider Park near the south end of Durango. About a mile (1.6 km) downstream is the biggest rapid on the Lower Animas, Smelter (Class 3). Santa Rita Hole, just below the highway bridge, is the site of the Animas River Days hole-riding contest. The last good take-out is at mile $19\frac{1}{2}$ (31.2 km), on the left bank $\frac{1}{2}$ mile (0.8 km) upstream from Bondad Bridge.

LOBATOS BRIDGE TO LEE TRAIL (UTE MOUNTAIN RUN)
Difficulty: Class 2
Length: $24\frac{1}{2}$ miles (39.2 km)

LEE TRAIL TO LITTLE ARSENIC SPRINGS (UPPER BOX RUN)
Difficulty: Class 3 to 6p
Length: 13 miles (20.8 km)

LITTLE ARSENIC SPRINGS TO JOHN DUNN BRIDGE (LA JUNTA RUN)
Difficulty: Class 3–
Length: $9\frac{1}{2}$ miles (15.2 km)

JOHN DUNN BRIDGE TO TAOS JUNCTION BRIDGE (TAOS BOX, OR LOWER BOX, RUN)
Difficulty: Class 4
Length: 15 miles (24 km)

(continued on following page)

◁ Rio Grande (New Mexico)

From its headwaters on the slopes of 13,000-foot (3,965 m) peaks in the San Juan Mountains, the Rio Grande flows 1,887 miles (3,019 km) to the Gulf of Mexico. Among rivers in the United States, only the Mississippi-Missouri system is longer.

Today, much of the river's flow is diverted for irrigation, especially in southern Colorado's San Luis Valley. In dry years the Rio Grande is nearly dewatered. The river is usually replenished below Alamosa, Colorado, by a major tributary, the Conejos, which drains the southeastern flank of the San Juans. Except in dry years, there is enough water for river running downstream on the Rio Grande. The vast majority of boaters are to be found on either the Taos Box run or the Racecourse run below Pilar.

Those whose skills match the demands of the box canyons of the Rio Grande will find a dramatic wilderness, a major bird sanctuary, and some of the finest whitewater around. Here, where the Rio Grande has carved its dramatic canyons through the flat lava flows of the Taos Plateau, the sheer black basalt walls of the narrow Upper and Taos boxes rise to heights of 700 to 800 feet (214 to 244 m).

The Ute Mountain run, upstream from the Upper Box, starting from Lobatos Bridge, is a rewarding but little-known and very isolated stretch of the river. Eagles, falcons, owls, geese, and mergansers are more common here than kayakers and canoeists. Many more lovers of bird life, solitude, and high-desert scenery would float this section of the Rio Grande if it weren't for the tough climb up steep Lee Trail at mile $24\frac{1}{2}$ (39.2

km), the last take-out above the Upper Box. Don't miss the take-out and enter the Upper Box by mistake.

The next stretch is the Upper Box, beginning at Lee Trail. If the Taos Box is the most famous section of the New Mexico Rio Grande, the Upper Box is the most notorious. This is an extremely hazardous and rarely boated stretch of river accessible only by long, steep trails. Those running the Upper Box should be prepared for difficult portages around some of the short, steep falls. Boaters unfamiliar with the river should consult local kayakers before making this run.

Below the Upper Box is the La Junta Run, from Little Arsenic Springs to John Dunn Bridge. This run offers good scenery, good camping, and two Class 3 rapids. Scout the take-out in advance and do not continue on by mistake into the Upper Box. The trail rises 220 vertical feet (67.3 m) in 500 yards (458.6 m).

New Mexico's premier run is the Taos Box, also known as the Lower Box, a splendid 15-mile (24 km) Class 4 reach from John Dunn Bridge to Taos Junction Bridge. The Taos Box offers ideal conditions for advanced boating: challenging rapids, good road access at the put-in and take-out, and a beautiful wild canyon where only a few trails reach the river. Action is fast and nearly continuous in the Rio Bravo stretch near the end of the run. Both private boaters and guests on commercial rafting trips flock to the Taos Box in good snowpack years.

Boaters who like their scenery without too much anxiety should consider one or more sections of the Lower Gorge of the Rio Grande between Taos Junction Bridge and Velarde. The Orilla Verde run (formerly called the State Park run) is a relatively easy 6½-mile (10.4 km) float through Orilla Verde Recreation Area. Downstream from the recreation area, around Pilar, private property lines both banks, and the next river access is ½ mile (0.8 km) south of the town. Below Pilar the action picks up again in the Racecourse run. The Class 3 rapids are friendlier than the bone-jarring drops of the Taos Box, and all can be scouted from the highway. Here runnable flows usually last through the summer.

Rio Chama (New Mexico) ➤

The Rio Chama is one of the West's best-loved rivers—not for its whitewater, though the rapids are pleasant enough, but for its quiet beauty.

The Chama begins on the east slope of the Continental Divide in southern Colorado, and its flow is enhanced by trans-divide diversions from the Navajo River. Its southerly course into New Mexico cuts through layers of sedimentary rock. Just below El Vado Reservoir the river makes its deepest cut, Chama Canyon, where the walls rise as high as 1,500 feet (458 m). When the canyon finally opens up, the Chama, filled with sediment, flows southeastward toward its confluence with the Rio Grande northwest of Santa Fe.

The wilderness run through Chama Canyon is a favorite of open-canoeists, but almost any type of river boat is suitable. In 1988 Congress declared the Chama a National Wild and Scenic River, protecting 25 miles (40 km) of river below El Vado Dam. An additional 4-mile stretch (6.4 km) is under study for possible Wild and Scenic designation. In recent years the Chama's popularity has increased dramatically, and in 1991 the Bureau of Land Management (BLM) began restricting use under a new permit system.

Taos Junction Bridge to Pilar
(Orilla Verde run)
Difficulty: Class 2
Length: 6½ miles (10.4 km)

Pilar to Taos County Line
(Racecourse run)
Difficulty: Class 3
Length: 4½ miles (7.2 km)

Season: Usually April through July, but it varies considerably from year to year; some sections all summer
Character: Widely varied runs, high desert

El Vado Ranch to Big Eddy
Difficulty: Class 2+
Length: 31 miles (49.6 km)

Season: April through August
Character: Natural runoff in spring and early summer, dam-release mid- and late summer

Below El Vado Dam the Chama continues at a relatively constant gradient. The first 5 miles (8 km) are fairly flat; then, as the walls of Chama Canyon rise, occasional Class 2 rapids appear. The upper 22 miles (35.2 km) from El Vado Ranch to just below Christ in the Desert Monastery are wilderness, while a rough road follows the final 9 miles (14.4 km). Because most of the whitewater is in the lower stretch, one-day runs are popular here.

◁ Green River (Utah, Colorado)

FLAMING GORGE RESERVOIR TO LODORE
Difficulty: Class 2–
Length: 46 miles (73.6 km)

GATES OF LODORE, LODORE TO SPLIT MOUNTAIN boat ramp
Difficulty: Class 3
Length: 44 miles (70.4 km)

DESOLATION AND GRAY CANYONS, SANDY WASH BEACH TO SWASEY'S BEACH
Difficulty: Class 2+
Length: 84 miles (134.4 km)

LABYRINTH AND STILLWATER CANYONS, GREEN RIVER STATE PARK TO MINERAL BOTTOM
Difficulty: Class 1+
Length: 68 miles (108.8 km)

Season: April through November
Character: Varied runs, but almost all are mild, high-desert wilderness runs

Beginning as a Rocky Mountain stream in western Wyoming's Wind River Range, the Green River flows generally south through Utah—and some of the most magnificent desert canyons in the West—to its confluence with the Colorado. Downstream of the town of Green, Wyoming, the river is impounded in the Flaming Gorge reservoir, which floods several lovely canyons as the river crosses the Wyoming-Utah border.

Below Flaming Gorge Dam in northeastern Utah, boaters can still enjoy the remaining half of Red Canyon and all of Swallow Canyon, both of which have fine scenery and easy rapids. Most popular is the first 7 miles (11.2 km) where the river flows beneath 1,500-foot (458 m) bright red canyon walls. Below Swallow Canyon, the Green wanders placidly eastward across the open flats of Browns Park and into the northwestern corner of Colorado. Put in below Flaming Gorge Dam and take out at various access points, the last of which is Lodore boat ramp just upstream of the next run, which requires a permit.

Since William Ashley's first descent in 1825, the Green River through today's Dinosaur National Monument has become known as one of the West's great river trips. The stretch begins with a run through the Canyon of Lodore. At the end of Lodore is the confluence with the undammed Yampa River, which during peak snowmelt adds 10,000 to 15,000 cfs (283 to 425 cumecs) to the Green's dam-controlled flow. Downstream lie Whirlpool and Split Mountain canyons. The three canyons present a constantly changing riverscape, from steep walls of red sandstone in Lodore to dramatically folded layers of gray limestone and pale sandstone in Split Mountain. The open flats of Browns Park, Island Park, and Rainbow Park offer outstanding views of some of the most dramatic and abrupt canyon entrances in the West. Below Dinosaur the Green winds through open terrain in the Uinta Basin. Take out at Split Mountain boat ramp.

The nearby Dinosaur Quarry Visitor Center makes a fascinating side excursion for river runners, detailing the excavation of some 350 tons of dinosaur fossils here since 1909.

Downstream the White and Duschene rivers join the Green near Ouray, Utah, and the river slices southward into the broad uplift of the Tavaputs Plateau. The ensuing run down Desolation and Gray canyons is one of the Canyon Country's best wilderness floats, offering inspiring scenery, easy to moderate whitewater, superb side hikes, expansive campsites, and wildlife viewing. Put in at Sandy Wash Beach and take out at Swasey's Beach. River running in Desolation and Gray has increased more slowly over the years than on a number of other Canyon Country runs.

The last 68 miles (110 km) of the Green are calm and quiet. This is one of the West's finest flatwater wilderness trips, well suited for open canoes except at high water. Labyrinth and Stillwater canyons require little in the way of whitewater skills, just basic boating ability and solid outdoor experience. Floating these canyons imparts a profound

Green River, Utah/Colorado. *(Edie and Vladimir Bazjanac)*

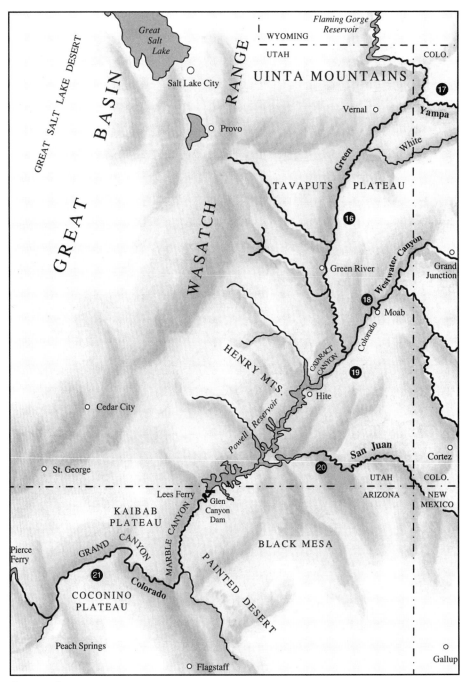

Canyon Country

sense of isolation and peace. Put in at Green River State Park and take out at Mineral Bottom (mile 68). Downstream there is no access.

Yampa River (Colorado) ➢

The Yampa is the last major river in the entire Colorado Basin with no large dams and reservoirs. It runs wild and free for almost its entire 300-mile (480 km) length. For river running we divide the river into three sections: Little Yampa (Duffy) and Juniper canyons, Cross Mountain Gorge, and Yampa Canyon.

Near its beginnings the Yampa is very much a river of the Colorado Rockies. Rising high on the White River Plateau in northwestern Colorado, the Yampa flows north to the famous ski resort of Steamboat Springs, then turns west toward its ultimate destination, the confluence with the Green River in Dinosaur National Monument. In Steamboat Springs local boaters enjoy a permanent slalom course, and each June the Yampa River Festival is held here. Below Steamboat Springs the Yampa changes, metamorphosing from a Rocky Mountain river into a Canyon Country classic. Downstream from Craig, the river picks up a thick load of silt as it carves through a series of four sandstone canyons.

The first and longest canyon begins a few miles below Craig. In Little Yampa Canyon (also known as Duffy Canyon), the river cuts through sloping sandstone walls that rise more than 500 feet (153 m) on either side. Here the Yampa is smooth and peaceful.

The next canyon on the Yampa is short but beautiful and covers a bit more whitewater. Juniper Canyon makes a fine run by itself, or boaters can combine Little Yampa and Juniper for a continuous 51-mile (81.6 km) float lasting three to five days. This second canyon sees even lighter use than the first, in part because of access problems. Boaters using the put-in at Government Bridge must cross 8 miles (12.8 km) of flatwater through open terrain to reach the canyon entrance. There is an alternate put-in at Juniper Canyon Access, 7 miles below Government Bridge. A rock diversion weir for the Maybell Ditch creates the biggest whitewater on the run just under a mile below the canyon entrance. The take-out for this section is at U.S. Route 40.

For 30 miles (48 km) below Juniper Canyon, the Yampa drifts westward past hills, mesas, and ranches as it gradually approaches Cross Mountain, a rugged 7,000-foot (2,135 m) north–south barrier bisecting the river's path. The river plows directly into the mountain, carving a dramatic gash 3 miles (4.8 km) long and a thousand feet deep. Cross Mountain Gorge is by far the toughest section of the Yampa. The standard put-in is only ¾ mile (1.2 km) above the jaws of the gorge. Just below the entrance is the biggest drop, Osterizer, also known as Mammoth Falls, a Class 4+ rapid that should be portaged at high water. A half mile (0.8 km) of Class 4 rapids follow leading to the Snake Pit (Class 4+). Downstream is Pourover City (Class 3) and Sherm's Hole. Just 4 miles (6.4 km) after it began, the Cross Mountain Gorge run ends; take out at Lily Park.

The Yampa's final canyon is known as Yampa Canyon. This beautiful 2,500-foot-deep (763 m) canyon is one of the West's most popular river trips as the river passes through Dinosaur National Monument. A breathtaking panorama of sheer cliffs, rounded buttes, slickrock walls, and hoodoos provides the scenery. For some 25 miles (40 km) below Deerlodge Park, the Lower Yampa River follows a relatively straight course. Below Harding Hole the canyon's character changes as the Yampa enters a deep

LITTLE YAMPA AND JUNIPER CANYONS, YAMPA PROJECT PUMP STATION TO U.S. ROUTE 40
Difficulty: Class 2–
Length: 51 miles (81.6 km)

CROSS MOUNTAIN GORGE, CANYON ENTRANCE TO LILY PARK
Difficulty: Class 4+
Length: 4 miles (6.4 km)

YAMPA CANYON, DEER PARK LODGE TO GREEN RIVER CONFLUENCE
Difficulty: Class 3–
Length: 71 miles (113.6 km)

Season: April through July
Character: Scenic desert canyons away from civilization

layer of pale sandstone. Four miles above the Green River confluence, the Yampa thunders through one of the West's most famous rapids, Warm Springs, created in 1965 by debris from a side canyon.

Not far below Warm Springs the Yampa merges with the Green at Echo Park. Most boaters prefer to continue down the Green River—either 17 relatively easy miles (27.2 km) to Rainbow Park, or 25 miles (40 km) to better access at Split Mountain Boat Ramp.

◁ Colorado River, Westwater Canyon (Utah)

Here in Westwater Canyon, one of the roughest reaches of the Colorado churns between some of its quietest stretches, much through polished stone known as the Black Rocks. This layer of ancient black schist is similar to the famous Vishnu Schist of the Grand Canyon. Throughout the run, the rapids appear when steep walls constrict the river and massive ebony boulders litter the riverbed.

There is a fairly natural runoff pattern: a sharp snowmelt peak, usually in late May or early June, followed by a steep decline to late summer lows—yet it never falls too low for boating.

At almost any water level, the action peaks at Skull Rapid (Class 4), one of the most famous pieces of rough water in Canyon Country. Skull throws up a variety of obstacles, including a remarkable whirlpool-like eddy known as the Room of Doom. The rapid's alternate name, Dead Sheep, refers to livestock seen floating and bloating in this eddy in times past.

Although Westwater Canyon can be run in one day, many parties prefer to linger. For a longer trip, boaters can start 25 miles (40 km) upstream at Loma and run through Horsethief and Ruby canyons or continue downstream.

The Bureau of Land Management controls river traffic by requiring permits.

◁ Colorado River, Cataract Canyon (Utah)

First descended by John Wesley Powell's expedition in 1869, the rapids of Cataract Canyon result from its unique geology. Extensive faulting has fractured the riverside cliffs into discrete blocks, many of which have sheared away. Cataract is the only stretch of the desert Colorado where the major rapids were not formed by debris flows from side creeks.

Sadly, more than half of Cataract's magnificent whitewater lies buried beneath Powell Reservoir. Of the 52 rapids identified by surveyor William Chenoweth in 1921, only half remain. The reservoir covers 23 of the original 36 miles (57.6 km) of whitewater, reaching to within $1/2$ mile (0.8 km) of the largest rapid, Big Drop. Nevertheless, the surviving remnant of Cataract Canyon still stands as one of the West's grandest river trips.

Cataract Canyon experiences a remarkably wide range of flows within each season and from one year to the next. Boaters should choose a starting date carefully, then keep track of snowpack and runoff. Many launch in July and August to avoid May and June high water. Another consideration for Cataract trips is that when Powell Reservoir is full, flatwater begins 34 miles (54.4 km) above the take-out. Few attempt to paddle or row this distance; the effort is likely to take more than one day, campsites are few and far between, and upstream winds can make the experience a living hell. Most groups bring a motor or arrange to be towed out by a motorboat or houseboat from Hite Marina.

Since Cataract Canyon lies just below the Green-Colorado confluence, boaters can approach it on either river. Both are essentially flat for many miles above the confluence. Most Cataract trips launch at the Potash access on the Colorado and drift 48 miles (76.8 km) to the confluence. Four miles (6.4 km) downstream of the confluence the Colorado loses its composure. Then the "Cat," as river guides know it, erupts into 10 miles (16 km) of big-water rapids. At low flows boaters may count 26 distinct drops, though some are only Class 2. At high water many of the rapids blend together.

Many rapids are known only by the numbers that Mr. Chenoweth and the U.S. Geological Survey assigned them. The first real challenge comes at Mile Long (Rapids 13 through 18 combined). Just above Powell Reservoir is Bid Grop. Here Rapids 21 through 23 combine in one of the West's most famous whitewater gauntlets.

San Juan River (Utah) ➤

At one time the San Juan ran free all the way to its confluence with the Colorado. Now it is impounded by Powell Reservoir, and its flow is diminished. What remains of the Lower San Juan still ranks as one of the West's great wilderness river trips. It is often described as the Grand Canyon without the big rapids. These days, river runners float the 27-mile (43.2 km) upper canyon from Sand Island (near Bluff) to Mexican Hat and/or the 57-mile (91.2 km) lower canyon from Mexican Hat to Clay Hills. Sand Island launches outnumber Mexican Hat starts by more than three to one.

Below Sand Island the river cuts through a plateau of sedimentary rock known as the Monument Upwarp. Colorful layers of sandstone and limestone rise $\frac{1}{4}$ mile (0.4 km) above the river in places. Downstream from Mexican Hat a seemingly endless series of meanders, the famous Goosenecks of the San Juan, send river runners back and forth through 13 miles (20.8 km) of twisting canyon to gain just 3 air miles (4.8 km).

The river's prehistory is equally rich. For more than a thousand years the San Juan and its side canyons were home to the Anasazi. Today, their cliff dwellings, petroglyphs, and scattered artifacts can be found throughout the canyons.

For many, side hikes are the biggest attraction of a San Juan trip: the swimming holes of Slickhorn Canyon, the Anasazi ruins and dramatic slickrock in Grand Gulch, and the sheer solitude of Steer Gulch.

The San Juan is also famous for sand waves. A chain of standing waves 2 to (rarely) 8 feet (2.4 m) high slowly rises in a stretch of smooth water. The waves are short-lived, lasting only a few seconds or minutes before fading away, caused as temporary ripples or bulges develop in the sandy riverbed formed by the river's tremendous silt load.

At present no one should boat below the Clay Hills Crossing take-out due to an unrunnable and virtually impassable waterfall resulting from the river's recent deviation from its former course at Powell Reservoir.

Colorado River, Grand Canyon (Arizona) ➤

For most people, floating the Grand Canyon of the Colorado, universally referred to as simply as the Grand Canyon, is the trip of a lifetime. The four million tourists that view the canyon from the rim each year see only a slice of the Canyon's profound scale and boundless variety. The 21,000 who boat the river each year enjoy much more. The stun-

SAND ISLAND (NEAR BLUFF) TO MEXICAN HAT
Difficulty: Class 2
Length: 27 miles (43.2 km)

MEXICAN HAT TO CLAY HILLS
Difficulty: Class 2
Length: 57 miles (91.2 km)

Season: April through September
Character: Scenic, remote with just minor whitewater

LEES FERRY TO PIERCE FERRY
Difficulty: Class 4+
Length: 280 miles (448 km)

(continued on following page)

Season: All year
Character: Absolutely
  spectacular, what all
  other rivers are
  compared to

ning vistas, the fascinating geology, the massive rapids, the long calm pools, and the tapestry of human history impart on most a feeling akin to spiritual regeneration.

A Grand Canyon float trip is surely the geology lesson of a lifetime. The 250-million-year-old Kaibab limestone that appears at river level just below the Lees Ferry put-in rises quickly to form the rim rock of the canyon. Only 30 miles (48 km) downstream it reaches 2,500 feet (763 m) above the river. It is followed at river level by older formations which appear one after another and climb ever higher. In the heart of the canyon, over a mile below the rim, the dark, twisted walls of the V-shaped Granite Gorge are made of 1.7 billion-year-old metamorphic rock: black Vishnu schist and pink Zoroaster granite.

Though the rocks are old, the deep cut of the Colorado River that made the Grand Canyon is relatively young. It is the result of the rapid uplift of the southern Colorado Plateau. From roughly 17 million to about 5 million years ago the plateau rose some 4,000 feet (1,220 m).

Four thousand years of human habitation, made possible when the climate was wet enough to support agriculture, can be seen, especially at the Nankoweap and Unkar areas. Remnants of the Anasazi (the Ancient ones) and the nearby Hopi are most notable. The Havasupai and the Hualapai now occupy reservations in the Grand Canyon.

It took the historic river journey of Major John Wesley Powell, a Union officer who lost his right arm in the Civil War, to reveal to Europeans the nature of the canyon. On May 24, 1869, his party of ten set off from Green River, Wyoming, in four wooden boats on an expedition down the Green and Colorado rivers and through the unknown expanses of the Grand Canyon. After much hardship, the crew reached the mouth of the Paria River (later the site of Lees Ferry) on August 4 and Bright Angel Creek in the heart of upper Granite Gorge on August 15. They struggled on to Separation Rapid at mile 239 (382 km), where on August 29 three more crew members walked out. Abandoning one boat, the rest of the party continued downstream, emerged from the canyon at the Grand Wash Cliffs, and floated down to a Mormon settlement at the mouth of the Virgin River.

The Grand Canyon was declared a National Park in 1919, but the park boundaries included only 82 miles (131.3 km) of the river corridor. Left outside the park were the first 52 miles (82.3 km) below Lees Ferry (most of the stretch that Powell named Marble Canyon) and everything below Tapeats Creek at mile 134 (214.4 km). In 1962, after the threat of Marble Canyon Dam was beaten back, Marble Canyon was made a National Monument. In 1975 the various components were consolidated as Grand Canyon National Park, which now covers nearly 1,900 square miles (4,921 sq. km) and the entire river from Lees Ferry to Pierce Ferry (including 40-plus miles usually under "Lake" Mead).

May through September is peak boating season in the Grand Canyon. June and July are the hottest months, with air temperatures regularly surpassing 100°F (38°C). But the river is so cold that wetsuits are sometimes advisable. Thunderstorms break the heat in late July and August (the latter is the rainiest month of the year). Flash floods in side canyons can be a hazard, especially at this time. Late September and October trips usually have the best daytime weather, though autumn days grow short and nights can be chilly. Some tough-hided boaters run the canyon in winter. Upstream winds are common, and rowing or paddling a heavily laden raft against the wind through slack water can be a chore. When dam-releases fluctuate, boaters need to be aware of when the water rises and falls in the various parts of the canyon—not just for running rapids, but also for deciding where to make camp and tie boats.

The Colorado in the Grand Canyon is a classic pool-and-drop river. Its rapids are caused by debris washed down the side canyons by flash floods. Aside from Lava Falls, the biggest rapids today are in the Upper Granite Gorge. (Two of the Canyon's most imposing rapids, Separation and Lava Cliff, are now under the waters of Mead Reservoir.) The drops are often quite substantial—15 or 20 vertical feet (4.5 or 6 m) and sometimes more, over a hundred yards long or so.

Most rapids in the canyon require only one or two maneuvers; a few are more complex. Big-water experience is essential for all boaters. The biggest rapids are: Hance at mile $76\frac{1}{2}$ (122.4 km), Sockdolager at mile $78\frac{1}{2}$ (125.8 km), Granite at mile $93\frac{1}{2}$ (149.4 km), and Crystal at mile 98 (156.8 km), all Class 4+; Horn Creek (Class 4) at mile $90\frac{1}{4}$ (144.3 km); Dubendorff at mile $131\frac{3}{4}$ (210.8 km) and Upset at mile $149\frac{3}{4}$ (239.7 km), both Class 4; and Lava Falls (Class 5) at mile 179 (286.9 km).

Many Grand Canyon veterans consider the side hikes the real reason to be here. One of the best-known side hikes, up Nankoweap Canyon at mile 52 (83.2 km), leads to Anasazi granaries high above the river. Another noteworthy hike is to an Anasazi fort atop a bluff overlooking Unkar Rapid at mile $70\frac{3}{4}$ (113.3 km). Tapeats Creek, at mile $133\frac{3}{4}$ (214 km), is one of the canyon's best lengthy hikes, leading to Thunder River, a tributary which cascades almost straight down from Thunder Spring in the limestone wall.

Much of the best scenery can be found next to the river, including Redwall Cavern on river left at mile 33 (52.8 km), a huge natural amphitheater, and Elves Chasm on the left at mile $16\frac{1}{2}$ (26.4 km), a refreshing oasis of moss, ferns, and waterfalls. Other attractions include Deer Creek at mile $136\frac{1}{4}$ (217.6), with a short hike to a spectacular, much-photographed waterfall; Matkatamiba Canyon at mile 148 (236.8 km), on the left; and Havasu Creek at mile $156\frac{3}{4}$ (251.2), a great side hike up a travertine stream.

Lower Rio Grande (Texas, Mexico) ➤

The Lower Rio Grande is the classic off-season wilderness float in the United States. Both private boaters and guests on commercial rafting trips enjoy the spectacular scenery in these remote reaches along the Texas-Mexico border. In the Big Bend region, river runners can choose one or more consecutive sections through a series of dramatic desert canyons, each with its own character. Farther downstream and far less known are the Lower Canyons, where deep, narrow gorges alternate with open desert and rugged hills on one of the remotest river runs in the country.

The Rio Grande, the second longest river in the United States, runs some 1,900 miles (3,057 km) from the lofty Rocky Mountains of southern Colorado to the shores of the Gulf of Mexico. From Colorado Canyon to Dryden Crossing, the Lower Rio Grande offers 230 miles (368 km) of continuous floating, though this distance is divided among a

RANCHERIAS CANYON TO LANGTRY
Difficulty: Class 1+ to 3
Length: 280 miles (448 km)

Season: All year
Character: Southernmost whitewater river in the U.S.; isolated, scenic, little whitewater

I was the 70th person to go down the Grand Canyon. Now over 20,000 people go down the Grand Canyon every year. . . . I photographed the trip in Kodachrome, then went on a tour showing it. I did about four shows a week for about a year and, frankly, that is how I got into politics. I figured I had been to just about every town and village in the state, so I ran for public office.

—Barry Goldwater, on his 1940 Grand Canyon trip

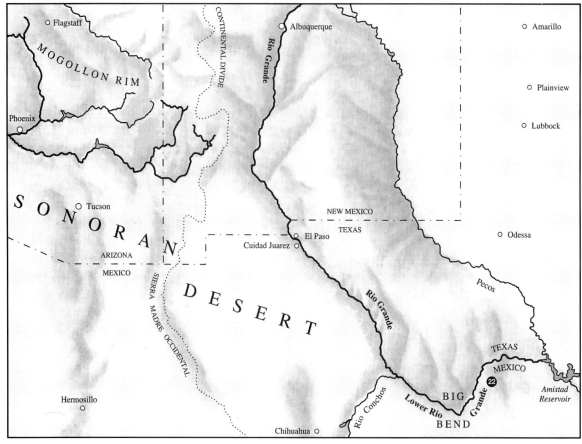

Southwestern U.S.–Mexican Border

number of canyons separated by open desert or low hills. Few boaters make the complete trip. The longest run most parties consider is 145 miles (232 km) from the head of Mariscal Canyon to Dryden Crossing.

Colorado Canyon, considered the first run, is upstream from Big Bend National Park. Just under 10 miles long, it is a popular one-day trip with easy access and enjoyable Class 2+ rapids against a background of rugged, reddish walls.

Below Lajitas the river flows for 118 miles (188.8 km) along the boundary of Big Bend National Park. Big Bend's first and most popular canyon, Santa Elena, is an 8-mile-long gorge bisecting the Mesa de Anguila with walls rising some 1,500 feet (458 m) high. Nearly 50 miles (80 km) of open desert and easy water separate Santa Elena from its downstream cousin, Mariscal Canyon. Like Santa Elena, Mariscal Canyon is an impressive gorge with rapids formed by rockfalls. After Mariscal the river makes two shorter, shallower cuts through San Vicente and Hot Springs canyons.

Continuing along the east side of the national park, the Rio Grande carves deep into the Sierra del Carmen mountain range through beautiful Boquillas Canyon, the longest and mildest in the park. For 33 miles (52.8 km) the river flows through nothing but easy riffles.

Below Boquillas Canyon and the Mexican village of La Linda, the river leaves the Big Bend and any remaining semblance of civilization far behind. Its course through open desert and rugged hills is punctuated here and there by the Lower Canyons of the Rio Grande. Use is gradually increasing, but the Lower Canyons are still rarely floated.

Kern River (California) ➢

The Forks of the Kern, with its alpine scenery and relentless rapids, is one of the finest expert runs in the West. Much of the attraction of this run is its remote location, high in the southern Sierra where few trails penetrate.

Put in at the confluence of the Little Kern on the right bank after a 2-mile hike down the trail from the top of the canyon. The 17-mile (27.2 km) run includes many Class 4 rapids; a number of long Class 4+ passages; and half a dozen Class 5 rapids, two of which are rated Class 6 at certain flows. The biggest include Lower Freeman Creek Falls, Big Bean, and Westwall, all Class 5; Vortex and Carson Falls, both Class 5–6. Several side hikes and side falls add to the scenery, including Dry Meadow Creek which drops over a series of spectacular falls into the river on the right upstream of Carson Falls. This series of teacup-like drops is now one of the top waterfall runs in the state for expert kayakers.

Unlike the Forks run, the Upper Kern has road access along its length but lacks continuity. We have split the Upper Kern into six runs, divided either by a dramatic change in difficulty, by unrunnable rapids, or by Fairview Dam. They include the Limestone run, Class 4, 2½ miles (3.8 km); the Fairview run, Class 3, 2¾ miles (4.5 km); Chamise Gorge, Class 4+, 2¼ miles (3.5 km); the Thunder run, Class 5p, 7 miles (11.2 km); the Camp 3 run, Class 4, 2½ miles (3.8 km); and the Powerhouse run, Class 3–, 2 miles

THE FORKS, LITTLE KERN CONFLUENCE TO JOHNSONDALE BRIDGE
Difficulty: Class 5
Length: 17 miles (27.2 km)

UPPER KERN, JOHNSONDALE BRIDGE TO RIVERSIDE PARK, KERNVILLE
Difficulty: Class 3– to 5$_p$ (many separate runs)
Length: 20 miles (32 km)

LOWER KERN, BELOW ISABELLA RESERVOIR TO DEMOCRAT HOT SPRINGS
Difficulty: Class 4$_p$
Length: 18 miles (28.8 km)

Season: April to mid-July for the Forks and Upper Kern, May through September for the Lower Kern
Character: Varied runs: the Forks, undammed wilderness; the Upper Kern, undammed with road near; the Lower Kern, dammed, secluded

Dry Meadow Creek above Forks of the Kern, California. *(© Michael Neumann)*

(3.2 km). The Upper Kern's wide range of whitewater attracts boaters from all over southern California. All but a few of the rapids can be seen from the road.

Below Isabella Reservoir the Kern turns southwest and cuts a deep canyon through the Greenhorn Mountains. The Lower Kern run, with excellent advanced whitewater below Miracle Hot Springs, is probably the most popular run for boaters from the Los Angeles area. The boating season (June–August in average years, May–September in wet years) coincides with summer irrigation releases. Watch for the largest rapid, Royal Flush, usually portaged on the right.

◄ Kings River (California)

UPPER KINGS, MIDDLE AND
SOUTH FORKS CONFLUENCE
TO GARNET DIKE
CAMPGROUND
Difficulty: Class 5+
Length: 10 miles (16 km)

MAIN KINGS, GARNET DIKE
CAMPGROUND TO KIRCH
FLAT CAMPGROUND
Difficulty: Class 3
Length: 9½ miles (15.2 km)

Season: Main Kings, April through July; Upper Kings, at the end of the main Kings season
Character: Upper run, extremely difficult low-water run through deep canyon; lower run, popular big-water run with long season

The Kings River is one of California's biggest rivers. Its large, high-elevation watershed near the southern end of the Sierra Nevada holds its deep snowpack well into summer, giving the Kings the longest boating season of any undammed river in the state.

In May and June of a wet year, when a heavy snowpack combines with warm weather to swell the river, the main Kings River gives California boaters a chance to test their skills against hydraulics on the scale of the Grand Canyon. The riverbed in this stretch just above Pine Flat Reservoir is wide and not heavily obstructed, so even at high flows the main Kings isn't exceptionally hazardous.

This is a popular meeting place for boaters from northern and southern California. Kayak races are often held here in the spring, and commercial outfitters run daily rafting trips throughout most of the summer.

Put in on the right at Garnet Dike Campground, and take out on the right at Kirch Flat Campground at mile 9½ (15.2 km). The best-known rapid is Banzai (Class 3+)

Upstream is a contrasting run in a deep, spectacular canyon just downstream from the confluence of the Middle and South Forks. This is the rarely attempted Upper Kings run—emphatically for experts only. The Upper Kings is among the most difficult runs in the West. It is for those who don't mind carrying gear down a 2-mile (3.2 km) trail, portaging several rapids, and running many others at the limits of navigability. Only expert kayakers and rafters have seen this isolated, rugged stretch of river. Even hikers and fishermen can reach only the area around the put-in at the end of the trail, which drops about 2,000 feet (610 m) to the river.

Put in for the Upper Kings where a 2-mile (3.2 km) trail from Yucca Point reaches the left bank at the confluence of the Middle and South forks of the Kings. At mile 4½ (7.2 km), Rough Creek enters on the right via a spectacular waterfall. At mile 5 (8 km), Garlic Falls cascades down the right wall. Garnet Dike Campground is on the right at mile 10 (16 km).

◄ Tuolumne River (California)

UPPER TUOLUMNE, CHERRY
CREEK TO LUMSDEN FALLS
(CHERRY CREEK RUN)
Difficulty: Class 5$_p$
Length: 9 miles (14.4 km)

(continued on following page)

The Tuolumne—known affectionately as the "T" among river runners—drains the western slopes of the Sierra crest. Upstream of these runs is the Grand Canyon of the Tuolumne and the Hetch Hetchy Valley, described by John Muir as "another Yosemite Valley." Much of that valley has long been buried under the waters of Hetch Hetchy Reservoir, a San Francisco city project approved by Congress in 1913 over the objections of Muir's young Sierra Club and completed in 1923. Between Hetch Hetchy and the backwaters of New Don Pedro Reservoir some 36 miles downstream, the Tuolumne still flows. What remains of the Tuolumne was admitted to the National Wild and Scenic Rivers System in September 1984.

This is California's premier whitewater river. It courses through outstanding rapids in a spectacular wild canyon in the central Sierra Nevada. Many of California's best rafters and kayakers cut their teeth on the exciting, pool-and-drop rapids from Meral's Pool to Ward's Ferry. This is perhaps the best-loved river trip in the state. The reasons are simple: it offers an overnight float in a region where extended trips are rare, the scenery is striking, and the wilderness solitude is deep and unspoiled. Well-known, regularly spaced Class 4 or 4+ rapids include Rock Garden, Nemesis, Sunderland's Chute, Hackamack Hole, Ram's Head, India and Lower India, Stern, Clavey Falls (Class 5–), Gray's Grindstone, Thread the Needle, Cabin, Hells Kitchen, and Pinball. The last rapid, just above the take-out, is often covered by the waters of New Don Pedro Reservoir.

Some 6,000 people float the Tuolumne every year, a number that would be considerably higher without the Forest Service's tight restrictions.

Upstream, on the Upper Tuolumne (also known as the Cherry Creek run), the river is truly fierce. Clavey Falls, the biggest drop below Meral's Pool on the lower run, would be just an average rapid on the Cherry Creek run. The Upper Tuolumne is one of the toughest stretches of regularly boated whitewater in the country and the most popular Class 5 run in California. Here in Jawbone Canyon, the Tuolumne crashes down at an average rate of more than 90 fpm (17.4 mpk) over granite boulders. In one mile-long section the river falls 200 feet (61 m). The rapids are separated by very short pools. Aside from Lumsden Falls, which is usually portaged, the three most feared by boaters are Mushroom, Lewis's Leap, and Flat Rock Falls. More than a dozen drops rated Class 4 or higher punctuate the run.

Meral's Pool to Ward's Ferry
Difficulty: Class 4+
Length: 18 miles (28.8 km)

Season: March through October
Character: Excellent wilderness whitewater runs when flow is right

Tuolumne River, California. *(Howard Weamer/ECHO)*

◄ South Fork American River (California)

The American is California's classic gold-country river. In 1848 James Marshall discovered gold at John Sutter's mill on the South Fork and touched off the great invasion that made California irretrievably American.

The American River is also the birthplace of whitewater boating in California, and the South Fork is easily California's most popular whitewater river. It provides 100,000 people a year with a thrilling ride through the heart of gold-rush country. Dam-controlled flows often make the South Fork runnable year-round.

Below the Chili Bar put-in the South Fork drops quickly through a remote, steep-walled canyon cut into metamorphic volcanic rock. Rapids of local legend include Meatgrinder (Class 3), Racehorse Bend, Maya, and Triple Threat (Class 3). Five miles (8 km) farther, where the canyon opens up into the gentle Coloma Valley, Troublemaker (Class 3+) provides the climax of the Chili Bar stretch. Civilization is close at hand for the next 4 easy miles (6.4 km) between Coloma and Lotus. Then the river heads into backcountry again, winding through foothills and finally plunging into the exhilarating rapids of the South Fork Gorge. Big pool-and-drop rapids including Fowlers Rock (Class 3), Satan's Cesspool (Class 3+), Haystack, Bouncing Rock, Hospital Bar (Class 3), and Surprise come one after another as the river passes through a series of small mini-gorges. Just below here are the waters of Folsom Reservoir. Depending on the level of the reservoir there may be a flatwater paddle to the take-out at Salmon Falls Bridge.

Leading the effort to protect the river from uncontrolled growth is the American River Land Trust, which has purchased sensitive parcels in the South Fork Gorge and is working to buy more land along the river.

More excellent boating and spectacular scenery can be found on the North Fork of the American with the challenging Generation Gap, Giant Gap, and Chamberlin Falls runs; however, these runs have are not dam-controlled and have a much shorter season.

(continued on page 84)

◄ Trinity River (California)

The Trinity, the Klamath River's largest tributary, rises some 20 miles (32 km) west of Mount Shasta. At first a small river, the Trinity runs south, then west and north through rugged terrain. By the time it joins the Klamath at Weitchpec, the Trinity is a big river winding through a lush, green canyon. The Trinity and its North and South forks are part of the National Wild and Scenic Rivers System.

The Trinity—called the Hoopa by local Indians—was given its present name by Pierson B. Reading, a pioneer who mistakenly thought it flowed into Trinidad Bay. Reading discovered gold here in July 1848. As a result, the Trinity suffered huge placer and hydraulic mining dredging operations. Fortunately, the runs recommended in this guide are downstream from most of the damage. Water projects are another factor. The biggest of these is Trinity Dam. Just downstream, smaller Lewiston Dam diverts 80 percent of this water through a tunnel to the Sacramento basin and the Central Valley. Aside from high spring runoff flows, the highest releases, 800 to 3,000 cfs (22.6 to 84.9 cumecs), have usually been in late May and early June, to wash smelts (young salmon and steelhead) downstream.

The upper river offers about 5 miles (8 km) of Class 3 whitewater with frequent vehicle access, making it possible to start and end the float at many different points. We di-

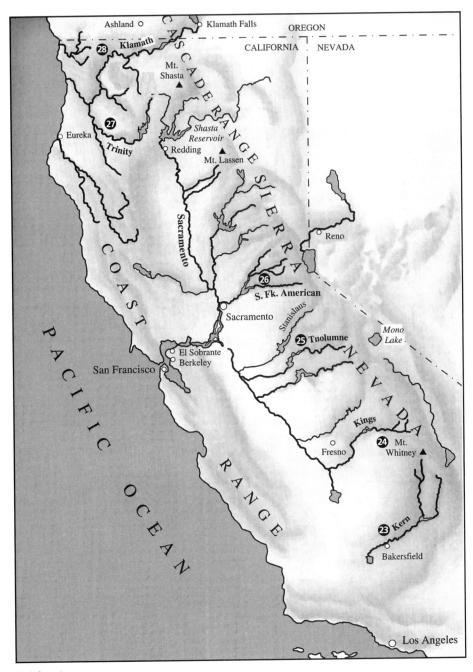

California

Season: All year; Burnt Range Gorge is only runnable at lower flows

Character: Dam-controlled, scenic runs ranging from easy to experts-only

vide the upper river into two runs, from the North Fork confluence to Big Flat Campground and from Big Flat Campground to China Slide.

The river changes character for Burnt Ranch Gorge, the reach from China Slide to Hawkins Bar. This is one of the best expert runs in the west through a narrow and inaccessible canyon. Though the overall gradient is moderate, this pool-and-drop run is laced with major rapids and is definitely for experts only. Don't make the mistake of attempting Burnt Ranch Gorge at high water. Major rapids include Tight Squeeze (Class 4+), Upper Burnt Ranch Falls (Class 5), Middle Burnt Ranch Falls (Class 5), Lower Burnt Ranch Falls (Class 5), Hennessy Falls (Class 5), Origami (Class 5), Table Rock (Class 4–6), and Gray's Falls (Class 5).

The Lower Trinity below Hawkins Bar is a scenic, easy float past the mouth of the South Fork, through the Hoopa reservation, and on to the Klamath confluence at Weitchpec. This is a fine summer run for boaters who enjoy Class 2+ whitewater. The final cut through Weitchpec Gorge is spectacular. Take out at Weitchpec or various access points on the way.

◄ Klamath River (California)

IRON GATE DAM TO HAPPY CAMP

Difficulty: Class 2+

Length: 83 miles (132.8 km)

HAPPY CAMP TO ABOVE ISHI PISHI FALLS

Difficulty: Class 3

Length: 24 miles (60 km)

BELOW ISHI PISHI FALLS TO WEITCHPEC

Difficulty: Class 3₄

Length: 24 miles (38.4 km)

Season: All year

Character: Lush scenery, easy whitewater

The Klamath downstream of Iron Gate is California's longest and biggest whitewater river, with 184 runnable miles (294.4 km) and an average flow at its mouth that surpasses that of the Colorado in the Grand Canyon. In 1980 it became the longest Wild and Scenic River segment in the state. Civilization retains only a small foothold in the largely unpopulated Klamath region. Route 96 is generally nearby, though usually unobtrusive.

For whitewater boaters the Klamath remains one of California's finest and most reliable rivers. It is never too low, even in California's severest droughts. It may be California's best river for open canoes, at lower summer flows. Thanks to its relatively low elevation, the Klamath also remains boatable in winter.

Few boaters run the full section described here. In fact, a continuous run is impossible without an arduous portage at dangerous Ishi Pishi Falls. The most popular section of river is the 36-mile (56.7 km) Class 3 run from Happy Camp to a few miles above Class 6 Ishi Pishi. Bigger rapids below Ishi Pishi Falls include Little Ike and Super Ike (Class 3+) and Bluff Creek Rapid (Class 3). Few go downstream of Weitchpec.

◄ Rogue River (Oregon)

GRAVE CREEK TO FOSTER BAR

Difficulty: Class 3+

Length: 34 miles (54.4 km)

Season: All year

Character: Classic mountain, wilderness, whitewater river

From its headwaters along the crest of the Cascade Range near Crater Lake in southwestern Oregon, the Rogue runs generally west some 200 miles (320 km) to the Pacific. This is one of the West's most famous and loved waterways. Its canyon is an assemblage of deep green pools, lush forests, and sparkling waterfalls. The canyon's dark forests shelter an abundance of wildlife, while the river itself has long been famous for world-class fishing and fine whitewater boating. In 1968 the Rogue's beauty earned it a place among the eight charter members of the National Wild and Scenic Rivers System.

The wilderness run described here is the heart of the oldest and most famous river trip in the Pacific Northwest. The run is regarded as a classic family float. Even Rainie Falls is now run fairly frequently. For the vast majority who still take a sneak chute around Rainie, the biggest challenge comes at Blossom Bar, a Class 4– boulder garden. Elsewhere the rapids are Class 3 or easier, and they are often separated by long, placid pools.

Rogue River, Oregon.
Left: © Larry Harrel/ECHO Right: Dan Dunlap

Man has done much to tame the Rogue. Upstream dams tame its periodic wild floods and capture logs washed down from the heavily forested upper watershed. Even more significant was the wholesale dynamiting of the Rogue's rapids by early river runners. Using explosives supplied free by the Forest Service, they blasted dozens of boulders out of the main channel. The result was the smooth, glassy drops that seem so easy today.

The canyon from Grave Creek to Foster Bar is an unspoiled wilderness except for occasional rustic riverside lodges. Hikes up crystalline side creeks lead to waterfalls and deep swimming holes. Wildlife is remarkably abundant, and deer, black bear, otters, eagles, ospreys, and herons are common.

Annually 650 private boating permits are issued on the Rogue during its permit season, allowing 120 river runners to launch each day. Jet boats prowl the river below Blossom Bar.

◁ Clackamas River (Oregon)

The Clackamas is one of Oregon's most popular rivers, offering a variety of whitewater and scenery, good access, short shuttles, fine fishing and camping, all close to nearby Portland.

In its journey northwest from the Cascades to its confluence with the Willamette River south of Portland, the Clackamas passes through two distinct sections separated by dams. In its upstream reaches, the river tumbles over challenging rapids in a heavily forested canyon. Below the dams, by contrast, the Clackamas is a river of easy rapids and light riffles, winding through open terrain wearing a relatively smooth channel.

The most popular section of the Upper Clackamas is the Three Lynx run, the 13 miles (20.8 km) from Three Lynx to North Fork Reservoir. This reach offers a combination of powerful intermediate to advanced whitewater, fine scenery, good camping, and a relatively long season. Well-known rapids include Hole-in-the-Wall, Carter Bridge Rapid, Toilet Bowl, and Bob's Hole, a renowned kayak playspot and site of an annual whitewater rodeo. Logs can still be a hazard on this section, so stay alert. Oregon Route 224 follows this reach closely, offering frequent access and allowing boaters to choose the sections best suited to their skills. Upstream of Three Lynx is the difficult Killer Fang run.

The Upper Clackamas ends where the river stills in North Fork Reservoir. In the next 10 miles, three dams block the Clackamas. The middle of these, Cazadero Dam, collapsed in the December 1964 flood, sending a torrent of water down on the town of Estacada.

The Lower Clackamas, below the third reservoir, flows freely through scenic pastoral terrain for some 22 miles (35.2 km) to its confluence with the Willamette. Although a few Class 2 rapids punctuate this section, at moderate flows the Lower Clackamas is generally forgiving and well suited to less experienced boaters. The river divides frequently around islands as it reworks its gravelly channel.

Most of the whitewater is concentrated near the beginning of this section, and boaters often repeat a short run of the first couple of miles within McIver Park or continue down to Barton Park.

◁ Deschutes River (Oregon)

The Deschutes is Oregon's most popular whitewater river, thanks to a long season, fun rapids, convenient location for urbanites, and sunny weather. Its popularity is soaring, with well over 138,000 users annually.

The Deschutes is fed primarily by groundwater flowing from porous volcanic rock in the upper watershed. The river can be traced upstream only as far as Lava Lake, 5 miles east of the Cascade crest, where it emerges fully fledged from a lake with no above-ground tributaries. The groundwater flow is so steady that, according to the USGS, "the Deschutes has a more nearly uniform flow than any other river of its size in the United States."

The described 96-mile (153.6 km) run is a long Class 3 stretch from the last dam near Madras to the confluence with the Columbia. The whitewater on the Lower Deschutes is generally forgiving and enjoyable except for Sherars Falls, a Class 6 cataract and mandatory portage, which divides this section roughly in half. The bulk of the rougher water is concentrated near the end of each of the two main sections. Alternate accesses allow boaters to choose from a variety of shorter runs.

Most Pacific Northwest rivers emanate from the furrowed flanks of the Cascade Mountains and work their way westward toward the Pacific Ocean. Formed by extensive volcanic activity, the Cascades are a geologically young mountain range. Cataclysmic eruptions, such as the 1980 eruption of Washington's Mount St. Helens, have lined the region's river corridors with thick layers of ash, pumice, and basalt. In more recent years, a series of devastating floods have torn at these volcanic materials, leaving altered riverscapes in their paths.

For kayakers, few changes are more noticeable than those that modify favorite playholes and surf waves. In Washington state, one awe-inspiring flood erased Snapdragon—a forgiving hole that had attracted playboaters for over fifteen years—from the face of the river without a trace. Heading south, another flood scoured deep layers of gravel from the riverbed of Oregon's Deschutes River, effectively creating a new playspot known as Trestle Hole. Still, the wildest series of changes in Northwest playspots took place on Oregon's Clackamas River, a popular Class 3 run less than an hour from downtown Portland.

Bob's Hole on the Upper Clackamas run has been a backyard favorite of Portland paddlers for two decades, and has hosted international rodeo competitions which have attracted dozens of paddling's superstars. Paddled at a wide range of water levels, every facet of Bob's personality was known to the boating community—until, one day, it disappeared. Dejected Oregon paddlers scorned the same Northwest floods that had improved other runs, and cursed the demise of Bob's. However, their bellyaching ebbed as a new hole— Re-Bob's—emerged just upstream. Re-Bob's provided some consolation for playboaters and was starting to reveal its own multifaceted personality when another flood hit. Today, Bob's Hole is more diversified than ever. A 50-yard section of rolling holes and dynamic surf waves surround Bob's Hole, providing enough variety to keep all but the most nostalgic pessimists entertained to the fullest.

Even as World Whitewater *goes to press, Mount St. Helens's lava dome—a giant cork that holds a subterranean magma bubble in check—simmers away while small earthquakes intermittently rumble along the region's fault lines. It is possible that the rivers described among these pages will change once again, carving new channels with future floods or disappearing beneath thick deposits of volcanic dust. Yet this is the nature of paddling in the Pacific Northwest, and the reason why every trip on Northwestern rivers feels exciting, fresh, and unique.*

—*Jeff Bennett*

In 1988 Congress designated the Lower Deschutes a National Wild and Scenic River. However, scenery, like solitude, is not the Lower Deschutes' strongest suit. Lying in a strong rain shadow, the canyon usually gets less than 10 inches (0.3 m) of rain a year. Grasslands predominate and trees are few and far between, though recent efforts to fence out cattle and replant riparian trees have helped regreen the canyon somewhat. Powerful winds that delight boardsailers in the Columbia Gorge continue right on up the Deschutes, and on some afternoons these gusts pose a real obstacle for river runners.

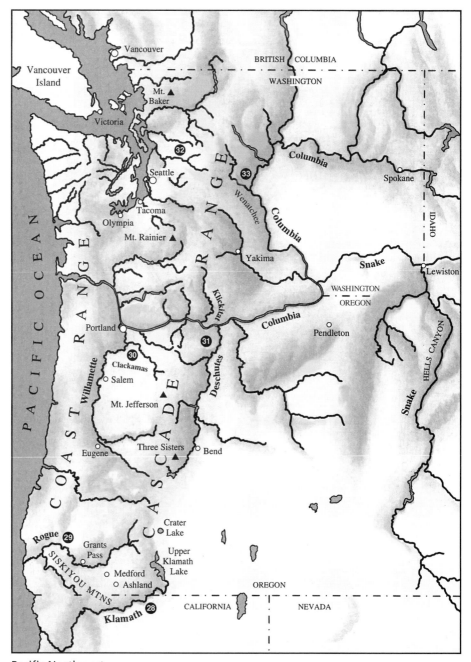

Pacific Northwest

Skykomish River (Washington) ➢

With easy access from Seattle, idyllic mountain scenery, a nearly year-round season, good whitewater, and one big drop, the Skykomish has long been one of the Evergreen State's most popular river trips. Local boaters know it as the "Sky"—an appropriate nickname given the river's clear, blue-green waters.

Above the town of Gold Bar, the Skykomish and its two tributary forks produce a rugged, narrow riverbed scattered with large boulders. Below Gold Bar, in contrast, the river courses easily with few resistant boulders in a broad, gentle channel.

The North Fork Skykomish is secluded, in contrast to the South Fork and main Sky. Above the town of Index, only a lightly used county road follows the left bank. The North Fork is steeper and narrower than the main stem, with nearly continuous Class 3 whitewater and a couple of larger Class 4- drops. The rapids are mostly long, technical rock-and-hole gardens where the river drops steeply through fields of polished granite boulders. Logs are a major potential hazard, and anyone contemplating a run should inquire with local boaters or outfitters first.

The run from Index to Gold Bar on the main stem of the Skykomish gets heavy commercial and private use. Boating begins just above the confluence of the North and South forks. Most river runners launch on the South Fork, but some prefer to start on the smaller North Fork when flows are adequate. Below the confluence lie nearly 3 miles of good Class 3 rapids, punctuated by a long Class 5 passage known as Boulder Drop. Technical and challenging at low and moderate flows, Boulder Drop gets big and intimidating at higher levels.

In addition to exciting whitewater, boaters on the main stem enjoy outstanding mountain scenery. Rugged peaks rim the glacial valley, with the soaring pinnacles of Mount Index, 5,979 feet (1,824 m), and Mount Persis, 5,464 feet (1,667 m), dominating the view from the river.

Wenatchee River (Washington) ➢

The Wenatchee is Washington's most popular river. With over 20,000 user days annually, the Wenatchee accounts for roughly half of all commercial rafting use in the state.

Snowmelt from the Cascade crest gathers in 5-mile-long Lake Wenatchee, then tumbles down the gentle, forested Upper Wenatchee. Suddenly the river turns due south and plummets down the narrow, rugged Tumwater Canyon's Class 5+ rapids. At the town of Leavenworth the Wenatchee abruptly emerges from Tumwater and turns east. For the final 30 miles (48 km) to the Columbia River confluence near the city of Wenatchee, the river bounces through big, playful rapids in a broad pastoral valley.

River lovers come to the Lower Wenatchee for exciting whitewater and reliable weather, not so much for scenery and solitude. The view begins with nice upstream landscapes of nearby mountains but quickly shifts to a semirural setting of small towns and orchards for most of the run. A four-lane highway and a railroad parallel the river as it winds down its broad, semiarid valley.

In many respects the Upper Wenatchee is the exact opposite of the lower river; about the only thing the two sections have in common is reliable summer weather. For 19 miles (30.4 km) below the outlet of Lake Wenatchee the upper river winds easily through a secluded pine forest in a scenic, gentle valley. The Upper Wenatchee is a quiet float much favored by open-canoeists with just a few mild Class 2 rapids.

NORTH FORK, GALENA TO INDEX
Difficulty: Class 4–
Length: 9½ miles (15.2 km)

INDEX TO GOLD BAR
Difficulty: Class 3₅
Length: 6½ miles (10.4 km)

Season: October to late summer
Character: Wet, scenic, road near

UPPER WENATCHEE, LAKE WENATCHEE TO ROUTE 2
Difficulty: Class 2
Length: 19 miles (30.4 km)

TUMWATER CANYON, LAKE WENATCHEE TO LEAVENWORTH
Difficulty: Class 5+ₚ
Length: 8 miles (12.8 km)

LOWER WENATCHEE, LEAVENWORTH TO MONITOR
Difficulty: Class 3
Length: 18 miles (28.8 km)

Season: April through October, though by late summer the river may be too low
Character: On dry side of mountains, varied runs; upper section is mild canoe run, middle section (Tumwater Canyon) is very difficult, lower section is popular intermediate run in May and June

Alaska

*A*laska has the northernmost rivers in the Western Hemisphere, most of them set in a landscape of isolation and wilderness surrounded by extraordinary beauty. Hardy pioneers opened up many of these rivers in the last two decades, particularly in the south-central region. However, with some 365,000 miles (584,000 km) of waterways, many are still unknown and unexplored.

If anything can be said about the terrain of Alaska, it is that it takes the concept of size and beauty to another level, even another dimension. This is a land of colossal mountain masses filled with glaciers and huge rivers. Whereas in the Grand Canyon of the Colorado river runners might feel they are in the focal point of the riverscape, those traversing the open valleys of the massive Alsek and Copper rivers can be overwhelmed with a feeling of their own insignificance.

The rugged landscape is the result of very active tectonic plate movement and glaciation. It holds North America's highest point, Mount McKinley, often called by its native name Denali, at 20,320 feet (6,194 m). McKinley is part of the Alaska Range, while peaks in the Wrangell and St. Elias mountain ranges easily top 16,000 feet (4,880 m). High altitudes, high latitudes, moderate to heavy precipitation, massive glaciers, long days, and little human development result in some great wilderness whitewater with unparalleled scenery and wildlife-spotting opportunities.

Alaska's rivers are one of the best ways to explore this vast land. For centuries natives in light boats poled up and down many of these waterways for seasonal hunting and

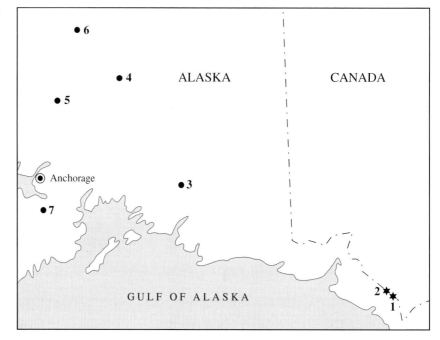

fishing in the interior. European fur traders came in the eighteenth century, followed by waves of gold prospectors, all using the rivers to reach the country's wealth. Even today roads are rare here. The ubiquitous small airplane is the vehicle of choice to foray to and from the wilderness. As roads reach few of Alaska's rivers, a bush plane is often needed at either the beginning or end of many trips. We have chosen rivers with good access by Alaska's standards. The Tatshenshini and Alsek are included here; although both flow in part in Canada, they are usually accessed from Alaska. Those wishing to learn more about other whitewater possibilities and true tales of some of the toughest whitewater to be found anywhere should get a copy of Andrew Embick's aptly named *Fast and Cold*.

River running in Alaska is a serious undertaking. Not only is getting on and off these rivers a task, but most of the rivers are so remote and trails so rare that rescue is not to be expected for days or weeks, if at all. The latitude of all the runs described here is above 59° north, and much of the water has been frozen for decades if not centuries in glaciers. Although temperatures vary, many of these rivers are among the coldest on the planet. Wetsuits, or better yet drysuits, are de rigueur, although rafters have developed a wardrobe of tough raincoats, layers of clothes, wool socks, and heavy rubberized boots that is more comfortable on and off the river on long trips.

The season for most rivers starts in June and ends in mid-September. The early season has higher snowmelt flows, with glacial flows peaking in July. Only the hardiest of river runners venture out in the shoulder seasons or in the winter when most rivers freeze over. Even in summer, most boaters prefer to wait until later in the season to avoid bugs. Camping on windy gravel bars with a smoky fire is most helpful, although full-coverage clothing and repellents are sometimes used. Rain, winds, and cold weather can visit without warning, as can bears. Campers should avoid clear side streams where bears often fish. Be sure to store all food well away from camp. Carrying firearms for protection from bears is common for experienced Alaska river runners.

As Alaska evolves from a frontier to a more modern, mainstream culture, there is reason to believe that Alaska's fine wilderness will remain. Much is still untouched, notwithstanding several major construction projects. The Alaska Highway was built shortly after World War II, opening the land to vehicle traffic from Canada and the Lower Forty-Eight. In the late 1970s the Trans-Alaska Pipeline was constructed from Valdez to the Arctic Ocean. Fortunately, this controversial project focused attention on Alaska's environment and spawned an influx of workers and money to the state. Federal protection has preserved much of the state's wilderness heritage as vast tracts were set aside in a series of parks and preserves, making it likely much of this unique wild area will endure.

Tatshenshini River (Alaska, Canada) ➢

The Tatshenshini and Alsek rivers combine for a floatable journey of some 130 miles (208 km) westward through the immense St. Elias and Fairweather mountain ranges, running through the world's largest non-polar glacier system. Just before crossing the border between British Columbia and the Alaskan Panhandle they join and flow as the Alsek to Dry Bay on the Gulf of Alaska. In terms of wilderness, wildlife, and glacial scenery, these runs are tough to beat.

The river landscape is a rich collage of unsullied north-country wilderness, with dramatic peaks and glaciers everywhere. The latitude of 60° north assures almost eighteen hours of light at the peak of the boating season. During the short nights, the aurora

HAINES HIGHWAY TO DRY BAY ON THE ALSEK RIVER
Difficulty: Class 3–
Length: 130 miles (208 km)

Season: June through mid-September
Character: Classic Alaskan wilderness run

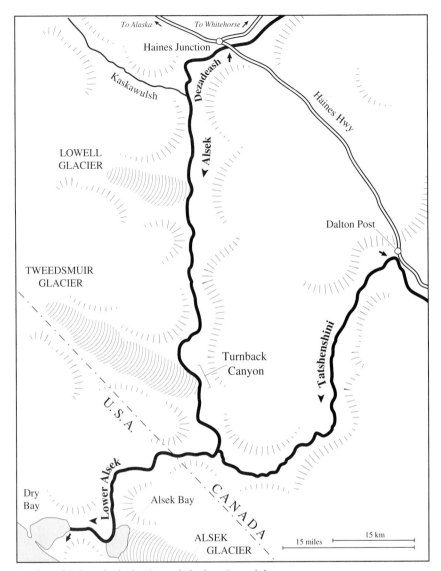

Tatshenshini and Alsek Rivers (Alaska, Canada)

borealis often pulses overhead. Wildlife is abundant. The Yukon moose, the world's largest at 1,800 pounds, is common and grizzlies, bald eagles, and otter chase the millions of spawning salmon. Sharp-eyed boaters may spot mountain goats or Dall sheep high above the river. There are countless waterfalls and fields of wildflowers as well as glacier walks. Foraging for wild edibles is possible, with sourgrass, wild cucumbers, wild celery, and low-bush cranberries. For those who know what they are doing, mushrooms are abundant. The nearby mountains are among the tallest in the continent, with Mount Logan second only to Mount McKinley at 19,850 feet (6,050 m). Those with the good fortune to float either the Tatshenshini or the Alsek concur that these are among the most visually spectacular river trips anywhere.

For all this, the Tatshenshini was a forgotten river for eighty years after Edward James Glave led a geological expedition here in 1890. Apart from a few native villagers, most of whom disappeared in the interim, few saw and none floated the length of the Tatshenshini until Dr. Richard Norgaard led a small group down the river in 1972. Since then, the legend of the river has spread and a strict permit system has been implemented to limit river traffic. The river system has received protection as part of the U.S. Glacier Bay National Park and Preserve in Alaska where the right shore of the river below Lake Alsek borders Tongass National Forest. British Columbia accorded protection to the "Tatshenshini-Alsek Wilderness Park" in 1993. The combined parks comprise the largest protected parkland in the world.

Most boaters put in at Dalton Post, a long-abandoned remnant of the gold-rush era once operated by early explorer Jack Dalton. The Post is now run by the Champaign-Aishinik Nation. Small rafts or kayaks may also put in near the Blanchard River confluence about 20 miles upstream to run an additional Class 3 canyon. Either way, most of the whitewater on the Tatshenshini is in the upper reaches where the river is still relatively small. Here the gradient is 50 fpm (9.7 mpk), compared to 15 fpm (2.9 mpk) overall.

Below Dalton Post are some easy rapids until steep, brown sedimentary walls rise above the river and it enters a rocky canyon. For the next 8 miles the rapids are fairly continuous until Silver Creek joins on the right. Things are mellow until just upstream of the O'Connor River confluence where debris from a slide near a tributary again squeezes the river, leaving a narrow passage and the beginning of another stretch of continuous rapids and big waves. From here on there are no extended rapids, but boaters should be wary of occasional big holes and waves along the river. Repeated interludes of braiding and shallow gravel bars require heads-up boating, as do strange hydraulics as the volume and speed builds. The river moves quickly, and boaters can usually put away many miles in a day, though headwinds can make going tough in slow sections.

After passing from the Yukon into British Columbia the river goes through the Alsek Range, which separates the Alsek River from the Tatshenshini. As boaters pass through the massive coastal barrier of the larger St. Elias Range, they meet the cooler, wetter weather of the Pacific.

The Tatshenshini and the Alsek meet at mile 75 (120 km), and the resulting lower Alsek is more than a mile wide in many places. The river enters Alaska 9 miles below the confluence. Although there are no major rapids along the 54 miles (86.4 km) of the Alsek, big flows can push boats around. The river is so broad that boaters often choose to stay near one bank or the other as a safer route than the center.

The scenery builds to a crescendo in the lower reaches, with glaciers providing the main entertainment, some reaching the river's edge. The Noisy Range, located on the left near the Tatshenshini-Alsek confluence, holds more than a dozen glaciers, all visible from the river. The name comes from the roar of the ice falling off the peaks in the distance, a music sometimes intertwined with the audible hiss and cracking of pebbles and rocks beneath the boats and at other times with the "snap, crackle, and pop" of blackflies hitting the tent walls on windless days.

Walker Glacier is a popular camping area. The glacier was named by river runners for the easy hiking access to the glacier face. Mount Fairweather is perhaps the most dramatic sight of the trip, rising 15,300 feet (4,667 m) from almost sea level and visible above Alsek Lake. Most boaters spend some time at the lake exploring as immense icebergs calve from the snout of the Alsek and Grand Plateau glaciers, generating a sound of rolling thunder and tsunami-like waves. The lake is usually filled with icebergs and debris which constantly break and move. These fascinating giants can fracture and flip without warning, so keep your distance. The entry to Alsek Lake demands some care. The entry is dominated by Gateway Knob, a small mountain forming an island at the inflow. The preferred route is the smaller channel to the right of the Knob, but this is not possible at low flows. Some outfitters even bring extra thwarts and use them to roll rafts along the dry channel to the right of the knob. The left channel, sometimes melodramatically called the Channel of Death, must be scouted as prevailing winds can clog it with icebergs and trap boats. Boaters must also be aware of currents, which can pull unwary boaters to the left at the entrance.

Below Alsek Lake the river enters the wetter coastal area, and lush vegetation and waterfalls decorate the surrounding slopes. Inquire locally regarding routes through the delta to the sometimes difficult-to-locate Dry Bay take-out. Most people charter flights out to Haines or Yakutat.

Some of the popularity of the Tatshenshini can be traced to the fight to preserve it

Rafting the Tatshenshini in 1972

Having spent the summer of 1972 as an academic participating with a University of Alaska team investigating the environmental and economic ramifications of the Trans-Alaska Pipeline, I was ready for adventure. Throughout the summer of 1972, my friend Jack kept mentioning the Tatshenshini River. Walt Blackadar's tale of running the Alsek River the year before [see sidebar on page 98] was already legend. Jack had flown the Tat recently in anticipation of running it.

So, on our way back to California in late August, Marida and I, along with Pete Tryon and Georgianna Davis, scheduled eight days to run the Tat. Though Jack was dying to go, his future depended on his being in the Lower Forty-Eight at an important meeting with the Sierra Club. It was crazy to make a first descent with just one raft, but that was what we had. No one we talked with knew anything about the Tat. We had topo maps with 500-foot contour lines. Since this only assured us that there were no 999-foot waterfalls along the way, we planned to carry backpacks, climbing ropes, and plenty of extra food, just in case the river proved unrunnable.

At Dalton Post, we inflated our nearly state-of-the-art neoprene raft, a 16-foot Yampa made by Rubber Fabricators Inc. following the design of the assault rafts of World War II. I had difficulty finding adequate oars in Alaska, and had to settle for 8-foot oars with 2-inch electrical conduit over the handles to give them another foot of length. I had constructed a wood frame at the beginning of the summer in Alaska.

We shoved off into the small, brisk stream with some anticipation. The first 15 miles drop at about 70 feet to the mile as the Tat cuts through the Squaw Range within the Kluane Range, so the potential for trouble was high. But this first reach proved to have simply long stretches of Class 3, though we did stop and look around some of the tighter bends, just in case. The cloudy weather and occasional light rains added to the adventure and sense of being all alone in unmapped territory. Within a few days, we were amidst the Alsek Range, which was absolutely incredible.

As the river increased in volume, its whirlpools, boils, and eddy fences commanded increasing respect, but none of these took us by surprise. Below the (continued next page)

from a proposed massive open-pit copper mine atop Windy Craggie Mountain, near the confluence of the Alsek and Tatshenshini rivers. The project was to have required access roads and a slurry pipeline as well as tailings, which would have created a massive sulfuric acid waste. Fortunately, this project was shelved, and the dispute caused more river runners to appreciate the value of the river system.

Alsek River (Alaska, Canada) ➢

A journey down the Alsek is a voyage through the spectacular landscape of the last ice age. Although many claim that the Alsek is, if anything, more impressive in beauty and scale than the nearby Tatshenshini, it is also more of a throwback. It bears little resemblance to the Tat's calm rapids, gentle landscape, and thick woods. The Alsek bears testament to a time when glacial megaevents stripped valleys bare, blocked rivers behind huge ice dams, and gave birth to colossal rapids.

HAINES JUNCTION TO DRY BAY
Difficulty: Class 3+ (Class 5+ to 6 in Turnback Canyon)
Length: 180 miles (288 km)

(continued on following page)

O'Connor River, as the Tat cuts through the Alsek Range, the gradient increases again, and we could look 10 miles down the valley and see that we were again descending dramatically.

Camping on the right bank just above Henshi Creek, we nearly lost the raft when the river rose several feet and our "dead man" pulled out during the night. I awoke early in the morning sensing that something was wrong, and panicked when I realized the raft was no longer where we had left it. I spotted it 100 yards away bobbing freely in an eddy that had not been there the evening before. Swimming after the raft completed my rude awakening.

The mountains got better and the sun came out for the best, the stretch through the Noisy Range intercepting the Alsek and then on through the St. Elias Range, with glaciers coming to the river. We camped at Four Mile Creek before the Alsek on the right bank and found we could avoid the devil's club in the forests by ascending the creek's rocky banks to get some elevation. The next day we scrambled up One Mile Creek for a spectacular view of the Noisy Range, the St. Elias Range, and the junction of the Alsek and Tat. The next night we camped at what is now called Walker Glacier on the right bank of the Alsek and explored the lateral moraine, leading us up into the upper valley.

The weather closed in again as we approached Alsek Lake. We went into the lake and camped at its northern end for our last night on the river. The clouds broke just enough in the evening for a fantastic view of Mount Fairweather to the south. Having not yet seen any bear, I put our tent next to a very large bear track; still did not see any bear.

For a first run in some eighty years, first run in this century, second run ever, and nobody having explored this territory by foot, the trip was surprisingly easy.

In early July 1993, I returned for a twentieth-anniversary run with our two children, Kari and Marc, by then twenty-five and twenty-two, and half a dozen friends. We took the Yampa along again, though this time accompanied by two Avon Pros. For this trip, the weather was spectacular nearly every day.

—Dick Norgaard

Season: June through mid-
September
Character: Even more
dramatic than the Tat,
but Turnback Canyon is
an obstacle

The biggest practical problem in running the Alsek is dealing with the 4-mile-long (6.4 km) Turnback Canyon, an aptly named stretch where the river is squeezed between the Tweedmuir Glacier and on which the Alsek's fierce reputation rests. Although the Alsek is almost a mile wide (1.6 km) just downstream, in Turnback it is constricted against sheer walls to as little as 30 feet (9 m) as it rumbles over a series of bone-crushing drops, massive holes, and powerful eddies. Upstream Lowell Glacier also calves icy obstacles into the maelstrom. The portage of Turnback has been described as the "gnarliest in North America," but this is probably overstated. The carry usually takes at least four to six hours as boaters must carry boats and gear, mostly over the rugged terminal moraine of Tweedsmuir. Commercial companies hire helicopters to carry guests and gear. Some 25 miles (40 km) below Turnback, the Tatshenshini joins on the left, and river runners on both trips follow the same spectacular route to Dry Bay.

The landscape of the Alsek above Turnback shows how recently and dramatically the glaciers have flexed their muscles. At regular intervals, the last of which was probably in this century, the Lowell Glacier upstream of Turnback surged across the river and piled up against Goatherd Mountain. Behind it an ancient lake would fill more than 60 miles (96 km) in the upstream valleys with as much as one trillion cubic feet of water. Eventually the buoyancy of the ice and sheer volume of the lake would weaken and break the dam, emptying the lake in two or three days and causing massive downstream floods. The phenomenon, known as glacial lake outburst flood (GLOF), is not uncommon in glacier country, although the scale of the floods varies greatly. The Alsek Canyon is a much smaller duplication of events that played out again and again in what is now western Montana and northern Idaho during the last ice age as Glacial Lake Missoula repeatedly breached a much larger glacier dam, inundating the Columbia drainage to the Pacific with flows estimated to equal the volume of Lake Ontario.

A voyage down the Alsek begins on the Dezadeash River at the small town of Haines Junction on the Haines Highway. The Dezadeash is an easy float through a pleasing valley. As it flows into the Kluane Range, the river hooks south about 10 miles (16 km) from the put-in, and signs of ancient flooding first become visible as the river narrows and trees and vegetation become scarcer. The river joins the Kaskawulsh at around mile 18 (28.8 km), and the two rivers form the Alsek.

The austere scenery continues through various canyons, alternating with flatter areas where the river becomes shallow and braided. At about mile 48 (76.8 km) the Alsek drifts into Lowell Lake, formed by the Lowell Glacier, on the left. River runners can watch upstream winds blow icebergs from the glaciers across the lake. There are some good side hikes up Goatherd Mountain, although camps at the base of Goatherd have been closed due to bears.

The biggest rapids on the Alsek, other than Turnback, are just downstream of the lake. Named for early river explorers, with such names as Sam's and Bill's, they feature big waves, holes, and hydraulics. Be particularly careful of icebergs on the river from Lowell Lake on downstream.

The river valley becomes greener and damper as it cuts through the Alsek ranges and passes from the Yukon into British Columbia at mile 75 (120 km). The Alsek receives protection here as part of Canada's Kluane National Park in the Yukon Territory.

Downstream, the massive Tweedsmuir Glacier becomes visible on the right from a distance as it reaches the river at mile 95 (152 km). The primordial power of glaciation is obvious from the otherworldly terrain nearby. Boaters can examine the spectacular entrance rapid, with waterfalls tumbling down Mount Blackadar across on the left side of the river. Those portaging will have plenty of time to get a close look at the Tweedsmuir.

First-timers bent on running Turnback Canyon (Class 5+ when less than 15,000 cfs, Class 6 if higher) should carefully monitor the flows and try to catch a low flow. Major rapids in the canyon include First Drop, Dynaflow, First and Second Island, Looking for Shelby, Hour Glass, Percolator, Walt's Falls, and Ducci's Ruse, as well as a final major constriction at the bottom. Huge drops, overpowering hydraulics, blocked routes, and boat-eating holes test boaters' skill and mettle, especially at higher flows. Even salmon cannot make it up a current that flows some 25 mph (4.8 mpk). Neither rescue nor climbing out of the canyon is a reasonable alternative, and a swim or the loss of a boat or paddle could spell disaster.

After Turnback, things ease up. From the bottom of the canyon it is 25 easy miles (40 km) to the confluence with the Tatshenshini as the river valley opens. Currently the Alsek may be run to Turnback without a permit; however, below here, a permit for Glacier Bay National Park is required.

Kennicott, Nizina, Chitina, and Copper Rivers (Alaska) ➢

McCarty to Copper River Highway
Difficulty: Class 3–
Length: 171 miles (273.6 km)

Season: June through mid-September
Character: Very long, moderately difficult north-country wilderness run

This is yet another classic Alaskan odyssey with good camping and spectacular scenery. It offers more big-water action than the Tatshenshini River and perhaps even more wildlife-spotting opportunities. The Nizina, Chitina, and Copper rivers are each venerable in their own right and this route is just one of many, but it offers road access at both ends and most of the best reaches of each river.

This is copper country. Chitina means "Copper River" in the tongue of native Ahtna Indians. The Kennicott is named for Robert Kennicott, an early expedition leader whose name was taken, although misspelled, by the giant Kennecott Copper Corporation born here. The history and even the prehistory of the area is shaped by this metal. The Ahtnas even made use of the copper long before modern intrusion in the region.

The rivers in this system flow out of the south of the Wrangell Mountains, and much of the route is in the Wrangell–St. Elias National Park and Preserve. The put-in for the Kennicott is in the town of McCarty and its headwaters in the Kennicott and Root glaciers. The Kennicott is a fast-moving shallow river with easy waves, a few boulders, and a preview of the fine scenery to come. The Nizina originates from the upstream Nizina Glacier. The 15 miles on the Nizina are more difficult (Class 3–) with bigger water and waves, especially in Nizina Canyon in the lower part of this stretch. The canyon is steep-walled and narrow as the river cuts through limestone walls up to 500 feet (153 m) high. The volume increases five-fold from the Kennicott to the Nizina. While the canyon is only Class 3–, there are several tight, often blind, turns and the hydraulics in the eddies and whirlpools can play havoc on smaller craft at higher water. The river leaves the canyon before emptying into the Chitina.

The Chitina River offers about 50 miles (80 km) of even bigger-volume, very silty Class 2 water. The Chitina is often braided with complex channels, gravel bars, and islands. Although this stretch will test boaters' river-reading and route-choice skills, it is ideal habitat for wildlife and side hikes. This wild country provides a home for brown bear (grizzlies) that can often be seen fishing at the mouths of the clear tributaries. Dall sheep, moose, bald eagles, and waterfowl can also be spotted, as can bison transplanted from Yellowstone Park in the early 1900s.

The Chitina keeps adding volume through its length, so it is quite large as it reaches the Copper, which is even bigger. There is good vehicle access at this point. The Copper takes boaters the last 100 miles (160 km) to the take-out. Originating from the Copper Glacier on Mount Wrangell, it is one of Alaska's great river highways, providing transportation over the years to natives, explorers, miners, and now recreationalists.

About 10 miles (16 km) downstream of the Chitina-Copper confluence, the river cuts through Wood Canyon with a steady powerful current. In these reaches the vegetation is coastal, and seals, normally seafaring, can usually be spotted in search of king and sockeye salmon.

Farther downstream the Copper cuts through the Chugach Mountains, creating another narrow cataract, Baird Canyon. About 40 miles (64 km) upstream of the delta in the Gulf of Alaska, several glaciers come in from the right. Here Abercrombie Rapids provide the best whitewater on the stretch between the Allen and Miles glaciers. However, these rapids are not nearly as exciting as Childs Glacier just downstream on the right where huge icebergs calve directly into the river from the 300-foot-tall (92 m), 2½-mile-wide (4 km) snout. The massive blocks of ice create surge waves, and boaters cursed with bad timing can get surfed.

Most boaters take out near Cordova on the Copper River highway. Those willing to slosh through the mud can take out 20 miles (32 km) upstream at the Million Dollar Bridge. The bridge is not just a bargain version of the Three Million Dollar Bridge over the Stikine River. This engineering marvel was built around 1906 at what was then a staggering cost to transport ore from the mines.

Notes from Walt Blackadar's first descent of Turnback Canyon, August 21, 1971

I want any other kayaker or would-be expert to read my words well. The Alsek Gorge is unpaddleable! Class 6+ on the AWA scale and 12+ on the Grand Canyon Scale. Unbelievable! After a careful scout, it's twice as bad out in it. I have scouted on shore all but one horrendous mile of HAIR—30 feet wide, 100,000 cfs, and seeming like a 45-degree grade going HOME. Incredible. I never flipped in that mile, or I wouldn't be writing.

But to go back. I scouted the first half mile and ran it with only two flips and tremendous respect for the rapids I saw. Stopped on the left and scouted another mile or two to a huge drop—20 feet or more—into a boiling hell. Looked it over carefully and decided to carry on the left for about 100 yards. I could avoid the drop with an apparently quite easy stop into an eddy on the left. There are huge icebergs that have calved off of Tweedsmuir Glacier running with you in the gorge. I hit two already, very hard in the big water. Boat okay and surviving well. I paddled down to the eddy, and in seemingly quiet water a whirlpool suddenly appeared. The boat was sucked by the stern into a perfectly vertical position. I was whirled one-and-a-half times around and plopped in upside down. I rolled up, however, immediately and caught the eddy as planned but at the upstream edge. I could stay here all day but couldn't get out because of the cliffs and had to work my way to the extreme lower end of the eddy in order to get out. This I couldn't do by going along the shoreline as I had planned because of the terrific current. I would judge that the lower end of the eddy was 10 feet higher than the top where I was. Consequently, I had to go out into the current in back into the bottom of the eddy, which I did twice but never caught the (continued next page)

Susitna River (Alaska) ➢

Like the Alsek and the Stikine, the Susitna River is another northern odyssey punctuated with a remote, extremely difficult and dangerous whitewater canyon. A measuring stick of cutting-edge whitewater in this land is whether salmon can pass upstream to spawn. A few huge salmon in the 50- to 70-pound range make it through Devil's Canyon every year. By this measure it is easier than Turnback Canyon of the Alsek or the Grand Canyon of the Stikine. However, the Susitna is even more remote, and the Class 5+ section of Devil's Canyon rumbles on for 15 miles (24 km).

The Susitna drains from upstream glaciers including the massive Susitna Glacier. Susitna means "Sandy River" in the tongue of Tanaina Indians, a name that may derive from the silt collected in its three glacial tributaries in the southern portion of the Alaskan range. The Susitna is already a large river at the easiest put-in at a bridge over the river on the Denali Highway, about 130 miles (210 km) upstream from Devil's Canyon.

The first 60 miles (96 km) downstream of the Denali Highway traverse open country. The river has several shallow sections as it braids its way through the valley bottom, rich in waterfowl, moose, and caribou. This continues until just past Goose Creek. As the Tyone River enters on the left, the stream narrows between high banks and winding turns. The Oshetna, entering on the left, signals the beginning of the mile-long (1.6 km) Watana Canyon where the river cuts a path through sheer 1,000-foot (305 m) vertical walls and several big Class 4 rapids, the toughest being at the canyon exit.

The river then flows through a wooded canyon in the Talkeetna Mountains where

DENALI HIGHWAY TO UNNAMED LAKE NORTH OF STEPHAN LAKE
Difficulty: Class 2 (Class 4 in Watana Canyon)
Length: 130 miles (208 km)

DEVIL'S CANYON, UNNAMED LAKE NORTH OF STEPHAN LAKE TO GOLD CREEK
Difficulty: Class 5+
Length: 30 miles (48 km)

GOLD CREEK TO TALKEETNA (LOWER SUSITNA RUN)
Difficulty: Class 1+
Length: 40 miles (64 km)

Season: June through mid-September
Character: Large river with access problems

apex and ended up back at the top of the eddy where I had started. So, on the third trip out I went a little farther out and, you guessed it, I went too far. I knew I had a paddle ahead. Just then I saw an iceberg the size of my bedroom immediately alongside me and both of us charging for the thirty-foot drop. I had to hurriedly turn around and do an upstream ferry, all the time dropping backward into the "falls". . . . [Blackadar missed the iceberg, flipped and rolled, and continued through several more swollen rapids until his fiberglass boat began to give way.]

Missed my roll, and in fact I found I was not in the boat, so I snuggled back in, probably as I hit the next hole. I got scrubbed and washed and scrubbed, rolled and missed, rolled and missed. Finally came up on probably my sixth try. Found the boat swamped. It was in the middle of the river heading for the Lava 6+ below me. Suffice it to say that I caught the last and only eddy on the right. And at that, a hundred yards downstream of the eddy, I rolled out on the bank and said thanks. I found that I had torn the left thigh hook off the deck and part of the deck as well. That popped the skirt and swamped me. I am trying to dry the boat now and fix it. If I don't get it fixed I will scout the canyon further, and if it is just the Lava 6+ below me, I will have to try it crippled. I'm not coming back. Not for $50,000, not for all the tea in China. It's a no-no. Read my words well, and don't be an ass. It's unpaddleable.

—edited from "Caught Up in a Hell of White Water," Sports Illustrated,
    August 14, 1972

several tributaries add to the flow, building its volume for some 90 miles (144 km) as it approaches Devil's Canyon.

Devil's Canyon is one of the toughest stretches of river in this book. It is at least a Class 5+, with 10,000–12,000 cfs (283–340 cumecs) considered low water and above 20,000 cfs (566 cumecs) considered high water. The canyon has four major rapids and several holes which are probably inescapable. The first big rapid is Devil Creek Rapid, just below the Devil Creek confluence on the right. It is followed by the Nozzle where the river shoots through a narrow passage, creating dangerous whirlpools. Just downstream is Hotel Rock, named for the giant boulder in the center which submerges and creates a massive river-wide ledge at high flows. The action eases for 2 miles (3.2 km) until the river comes to False Screaming Left-hand Turn, followed by Screaming Left-hand Turn, a jumbled mess of boulders and holes around a blind turn. Soon after a cable bridge the river bends to the right and over a series of titanic waves as the river exits the canyon. At high water the exit waves crest at about 25 feet (7.6 m), probably the largest standing waves in North America. The river runner's reward for negotiating one of the toughest stretches of whitewater anywhere is riding out the immense wave train. Boaters planning to run Devil's Canyon should talk to some of the few boaters who have been there.

The history of attempts on this great canyon (along with Turnback Canyon) is detailed in Andrew Embick's book *Fast and Cold*. Several ventures into the canyon have ended badly and even tragically. Failed assaults in rafts in the 1950s by the U.S. Army and later its Corps of Engineers ended in dramatic air rescues. Somewhere under the river is a 22-foot (7 m) jet boat that flipped near the bottom of the canyon in an attempted first ascent in 1982, resulting in yet another sensational rescue. Incredibly, in 1985, Steve Mahay successfully ascended Devil's Canyon in a 27-foot (8 m) jet boat with a helicopter providing scouting and dropping fuel between rapids. Paddlers taking on the canyon can at least count on upstream traffic being light.

Due to lack of float plane landing options, it is difficult to exit the river above Devil's Canyon or to put in to run Devil's Canyon. One reported option is to work your way up Log Creek to fly out from the lake above Log Creek or nearby Stephan Lake. A combination of portaging and paddling the canyon is possible but risky. Portage routes can reportedly be found on Devil Creek Rapid, Nozzle, Hotel Rock, and Screaming Left-hand Turn. This strategy apparently proved successful for the crew of a 14-foot (4 m) raft who made the run without incident at lower flows, but Devil's Canyon has proven fatal to at least one rafting group.

To run the lower Susitna, put in at Gold Creek via the Alaska Railway for an enjoyable scenic float within view of Mount McKinley (Denali). The biggest danger on this shallow, braided run are the occasional sweepers along the river. Take out where the river rejoins civilization at Talkeetna.

YELLOWJACKET CREEK TO
TALKEETNA
Difficulty: Class 4
Length: 70 miles (112 km)

(continued on following page)

◁ Talkeetna River (Alaska)

Talkeetna means "River of Plenty" in the language of the ancient Dena'ina Indians, who traveled the river in birchbark canoes in the summer and on dog sleds in the winter. The Dena'inas are gone, but the Talkeetna remains a whitewater blessing under the visage of Mount McKinley (Denali) in the heart of the Talkeetna Mountains. The river has everything one could ask for from an Alaskan wilderness trip: continuous, challenging white-water, an abundance of salmon and wildlife, spectacular scenery, and more. It is usually considered the best wilderness whitewater trip in Alaska.

Most kayakers reach the Talkeetna via seaplane to Murder Lake and run Prairie Creek to the river. This 8-mile (12.8 km) stretch is narrow, and logjams are a hazard. Commercial rafters usually fly into the airstrip at Yellowjacket Creek upstream of the Prairie Creek confluence.

For the first 22 miles (35.2 km) downstream of Yellowjacket Creek the river flows quickly through an enjoyable valley with spruce and birch trees and caribou and Dall sheep. About 7 miles (11.2 km) downriver of the confluence with Prairie Creek is Talkeetna Canyon, 14 miles (22.4 km) of relentless whitewater through a deep granite canyon. The most difficult rapid on the river is Toilet Bowl, near the entrance to the canyon. A scout right is advised, as a swim here, especially at higher flows, will be an ordeal. The balance of the canyon is some 14 miles (22.4 km) of waves and holes that can excite and exhaust any river runner. Self-bailing rafts are recommended due to the difficulty in stopping, and measures must be taken not to lose boats or equipment due to the extreme remoteness of the area. When camping or hiking, remember that this emphatically is grizzly country, and take precautions.

The action settles down after Iron Creek at mile 40 (64 km) to the take-out at Talkeetna where the river joins the Susitna.

Season: June through mid-September

Character: Outstanding whitewater and wilderness run

Nenana River (Alaska) ➢

Located near the highway between Alaska's two largest cities, Anchorage and Fairbanks, the Nenana River combines great whitewater and fine scenery with good access. It is Alaska's most popular river. Like many Alaskan rivers, the Nenana begins at the glacier of the same name. Flowing north from near Broad Pass in the Alaska Range, it ultimately joins the Tanana.

The section upstream of the Nenana Gorge is a wilderness float with some good scenery. The gorge itself is 24 miles (38.4 km) of big-water action for all types of craft from kayaks to 18-foot (5.5 m) commercial rafts. Although the river is not technically exacting, a swim here can be long and cold.

Road access along the river provides some options. A popular put-in for the upper section is east of Cantwell on the Denali Highway. River runners can go 20 miles (32 km) downstream to the Parks Highway or can continue farther downstream to McKinley Village for an another 18 miles (28.8 km) of great scenery. Although a road and railway are nearby in this 18 miles, they are unobtrusive. One rapid in this section, Panorama, rates as the most difficult.

Below McKinley Village a few rapids and waves appear as the current picks up. The first big rapids do not start until downstream of Riley Creek Bridge, including Terror Corner. Below the Jonesville Bridge are Squirrel Corner, Rooster Tail, Ice Worm, Twin Rock, and Cable Car rapids (even the big commercial rigs have reportedly flipped in the big holes on Cable Car). Below Moody Bridge are Split Rock, Boxcar, and The Narrows. Take out at a bridge near Healy or continue to a railroad bridge 10 miles (16 km) downstream. Some boaters add an additional 50 miles (80 km) of Class 2, taking out at the town of Nenana.

DENALI HIGHWAY TO MCKINLEY VILLAGE
Difficulty: Class 2–
Length: 38 miles (60.8 km)

MCKINLEY VILLAGE TO 10 MILES (16 KM) DOWNSTREAM OF HEALY
Difficulty: Class 4–
Length: 24 miles (38.4 km)

Season: June through mid-September

Character: Popular, road nearby

◁ Sixmile Creek (Alaska)

Located close to Anchorage with clear water, lush vegetation, deep canyons and superb rapids, Sixmile Creek has all the elements of a classic Class 5 run. Although not the most difficult river in the state, most Alaskan boaters are familiar with it and hold it as the standard by which other tough rivers are measured.

With a medium flow of about 2,000 cfs (56.6 cumecs), Sixmile Creek is a river in all but name, although not a big-volume river by Alaska standards. It has been the site of several mishaps, including fatalities. Its big drops, undercut ledges, and occasional log-jams deserve respect, especially from those unfamiliar with it. Sixmile Creek is occasionally rafted commercially by those who pass a rigorous whitewater test. The road from Anchorage to Seward on the Kenai Peninsula follows the run and provides unusually good access for these parts.

The put-in for the upper canyon is on the Seward Highway upstream where it crosses the East Fork of Sixmile Creek. After a short warm-up, Gulch Creek enters on the right and the combined flow plunges into the canyon. This stretch of tough rapids slowly eases to a flatwater section above the confluence with Canyon Creek on the left where the volume is almost doubled, marking the beginning of Sixmile Creek proper. A gravel road on the left provides access along a long 3- to 4-mile (4.8–6.4 km) flatwater section that separates the upper and middle canyons. Some boaters put in at Boston Bar, just above the entrance to the middle canyon. The action starts immediately below Boston Bar as the current narrows and tumbles over a series of ledges, scoutable from the left. Exiting the river is possible here before committing to the more difficult lower canyon.

Although only 2 miles (3.2 km) in length, the flow in the lower canyon is squeezed between rock walls, and the action is continuous. Rapids include Staircase, Suckhole, Merry-Go-Round, Jaws, and Junkyard Dog. Scouting is mandatory, and some drops should be portaged at certain flows. Take out on the gravel road on the left, half a mile (0.8 km) below Junkyard Dog. Shortly after the take-out, Sixmile Creek flows into the sea.

Along with the good whitewater, Sixmile has some history. This was the site of a gold rush at the end of the nineteenth century, and placer miners still ply their trade along its banks.

Eastern Canada

*T*he rivers of Eastern Canada attract boaters from all along the East Coast for a number of reasons. Both Quebec and Ontario have vast expanses of wilderness, most easily explored by boat. The French-speaking province of Quebec provides an exotic change of pace; it sometimes seems more European than American. While there are no Alps here—Mont Tremblant is the region's highest peak at 3,100 feet (968 m)—river runners will find big water. The major whitewater river, the Ottawa, showcases pure volume as the main attraction. Other runs, including the Rouge, are more technical but can still have plenty of push. As in western Canada, high latitude makes for a later, shorter season, with boating weather not arriving until late April and cold weather arriving by mid-October.

The Canadian Shield, a massive carved landscape of immense Precambrian rock, dominates the area. Ancient mountains higher than the Rockies once stood here, forming the origins of the North American continent. Over time the rest of the continent accreted onto the shield, and later, ice age glaciers flattened the mountains and scraped the bedrock bare. The result is rivers with long, calm stretches broken by ledges and falls. Glaciers carried huge boulders, called erratics, for miles before leaving them behind during glacial retreats. Many of them now serve as obstacles along Eastern Canada's rivers.

While Eastern Canada has some great whitewater runs, the region is probably best known for flatwater touring and camping. Calm rivers and hundreds of thousands of lakes offer countless quiet-water runs.

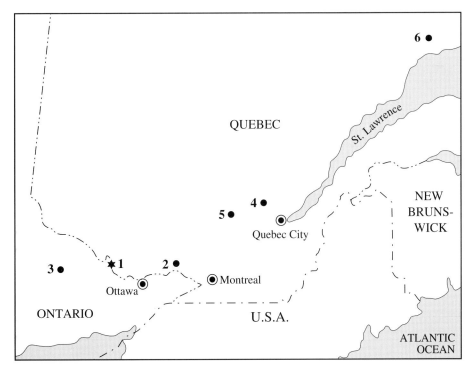

1 Ottawa River (see page 104)
2 Rouge River
3 Madawaska River
4 Jacques Cartier River
5 Batiscan River
6 Magpie River

Eastern Canada

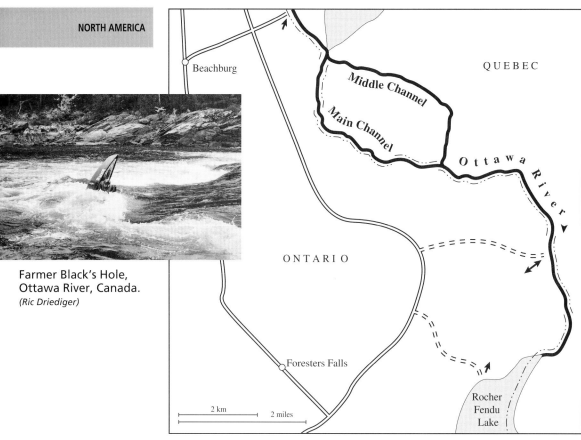

Farmer Black's Hole, Ottawa River, Canada.
(Ric Driediger)

Beachburg

Middle Channel

Main Channel

QUEBEC

Ottawa River

ONTARIO

Foresters Falls

2 km   2 miles

Rocher Fendu Lake

Ottawa River (Ontario, Quebec)

THE ROCHER FENDU, ABOVE
McCOY'S RAPID TO ROCHER
FENDU LAKE
Difficulty: Class 4–, Class
1+ after the rapids
Length: 10 miles (16 km)

Season: April through
October
Character: Popular, large,
big-volume river

◄ Ottawa River (Ontario, Quebec)

The Ottawa River originates in the Laurentian Highlands and flows along the Laurentian Shield, with glacial scouring predominating in the area. Boasting a drainage of some 50,000 square miles (129,500 sq. km), it quickly mushrooms into a huge river, boasting flows from 10,000 to 200,000 cfs (283 to 5,660 cumecs), and provides some of the best big-volume rapids in the East.

The Ottawa was the main route to the West as far back as the days of explorers and fur traders. Modern river runners have found relics of early ascents along its portage trails, including an astrolabe mislaid by Samuel de Champlain's crew in 1613. In the 1700s the Ottawa River came to divide what was then all of Canada, forming the 400-mile (640 km) border between Ontario and Quebec. English-speaking "Upper Canada" in the upper St. Lawrence drainage became Ontario, and French-speaking "Lower Canada" in the lower St. Lawrence drainage became Quebec.

The whitewater section of the Ottawa is about 70 miles (112 km) west of the Canadian capital of Ottawa, after the river's slow upstream journey has taken much of the chill out of the water. The most challenging and popular run is the Rocher Fendu

(French for "split rock"), just east of Beachburg, Ontario. Rocher Fendu is the aggregate name for the many mammoth rapids as the river falls off the Laurentian Shield. During peak season big commercial rafts can be seen blasting through big holes or negotiating calm stretches while guides lead customers in French boating songs. When not dodging rafts, kayakers enjoy well-known and oft-discussed holes, waves, and playspots.

The current of the Rocher Fendu splits into two main and several smaller channels, giving boaters several choices as they go. It's possible to have two or more almost completely different runs with the same put-in and take-out. The braided channels have been compared with the Potomac between Great Falls and Tidewater at Washington, D.C., with isolated islands and beaches scattered everywhere. Rapids this big also bring comparisons to the big-volume rapids in Grand Canyon of the Colorado. These comparisons are apt in the sense that the wide channels and multiple routes make it hard to get into too much trouble; rocks are usually rounded, pools follow the big drops, and the holes rarely hold swimmers. Even with the multiple channels, flows are still huge, running from 10,000 to 80,000 cfs (283 to 2,264 cumecs) in the main channel.

Ottawa River, McCoy's Rapid, Canada. *(Henry Georgi/Madawaska Kanu Centre)*

The one either-or choice for boaters is the first major rapid, McCoys, which must either be run or carried around. McCoys features three big staggered holes called Sattler's, Phil's, and Sandy's, the biggest of which is Phil's, especially at lower flows. These holes force hard-boaters to make the most difficult moves on the run without much of a warm-up. A sneak route near the right bank appears at medium to high flows, and a

Ottawa River

The Ottawa River has many moods—serene flatwater sections that can be whipped into a wind-blown seascape, stretches that pass though urban centers, and whitewater that rates up there with the Colorado for huge, mountainous waves. Each year the renowned whitewater near Beachburg, Ontario, attracts boaters from all over eastern North America. They come every summer with kayaks, rafts, canoes, duckies, and boogie boards. And some 40,000 thrill-seeking novices sign up for river trips with one of the five commercial rafting companies.

Experienced paddlers consider the Ottawa to be a friendly river. Familiarity is no substitute for common sense, however, and I recall one memorable occasion when the latter was disregarded. Mark and I realized that by leaving for the Ottawa after work we could be on the water before dark, squeeze in a night run, and then, after catching some shut-eye at the put-in, paddle the river a second time at dawn. We could make it back to work by noon, only missing half a day of work but getting in two days' worth of paddling. Perfect! So it was that I now found myself using the bright moonlight to pick out Mark's white helmet in the eddy at the bottom. I splashed my face, a ritual I use to acclimate to the water temperature. Then I lined up on the downstream V and began picking up speed. A few power strokes later, and after lots of bracing, I cruised into the eddy beside Mark.

The next rapid, the well-named Coliseum, is the last big one. Running this rapid involves cutting throughout several diagonal waves to line up a V that is messy at best. It twists and plunges under boils past a hole, or pushes it left into a strong eddy that will carry you around for another dose of swirls. It was now 10:30 P.M. and Mark and I were becoming quite adept in sensing the different waves, currents, and reading the rapids by moonlight. I watched Mark run through Coliseum; I was prepared to offer assistance if necessary, but he floated through the usual route with practiced ease. Encouraged, I peeled out and started to punch the first diagonal waves in my quest for the V. Where is it, anyway? I blinked, but closing my eyes didn't make much difference. The moon was gone, squelched by a cloud. Fortunately, whitewater is aptly named. Spotting a pile of white foam, I quickly pivoted and punched through it to the dark-water V, which carried me directly into the boils. But boils are not white, and definitely not friendly. I was not having a good time and was now having second thoughts about paddling at night. But once again the old low brace paid off, and I eventually ended up in the calm water with Mark. I could have sworn I heard someone giggling in the dark, but as the moon reappeared Mark had a remarkably straight face.

One last stop was at Farmer Black's Hole, a small eddy spot just before the take-out. I pulled out my camera and we took turns doing eddies and pirouettes by moonlight, punctuated by the strobe, then shuttled back to the put-in to catch some sleep. As I snuggled down in my sleeping bag, I reflected on the thought that we only had to wait five hours until our next paddling fix.

—Paul Mason

portage route is also available. Big commercial rafts usually punch the holes. McCoys is a favorite playspot and the site of an annual rodeo competition.

Just downstream the river splits, with the Main Channel on the right and the Middle Channel on the left. Although either can usually be run, most boaters go for the Middle Channel at higher water. At low summer flows, most boaters put the Main Channel on their itinerary. Both channels are laced with regularly spaced big drops and holes.

In the Middle Channel the current splits around an island, with tough rapids on either side. To the left are Iron Ring and Butterfly, and on the right are Little Trickle and Angel's Kiss. Iron Ring becomes tough at higher flows. Downstream islands divide the river into Garvin's Chutes, usually the most difficult rapids on the river with a series of ledges above big hydraulics, standing waves, and holes. Two such rapids, dubbed Upper Noname and Lower Noname, wait farther downstream.

The Main Channel has more continuous action after the first rapid, Black Chute (also known as the Lorne). Other rapids are Wakiki, Butcher Knife (named for sharp quartzite rocks on the right), Hair (also known as Norman's), Coliseum, and Dog Leg. At high flows the latter three rapids merge and end with a huge hole at Dog Leg. At lesser flows most rapids culminate in big wave trains and eccentric hydraulics.

Just after the last rapid on the Main Channel or parallel to the convergence of the Main and Middle channels, it is possible to take out at Farmer Black's for a small take-out/parking fee. Otherwise, it's 4 easy miles to Rocher Fendu Lake. Access may also be available at River Run Paddling Centre on a small bay on the right about 1½ miles (2.3 km) below Coliseum.

Owl Rafting/Madawaska Kanu Centre provides free parking and put-in access just above McCoys Rapid as well as a map of the various river routes on the bulletin board. Wilderness Tours and River Runs own launch sites just upstream. Beachberg is located near Cobden off Route 17, 68 miles (110 km) west of Ottawa. The river also passes through Ottawa where spring runoff brings paddlers out to run big surf waves dancing within sight of the parliament buildings.

Rouge River (Quebec) ➢

Although Mont Tremblant is only 3,172 feet (968 m) tall, it is the highest peak in this region. It overlooks the headwaters of the Rouge (sometimes referred to in English as the "Red River"), a northern tributary of the Ottawa that joins the larger river between the population centers of Montreal and Ottawa. Nearly all of the more than 100 miles (160 km) of the Rouge can be floated, but the Harrington and Seven Sisters runs are the most popular whitewater reaches and they are only 5 miles (8 km) apart. Unfortunately, several dams situated between the two runs make a combined trip impractical. Both runs are considered to be big-volume, but riverbed boulders, including glacial erratics, make the Seven Sisters run more technical and less forgiving than the Ottawa.

The Harrington run, sometimes called the Middle Rouge, begins upstream of the town of Rivington and provides the best springtime whitewater on the river. Boaters put in upstream of the town on the road to Huberdeau. Take-out access is either at Rivington or upstream of Bell Falls. The whitewater in this stretch is forgiving, and boaters are drawn by the wooded and mountainous scenery and the solitude of detachment from roads and civilization.

The lower section, called the Seven Sisters run for the seven big drops near the end,

MIDDLE ROUGE, HUBERDEAU ROAD TO RIVINGTON (HARRINGTON RUN)
Difficulty: Class 3+
Length: 6 miles (9.6 km)

LOWER ROUGE, CALUMET ROAD TO ROUTE 148 (SEVEN SISTERS RUN)
Difficulty: Class 4–
Length: 8 miles (13 km)

Season: April through October
Character: Big volume in heavily wooded hill country

is usually better later in the season after flows have peaked. The put-in is off the road from Calumet to Rivington at a commercial launch, Eau Vive, upstream of the first big rapid, a double-drop called Elizabeth's Sill. The road follows the river for the first 5 miles (8 km), then turns away. The drops continue, including Slice 'n' Dice, Monster, Mushroom, and another major drop, Washing Machine. Be careful to take out on the left upstream of a midcurrent warning sign to avoid the Seven Sisters. The Seven Sisters are the toughest drops and are concentrated near the end of the run. Commercial outfitters usually pass on the last five, but expert boaters can try their hand at some of these waterfalls at low levels. A path along the right allows a safe stroll and great views. Just downstream the Rouge empties into the Ottawa.

A 21-mile (33.6 km), Class 3+ run upstream near Mont Tremblant Park is another option.

◁ Madawaska River (Ontario)

In 1827, while exploring the Madawaska River for the possibility of establishing a navigational canal, Lieutenant J. Walpole recorded his observations: "The extraordinary rapidity with which it descends into the Ottawa are circumstances which would render the operation, if not feasible, extraordinarily expensive and laborious." Two other noteworthy explorers in the early 1800s, Lieutenant Catry and David Thompson, recorded that the canal project was impractical due to the many rapids, falls, and shallows along the Madawaska. Today, the same bellowing whitewater that kept the early explorers away draws paddlers in droves. The Madawaska may be the most popular paddling river in Canada.

The Madawaska flows out of the east side of Algonquin Park, a pristine north-country park in Ontario, filled with low hills and covered with pine and hardwood forests. Countless upstream lakes, the remains of the last ice age, warm the water, as does the dam spill above the thermocline of Bark Lake. It is not uncommon for temperatures to approach 70°F (21°C) in midsummer—balmy for the north country. Dam-releases provide for regulated flows, currently scheduled for Monday through Thursday all summer.

The run from Bark Lake to Mud Bay is the home of one of North America's premier canoe and kayak schools, the Madawaska Kanu Centre (MKC). Here students and the public can take full advantage of the forgiving, warm rapids (such as Staircase, Chalet, Gravel Pit, and Cottage) as they ready themselves for bigger challenges elsewhere. Put in below Bark Lake Dam. MKC owns the Mud Bay take-out, so get permission or take out upstream on River Road below Cottage Rapid.

Downstream, below Latchford Bridge, is a popular, much longer run, usually called the Lower Madawaska. The first 5 miles (8 km) take one down to Aumonds Bay and Aumonds Rapids. Downstream of the Aumonds Bay the river enters the Lower Madawaska Provincial Park and leaves all roads and civilization behind. This stretch has some good campsites and is popular with whitewater tandem canoes. There are a number of rapids that are usually portaged by experienced canoeists, generally about a dozen. Many are in a difficult reach called the Snake Rapids, a series of about eight tough rapids that have each earned names from the locals. Some boaters shorten the run by putting in at Aumond Bay and taking out at Buck Bay for an easy one-day trip. The lower take-out is where the Route 41 bridge crosses the river at Griffith.

BARK LAKE TO MUD BAY
Difficulty: Class 2
Length: 3 miles (4.8 km)

LOWER MADAWASKA,
  LATCHFORD BRIDGE TO
  GRIFFITH
Difficulty: Class 3p
Length: 20 miles (32 km)

Season: April through
  September
Character: Dam-controlled;
  heavily wooded

Lower Madawaska River, Ontario, Canada. *(Henry Georgi/Madawaska Kanu Centre)*

Group of canoeists at dam on Madawaska River, Ontario, Canada.
(Henry Georgi/Madawaska Kanu Centre)

Other reaches are boatable as well, though less popular. Between the featured runs is a beginner's run just downstream of Lake Kamaniskeg at Palmer Rapid. An upstream run, usually called the Upper Madawaska, starts just below Whitney and passes through Upper Madawaska Provincial Park, ending at the Victoria-McCanley Lake road crossing.

A 1-mile (1.6 km) stretch of the Gull River southwest of Madawaska near Minden holds some Class 3 and 4 rapids and is popular with slalom kayakers and playboaters.

Algonquin Park is the definitive north-country setting for recreational paddling in Eastern Canada. It sits at the southern tip of the Canadian Shield, the flattened remnant

Slalom course, Chalet Rapid, Middle Madawaska River, Ontario, Canada.
(Henry Georgi/Madawaska Kanu Centre)

of what was once the genesis of the North American continent. The highest hills in the area are below 2,000 feet (610 m), but glacial scouring has left a maze of carefully rounded hills, lakes, and rivers with rich pine forests clinging to a marginal soil bed.

◁ Jacques Cartier River (Quebec)

The charm of Europe is no better represented in the Americas than in Quebec City, an antiquated walled burg overlooking the St. Lawrence Seaway. Francophiles who love the *eau l'vive* (rapids), or simply whitewater buffs who love the French, will love Quebec City. For river runners with no budget for the French Alps, this is the place to stay and the Jacques Cartier, only half an hour away, is the river to run.

La Riviere Jacques Cartier drains the 3,000-foot (915+ m) Laurentian Highlands north of Quebec City, providing several varied whitewater runs as it journeys to its confluence with the St. Lawrence River upstream of Quebec City. River runners can find everything here from flatwater to playboating to multi-day wilderness sojourns.

The Jacques Cartier is divided into four sections. The first is the Taureau Gorge, found just before the river enters Parc de la Jacques Cartier. This hair run, one of the most difficult stretches of river on the eastern continent, usually has enough water for boating only in the spring. With a gradient of more than 100 fpm (19 mpk), it has continuous tough rapids and some difficult portages. In any given year, only a few groups are willing to take it on. Set in a tight canyon with walls more than 1,500 feet (458 m) above the river, this steep creek holds some thirty major technical drops. A significant

TAUREAU GORGE (UPPER GORGE
RUN)
Difficulty: Class 5+p
Length: 25 miles (40 km)

PARC DE LA JACQUES CARTIER
(PARK RUN)
Difficulty: Class 1+
Length: 10 miles (16 km)

UPSTREAM OF TEWKSBURY TO
ROUTE 371 (TEWKSBURY
RUN)
Difficulty: Class 4
Length: 5 miles (8 km)

(continued on following page)

enhancement is the length of the trip. It usually takes at least two days to run. Kayakers generally run self-contained, placing some limits on the type of craft and raising the stakes in the event of a wipeout. The canyon is remote and help hard to come by in case of trouble. To get to the put-in, take Route 175 to Route 14 to a bridge over a side stream between Lac Lapointe and Lac Lanoiraye. To get to the take-out, use Route 175 to Route 4 to the end of the road (between Camp 3 and Camp 4).

By contrast, the next section in the lower part of the Parc de la Jacques Cartier is an easy, mostly flatwater float through dense forest with good opportunities to spot moose, bear, and deer. The river leaves the park near the Nature Center (centre d'accueil). The park itself draws hordes of canoe-campers. Downstream the river flows through a military base that is closed to boating. Check at the Nature Center for updated information about river logistics.

The third run is near the town of Tewksbury and is the most popular stretch. It has a good gradient of some 40 fpm (7.7 mpk) and usually affords some big water requiring technical moves with plenty of boulders, drops, and slippery eddies. Hard-boaters will find plenty of playspots. The run is less forgiving than the Ottawa River, as boaters must dodge some hazardous pour-overs. At all but high flows this stretch is popular with nearly every type of craft, from squirt boat to open canoe to commercial raft. If you are new to the area, the locals will give you advice, and if you are lucky, it will be in English. Put in at a bridge upstream of the town of Tewksbury near a rafting company lot. Take out downstream of Tewksbury on Route 371 as the road again meets river.

The last section, the Donnacona Gorge from Pont-Rouge to Donnacona, is an easy float. Although it runs through farmland, the river is in a deep limestone canyon where boaters can leave civilization far behind. Ledges in the riverbed provide innumerable small drops and fine playspots for kayaks, especially at higher flows. The put-in for the Donnacona section is north of Pont-Rouge on Route 365. Go north on Route 365 to the Pont-Rouge Chamber of Commerce sign and turn left onto a dirt road. A Class 6 rapid is just above the launch point. Take out upstream of the bridge in Donnacona.

Batiscan River (Quebec) ➢

The Batiscan rises out of Lac Edouard, nestled among 2,000-foot (610+ m) highlands, and flows south to join the St. Lawrence at the town of Batiscan. It is located about an hour northwest of Quebec City. This is a big-volume river known for its magnificent scenery and long wave trains. It runs through Parc Portney, an area scattered with glacial lakes. The described run is often called Les Portes de l'Enfer ("Hell's Gate"), and boaters can extend the run an additional 5 miles (8 km) by putting in upstream at the Jeannotte River. A road follows the Batiscan.

To reach the put-in, follow the road north for 12 miles (19.2 km) from Riviere-a-Pierre ("Stony River"). Put in at the bridge at Miguick just above the first big rapid, Rapide des Trois Roches ("Three Rocks Rapid") where three huge granite boulders choke the river. Below Rouleaux the action eases until Pierre-Antione, where the Serpentine River enters on the right. A recirculating eddy here on the left was the cause of a multiple-fatality accident during a military training exercise. The eddy may be decorated with warning signs and a rescue rope. The Canadian National Railroad follows the river on the left but turns away at this point as the river drops into Les Portes de l'Enfer for some 6 miles (9.6 km) of challenging rapids, the largest of which is La Tour. The run

DONNACONA GORGE, PONT-ROUGE TO DONNACONA (LOWER GORGE RUN)
Difficulty: Class 2
Length: 7 miles (11.2 km)

Season: April through late summer; early snowmelt, then rain runoff
Character: Various whitewater possibilities

MIGUICK BRIDGE TO BATISCAN BRIDGE (HELLS GATE RUN)
Difficulty: Class 4–
Length: 15 miles (24 km)

Season: April to late summer, snowmelt and rain
Character: Isolated, in backcountry

continues through beautiful mountain country to the bridge at Batiscan just upstream of where the river leaves the park.

The run can be extended upstream 5 miles (8 km) to the Jeannotte River. Local outfitters offer helicopter access to run from even farther upstream.

◀ Magpie River (Quebec)

MAGPIE LAKE TO ST. LAWRENCE RIVER
Difficulty: Class 4+ₚ
Length: 40 miles (64.4 km)

Season: May through September
Character: Exotic multi-day run far from civilization

The Magpie River is one of several great multi-day runs in the northwoods of Eastern Canada. The put-in is via float plane to Magpie Lake, although some have put in 43 miles (70 km) upstream at Eital Lake. The river flows through a vast wilderness area, often cascading through deep, glacier-carved gorges and drifting through expanses of untouched virgin forests.

The river is usually big-volume, 4,000–5,000 cfs (113–42 cumecs), and mostly pool-and-drop with an average gradient of 17 fpm (3.3 mpk). This does not include the 1-mile (1.6 km) portage of 80-foot (24.4 m) Magpie Falls near the bottom. There are also a couple of easier portages upstream. The take-out is at the road that follows the north shore of the St. Lawrence. Boaters not wishing the attention of blackflies and mosquitoes will want to wait until the later part of the season.

Western Canada

The geography of Western Canada is dominated by three geological formations: the Rocky Mountains, the Columbia Plateau, and the Cascades in the Pacific Coast Range. Each provides a number of great river-running opportunities.

For some half-billion years a large, shallow sea deposited layer upon layer of sediments and fossils on what is now the Canadian Rockies. The waters receded 90 million years ago as the Rockies formed, with massive forces thrusting and folding the carbonate sediment skyward. Repeated cycles of glaciation began an ongoing process of sculpting the mountains to their present shape. The result is quite a sight, a seemingly endless

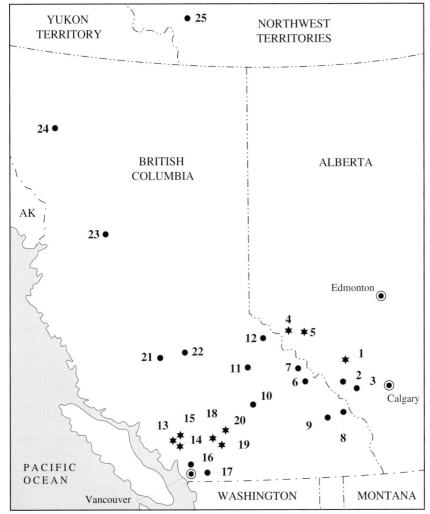

1   Red Deer River
    (see page 115)
2   Kananaskis River
3   Bow River
4   Athabasca River
    (see page 118)
5   Maligne River (see page 118)
6   Kicking Horse River
7   Blaeberry River
8   Kootenay River
9   Toby Creek
10 Upper Fraser River
11 Adams River
12 Clearwater River
13 Elaho and Squamish Rivers
    (see page 127)
14 Cheakamus River
    (see page 127)
15 Soo River (see page 127)
16 Capilano River
17 Chilliwack River
18 Fraser River (see page 132)
19 Nahatlatch River (see page 132)
20 Thompson River
    (see page 132)
21 Chilko River
22 Chilcotin River
23 Babine and Skeena Rivers
24 Stikine River
25 Nahanni River

Western Canada

assemblage of jagged peaks, glacier valleys, and exceptional rivers. Today most of the peaks in Western Canada are between 8,000 and 13,000 feet (2,440 and 3,965 m).

The Columbia Plateau is named for the large drainage of the Columbia River west of the Canadian Rockies. Intense volcanic activity left one of the largest lava surfaces in the world here, extending in places as deep as 10,000 feet (3,050 m). The Columbia River and its tributaries cut several deep, winding gorges through these lava features.

Farther west, along the Pacific Coast, the North American plate overrides the Pacific plate, forming the Cascade or Pacific Coast Range. These set the table for yet another series of fine rivers wandering inland or spilling into the Pacific Ocean.

All these mountains, glacier flows, snowmelt, rain, and well-developed access combine for fine river running throughout the region. It is no coincidence that about one in ten of the rivers in this book is in Western Canada.

Other factors make Western Canada an outstanding place to paddle. Much of the country is pristine, and the sumptuous scenery is filled with wildlife. Elk, bighorn sheep, mountain goats, deer, black bear, and moose frequent the rivers and roads. The facilities are modern, road access is good, and the locals are usually friendly to boaters, in part because many of them are paddlers. You will recognize the Canadian family on vacation: they will likely have a canoe strapped to the station wagon roof.

Western Canada is lightly populated, with most folks in the southwestern corner of British Columbia where the moderating influence of the Pacific allows for year-round river running. A few hardy souls venture out even in the winter. In the Rockies the high altitude, latitude, and river volume make for a later season, with many glacial rivers too high until July or August when the area becomes a haven for local and visiting river runners.

We arrange the rivers starting with the Canadian Rockies near the British Columbia and Alberta border, moving toward the southwestern corner of British Columbia. We then move northward toward Alaska. Few people inhabit the coastal region above the Vancouver area. This is a treasure trove of spectacular, barely explored rivers, similar to those of neighboring Alaska. The difficult access and terrain assure that they will remain wild and lonely for some time.

◁ Red Deer River (Alberta)

Big Horn Creek to Coal Camp Ledge

Difficulty: Class 2+ to 4–
Length: 42 miles (67.2 km); shorter trips possible

Season: May through September
Character: Eastern-slope river flowing to central plains

The Red Deer is one of Alberta's few runnable rivers on the east slope of the Continental Divide. It drains a large area, including parts of Banff National Park, but sits in a rain shadow and rarely generates the volume of the rivers to the west. Still, the Red Deer is a significant river with a character that changes continually as it moves downstream. Its location makes it a favorite with boaters from nearby Calgary and Edmonton.

From its headwaters, the Red Deer flows east through the scenic Rocky Mountain Forest Reserve, an area laced with alpine meadows and steep, forested gorges. The best whitewater is found between Big Horn Creek and Coal Camp Ledge where the river makes its way over a series of well-spaced ledges forming big drops and good playspots. In this stretch the river gradually drops from the mountains into the coastal plains. It then flows into the flatlands near the town of Sundre and begins a long, slow meander across the heartland of Canada.

The upper put-in at Big Horn Creek is about 12 miles (19.2 m) outside Banff National Park. A road follows the river most of the way, with convenient access for shorter

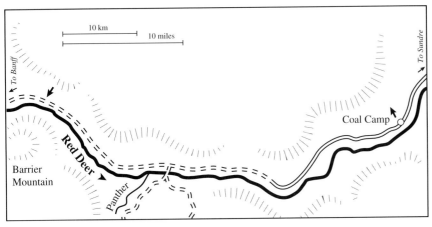

Red Deer River (Alberta)

runs. Most of the best rapids pour over tilted sedimentary formations in intervals along the river. The ledges form big chutes, drops, and some big holes. Because of the large drainage, the Red Deer reacts quickly to big rains, and boaters should be wary—many rapids become much tougher at high flows. Boaters should also keep an eye out for logs and sweepers, especially in the braided sections.

The first section from Big Horn Creek to Mountain Air Lodge is a mellow float at most levels, with braided channels, rocks, logs, and sweepers the only concern. Put in on the gravel road on the north side of the river. The Panther River enters on the right just upstream of Mountain Air Lodge.

More serious whitewater begins downstream of Mountain Air as the river builds from an easy float to good rapids. This reach has some continuous action, with rapids including Gooseberry Ledge, Big Rock, Big Ledge, and Jimbo's Staircase. A slalom course site is just above the Deer Creek confluence. Below Deer Creek, ledges continue as the gradient slackens.

Double Drop Ledge is the biggest drop in the next section from Deer Creek to Coal Camp Ledge. Here the second of two ledges forms a big hole which gets bigger as flows increase.

At this point the river runs through farmland as it heads to the wheat and oil country of the midlands.

If you're looking for a little more adventure on the eastern slope, check out the Ram River, just north of the Red Deer. The Ram offers 34 miles (54.7 km) of fine wilderness, some tough rapids, and a few portages. The put-in for the Ram is a steep carry from the viewing stand just below the splendid Ram Falls on the South Ram. The take-out is just upstream of the mouth of the North Saskatchewan River.

Kananaskis River (Alberta) ➤

The Kananaskis is a southern tributary of the Bow River and just a short drive from Calgary. The fine mixed forest and jagged mountains of the Kananaskis Valley make a good backdrop for this run, which gets a lot of use from Calgary boaters.

The Kananaskis River comes off the east slope of the Rockies south of Banff National

LUSK CREEK, 1½ MILES (2.4 KM) BELOW BARRIER DAM, TO TRANS-CANADA HIGHWAY
Difficulty: Class 3–
Length: 6 miles (9.6 km)

(continued on following page)

Season: May through
  September
Character: Dam-controlled
  river in scenic area

Park and flows north through the glacier-carved Kananaskis Valley. After a brief impoundment behind the Barrier Dam it drops into the described section and then empties into the Bow near the Trans-Canada Highway.

The Kananaskis Valley is a good place to blow off any pent-up resentment from the oil crisis of the 1970s. The recreational resources of the valley were developed with surplus oil revenues collected from that era. Just upstream from the put-in is the Nakiska ski area, site of the skiing events of the 1988 Winter Olympics.

Most boaters put in at Lusk Creek near Widowmaker, the biggest drop on the run 1½ miles (2.4 km) downstream of Barrier Dam. Widowmaker is an immense tilted rock ledge that spans the river as the river pours over a gap in the center. Boaters can launch above the rapid or use the easier put-in just below. Two kilometers downstream is a slalom course with artificial jetties and gates hung above a series of playful rapids, eddies, and holes. The rapids ease below Canoe Meadow, and kayakers often take out there and shuttle back up to Lusk Creek for additional runs on the course. From Canoe Meadow down it's a scenic float to the Trans-Canada Highway. Take out on the right just upstream of the highway bridge and carry up to small parking area off the highway. Although the river joins the Bow just downstream, weirs block this passage.

◁ Bow River (Alberta)

Bow Falls to Canmore
Difficulty: Class 2–
Length: 3 to 12 miles (4.8
  to 19.2 km) (various
  access points)

Season: May through
  September
Character: Mild float with
  grand panorama of
  Banff area

Nowhere is the beauty of Banff more striking than at the put-in for the Bow River, one of the most beautiful launch sites in North America. Boaters embark below two of Canada's finest attractions, Bow Falls and the Banff Springs Hotel. Access is on the right at the Spray River confluence.

Bow Falls is a sloping jumble of some 60 vertical feet clogged with rocks, ledges, and holes. It has been run at favorable levels, but some attempts have ended in tragedy. Movie buffs may want to check out an early descent in the 1954 film, *River of No Return*. In the climactic scene, a double for Marilyn Monroe shoots the falls on a wooden raft. Although Marilyn's character is able to shake a band of fleeing Indians, she doesn't shake Robert Mitchum's character, last seen clinging to the rudder above the falls and reappearing below (apparently no stunt double was interested in running Bow Falls from that position). Other scenes in the movie were filmed along the Athabasca River near Jasper to the north.

The Banff Springs Hotel also dominates the put-in with its massive roof line and grand architecture. Built in 1888 by the Canadian Pacific Railway, it once held bragging rights as the world's largest hotel in an era of one-upmanship.

The stretch below Bow Falls offers mild whitewater and a gradient of about 15 fpm (2.9 mpk). Few come here for big whitewater action. Commercial rafts filled with tourists make up much of the traffic as the river winds its way around several channels and islands. Logjams occasionally dictate routes and are often, but not always, marked by upstream signs.

The scenery is unsurpassed. Among the sights gracing the banks are hoodoos. Like clouds, they invite the imagination to transform them into recognizable figures. These curious presandstone formations arise from different rates of erosion and variations in calcium carbonate cementing of the ancient sediments.

Wildlife abounds along the river. Elk are particularly common in the upper reaches, with herds often visiting in late afternoon. Errant-footed elk have reportedly been swept into Bow Falls only to emerge kicking from the huge pool downstream.

Boaters can choose from several access points along the river. The first take-out is off a loop road downstream of the hotel golf course for a short half-hour float. Boaters can continue for a two-hour float around the bases of beautiful Tunnel Mountain and Mount Rundll and take out at Canmore near the bridge on Eighth Avenue.

Athabasca River (Alberta) ➢

The Athabasca is one of Canada's major glacial rivers, running big and silty northward from the Columbia Icefield. The river passes the resort town of Jasper and continues north, eventually joining the Mackenzie River en route to the Arctic Ocean. The icefield itself is the remnant of a huge glacial mass that included the old Athabasca Glacier, a leviathan responsible for carving much of the present drainage. It sits astride one of only two triple continental divides in the world as its icy runoff finds its way to the Atlantic, Pacific, and Arctic Oceans.

The Athabasca shares its name with the descendants of some of the first group of humans to traverse the Alaskan land bridge and inhabit the interior areas of Alaska and northwestern Canada. The name literally means "there are reeds here and there," perhaps in reference to Lake Athabasca, a major lake into which the river empties.

European exploration began here with the intrepid David Thompson, who picked the dead of winter in 1811–12 to scout the valley and ascend the frozen Whirlpool River in search of the Northwest Passage. Those of his party who remained had an easier task, establishing a small trading depot that later became Jasper.

The glacial character of the Athabasca is hard to miss. Its color varies from to greenish white to gray. The rapids are easy, and the overall gradient varies from 15 to 25 fpm (2.9 to 4.8 mpk). The river braids, especially in the lower reaches, giving boaters the opportunity to guess the best routes around several islands. Gravel bars predominate at low flows.

Athabasca Falls, just above the mouth of the Whirlpool River about a third of the way down the run, is a big attraction for tourists and river runners. This is an unrunnable, 100-foot (30.5 m) drop over bedrock ledges into a deep, potholed chasm laced with undercuts. Boaters running the entire river usually opt to exit right, drive the mile-long (1.6 km) portage, and put in on the left after crossing the bridge over the falls. Downstream the river goes through a small canyon away from the road.

Most of the usage downstream of the Athabasca Falls consists of day trips, using various intermediate access points along Route 93. What is locally called the Five-Mile run is the most popular. Put in at Alpine Bridge and take out at Alpine Village, or continue to just downstream of the Miett confluence at Fort Point. The biggest rapid is Becker's, just below the put-in on a right-hand bend. It is named for the resort on the right where guests watch boaters frolic in the good surf waves and dodge massive oar rafts filled with commercial tourists.

Jasper is a five-star resort town where elk freely roam the streets. Pass on the wine at dinner, and try the delicious tap water that comes directly from the glacial source.

MOUNT CHRISTIE VIEW POINT TO JASPER
Difficulty: Class 2 and 3 (one portage)
Length: 30 miles (48 km), shorter trips possible
Season: May through September
Character: Scenic big-water run with many trip options

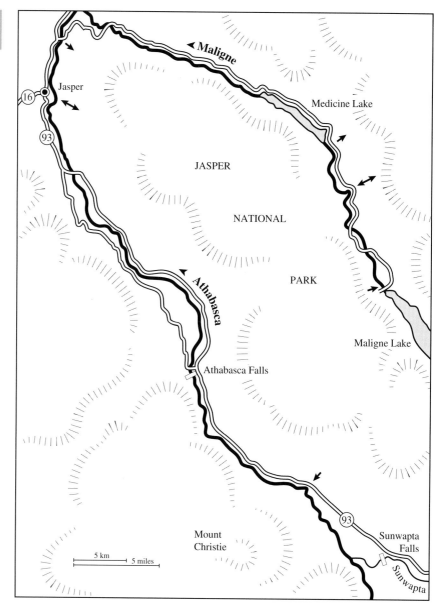

Athabasca and Maligne Rivers (Alberta)

Maligne River (Alberta) ➢

French-speaking Father Pierre DeSmet must have been having a bad day when he came to this tributary of the Athabasca River in 1822. Struggling to ford his horses across the high waters, he dubbed it La Riviere Maligne, or "Evil River." It was not until 1908 that mushers Billy Warren and Mary Schaeffer were the first Europeans to reach its upstream origins at Maligne Lake, an area they dubbed "the most beautiful area in Western Canada." Warren and Schaeffer accurately described the valley, but by then the river and valley were already named for DeSmet's frustrated curse.

The Maligne drainage is among the most interesting of the world's natural phenomena. This superb hanging valley came to be in the last ice age when the huge, ancient Athabasca Glacier carved the massive Athabasca Valley to the west, and the smaller Maligne Glacier sculpted the less imposing Maligne Valley. As the smaller glacier could not cut as deeply, the Maligne Valley "hangs" some 328 feet (100 m) above the Athabasca River. The river now drains a smaller area that includes many large glaciers and the Brazeau Ice Fields. It also holds what is reportedly the longest underground drainage system in the Western Hemisphere. Medicine Lake befuddled both Indians and early European explorers, as most of the year it had no outlet and in late summer it seemed to dry up completely. In fact, most of the outflow goes underground, and at low water the lake recedes completely into the aquifer. The current dips below the riverbed elsewhere as well.

The upstream lake, Maligne Lake, is the second deepest glacier-fed lake in the world. It sits below remarkably jagged, blade-like peaks. Put in for the upstream run at the bridge at the outlet of Maligne Lake, and take out either at a picnic site 4 miles (6.5 km) downstream or at a primitive campsite 3 miles (5.1 km) farther downstream at mile 7 (11 km). The river runs through an open valley mostly covered with lodgepole pine. The road is never too far from the river but usually not visible. Several large boulders and occasional constrictions create some challenging waves and holes at higher levels. Z Drop is the most difficult rapid. Sweepers and logjams may be anywhere on the river.

The lower section is for experts only. The gradient increases dramatically, and the continuous, technical rapids command precise maneuvering. Kayakers will need good paddling skills and a reliable roll. This reach of river is also well away from the road, making quick rescue improbable. The biggest drops, Hypertension, Slot Machine, and Staircase, may be difficult to recognize for first-timers. Staircase, just past the halfway point, is the crux. This long, steep collection of ledges and holes is littered with huge boulders. A mishap here could result in a torturous swim and give reason to believe DeSmet named the river aptly. The portage on the right involves a scramble up a steep embankment, a romp through the woods, and lowering boats back down to the river with lines. Take out at Medicine Lake.

Downstream of the sections described here the Maligne tumbles to the floor of the Athabasca Valley, cutting the impossibly narrow Maligne Canyon. Here the river passes through a cataract a few feet wide with some of the current passing underground in a study in tightly focused erosion.

In recent years boating on the Maligne was prohibited before July 1 to protect harlequin ducks that breed on the river. As of the spring of 1999 the Maligne will be *closed to all river running*. This closure is based on studies claiming to show that commercial

MALIGNE LAKE TO CAMPSITE
Difficulty: Class 3
Length: 7 miles (11.2 km)

CAMPSITE TO MEDICINE LAKE
Difficulty: Class 5
Length: 4 miles (6.4 km)

Season: May into August (currently closed to all boating)
Character: Small, scenic mountain run

rafting on the Maligne interrupted courtship rituals of this resplendent waterfowl. While it was far from clear that other factors may not be responsible for declines in harlequin population, it is hoped that further study or revival of the population will allow at least limited boating in the future.

◁ Kicking Horse River (British Columbia)

The Kicking Horse River rises in the mountains and glaciers of Yoho National Park and drains the west slope at the Continental Divide. Its present course is a relatively new one. The river once flowed into the Kootenay drainage. Glacial material deposited during the last ice age about 10,000 years ago blocked its route and forced it to take its present steep and torturous route westward to Golden and the Columbia. The Kicking Horse is the quintessential Canadian glacier-fed river, its milky greenish waters tumbling down a boulder-strewn streambed in a deep, scenic canyon with a gradient of 15 to more than 50 feet per mile (2.9 to 9.7 mpk). This is a prime area for viewing bighorn sheep and mountain goats, both near the river and in the surrounding mountains.

The name Kicking Horse comes from an incident here in 1858 when a boisterous horse threw geologist Dr. James Hector and added a kick in the head for good measure. Given up for dead and moments from burial in a shallow grave, Hector blinked his eyes, forcing attendees to take a rain check on the solemn proceedings and lending a colorful name to the river.

The first section of the described run is from Beaverfoot (also known as Cozier) Bridge to Hunters Creek. This is a popular commercial rafting run in a broad canyon with easy rapids. The put-in is off a side road just outside the Yoho National Park boundary. The take-out is at the bottom of a dirt side road off the Trans-Canada Highway, 1½ miles (2.5 km) upstream of a brake-check station.

The section below Hunters Creek begins easily, then builds to bigger action. The toughest stretch is Portage Rapid, a long boulder-cluttered passage beneath a cliff wall on the right. A "slow" sign just upstream on the right marks the entrance. Portage leads to Shotgun, the largest drop on this reach, where the river pours over a constricted ledge. The hole and wave at the bottom can be immense at high flows.

Most kayakers and all rafters exit at Rafters Take-Out (sometimes called Glenogle, as it is opposite Glenogle Creek) to avoid the long, difficult rapids near the Yoho Bridge (sometimes called Five-Mile Bridge). The section between Glenogle and Yoho Bridge invites some boaters to flirt with disaster in the form of the Yoho Bridge Rapid, a hideous frowning hole that is unavoidable at most flows and nearly always portaged. Construction of the railway probably had a hand in creating the hole, and it reportedly harbors construction debris from the bridge as well. Kayakers sometimes play a game of chicken with the hole in the rapids upstream, choosing between obstructed runs on either side of an island to catch an eddy from which to carry around the hole. The entire stretch could be dubbed the "Brown Mile," as the "miss the eddy and you die" scenario has been played out here at least once. If you carry or want to put in here you can launch either above or below two more drops just downstream of the bridge. The entire stretch is an enjoyable scout from paths below the bridge.

Below the bridge the highway rises high above the river on the right, leaving only the railway along the banks. The river then plunges into a deep canyon for more big drops before emerging finally at the town of Golden. The Trans-Canada Highway and railroad follow the river upstream of the Yoho Bridge.

The best way to access the canyon is to put in at a commercial rafting launch site downstream of the bridge on the right. To reach this launch site, find a railroad service road off the highway but still within sight of the bridge. The road leads to parking and a broad trail to the river directly across from a lofty side-creek waterfall.

The solitude of the lower canyon is tempered a bit by the railroad that crosses the river four times but does afford emergency access. This is a big-water run with ledges often following each other in quick succession, the biggest of which is called Town House. The action is mostly nonstop at the beginning but starts to ease at the first of the four railroad bridges, with bigger rapids appearing periodically after that. Take out on the left at a college or at several alternate sites downstream in Golden.

Blaeberry River (British Columbia) ➤

The Blaeberry River drains the west slope of the Canadian Rockies northwest of the Kicking Horse River and Yoho National Park. Its clear blue waters wander west and then south through a lightly populated area before emptying into the Columbia River. The scenery here includes some splendid multicolored rock formations on the mountains that dominate the right side of the river. The gradient on this stretch is 15 fpm (2.9 mpk), and a gravel road follows much of the way. Although the rapids are easy, keep an eye out for logs and sweepers in the braided sections. Expert kayakers may want to explore some very tough whitewater upstream.

The convoluted and poorly marked roads don't make finding the put-in easy. Even the locals confess to some confusion. Approach the put-in as follows, or ask locally for directions: Take the Blaeberry School Road north of the Route 1 (Trans-Canada Highway) bridge over the Blaeberry for 1 mile (1.7 km) to a junction with the Golden-Donald Upper Road, turn right, and go 1¼ miles (2 km) to the take-out, near the Route 1 bridge near the Columbia confluence. To reach the put-in, go south for just under 1 mile (1.4 km) to the junction with Oberg-Johnston Road, turn left, and proceed for 1 mile (1.8 km) to the junction with the Moberley School Road. Turn left and go 650 yards (600 m) to a fork where you stay right on the Blaeberry Road. Continue on Blaeberry Road for 4 miles (6.5 km) to a junction with a bridge.

BRIDGE NEAR REDBURN TO COLUMBIA RIVER CONFLUENCE
Difficulty: Class 2
Length: 8 miles (12.8 km)

Season: May to September
Character: Mild; mountain scenery, followed by gravel road

Kootenay River (British Columbia) ➤

The Kootenay and Columbia rivers begin their journeys in the same area and pass so close to each other they could literally wave and say hello. At one point only 1 mile (1.5 km) and less than 13 feet (4 m) in elevation separate Columbia Lake and the Canal Flats section of the Kootenay; they then flow in different directions along the Rocky Mountain Trench, a combined journey of some 800 miles (1,280 km), before they finally meet. In the 1880s a visionary named Wabaille-Grohman tried to bring the two rivers together. He concocted a plan to dig a canal to divert Columbia floodwaters that threatened the potentially rich farming areas in Kootenay Flats. The Canadian Pacific Railway opposed the plan, arguing that the waters would instead flood its new track along the Columbia River. A lopsided compromise resulted in a marginal single-lock canal with no diver-

SETTLERS ROAD BRIDGE TO FOREST SERVICE BRIDGE
Difficulty: Class 3−
Length: 27 miles (43.2 km)

FOREST SERVICE BRIDGE TO CANAL FLATS
Difficulty: Class 3− upstream of Gibraltar Rock, Class 2− downstream
Length: 22 miles (35.2 km)

(continued on following page)

sions. Flooding continued, and the canal's final traffic tally was only two steamboats, the *Gwendoline* in 1894 and the *North Star* in 1902.

The headwaters of the Kootenay are in Kootenay National Park, and the best white-water is the first 27 miles (43.2 km) as the river leaves the park. For the described stretch, the river takes a southerly course, eventually dipping into northwest Montana and the Idaho panhandle before looping back to British Columbia and finally joining the Columbia River. The climatic scenes in the movie *The River Wild* were filmed at Kootenai Falls (U.S. spelling) in northwestern Montana.

The Kootenay's waters are usually a dazzling emerald green and always cold. The river flows through a canyon within a much larger forested valley set beneath glacial mountain peaks. Although roads follow the river on either side, they remain hidden behind canyon walls and stands of birch and aspen. Although not a steep descent, the big flow of the Kootenay is steady and swift. At higher flows one can put away many miles without much effort. Good camping on gravel bars or the occasional sandy beach make the Kootenay ideal for multi-day trips.

The put-in for the upper run is just downstream of the park boundary at the Settlers Road bridge. The primary intermediate access point is at the Forest Service bridge, although a few other access points can be found. Boaters can also do the entire run down to Canal Flats.

The larger rapids above the usual intermediate take-out include Ledge, Horseshoe, and Palliser and are usually accompanied by bends and curves on the river. The Palliser Rapids are at the mouth of the Palliser River on the left at 18 miles (28 km) downstream of the put-in. Pedley Falls, a beautiful 82-foot (25 m) cascade on the right at 18½ miles (30 km), is a popular stop. The Forest Service bridge crosses the river at mile 27 (43.2 km).

About 1 mile (1.6 km) downstream of the Forest Service bridge is an impressive set of hoodoos on the left. The White River enters on the left about 1 mile (1.6 km) farther downstream, and 3 miles (4.8 km) below that is Gibraltar Rock. This was once considered as a site for a hydroelectric dam. Gibraltar Rock to Canal Flats is about 18 miles (28.8 km) of easy drifting, with some braiding before the take-out.

To get to the put-in, turn off at Settler's Road just inside the park on Route 93. The Settler's Road bridge is less than ½ mile (0.8 km) downstream of the park boundary. Although roads follow the river on either side, Ravens Head Road on the right is the faster and better-maintained route, connecting to both the intermediate access and the take-out on the Route 95 bridge, near Canal Flats.

UPPER BRIDGE TO PANORAMA
Difficulty: Class 3–
Length: 6 miles (9.6 km)

PANORAMA TO ACCESS ROAD BELOW SLIPPERY ROCK FALLS
Difficulty: Class 3; Slippery Rock Falls Class 5
Length: 4 miles (6.4 km)

(continued on following page)

◁ Toby Creek (British Columbia)

Toby Creek drains a small, high watershed in the Purcell Mountains, beneath jagged Mount Nelson (10,850 feet, 3,309 m) and the Toby Glacier. It tumbles down a steep, narrow canyon and empties into the Columbia at Invermere. Development has come to the valley in the form of Panorama Resort, a modern ski area that boasts the second largest vertical skiing drop in North America. The road up to the resort is paved, turning to a good-quality gravel road above the resort.

There are several put-in options on the upper section. A good choice is a developed commercial launch site 4¼ miles (7 km) above Panorama or a bridge 2 miles (3 km) farther upstream. All put-ins are on river left off of the road. The run upstream of Panorama has a steady gradient of about 50 fpm (9.7 mpk) with a few rocks in the riverbed to dodge. As snowmelt tails off late in the season, the water becomes greenish-white with glacial runoff. Boaters seeking a little more challenge put in even farther upstream at Delphinia Creek confluence for a Class 3 stretch.

From Panorama down, the river gets more difficult, particularly at higher levels. About halfway down is Slippery Rock Falls (Class 5), a series of three boulder-choked drops. Boaters should choose their routes from the road in advance. The take-out for this stretch is where the road meets the river near the end of the next large set of rapids after Slippery Rock Falls.

From here the canyon walls narrow and the river drops away from the road. This is the last chance to take out before committing to run the difficult Seven Canyons run (Class 5+) as the river squeezes through seven short but distinct narrow canyons. This stretch is definitely for experts only, and some of the portages are trickier than the rapids. The drops are frequent and often continuous; the biggest include Placebo, Juniors, Smittys, Seventh Heaven, and Fangs. Take out at the bridge over the river near Invermere.

Upper Fraser River (British Columbia) ➢

The Fraser is the largest undammed river in North America. Its headwaters rise among a string of spectacular peaks on the western edge of Jasper National Park including Mount Robson, the highest of the Canadian Rockies at 12,960 feet (3,954 m). The mountains overlooking the Upper Fraser usually hold snow into September and drain a chain of glaciers nestled near the mountain peaks. The Robson River joins the Upper Fraser from the north about halfway down the run.

The Fraser is covered twice in this book. In this section, 600 miles (965 km) upstream of the big-volume Hell's Gate run, the Fraser is still a small- to medium-volume river. It crashes relentlessly through a canyon of lava and sedimentary rock, pours over Overlander Falls, and drops into a second, shorter—but no less difficult—canyon. Most boaters should stay away from either of these runs at higher flows. Downstream the canyon opens up for an easier Class 3 stretch with smooth ledges and rounded boulders interrupted by Rearguard Falls.

The run begins at Moose Lake where much of the glacial silt drops out and clears the water. Access the river at the outlet from a railroad yard just downstream of a railroad bridge at Red Pass off the Trans-Canada Highway. The legal status of this put-in is uncertain. From here it is a mile of flatwater before the current picks up speed. Boaters can avoid the paddle by finding a railroad track near the highway about $1\frac{1}{4}$ miles (2 km) downstream from Moose Lake, but this requires a carry to the river.

The action begins just above the first (and only) railroad bridge downstream of Red Pass where the river steepens and forms a long series of big waves. From here down, the action is incessant, especially at higher flows when a swim would be critical. The sheer gradient of the river is apparent in straight stretches of the canyon, giving the river the feel of a luge run. About 4 miles (6.4 km) below the put-in there is emergency access by a trail leading to a road from the right channel of an island. The channel may be dry at low flows.

Not far downstream of the island, the river constricts near a small building on the left marking Outhouse Rapid. This is the beginning of a long difficult stretch of Class 5– water. The river follows a series of steep, often blind turns with large boulders in the riverbed stirring up waves, holes, and small eddies. The most difficult passage is Eric's

SLIPPERY ROCK FALLS TO LOWER HIGHWAY BRIDGE NEAR INVERMERE (SEVEN CANYONS RUN)
Difficulty: Class 5+$_p$
Length: 10 miles (16 km)

Season: May through September
Character: Road nearby, snow runoff, mountains

MOOSE LAKE TO ROBSON CONFLUENCE
Difficulty: Class 5–$_p$
Length: $11\frac{1}{2}$ miles (18.4 km)

ROBSON CONFLUENCE TO TETE JAUNE CACHE
Difficulty: Class 3–$_p$
Length: $10\frac{1}{2}$ miles (16.8 km)

Season: May through September
Character: Mountainous headwaters of a huge river

Hole, a dangerous keeper blocking most of the main channel on the left along a left-hand bend. Most boaters portage or pick a route through the puzzle of boulders and ledges on the right and rejoin the main channel below the keeper. From here the canyon opens, giving boaters some time to breathe before the downstream rapids: Boulderdash, Holy Terror, Regurgitron, Toilet Bowl, Otter Slide, and Staircase.

Boaters willing to carry up a steep embankment to the highway can take out below Staircase or paddle easier rapids and carry out at the 1-mile-long (1.6 km) tourist trail at Overlander Falls.

Overlander is a 30-foot (9 m) river-wide drop into a pool just upstream of a tourist observation bridge. Although it has been run, the rule is to carry to the right. (The falls are named for an acclaimed group of fortune seekers who traversed Canada and camped at the falls in 1862 on their way to the gold fields of Tete Jaune Cache. Some in the group later took their place in Canadian whitewater lore by navigating the big-water runs downstream on the Fraser and on the Thompson on wooden rafts.)

Below Overlander the character of the river changes to pool-and-drop as it enters an intimate, narrow, sheer-walled gorge and drops over a series of boulders and ledges. Boaters can scout parts of this section from the bridge at Overlander Falls at the entrance and the Hargreaves Road bridge on the way to Mount Robson Ranch at the exit. There is also a nice footpath through the woods along the length of the canyon on the right. Getting a good look at the biggest drop, Terminator, is tough. Terminator requires boaters to catch a small eddy to scout/portage on the left. Take out from the big pool near the Robson confluence below the Hargreaves Road bridge.

From the Robson confluence the river is mostly Class 3 except Rearguard Falls at about 7 miles (11 km) downstream. This convoluted series of ledges can be portaged on the right. From here down it's an easy 3-mile float to the old mining town of Tete Jaune Cache. The Fraser remains a mild float for hundreds of miles before picking up volume for the rapids of Moran Canyon and the Hell's Gate section.

◁ Adams River (British Columbia)

ADAMS LAKE TO HIGHWAY BRIDGE 2 MILES (3.2 KM) UPSTREAM OF SUSWAT LAKE
Difficulty: Class 3
Length: 6 miles (9.6 km)

Season: Late April through October
Character: Short, mountainous gorge

Located in the Shuswap region, a recreational area in the interior of British Columbia, the Adams is a delight. It flows through a pristine wooded valley and a narrow mini-gorge. Unlike many of the silty glacial rivers in the region, these waters run warm and clear and teem with life. Beaver, otter, and waterfowl busy themselves near the banks. Trout surface to gulp insects. In late September, parts of the river turn red with what may be the largest sockeye salmon run in the world. Most of the land is owned by the Hustalen Indian Band.

For road access, turn north off the Trans-Canada Highway between Chase and Serrento and follow the signs to Anglemont. This road also leads to Shuswap Lake Provincial Park. The take-out is just downstream of the bridge on the left. To get to the put-in, go back across the bridge and turn right, following the signs to Adams Lake. Put in at the outflow of Adams Lake, near the remains of a burned bridge at the end of a dirt road.

The river runs at an even gradient, with steady Class 2 and 2+ rapids that continue throughout its length, providing kayakers with several good playholes. The upper section features a few islands, and boaters should be careful of logjams. The action is at Devil's Gate, sometimes called the Gorge, about two-thirds of the way down. Here the entire river funnels through a narrow slot between two high canyon walls, creating a progression of Class 3 hydraulics and standing waves out of character with the rest of the river. Rafters may find the excitement a bit short-lived, but kayakers are able to paddle up again and again, riding the excellent surf waves.

Clearwater River (British Columbia) ➢

Warmed in the lakes in the beautiful Wells Gray Provincial Park, the glacial waters of the Clearwater River course south through rock-walled canyons to the town of Clearwater where they empty into the North Thompson River. This entire stretch holds some of the best river running in Western Canada. The configuration is a little reminiscent of the great runs of Chile, with big glacial flows cleared of silt to an azure color and warmed in the thermocline of upstream lakes before dropping into a canyon filled with great pool-and-drop rapids and world-class surf waves. Although the gradient of the featured stretch is no more than 25 feet fpm (4.8 mpk), don't be fooled. The riverbed is largely volcanic, and the lava formations make for big drops, holes, and waves. The sheer volume of the river adds speed and power. At higher flows the waves are huge and the eddy fences are more like walls.

The shuttle road is Clearwater River Road, a good-quality dirt/gravel road along the right bank that begins near the bridge at Clearwater and ends about 23 miles (37 km) from town. The featured run begins at a riverside campground 8 miles (13 km) upstream of the bridge at Clearwater with Class 3 water for the first 2½ miles (3.2 km) to another access point. Below here the rapids increase to continuous Class 4, culminating at Kettle Falls (Class 6), a multitiered drop with a broad reversal on the bottom left that forms a huge boil line at high flows. This is the most difficult rapid in the canyon and is often portaged. Some boaters choose to avoid this difficult stretch by using a commercial put-in just below Kettle Falls about 4 miles (7 km) from the bridge at Clearwater, taking the short hike upstream to look at Kettle Falls.

Just below the commercial put-in, the river splits around an island. The left channel begins with the Wall, a big ledge and drop with a powerful side wave below. The rapids follow regularly, with some time to breathe between drops. Just below the Wall is the Hole-in-the-Wall, followed by M87. A nest high on the left marks the next rapid, Osprey. Below that is Pink Mountain, the best surf wave on the river. Its name comes from the huge granite wall on the left side just upstream. The last big rapid is Tube Snake Boogie, a series of waves and hydraulics off the left wall. Take out on the right shortly above the confluence with the North Thompson River, at the Old North Thompson Highway.

The Clearwater River features good upstream runs as well. Experts will want to take on Sabretooth Canyon, about 13 miles (21 km) up the shuttle road. Here a short canyon creates huge Class 5 hydraulics, especially at high water. After a short Class 3 interlude the river enters S-Bend where immense wave trains await at high water. The entire stretch is only about 1 mile long (1.6 km) but well worth the effort.

Farther upstream is Wells Gray Provincial Park, which is reached from a different route along Wells Gray Road (also known as Clearwater Valley Road). The park is rich in lofty mountain scenery, splendid azure lakes, and imposing waterfalls, including 175-foot (54 m) Spahats Falls.

The area also has some good flatwater paddling. Devotees of quiet water can start in the park, putting in at Azure Lake and floating a short stretch of the river to Clearwater Lake. Stay clear of the falls at the outlet of Clearwater Lake.

RIVERSIDE CAMPGROUND 8 MILES ABOVE CLEARWATER TO NORTH THOMPSON CONFLUENCE

Difficulty: Class 4_6
Length: 10 miles (16 km)

Season: May through September (in wet years may be too high until July)
Character: Large-volume, central British Columbia river

Below Clearwater Lake the water retains its fine azure hue, and boaters can put in for the challenging 6-mile (10 km) Upper Clearwater run. This Class 5 run has plenty of rapids and scenery as well as portages at Donkey Falls and Bailey Chute. Put in near the bridge over Falls Creek, where boaters have the option of running the 14-foot (4.3 m) waterfall just upstream of where the creek joins the Clearwater. This confluence is just downstream of Osprey Falls on the Clearwater.

◁ Elaho and Squamish Rivers (British Columbia)

Located north of Vancouver on the way to Whistler, the Squamish River and its much larger "tributary," the Elaho, offer silty gray-green waters, great scenery, and a little something for boaters of all levels. The first section, upstream on the Elaho, is experts-only boating. The rapids ease to intermediate whitewater for the second section as the river continues downstream past the Squamish confluence. About 7 miles (11.2 km) downstream of the confluence the third section begins as the rapids subside to an easy float ideal for sightseeing.

The scenery along the Elaho and Squamish rivers is almost reminiscent of Yosemite, with towering glacial carved-granite walls lined with rich forests. In clear weather the peaks reveal glacial bowls and waterfalls. Squamish is a native term meaning "mother of the wind"—perhaps a warning, as the canyon can get chilly. The glaciers overhead also give warning of the icy-cold, silty water in the rivers. Be forewarned: snowmelt, temperature, and occasional rainstorms can cause flows to surge, and fog along the river is common. River runners should be prepared with thermal gear for cold or overcast days. Sweepers and logjams can appear anywhere along the two rivers, an image suggested in the derivation of Elaho, the native word for "pile of salmon bones."

Put in for the uppermost section about 7 miles (11.2 km) above the Elaho-Squamish confluence. From here, the first 3 to 4 miles (4.8 to 6.4 km) are strictly Class 5 whitewater, fit only for experts and usually only runnable in fall as flows subside. This run features a 100 fpm (19 mpk) gradient, technical drops, and tight constrictions. The take-out here, the road, is also the put-in for the next run.

The second section begins at about 3 miles (4.8 km) above the confluence of the Elaho and the Squamish. Here the river eases to Class 3+ and the gradient to about 20 fpm (3.8 mpk). Playboaters will find some good surf waves here, but most are one-timers due to the lack of eddies. Care should be taken at Devil's Elbow, where the river takes an abrupt turn to the right in a tight canyon. The crook acts as a drain trap, catching flotsam and logs on the left. It is easy to bypass the jam, but pay attention. In 1987 an inattentive commercial rafting crew drifted into a jam, broached, and flipped, drowning five passengers beneath the logs and debris. Access is available just above the confluence with the Squamish.

Even though the Elaho is the "tributary," it is many times larger than the Squamish. The rapids ease below Devil's Elbow and then return to Class 3 for the first 7 miles (11.2 km) down the Squamish, with Steamroller the biggest rapid just below the mouth of Turbid Creek on the left.

The rapids then ease to a gradual float for the third stretch, with a gradient of 10 fpm (1.9 mpk). The canyon opens up into the valley for good views of the Tantalus Range along the west. Salmon runs bring scores of bald eagles to this stretch. From here there are 16 miles (25.6 km) of easy floating, with some braiding, to the take-out where the road moves away from the river.

Upstream of the Class 5 run on the Elaho is another easy float.

ABOUT 7 MILES UPSTREAM OF THE ELAHO-SQUAMISH CONFLUENCE TO ABOUT 3 MILES ABOVE THE CONFLUENCE
Difficulty: Class 5
Length: 4 miles (6.4 km)

ABOUT 3 MILES ABOVE THE CONFLUENCE TO ABOUT 7 MILES BELOW THE CONFLUENCE
Difficulty: Class 3+
Length: 10 miles (16 km)

FIVE MILES BELOW THE CONFLUENCE TO WHERE THE ROAD LEAVES THE SQUAMISH
Difficulty: Class 1+
Length: 16 miles (25.6 km)

Season: June through September (uppermost run only at low flows)
Character: Wet, lush area surrounded by glaciers, followed by an unimproved road

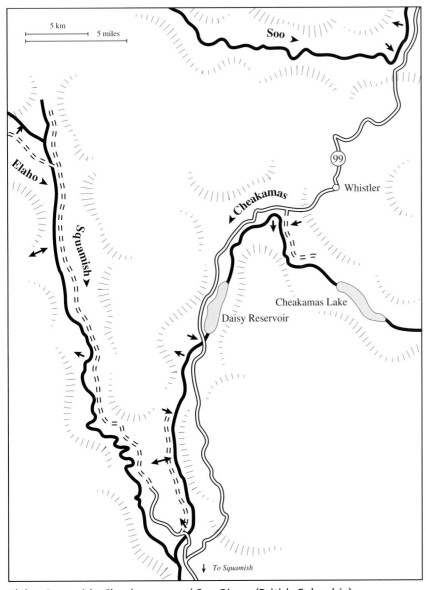

Elaho, Squamish, Cheakamus, and Soo Rivers (British Columbia)

Cheakamus River (British Columbia) ➤

Like the nearby Elaho and Squamish rivers, the Cheakamus (CHECK-a-mus) is a mixture of rain, snowmelt, and glacial melt, but the water here is usually clear. Aside from some clear-cutting in the upper valley, the scenery is excellent, and the river holds a little something for boaters of all abilities. Its popularity is assured by its location less than two hours from Vancouver.

The upper run is considered by many of the locals to be the premier run in the area and often the site of slalom competitions. Evidence of the reverence afforded to the run

UPSTREAM OF LOGGERS LAKE TO LAST ROAD BRIDGE (UPPER RUN)
Difficulty: Class 4+, Class 5 at higher water
Length: 2 miles (3.2 km)

(continued on following page)

Daisy Lake Dam to where the road leaves the river
Difficulty: Class 3+
Length: 3 miles (4.8 km)

Paradise Valley Road (near Brackendale) to Brackendale
Difficulty: Class 2+ and 1
Length: 8 miles (12.8 km)

Season: All but the lowest run, May into October; lowest run, all year
Character: Varied runs, mountain river

is a series of engraved stones mounted on a boulder just to the right of House Rock rapid. The memorial is easily accessible by trail from the road and honors three boaters who lost their lives on rivers in the area.

With a gradient of more than 100 fpm (19 mpk), the upper run is 2 miles (3.2 km) of steady action incorporating the best of big holes, pushy waves, and boulders. Most of the run can be scouted from the left. Big rapids include Bush's Drop, followed by Race Course Drop where a massive boulder called House Rock is situated in the middle of the rapid. The rapid is sometimes used as a very challenging slalom site. The upper run is sensitive to flow changes and is much more difficult at higher water. Roads follow on either side of the river. The take-out is the first bridge on a road off Route 99 beginning just opposite Function Junction. The put-in is 2 miles (3 km) upstream of a trail at a small parking area on the road to the left of the river.

Daisy Reservoir serves to divert much of the Cheakamus River's flow through a tunnel to the Squamish; however, massive runoffs usually allow dam-releases and good downstream flows into the summer. The section downstream of the reservoir begins at a put-in on a small bridge on Route 99 (Garibaldi Highway) just below Cheakamus Dam. The rapids are Class 3+ for about 3 miles (4.8 km) until the road leaves the river. Massive mudslides down the aptly named Rubble Creek in the mid-1850s choked the river with debris. The hazardous effects can still be seen in the series of tree stumps in the streambed as the rapid is regularly rearranged by erosion. Another big drop is just above the take-out.

Below here the river drops into a spectacular but unrunnable canyon for about 4 miles (6.4 km).

Below the canyon an 8-mile (12.8 km) runnable stretch begins not far upstream of the Culliton Creek confluence, with access off Paradise Valley Road near Brackendale. The canyon opens for this run as some Class 2+ rapids subside into a leisurely float. The ecological reserve along the river draws hundreds of bald eagles, especially from November to February, making this run good for beginners as well as hardy nature enthusiasts. In 1994 nearby Brackendale recorded a record count of more than 3,700 bald eagles.

Another run with a popular surf spot near the put-in is from the Route 99 bridge on Callaghan Creek to the Cheakamus, taking out above the wild canyon upstream of Daisy Lake. Locals refer to this expert run as the Cal-Check.

Along Route 99 north of Whistler
Difficulty: Class 5–
Length: 2 miles (3.2 km)

Season: May into October
Character: Boulder-choked, open-bottomed canyon

◁ Soo River (British Columbia)

North of the Cheakamus River on Route 99 (Garibaldi Highway) between Whistler and Pemberton is the Soo, another cold, silty glacial river with a gradient of over 100 fpm (19 mpk). The Soo has a short name, tough rapids, and reasonable access near the highway. A railroad runs along the river. Big drops include Bob's Drop and Deep Throat. Although the highway follows the river, it climbs well above it, providing excellent solitude along the "Sea to Sky Trail."

The put-in is from a dirt road at a break in the concrete guardrail marked by a 60 km speed limit sign on Route 99. This is about 1½ miles (2.5 km) downstream of Shadow Lake (measured from the railroad tracks). Boaters take out upstream of a bridge near the Green River confluence and the highway. A tough section farther upstream called the Railroad run is also available.

Capilano River (British Columbia) ➤

The Capilano is one of the best whitewater runs to be found in any large urban area and one of the most scenic runs anywhere. The technical pool-and-drop rapids of the "Cap" flow through a coastal rainforest of hemlock, cedar, moss, and ferns and a secluded, intimate canyon filled with side waterfalls, green pools, and sandy beaches. Set in North Vancouver, just minutes from downtown Vancouver, it is the ideal paddling escape for city dwellers, with a slalom course and technical, pool-and-drop rapids.

The Cleveland Dam, which holds drinking water for Vancouver, regulates flows on the river as does the salmon hatchery just above the put-in. This makes boating possible during releases. Unfortunately, sizable late-summer releases are rare, making this a difficult run for visitors arriving for the late season of nearby rivers. Even if it is too low, it is still worthwhile to take a walk along the Capilano's fine trails and appreciate its beauty.

The put-in is at the salmon hatchery at the end of Capilano Park Road, off Capilano Road. The hatchery is set up to accommodate self-guided tours and is worth the time to watch the fish work up the aquarium-like glass ladders during salmon runs. Launch near the parking area just below the weir above a site often used as a slalom course. The rapids include House Rock Drop, Dogleg, Big Mother, Head Wall, Woodkroft, and Nude Rock. Some boaters take out at Dog Leg after running the slalom course. About halfway down, a suspension bridge originally constructed in 1889 crosses high above the river and is the pretext for an elaborate private park along the shuttle route. Watch out for anglers who appear seasonally to try their luck with the steelhead and coho salmon runs; be courteous, and avoid conflicts.

Take out on the right just upstream of Park Royal Bridge on Marine Drive near a motel. The Seymour and Lynn are other nearby rain-fed drainages popular with local kayakers.

CABLE POOL TO PARK ROYAL BRIDGE
Difficulty: Class 3+
Length: 3½ miles (5.6 km)

Season: All year, except usually too low during late summer
Character: Scenic mountain canyon run neighboring an urban area

Chilliwack River (British Columbia) ➤

Draining headwaters in the North Cascades National Park in the United States, the Chilliwack is the southernmost whitewater river in Western Canada. Just a little over an hour from Vancouver, it is the destination of choice for local boaters of all skill levels in all type of craft. Boaters usually divide the Chilliwack into three progressively easier sections: the Canyon run, from Camp Foley to Slesse Creek, 5½ miles (8.8 km); Slesse Creek to Pointa Vista, 8 miles (12.8 km); and Pointa Vista to Vedder Crossing, 4½ miles (7.2 km).

The Canyon section lacks the sheer vertical walls and difficult access usually associated with a "canyon," but it does have a precipitous gradient, over 100 fpm (19 mpk), and continuous whitewater. Although the whitewater becomes technical pool-and-drop in character at the lowest flows, it is relentless at higher flows, as the drops and holes grow and merge together. This is great experts-only territory, but the possibility of long swims is a good reason for those with lesser skills to go elsewhere. Put in at Camp Foley, a public campground. The biggest drops include Picket Fence and Cable Pool near the top. Fish Hatchery Drop, a narrow slot built to divert water to the nearby fish hatchery was washed out by floods in 1995 and is now easily run. Take out on the left just below the mouth of Slesse Creek.

CAMP FOLEY TO SLESSE CREEK (CANYON RUN)
Difficulty: Class 5–
Length: 5½ miles (8.8 km)

SLESSE CREEK TO POINTA VISTA
Difficulty: Class 3+
Length: 8 miles (12.8 km)

POINTA VISTA TO VEDDER CROSSING
Difficulty: Class 2
Length: 4½ miles (7.2 km)

Season: April to early August
Character: Mountainous, road nearby, many options

The middle section, from Slesse Creek to Pointa Vista, provides lively rapids and is popular with all types of paddlers. On weekends it can get crowded as boaters and anglers converge. Slesse Creek is the uppermost limit of legal fishing, so expect a gauntlet of fishing lines here at peak season. Make sure any extra paddlers don't come from the correctional facility on the right. A popular spot to stop is a waterfall and cave on the right bank, just downstream of a shallow braided section.

The most difficult rapid on the middle section is Tamihi (TAM-ah-hi) at the bridge crossing the river about 2 miles (3.2 km) upstream of Pointa Vista. This is a popular place for playboating. The rapid is usually decorated with slalom gates and is the permanent training site for the Canadian National Team. Below Tamihi are Campground and Saw Hill rapids. All these rapids can be scouted from the bridge along the shuttle. Take out at Osborne Road just upstream of the Ponta Vista Cafe.

The lower section from Osborne Road to Vedder Crossing is popular with beginners and recreational floaters as well as those interested in sightseeing and fishing. There are several alternate designated access points along Chilliwack Lake Road. The access points are designed so as not to disturb gravel bars necessary for spawning, and boaters should use them exclusively.

BOSTON BAR TO YALE
Difficulty: Class 4+
Length: 28 miles (45 km); shorter runs are possible

Season: May through September
Character: A huge-volume river in a large canyon

◁ Fraser River (British Columbia)

With flows of over 100,000 cfs (2,830 cumecs) in the summertime and occasionally topping 400,000 cfs (11,320 cumecs), this is the largest-volume whitewater run in the Western Hemisphere. The sight and sound of the Fraser as it roars through the massive igneous formations of Hells Gate is a spectacle of astounding turbulence, brown boils, wide eddies, and whirlpools. The river is set in a great canyon, with sheer cliff walls and black crags overhead giving the entire area a feeling of immensity. The Fraser at this point has grown a hundred-fold from the Upper Fraser run in the Canadian Rockies some 600 miles (960 km) upstream (see Upper Fraser description).

The river is named for Simon Fraser, who explored the area for the Northwest Company in 1808 on his way to the Pacific. It is believed that Fraser, unprepared for the im-

In August 1985 I was part of a group running Hells Gate of the Fraser. At the put-in, the Canadian Mounties told us rafts had to be at least 22 feet long to run Hells Gate. We promptly drove to the police station, and there spouted some choice words about river running and freedom. We paraphrased liberally from Ed Abbey, but the fact that they couldn't find the law in question written down anywhere left them powerless to do anything but warn us and wish us good luck.

I had no plan on staying in the 14-foot raft in Hells Gate anyway. I was told that the biggest danger had been whirlpools that would suck swimmers down and pop their eardrums. At the top of the rapid I jumped in the water with about 70 pounds of flotation in the form of a survival suit (20 pounds) and two PFDs (2 × 25 pounds). Sure, I got sucked in a whirlpool, but no way was I going down. The next year I was working with Bob Carlson on a riverboard, an even better way to swim rivers.

—Jim Cassady

posing rapids, portaged his way downstream on shelves constructed by local Indians who offered assistance. Fifty years later this was the gateway for the gold rush to the north along the Cariboo Trail in 1913 and 1914. Blasting associated with construction of the railway narrowed Hells Gate to 70 feet (23 m), making it impossible for most salmon to pass upstream. Millions of spawning fish battered themselves to death at this new constriction as the upstream spawning grounds were decimated; particularly hard hit were some of the world's largest coho and sockeye salmon runs on the whitewater sections of the Adams and Chilko rivers. An elaborate series of mostly submerged fishways were constructed beginning in the 1940s, and they now line both sides of the rapid. Upstream salmon populations, however, are still recovering. Nonetheless, the Fraser still flows free and remains the longest undammed river in North America with a total length of over 700 miles (1,120 km).

The volume of water at Hells Gate has caused river runners to battle size with size. The boat of choice is a 28- to 35-foot (8.5 to 10.5 m) motorized J-rig with four tubes, and the governing authorities have gone so far as to purport to prohibit use of smaller inflated craft. The motorized rigs do have the advantage of easily powering through the flatwater sections on the run.

Boaters on the Fraser have a choice of several access points. A popular put-in is at Boston Bar, which is about 25 miles (40 km) downstream of Lytton. Rapids here, aside from Hells Gate, include Scuzzy Rock, Little Hells Gate, Black Canyon, Sailor Bar, and Saddle Rock. Boaters sometimes lengthen this run considerably by combining it with the upstream run on the North Thompson, which meets the Fraser at Lytton.

Upstream on the Fraser between Big Bar Ferry and Lillooet is Moran Canyon, a big-volume Class 3 section. Watch out for a constantly surging rapid of immense proportion called Bridge Rapid, formed from a ledge just above the confluence of the Bridge River on the right.

Nahatlatch River (British Columbia) ➢

The jade-green waters of the Nahatlatch (Na-HAT-latch) River flow eastward from the coastal mountains until they join the Fraser River about 10 miles (16 km) upstream of Hells Gate. The river is commercially run, and the stretch below Frances Lake is the site of the REO Rafting base camp.

The run from Hannah Lake to Frances Lake is a quick jaunt that entails a ½-mile (0.8 km) paddle across the glacial waters of Hannah Lake. Put in near the old ranger station along the Nahatlatch Forest Road or at two wooden raft launches along the road. The short stretch of whitewater between the lakes is only Class 3 but affords a pleasant warm-up before the more challenging downstream run.

The lower section pours through a tree-lined canyon beginning at the outlet of Frances Lake. Boaters can put in near the campground at the outlet. The action starts early with major rapids including Rose Garden and Meat Grinder near the top. Head Wall (Class 4+) follows about 1½ miles (2 km) farther downstream and is the toughest on the run. The whitewater after Headwall is less involved, but consistent and bouncy rapids and waves continue throughout. The canyon is particularly tough at high water, usually in June or early July. Tree hazards are significant as felled trees pile up on the upstream banks of islands and elsewhere. Inquire locally about the possibility of taking out

HANNAH LAKE TO FRANCES LAKE
Length: 1 mile (1.6 km)
Difficulty: Class 3

BELOW FRANCES LAKE TO FRASER RIVER
Difficulty: Class 4+
Length: 9 miles (14.4 km)

Season: May through September
Character: Medium-flow river in a scenic mountain area

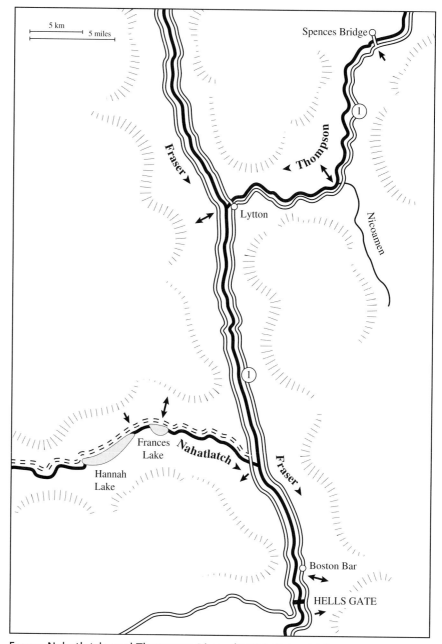

Fraser, Nahatlatch, and Thompson Rivers (British Columbia)

near the bridge to avoid the longer trip and shuttle on the Fraser. Below the bridge the river enters a vertical-walled canyon, but there are no more difficult rapids.

Thompson River (British Columbia) ➢

Although not quite to the scale of the Hells Gate section of the Fraser River, the Thompson River is another run of major proportions. The usual summer flows range from 15,000 to 60,000 cfs (425 to 1,698 cumecs). Although the locals proclaim this the "Whitewater Capital of Canada," this title may have more to do with the absence of much else going on in these parts than any consensus that this is the best Canada has to offer. The Thompson is, however, by any measure, a great whitewater river.

The high flows come early in the summer and sire waves in the 15-foot (4.6 m) range. Late summer brings clear water, baking sun, and lots of boaters to savor flows that are warmer than most Canadian rivers. Kayakers will find better surfing and easier eddy lines at lower levels, below 25,000 cfs (595 km). The abundance of water is in stark contrast to the environs. The Thompson rolls through the driest real estate in Canada. Though the banks have some enjoyable sand beaches, the surrounding country is sun-baked badlands complete with sagebrush, ponderosa pine, and prickly pear cactus. Most of this run is in a deep, heavily eroded canyon composed of a variety of unstable rock formations which often drop sharp rocks, talus, and rubble into the river. The Trans-Canada Highway and railroad follow the river.

Put in at Spences Bridge on the Trans-Canada Highway for a fairly easy float with some interesting hydraulics on the upper run. There is a splendid waterfall on Murray Creek on the right downstream of Spences Bridge. Some boaters put in at Big Horn, a mile or two (1.6 or 3.3 km) above Gold Pan Provincial Park, to avoid the less interesting stretches.

An intermediate access point is found where the Trans-Canada Highway crosses the Nicoamen River, where the Nicoamen joins the Thompson on the left and the river enters Devils Gorge. Don't be fooled by the gradient of only about 15 fpm (2.9 mpk) or the deceptive appearance of the rapids from the road. Many of the drops are formed by subsurface pourovers, making the hydraulics tricky and powerful, especially at higher flows. The larger rapids can surge, making timing an important factor. Newcomers are well advised to discuss recommended moves with the locals before committing.

Big, powerful rapids beginning just downstream of the Nicoamen confluence include Frog, named for the large mid-channel rock. Next is a big ledge called Devils Kitchen, followed by Cutting Board where the river is split by midstream boulders. Witches Caldron, sometimes called Jaws I, is next. The name of the biggest rapid, Jaws of Death, was not given by river runners but came from the demise of two Chinese workers who fell in and drowned while laying track. The rapid, sometimes called Jaws II, is formed by a constriction creating a playground of stupendous surfing waves. Take out at Lytton. Anyone willing to row or motor some flat stretches has the option of continuing downstream to Hells Gate on the Fraser River for some really big water.

River runners can also try an upstream run from Ashcroft to Martel where more big-water rapids, fine camping, and scenery await, including Black Canyon with its cathedral-like walls of sedimentary rock dating back some 150 million years.

The Thompson was given its name by Simon Fraser who mistakenly believed he was following a route blazed by David Thompson. Thompson himself never saw the river that bears his name. The intrepid Overlanders, the same group who left their name to

---

SPENCES BRIDGE TO NICOAMEN CONFLUENCE
Difficulty: Class 2+
Length: 11 miles (17.6 km)

NICOAMEN CONFLUENCE TO LYTTON
Difficulty: Class 4+
Length: 15 miles (24 km)

Season: May through September
Character: Big-volume river with big rapids

Overlander Falls on the Upper Fraser run described earlier, may have been the first to descend the Thompson using rafts made of lashed timbers, while others in the group floated the Fraser and even ran Hells Gate on the Fraser.

◁ Chilko River (British Columbia)

Draining the east slope of the wet coastal mountains, the Chilko would take its place among the world's great whitewater rivers even if it were not part of a longer river odyssey. When joined with downstream runs on the Chilcotin and Fraser rivers, it combines 140 miles (224 km) of varied whitewater, glacial lakes, forested canyons and valleys, rolling grassland prairies, and desert-like badlands. The combined trip is probably Canada's greatest extended whitewater voyage.

The most impressive part of the journey is on the Chilko, with its turquoise waters pouring through unremittingly difficult rapids, its spectacular scenery, abundant wildlife, and even the Native American fishermen along its banks enjoying the bounty of its massive salmon runs.

Put in at the outflow of Chilko Lake. The lake is more than 1,000 feet (305 m) deep and surrounded by towering mountains holding many of the great glaciers that feed the river. The lake settles out most of the glacial silt, leaving the water azure blue and transparent. The outlet provides a prodigious spawning grounds for sockeye salmon, a fortuity that has saved the Chilko from hydroelectric development.

The first 23 miles (36.8 km) downstream from the lake are easy with a gradient of 20 fpm (3.8 mpk) through woods of Douglas-fir and lodgepole pine. Boaters should be aware of sweepers and the cold glacial water. Just downstream of a farm on the left bank, the road reaches the river. This is the last access upstream of Lava Canyon and gives the option to shuttle around the difficult whitewater and relaunch at the Taseko River conflu-

CHILKO LAKE TO TOP OF LAVA CANYON
Difficulty: Class 2–
Length: 23 miles (36.8 km)

TOP OF LAVA CANYON TO TASEKO CONFLUENCE
Difficulty: Class 5
Length: 17 miles (27.2 km)

TASEKO CONFLUENCE TO CHILCOTIN CONFLUENCE
Difficulty: Class 3–
Length: 12 miles (19.2 km)

Season: June through September
Character: Isolated canyon in scenic wilderness

Chilko River, British Columbia, Canada. *(Dave Manby)*

ence. Another option is to put in on the road bridge on the way up to Taseko Lake and float the smaller, more technical Class 4 Taseko with the Chilko, Chilcotin, and Fraser rivers; this is a 143-mile (229 km) journey free of the trepidation instilled by Lava Canyon.

Those who stay on the Chilko experience the bottom falling out of the river as it roars through Lava Canyon for some 17 miles (27.2 km) of continuous whitewater. True to its name, the vertical-walled canyon has been carved by the river's thundering through basaltic and lava formations. This is an experts-only stretch, especially at high water when the rapids become continuous. Scouting is difficult, and hypothermia and exhaustion prey on swimmers. The first major rapid, Bidwell Falls, is also the most difficult, leading into seemingly endless wave trains including the White Kilometer and the White Mile. The action continues until about 1 mile (1.6 km) above the Taseko confluence. During the few calm moments boaters have time to take in some great scenery, with several side waterfalls and common sightings of bear and bald eagles. The gradient throughout the canyon is about 60 fpm (11.6 mpk). This reach was the site of a tragic rafting accident in 1987 in which five Americans drowned; it was later depicted in the made-for-television movie starring Alan Alda called *The White Mile*, filmed in California.

At the Taseko confluence the ivory, silt-laden waters of the Taseko cloud the transparent waters of the Chilko and double the flow. From here the gradient eases. The river enters a narrow canyon that is tricky at high water, and then opens and the gradient eases further. The Siwash Bridge crosses the Chilko 7 miles (11.2 km) downstream of the Taseko confluence above a rapid called The Gut. As the river joins the Chilcotin the resulting river takes the name Chilcotin, though the Chilko's flow is perhaps ten times larger; apparently early cartographers gave more weight to the Chilcotin's greater length than its size.

Chilcotin River (British Columbia) ➢

The Chilcotin takes its name from the nearby Chilcotin Indians. Chilcotin country is drier than the upstream terrain of the Chilko, but it is still spectacular with wide variations in climate, geology, wildlife, and vegetation.

After 12 miles (19.2 km) of the Chilko River from the last road access to the confluence of the two rivers (see Chilko description above) is the first section of the Chilcotin stretch, from the confluence to Hanceville Bridge. This is a comparatively easy float through and around rolling grassland, Bull Canyon, and Battle Mountain. Upstream of Alexis Bridge the river flattens out as it passes through the Anaheim Indian Reserve and some easy rapids in Stoney Canyon about 6 miles (9.6 km) above the take-out on the left bank below Hanceville Bridge.

The river then leaves the highway behind and enters Hanceville Canyon, the beginning of some more challenging and remote rapids. There is no access until a mile before Farwell Canyon, some 29 miles (46.4 km) downstream. Farwell is particularly tough at lower flows, as emerging rapids can flip even good-sized rafts. There are lots of California bighorn sheep above Farwell Canyon, and the area has been set aside as a sheep reserve.

Good camping can be found below Farwell Canyon, along with good hiking for those with the inclination to explore hoodoos, sand dunes, and wildlife habitats. From Farwell to the Fraser the river is big-volume, ranging up to 20,000 cfs (566 cumecs). The float is easy for the first 7 miles (12 km) before the river narrows again between the cliff walls of Chilcotin Canyon, sometimes called Big John Canyon after river pioneer John

CHILKO-CHILCOTIN CONFLUENCE TO HANCEVILLE BRIDGE
Difficulty: Class 2
Length: 29 miles (46.4 km)

HANCEVILLE BRIDGE TO FARWELL CANYON
Difficulty: Class 3
Length: 29 miles (46.4 km)

FARWELL CANYON TO FRASER CONFLUENCE
Difficulty: Class 4
Length: 12 miles (19 km)

FRASER RIVER, CHILCOTIN-FRASER CONFLUENCE TO GANG RANCH BRIDGE
Difficulty: Class 2
Length: 18 miles (29 km)

Season: April through September
Character: Dry, isolated region

Mikes Sr. Chilcotin Canyon is much tougher, with some Class 4 rapids. A landslide blocked the river here in 1972–73, creating a series of rapids called Railroad.

The canyon walls open again, and after a short stretch the Chilcotin adds its flow to the mighty Fraser. Lack of vehicle access at this point obliges most boaters to continue for 18 easy miles (29 km) to the Gang Ranch Bridge or just upstream at Dog Creek. Gang Ranch is one of the largest cattle ranches in the world, with more than one million acres. There are several abandoned ranches along the river waiting to be explored.

◁ Babine River (British Columbia)

ABOUT 1½ MILES (2.4 KM) DOWNSTREAM OF NILKITKWA LAKE TO KISPIOX INDIAN VILLAGE, UPSTREAM OF HAZELTON, ON THE SKEENA RIVER
Difficulty: Class 4 in the canyon, Class 3 elsewhere
Length: 90 miles (144 km)

Season: May through September
Character: Remote, scenic wilderness run

The Babine River flows through a beautiful wilderness valley which just happens to be North America's most prolific grizzly bear habitat, a fact that justifies its nickname "The River of Grizzlies," given by the native Babine Indians. With more than a hundred grizzlies making their home in the forests along the river corridor, a float here is as good a place as any on the planet to spot the mighty "griz." A particularly good bet is Grizzly Falls during salmon runs as fishing grizzlies occupied with the spawning fish can pose a unique hazard to river runners trying to get through. The Babine was designated a Provincial Park in 1997 and will likely be subject to boating permit requirements.

The Skeena is one of the largest untamed rivers in North America and drains a huge watershed. The name Skeena derives from K'shian, meaning "Water of the Clouds." It supports some of the largest salmon and steelhead populations found anywhere. The salmon are popular not only with river runners and bears but also with natives along the bank using nets. Along the way boaters can visit large, ancient totem poles and the remains of Gitksin villages. This is one of the world's classic wilderness multi-day trips, far enough north to remain untouched yet still within reach of roads and nearby towns.

To get to the put-in, take Route 16, which is the main road to Prince Rupert along the Pacific Coast and the major gateway to Lower Alaska. The best jumping-off spot is the town of Smithers, which has an airport. To get to the put-in go east, then north from Smithers until you get to the final outlet of Babine Lake at the northern end of Nilkitkwa Lake. Put in at the road bridge 1½ miles (2.4 km) downstream of the lake.

The Nilkitkwa River enters on the right 2 miles (3.3 km) downstream of the put-in, and easy rapids continue for 10 to 15 miles (16 to 24 km). Paddlers share this section of the river with jet boats used to reach lodges along the river accessible only by water. The whitewater then picks up to an easy Class 3 with a gradient of 10 fpm (1.9 mpk). Mountains and glaciers to the north provide the backdrop as the river doubles in size, eventually entering the 15-mile (24 km) Kisgegas Canyon, sometimes called the Babine Canyon, near the end of the Babine River. The canyon holds the toughest Class 4 whitewater.

During migrations in September, the river teems with sockeye salmon and steelhead, all bent on ascending Grizzly Falls, normally a Class 4 drop. The rating does not take into consideration any grizzlies found fishing on the rocks here. These bears are universally less predictable and almost always more dangerous than the rapid itself. When rating a rapid one can argue the weight to give to a fishing grizzly. Above all, avoid the tempting route between sow and cub, which will elevate the rating of the run at least a full class. Watch out for moose as well. They, too, are unpredictable and can charge without warning.

Several miles upstream of the Skeena confluence the Babine flows through the Kisgegus Indian Reserve, site of an abandoned Indian village. Smallpox from the missionaries reportedly decimated the locals, leaving the village as a haunting reminder.

As the Babine joins the Skeena the volume triples and becomes a force to be reckoned with, as hydraulics and boils become formidable. Giant cedars and hemlocks adorn the banks, and the glaciers of Mount Thomlinson crown the landscape. Signs of civilization eventually reappear along the shores. The take-out is at the abandoned Indian village of Kispiox. Here are some of the largest and oldest totem poles in the world, standing sentinel to a bygone era. Boaters can also continue downstream to Hazelton.

As with all multi-day rivers, private boaters should coordinate launch days and campsite plans with commercial companies and other private boaters. Campsites can be particularly scarce on the Babine.

Stikine River (British Columbia) ➤

Stikine means "Great River" to the Tlingit Indians, who still live in the coastal area and who historically paddled the Stikine to trade and fish for salmon. This is an ancient river that has run the same general course for some 50 million years while geological forces changed the land along its banks. Volcanic action in the interior left massive lava formations that are still evident in Mount Edziza Provincial Park, known as the "Valley of 10,000 Smokes." Near the headwaters in the Spatsizi Wilderness Park, ice-age glaciers carved and rounded the lower parts of the valley but spared the tallest mountains above 6,000 feet (1,830 m), which remain jagged. Gradual forces uplifted the Stikine Plateau and the Coast Mountains, but never fast enough to offset the erosive powers of the river. As a result, the Stikine slices dramatically through the Plateau at the Grand Canyon of the Stikine and the sheer 10,000-foot (3,050 m) peaks in the Coast Range.

For boating purposes, the Stikine is two very different rivers above and below the late-nineteenth-century boomtown of Telegraph Creek. Just upstream is the Grand

GRAND CANYON OF THE STIKINE, CASSIAR HIGHWAY (ROUTE 37) TO TAHLTAN RIVER UPSTREAM OF TELEGRAM LAKE
Difficulty: Class 5+ below 12,000 cfs (340 cumecs), Class 6 at other times
Length: 60 miles (96 km)

TAHLTAN RIVER TO WRANGELL (LOWER STIKINE)
Difficulty: Class 1
Length: 150 miles (235 km)

Season: August, September
Character: Grand Canyon is a difficult, remote, big-volume canyon run; lower Stikine is a flat, scenic paddle

Stikine River, "Great Glacier." *(John Muir/Alaska Vistas)*

Lower Stikine River, Alaska. *(Alaska Vistas)*

Canyon, one of the toughest runs in the world. Downstream is a scenic, easy float. Until recently the world could only reach Telegraph Creek by steamboat. In bygone days it was used to access and supply gold fields. John Muir visited the river he penned as the "Stickeen" between Telegraph Creek and the Pacific in 1879 and designated it a "Yosemite 100 miles long." Never a man prone to understatement, Muir somehow overlooked 50 miles (80 km) of the river. This lower stretch is so flat that sea kayaks are a good paddling choice, although large canoes are sometimes used. The scenery is fine, and boaters may even run into seals chasing salmon as many as 100 miles (160 km) or more inland, as they do in many other Northwestern coastal rivers.

The lower Stikine flows past some spectacular glaciers, most of which have been retreating in modern times. In Muir's time the Great Glacier and the Choquette Glacier on opposite sides of the river were perhaps half a mile apart. Indian legend recalls a time when the two glaciers collided, creating a massive ice bridge across the river. Indians traveling downstream often floated probes through the flow. Legend is told of old women volunteering to float beneath the ice in an act of sacrifice surrounded by much ceremony. If the women ultimately emerged safely on the other side, the leaders judged the route safe.

While much can be said for the scenery, wildlife, and hot springs on the lower section, the real whitewater action is upstream in the Grand Canyon of the Stikine. This is a stretch many of the top river runners in the world rank as the most difficult large-volume whitewater trip in the world. Parts of the canyon are so steep that none of the five varieties of coastal salmon can navigate it to spawn. Although the overall gradient in the canyon is only about 45 fpm (8.7 mpk), the flow is so powerful that the canyon stays ice-free year-round.

In fact, water volume is a big problem. Most of the year there is simply too much water to consider this run. Even the most accomplished boaters wait for the lowest possible levels, usually in August or September, so they have the best chance to scout or portage the big drops. Low flows also expose the best river-level campsites, as there are few at higher flows. This is a self-contained expedition trip of the highest order, with top skills, light gear, and emergency equipment a priority.

The only facet of the Grand Canyon of the Stikine that isn't tough is the access. Unlike other wilderness classics such as the Alsek, Susitna, and Landsborough rivers, boaters can drive to both the put-in on the Route 37 bridge and the take-out just upstream of Telegraph Creek.

The action begins as the river narrows not far downstream of the put-in. Giant sedimentary and sandstone cliffs rise above granite walls at the bottom of the canyon in turn above lava and basalt formations near the water level. Entry Falls, the first of many difficult rapids, provides fair warning to those who come to challenge the canyon. Downstream are other monsters including Wasson's Hole, Site Zed, and Garden of the Gods. Wasson's Hole was the site of a near-tragic swim filmed on the partial first descent in 1981. Site Zed is just downstream of shacks left over from work at a potential dam site of the same name. Inside is an old chalkboard to which river runners can add their names to a list of those who come before. The last difficult stretch ends with the Tanzilla Narrows about two-thirds of the way down the run. Here the river squeezes between canyon walls to a width of about 6 feet (1.8 m). After the Narrows the rapids ease, but the Stikine stays in the canyon. The rough road from Telegraph Creek to the Steward-Cassiar Highway provides access where the Tahltan River joins the Stikine.

The Grand Canyon of the Stikine was loath to give up its unrunnable reputation. An ABC camera crew assisted in the partial first descent in 1981 as helicopters carried the kayakers down much of the canyon in order to film a closing shot at the Tanzilla Narrows. The first full descent was by Bob Lesser, Lars Holbek, and Bob McDougall in 1985 along with a raft crew. Later a rafting expedition was caught in high water, resulting in a rescue. In 1992, Montanan Doug Ammons kayaked the canyon solo.

The canyon area is the native ground of the Tahltan Indians who led a fight in the 1970s to save the canyon from inundation under a series of five proposed dams. Although most of the upper Stikine drainage is now protected, timber interests, minerals claims, and hydroelectric power may still press for development of the area's many resources in the future.

Nahanni River (Northwest Territories) ➢

The Nahanni River, sometimes referred to as the South Nahanni, was the first area in the world designated as a United Nations World Heritage site. The name means "people from far away," referring to the Nahanni Indians who traveled west across the Great Divide to hunt and trap in the 1700s. This remote wilderness river, often called "the greatest canoe trip in the world," features an inspiring landscape; a haunted and storied past; impressive geothermal formations; and Virginia Falls, an eye-popping 300-foot (92 m) drop every bit as spectacular as Niagara or Victoria Falls. Much of the river is within the

MOOSE PONDS TO NAHANNI BUTTE AT LAIRD RIVER CONFLUENCE (BLACKSTONE LANDING IS DOWNSTREAM ON THE LAIRD)
Difficulty: Class 2, Class 3– above Little Nahanni

(continued on following page)

Length: 210 miles (336 km); 140 miles (224 km) from Rabbit Kettle Lake put-in

Season: June through August

Character: Classic wilderness canoe run in remote area

remote Nahanni National Park, so boaters usually have to share this area only with beaver, caribou, bear, wolf, and moose.

Like the Stikine, the Nahanni is an ancient river which maintained its west-to-east coarse by eroding and downcutting its streambed faster than the Mackenzie Mountains could rise during the Paleozoic era. The massive glaciation of the Pleistocene era spared a part of the Nahanni, leaving a series of narrower canyons between the broad U-shaped glacial valleys above Virginia Falls and farther downstream.

The watershed of the Nahanni sits among the Saskatchewan, Yukon, and Mackenzie river systems, all great transportation waterways of the Northwest, yet the Nahanni was forgotten among these giants. It remains virtually untouched today and accessible only by boat, plane, or strenuous hike; Nahanni National Park is completely roadless. Even Native American tribes chose not to settle here but came only seasonally to hunt or later to escape pressures from white settlers or other tribes.

Loneliness has bestowed on the Nahanni many legends. In the early 1900s Charlie and Willie McLeod came to the valley to prospect for gold. Their bodies were later found apparently beheaded. An early adventurer named Shebbach was found starving inside his cabin on which a sign read "dead man inside." These ghosts from the past have given the Nahanni names like Dead Man Valley, Headless Range, and Murder Creek. The lore of the Nahanni flourished when R. M. Patterson explored the river in the 1920s and chronicled his adventures in the classic canoe work, *Dangerous River*.

Although the Nahanni is navigable in just about any whitewater boat, it is most closely associated with the canoe, which is ideal for carrying gear and paddling slower

Two Southern boys stand at the edge of a canyon above the Arctic Circle plotting a zigzag, eddy-hopping run in eggshell fiberglass canoes through Bloody Falls on the Coppermine River in Northwest Territories. Thirty thousand cubic feet per second of fast, frigid water piles into a rock wall, preceded by standing waves, ledges, holes, and no previously successful runs, according to the local authorities. To this day, I question whether ours was a first descent. The run looked like a piece of cake for a kayak, but for an open canoe, the speed of the water alone made it an immense challenge. A swim would be long, perhaps fatal.

It was 1979, the days of all-out, gonzo paddling trips in the spirit of Hunter S. Thompson. The days before wives, kids, and IRAs. Ron Muller and I had quit our jobs, sold our houses, and left our girlfriends to the challenges from other suitors to spend the summer paddling in Canada. Ike was the third, driving us in his cranky Volvo 3,000 miles from Columbus, Georgia, to Yellowknife in the Northwest Territories, which for all practical purposes was the edge of the blinking earth. En route, we met burned-out pioneers heading south, retreating from a life half spent in darkness on this modern-day frontier.

The 400-mile paddle from the headwaters of the Coppermine to the Arctic Ocean was the final fete before our return to reality. We had been looking for the most extreme trip for the longest possible duration that could be accomplished in open canoes with no portaging. The selection process was complicated: look at map, point, grunt affirmatively. The famed chimpanzee selection process really worked. The extreme nature of the location was confirmed as we circled above mostly frozen Lac de Gras in a twin-engine Otter on July 10th looking for an open place to land among the ice floes. (continued next page)

sections. Particularly popular is a 30-foot (9.2 m) wooden canoe that can be broken down into three pieces for air transportation and for the Virginia Falls portage.

To reach the put-in, most boaters charter a plane at Fort Simpson, Watson Lake, or Fort Nelson. If running your own trip, it is a good idea to let the park superintendent at Fort Simpson know beforehand. The river between the put-in at Moose Ponds and the Little Nahanni confluence is relatively small and technical as it makes its way through a series of mountain meadows. There are some good Class 3– rapids in this stretch.

After the Little Nahanni confluence, the rapids ease and the river begins to build in volume. Many boaters put in farther downstream, flying into Rabbit Kettle Lake for an easy ½-mile (0.8 km) carry through the woods to a put-in above the confluence of the Rabbit Kettle River on the right. As with many other rivers in the great Northwest, you will find yourself walking on a cushion of mosses and an implausible variety of mushrooms. From the confluence of Rabbit Kettle River, it is a difficult 2-mile (3.2 km) hike up the tributary to Rabbit Kettle Hot Springs, an impressive layered formation of calcium carbonate. Rabbit Kettle Falls has crystal pools at the top of two imposing mounds some 90 feet (27.5 m) high. From here downstream, the river is in the national park.

The easy float continues downstream as the Sunblood Mountains eventually appear to the left. As the current begins to quicken, the roar of Virginia Falls becomes audible. Boaters hug the right shore to find the mile-long (1.6 km) Albert Faille Portage Trail. The falls area is popular for camping and laying over, and boaters usually have plenty of time to scout the big drop. Below the trailhead the river bends and drops into a series of rapids with most of the water moving to the left, leaving the right side littered with piles of logs.

There was nothing so remarkable about us really except for our Southern accents north of the Arctic Circle. The most remarkable phenomenon was the transformation that occurred on the trip: a release from all the usual bonds of civilization. A deep appreciation developed for a shard of the planet that man had not conquered—a revelation from the observations of the abundant wildlife that thrived despite the austere, Arctic ecology. The few glorious weeks of Arctic summer are protected from all-out tourism by legions of blood-sucking, winged insects that form a visible plume in the wind behind all bodily functions. The solitude and detachment from civilization, though not absolute anywhere on a planet with an atmosphere that supports winged aircraft, was ample.

All the layers of conditioning about how we should spend our lives delaminated in those two months. I realized it one evening while camping in an esker on an island in midriver as a flight of ducks whistled by just above my head, tilting from side to side as they flew into the sunset. The release from the psychology of deferred gratification was complete. I spent the next year living mostly in the wild and near wild places. It freed me to pursue only those endeavors for which there was a sincere personal commitment. On the eve of my fiftieth year, the energy given to my life is still with me. And so is my tolerance for civilization, granted in part by the knowledge that another Arctic adventure awaits me someday.

—David Brown

The entire river then plummets some 300 feet (91.5 m), much of it crashing into a massive limestone steeple that takes the brunt of the current and splits it in half. The portage trail is a scenic path, much of it along an older riverbed. Those with sharp eyes can find several species of orchid here.

Below the falls the river passes through a series of four canyons numbered in an order based on upstream travel. Aside from some Class 2 whitewater in the fourth canyon it is an easy float as the river drifts between limestone walls. The most difficult rapid is Hells Gate, also called Figure Eight, between the fourth and third canyons where the current piles into a cliff wall and splits into two eddys. Canoeists may elect to portage on the right bank. Downstream of the last canyon is Klaus Hot Springs, a popular stop. After drifting through open country the river splits into many channels before reaching Nahanni Butte Indian Village where most boaters take out.

A word of warning: as in many other Northwest Territories and Alaskan rivers, biting flies and mosquitoes can be a problem in the lower reaches, especially early in the season. Coverage, netting, and repellents are a good idea.

Mexico

$\mathcal{M}$exico has fine beaches, Aztec and Mayan ruins, and great native cuisine, and it considers its tourism industry a major success in its struggle from third-world obscurity to economic respectability. Although the coastal areas have drawn visitors for years, Mexico's exotic whitewater is a well-kept secret. On a trip to Veracruz we shared a shuttle with managers for the national airlines. They were on a mission to find new and different activities to draw tourists. One way or another, it is likely the rivers of Mexico will not be overlooked much longer.

Like most Latin American countries, Mexico is only slowly learning to understand and appreciate whitewater. In fact, we can find no Spanish equivalent for the term "whitewater," although *rapidos* will do in a fix. Over the last few years the locals have established a river-running community, and private boaters often organize into clubs overseen by the Federacion Mexicana de Dencenco de Rios. Most of these boaters hail from Mexico City, the "Big Enchilada," the world's largest city. Yet much of the river running is still done by "gringos" who realize great river adventures can start much closer to home than Chile or Costa Rica.

The boaters of Mexico should be proud. Their country is laced with off-season whitewater opportunities ranging from one-day trips near Veracruz to exotic multi-day trips on such rivers as the Santa Maria and the Usumacinta. Although the roads are not as good as those of more developed countries, nearly all the rivers have decent access.

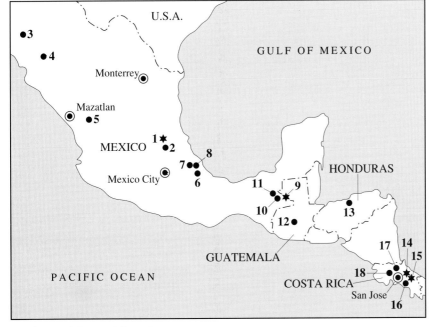

1 Rio Santa Maria (see page 145)
2 Rio Moctezuma
3 Rio Yaqui
4 Rio Urique
5 Rio Mezquital
6 Rio Antigua
7 Rio Actopan
8 Rio Filo-Bobos
9 Rio Usumacinta (see page 156)
10 Rio Jatate
11 Agua Azul and Shumulja
12 Rio Cahabon
13 Rio Cangrejal
14 Rio Reventazon (see page 164)
15 Rio Pacuare (see page 164)
16 Rio General
17 Rio Sarapiqui
18 Rio Corobici

Mexico and Central America

The locals usually show river runners the fun-loving hospitality that seems inherent in the Mexican soul.

Not only are many of Mexico's rivers flush with whitewater, they serve as a unique road to explore its past. Before Columbus and Cortez, natives built elaborate civilizations in and around the highlands of Mexico City, and in the tropical lowlands of Veracruz and the Yucatan peninsula to the east. This was the cultural center of North America, and it is estimated that some twenty million people lived here while less than a million lived in what is now the United States. Pyramids and other surviving ruins on the Usumacinta and Filo rivers testify to their advanced architecture, irrigation, and government. Other fascinating indigenous populations survive to this day. River runners are in a unique position to enjoy the Yaquis and the Tarahumaras whose cultures surround the Yaqui and Urique rivers, respectively.

The north of Mexico is dry, but the south gets plenty of rain. The wet season begins in June and lasts until September or as late as December in the extreme south. The Rockies take the name of the Sierra Madres in Mexico, and the highlands are divided into the Sierra Madre Occidental on the west and Sierra Madre Oriental on the east. Most of the storm fronts come from the Caribbean, so the eastern slope of the mountains, including Veracruz and Chiapas, have plenty of rainfall and a lush tropical habitat. Volcanoes ring the central highlands, some reaching nearly 19,000 feet (5,800 m).

Mexico is also home to the finest travertine streams in the world. Here the rains dissolve limestone and carry it through underground passages; it then percolates back to the surface, forming spectacular azure pools and dazzling falls. Those who hike Havasu Canyon in the Grand Canyon of the Colorado River see a smaller version of what can be found on a truly mammoth and blissful scale in Mexico.

Presently only a few rivers, including the Santa Maria, Antigua, Actopan, Jatate, and Usumacinta, are run commercially. Accurate maps and information have been scarce in the past, so be sure to obtain the newest maps and information you can.

Sierra Madre

◄ Rio Santa Maria

JALPAN–RIO VERDE HIGHWAY TO
OJO CALIENTE
Difficulty: Class 5p
Length: 43 miles (68.8 km)

LA BOQUILLA (OR OJO CALIENTE)
TO ROUTE 85
Difficulty: Class 4p
Length: 45 miles (72 km)

Season: September to April
(come after December to
avoid portage at Tamul
Falls)
Character: An exotic river
not far from United
States

The Santa Maria could be considered to be the definitive river trip of Mexico. Its beautiful clear blue waters course through a series of distinct limestone canyons filled with countless springs, caves, and profuse travertine throughout. At times the river even passes underground for a short time only to reemerge. The natural beauty reaches its zenith at Cascada de Tamul (Tamul Falls), as resplendent a sight as can be found on any river. Here the turquoise waters of Rio Gallinas drop more than 300 feet (90 m) into the Rio Santa Maria, turning the canyon into a curtain of water, mist, and rainbows. Such is the force of Tamul's hurricane-like winds that it's impossible to paddle under them at higher flows. Only after the rainy season at low flows can boats make it through.

The Santa Maria is born in the north-central highlands of Mexico and flows east through predominantly limestone formations. The runnable reaches are in the state of San Luis Potosi, far enough south to escape the cold, dry climate of northern Mexico, yet only a day-and-a-half drive from the Texas border. Ironically, the river gets little attention from the boaters of Mexico City due to the tedious mountain roads linking it to the capital.

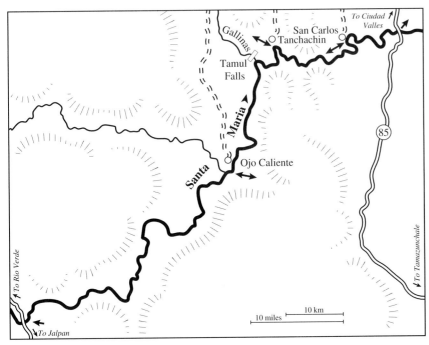

Rio Santa Maria (Mexico)

The Polish group Canoandes was probably the first to run the Santa Maria in 1979. Equipped with an Eastern Bloc military truck and outdated boats, this was but one of many impressive feats by this unlikely crew of university students from Krakow. Kayakers from the United States followed in the mid-1980s, and word of the river's wonders soon spread.

The first 43 miles (68.8 km) from Jalpan–Rio Verde highway near the town of Conca to Ojo Caliente and the Rio Verde include the first two canyons, both filled with several tough, boulder-congested rapids. This stretch requires expedition-style boating. As more than a dozen rapids are unrunnable, most boaters pass on this portage fiesta and concentrate on the more hospitable downstream canyons.

To run the lower sections, put in just below the Rio Verde confluence near the village of La Boquilla. Reach the river either at a gauging station upstream of La Boquilla or with permission of the owner of a private ranch, Ojo Caliente. The owner has been friendly to boaters in the past.

Downstream of here the river often takes the name Tampoan. A long one-day trip of about 18 miles (28.8 km) from Ojo Caliente past Tamul Falls and on to Tanchachin involves running the third and fourth canyons and portaging a few boulder-choked rapids, the biggest of which are Triple Falls near the entrance of the fourth canyon and Tamul Falls farther down the canyon. If flows are too high, boaters must portage Tamul. This entails a tough climb on a small path up the canyon wall upstream of the waterfall, crossing the Gallinas River and descending back down to the canyon bottom. Some commercial operators put in on the Gallinas and portage down to the Santa Maria below. Hard-boaters have the option to put in at Tanchachin and paddle upstream to witness the falls—tough, but worth the effort.

Not far below Tanchachin the river enters a short fifth canyon, Canyon Tampoan, with many technical but runnable rapids. Be sure to portage the extraordinary Puente de Dios (Bridge of God) near the end of the canyon where the river disappears underground for some 200 yards (180 m). From here it is 7 miles (11.2 km) of whitewater until the canyon walls open and access is possible via a dirt road from Route 70. If access is unavailable here, boaters can continue another 8 miles (12.8 km) to San Carlos or an additional 12 miles of flatwater to Route 85.

The overall gradient of the entire river is 20 fpm (3.9 mpk) but is much steeper in the upper canyons. Scouting can be onerous, and mishaps either on or off the river are perilous considering the limited prospect of rescue. Flows can vary greatly, and high flows can be very dangerous. Allow at least a day for each canyon and additional time if Tamul Falls must be portaged (generally mandatory for flows above zero on the Gallinas gauge).

While in the area, check out the Micos on the Rio El Salto (River of the Waterfalls) north of Ciudad Valles, 11.2 miles (18 km) off the Santa Maria shuttle road (Route 70). Seven of the nine travertine drops are considered runnable and range from 5 to 25 feet (1.5 to 7.6 m). Boaters have their choice of routes on most falls as the river drops 131 feet in a third of a mile (40 m in .5 km).

◁ Rio Moctezuma

RIO EXTORAX (ALSO KNOWN AS THE SANTA CLARA) TO PISA FLORES
Difficulty: Class 5
Length: 45 miles (72 km)

PISA FLORES TO TAMAZUNCHALE (LOWER STRETCH)
Difficulty: Class 3
Length: 30 miles (48 km)

Season: October to April
Character: Dam-controlled, isolated canyon; poor water quality

The Rio Moctezuma is a large river that drains the dry central highlands north of Mexico City before dropping off the Central Plateau to the northeast and into the rainforest. On its way it cuts through the southern spine of the Sierra Madre Orientals and passes through the states of Hidalgo, Queretaro, and San Luis Potosi. It drops nearly a mile (1.6 km) in elevation before emptying into the Rio Panuco and the Gulf of Mexico near Tampico. The Moctezuma is sometimes called the "River of Magic Pools" for the many springs and travertine pools along its banks.

The river is named for the celebrated Aztec leader (also known as Montezuma) who floated a boat full of gold down the river that bears his name to keep it from Cortez. It is no surprise that the gilded cargo was never seen again, considering the ruggedness of the uppermost canyons. The modern river explorers who first descended the Moctezuma in the 1980s probably couldn't help but be a bit disappointed not to stumble upon the treasure, but they did uncover an elaborately eroded limestone terrain and the maze of sink holes, underground rivers, and caves along the river. The lower reaches are home to one of the most congenial indigenous cultures in North America, the Huasteco Indians, long culturally separated from the Mayans from whom they descended.

The flow on the sections described here is controlled by upstream dams on the Moctezuma and its tributary, the Tula. Much of the water comes from reservoirs near Mexico City and has been polluted in the past. Fluctuating flows and poor water quality have limited boater traffic on the Moctezuma in recent years, and current information on the river is scarce.

Exploration of the upper reaches of the Moctezuma began before the construction of the newest upstream dam which dewatered the uppermost canyons. These trips involved many portages in three exceedingly demanding and boulder-clogged canyons. One portage requires a 40-foot (12 m) "leap of faith" into the river after heaving in boat and gear over the drop. The first group to run the river in the mid-1980s ran out of food days before reaching the take-out.

A new dam at the entrance to the uppermost canyon near Zinopan is now in place. Although some pollution settles out at the dam, water quality remains poor. A diversion to turbines 25 miles (40 km) below the dam at Los Adjuntos effectively dewaters the uppermost section. Boating the 40 miles (64 km) of difficult rapids below Los Adjuntos to Mizacinta is possible, but eight-hour releases create significant timing problems after the first day. Water from springs and side streams ease this problem for the next 30 miles (48 km) downstream of Mizacinta.

The featured reach described here, from the Rio Extorax (also known as Santa Clara) confluence to Tamazunchale, makes for a more hospitable adventure. Below Rio Extorax are some tough rapids and a gradient of about 30 fpm (5.8 mpk), easing to half that above Pisa Flores ("a walk through the flowers"). Another option is to put in after a 5-mile (8 km) hike from Puerta de Naranjas ("Port of the Oranges"). A primitive road meets the river at Pisa Flores. Below here the rapids are no more than Class 3.

For most of this run the river makes its way through tropical rainforest, steeply sloped farmland, and small remote villages. The Huasteco Indians grow corn, oranges, and sugar cane along the river and can also be seen in temporary camps along the banks herding stock or tending to wooden fishing baskets positioned in the river to catch fish. Many Huastecs do not even speak Spanish, but they are blessed with inquisitive children who find river runners a source of much excitement.

Side hikes through the rainforest or to waterfalls and plunge pools on side streams are a good diversion. The best known are the Magic Pools in the lower stretch.

Rio Yaqui ➤

The Yaqui, Mexico's northernmost river, winds its way through the hills of central Sonora, flowing westward to the Sea of Cortez. With its proximity to the United States, and good access along recently constructed roads and dam-controlled flows, it has all the usual requisites for an engaging off-season destination. Yet, the biggest allure of the Yaqui is its exotic high-desert drainage. The river's headwaters are at a lofty 10,000 feet (3,050 m), and the river wanders through the land of the Yaqui Indians and Carlos Casteneda's mythical Yaqui teacher, Don Juan. Although Don Juan may be concocted, the Yaquis are genuine, with a reputation for independence and a long history of resistance from the government.

The put-in is about 100 miles (160 km) east of Hermosillo, 4 miles (6.4 km) downstream of El Novillo Reservoir. The dam usually provides regular releases, except on Sundays and holidays during the dry season when releases are undependable. With an overall gradient of less than 10 fpm (1.9 mpk), the rapids are easy.

The one-day reach from Solarlpa to Soyopa begins in a scenic canyon, with some curious desert flora including strangler fig and tree cactus. The canyon has some good side hikes, and osprey and other birds will entertain birdwatchers. The canyon then opens to the rolling hills and the Sonoran plains, with kaypoc trees, bear grass, and signs of civilization, both past and present. Thorn junkies can check out a unique thorn forest where colonies of ants make their homes in the black thorn acacia. Common sights include turtles, white-tailed deer, and the usual suspects of the small-mammal variety including badgers, coyotes, and raccoons.

The river below Soyopa is mostly open flatwater, but the trip can be worthwhile for

SOLARLPA TO SOYOPA
Difficulty: Class 2+
Length: 16 miles (25.6 km)

SOYOPA TO OBREGON RESERVOIR
Difficulty: Class 1+
Length: 100+ miles (160+ km)

Season: Dam-releases year-round, but not recommended in hot summer months
Character: Dry area just south of Arizona

those looking for a multi-day desert experience. The Yaqui then flows into Obregon Reservoir, the lifeblood of the bountiful and heavily irrigated Yaqui Valley.

◁ Rio Urique

The Rio Urique rises on the plateau of the Sierra Madre Occidental west of Chihuahua, Mexico. Urique means "canyon" in the tongue of the Tarahumara Indians, the exotic natives who inhabit the majestic gorges around this river. The Urique flows at the bottom of one of the most beautiful canyons in North America, Barranca del Cobre ("Copper Canyon"), long a source of temptation and some frustration for river runners. Barranca del Cobre is about 6,000 feet (1,830 m) deep, roughly 1,000 (305 m) feet deeper than the Grand Canyon. Unlike the Grand Canyon, it is V shaped, not terraced, and the paths are steeper and fainter. Unfortunately, the flows are much skimpier, rarely large enough to clear boulder jams formed by side creeks, making for tough going in many places. Barranca del Cobre is just part of a 900-mile (1,440 km) complex of seemingly bottomless gorges laced with spectacular waterfalls where several rivers cut through a plateau of ancient uplifted volcanic flows.

If the allure of natural beauty is not enough, man has made a few contributions. The preferred mode of access is the Chihuahua al Pacifico Railway, an antique splendor which took over 100 years to complete. The railroad reaches the Pacific at Topolobampo, linking it across some 600 miles (1,000 km) to Chihuahua, the capital of Mexico's largest state. The take-out at Agua Caliente is about 100 miles (160 km) east of Topolobampo. The ride is unforgettable, rising 8,000 feet (2,440 m) from sea level, nearly all of it in a 22-mile section that took 20 years to complete.

The Tarahumaras are masters of distance running, and their messengers are known to have negotiated stretches of rough terrain in near world-class times. They guard and preserve their customs and ceremonies, and stage colorful festivals of body painting and dancing. The Tarahumaras celebrate life by playing hand-made violins, an art apparently learned from the Spanish centuries ago.

The history of river exploration begins as early as the 1960s, and the final chapter is yet to be written. Most of the early ventures focused on the stretch from Carmen Bridge downstream to the town of Urique, a spectacularly beautiful area. However, a steep gradient of over 100 fpm (19 mpk) makes this an ordeal to navigate. This stretch can be shortened by putting in after hiking down to the river from El Divisadero. However, the hike is onerous, and several difficult stretches of river remain to be run between El Divisidero and Urique. Some success has been reported using inflatable kayaks. Boogie boards and even inflated river mats with camping gear attached are low-water options.

A good way to see much of the beauty of this area by boat is to put in at Urique using road access from the railroad at Bahuichivo through Cerocahui. This area has some of the best vistas in the region. The first few days of this stretch are in a deep canyon with a gradient of 50 fpm (9.7 mpk) and the rapids generally Class 4. About 10 miles (16 km) below the put-in, boaters must negotiate a lengthy portage at Dos Arroyas. As the Rio Verde joins the Urique the gradient eases to 25 fpm (4.8 mpk) and the river is known as the Rio Fuerte. Take out at Agua Caliente where the river meets the railroad.

A word of caution throughout western Mexico: Marijuana cultivation is not uncommon, and harvests unfortunately often coincide with peak flows. Growers may be armed and suspicious of boaters, making side hikes risky.

Rio Mezquital ➤

River explorers with the bent and mettle to take on an extremely lengthy, difficult, and mostly unknown river need not fritter away tens of thousands of dollars trotting around the globe. The Mezquital, known downstream as the San Pedro, is a prize only a few hundred miles from the U.S. border near the readily accessed tourist city of Mazatlan. It is a river so overlooked that we have little guidance to give readers who may wish to run it.

The Rio Mezquital starts in the dry central highlands near Durango and heads south, descending into the rainforest near Ruiz. The stretch of water between the put-in and the take-out is so remote and rugged that the locals at the bottom call the river by a different name, the San Pedro.

Exploration of the Mesquital has been minimal. An aborted first descent ended in tragedy as expert kayaker Steve Daniels lost both legs as a result of an accident. The river has since been successfully run. It is known that the most difficult whitewater is in the first 80 miles (128 km) where the overall gradient exceeds 100 fpm (19 mpk). Many rapids are made of huge boulders, requiring some tough portages. At high flows the river would be potentially very dangerous. After the first 80 miles (128 km) the difficulty then eases, especially for the last half of the trip with a gradient of about 10 fpm (1.9 mpk).

Mezquital to El Venado
Difficulty: Class 5+
Length: 250 miles (400 km)

Season: October through December
Character: Wild and unexplored, difficult

Veracruz Region

The Veracruz region is rich in history, bustling with activity, and crossed by fine rivers. The city of Veracruz is Mexico's largest port, and the region is the fruit basket of Mexico, with bananas, limes, oranges, pineapples, mangoes, and papayas, as well as coffee and spices grown in abundance. The people are warm and friendly, and the area is well known for great seafood dishes.

The geology and topography provide for fine whitewater. Much of the area is situated on the high Central Plateau and a volcanic band that stretches across Mexico almost to the Gulf of Mexico. The high country is dotted with active and extinct volcanoes, including Orizaba, North America's third highest peak. The plateau drops dramatically into the lush eastern coast, and the resulting small river drainages provide steep, delightful rivers.

Rio Antigua ➤

Hernan Cortez landed near the Rio Antigua in 1519 to set up a permanent settlement and launch his conquest of the Aztecs. The sad history of what happened might have been avoided if he had only been looking for a fine whitewater river instead of gold.

The Antigua begins on the snowy upper slopes of volcanic Pico de Orizaba, then drops 18,700 feet (5,700 m) in just 100 miles (160 km), providing some of Mexico's most consistently challenging paddling. It is also the meeting ground for Mexico's whitewater community, centered around the town of Jalcomulco.

Like many Latin American rivers, this one goes by different names in different regions. The upper stretch is often called Los Pescados. Near the town of Jalcomulco it sometimes takes on the name of the town. Only near the bottom is it always called the

Barranca Grande to Puente Pescados (Barranca Grande section)
Difficulty: Class 5
Length: 20 miles (32 km)

Puente Pescados to Jalcomulco (Pescados section)
Difficulty: Class 4+
Length: 6 miles (9.6 km)

(continued on page 151)

Pescados-Antigua River (Mexico). *(Veraventuras)*

All right, so I was out of shape. And at forty-eight, a bit past my prime in river-running ability. Blame it on aging, lack of exercise, business demands, and fatherhood. I was float-ing along in the land that has all the appearances of our definition of paradise—tropical, lush, wild rivers, high mountains, and exotic native people. More specifically, I was on the Rio Antigua, in a rainforest, dropping off the east slope of the Sierra Madre Orientals, in the state of Veracruz, Mexico. It was high water (rainy season), and I was clutching the handles on my riverboard (an oversized ocean bodyboard) totally decked out in my body armor (leg guards, swim fins, helmet, webbed gloves, wetsuit, lifejacket), barreling down the river with the other contestants in the open class of the Antigua Whitewater Races.

I entered the races on a riverboard somewhat as a joke. I think riverboards are definitely the biggest kick on the river, but they are not fast racing downriver. Your principal means of power are your legs, aided by swim fins which allow for quick movements but can't compare to the sustained power of a paddle or an oar. On that day the other craft with me were a C-1, several inflatable kayaks, and several full-size rafts. The hard-shell kayak and four-person raft divisions had already left downstream in earlier heats.

The other river runners in my "race" were talking to one another, probably discussing how to run the rapids in this 11-mile stretch of river. Unfortunately, I didn't speak Spanish and the other river runners didn't speak English. The universal form of language, sign lan-guage, would be my only chance.

The best understanding I could get from them was that they wanted me to go first, sort of a live-bait, probe-unit craft. What the hell—big-water rivers like this are really pretty easy on a riverboard, the rocks are well covered, and the riverboard plows (continued next page)

Antigua. Mexican river runners sometimes adopt the local names and may talk of running Rio Antigua in one breath and Rio Pescados in the next.

By any name the river is a gem, set in a lush, exotic tropical valley. It was here that much of the footage of *Romancing the Stone* was filmed. It is also the home of the Banos Carrizal, a commercially developed hot-springs resort awaiting boaters whose weary muscles can enjoy respite from the relentless rapids.

The rapids of the Antigua generally tend to get easier the farther one is downstream. We divide the river into four sections, all of which can be run by raft or kayak.

The Barranca Grande section is narrow and tricky with a steep overall grade of about 100 fpm (19 mpk). Although generally pool-and-drop, many of the rapids are staircase style and continuous with some big holes, boiling waves, and boulder hazards.

The Pescado section drops through a narrow relatively remote gorge with sheer walls. This is a steep, boulder-choked run with huge waves and hydraulics in high water and technical rocky rapids at lower water. Although the overall gradient of 50 fpm (9.7 mpk) is half that of the upstream run, it can be more challenging. Take out at the bridge at Jalcomulco.

The Banos Carrizal section is the most popular run, with a gradient of 40 fpm (7.7 mpk). Most of the big rapids are at the top and bottom of the run, with things easing somewhat in the middle. Take out at the resort, and check out the Olympic-size hot pool as well as a monstrous concrete waterslide structure resembling a swarm of dragons.

JALCOMULCO TO BANOS CARRIZAL (BANOS CARRIZAL SECTION)
Difficulty: Class 4–
Length: 11 miles (17.6 km)

BANOS CARRIZAL TO PUENTE NACIONAL (PUENTE NACIONAL SECTION)
Difficulty: Class 2+
Length: 14 miles (22.4 km)

Season: All year, except after extended dry periods
Character: Popular whitewater river with varied sections

---

through the holes relatively easily. After each rapid I'd turn around and see that another boat or two had dropped out. The C-1 was the last craft to go, but soon it was history, too. About halfway down the run, I started thinking that I was alone.

Soon I realized this was a river through a third-world rainforest-type area that, typically, was slowly being sacrificed to civilization. Locals began to appear everywhere, peering at me in amazement from their yards and fields. They were probably getting used to those bizarrely outfitted river runners (surely to them only; river runners' appearance is mainstream, right?) that went by periodically, but here was a truly alien creature cruising by without even a boat.

People still have this notion that you need to be in a boat to go down a whitewater river. So primitive. As I passed, I usually smiled or waved. They would sometimes smile or wave, but more often they'd just stare or scurry away. Despite the idyllic setting, my mind was still racing: What was in their minds? What did they think of me? What did I think of them? What is the meaning of life? Is Elvis dead? In my head I was composing a new book, Zen and the Art of River Running. Things were getting real heavy. Way before I got to the appendix of the book, I rounded a corner and the river was lined with people, the finish of the race. From a cart that hung from a cable that crossed the river, a boy handed me a flower. I was enchanted. This definitely was not river running in the U.S.A.

The river gods are a moody lot. On this day, however, they shone down brightly on this river runner, even if he was an aging, out-of-shape one.

—Jim Cassady

The Puente Nacional (National Bridge) section begins at the resort or at the low-water dam just downstream. This section is easier, providing good training and a good warm-up for the upper runs. Although the scenery and solitude are not as good as on the upstream runs, the rapids are consistent, with one large rapid. The gradient is 30 fpm (5.8 mpk). The take-out is on a bridge on the "libre" (non-toll) highway to Veracruz. An inexpensive taxi shuttle from nearby Tamarindo is an option.

DESCABEZADERO TO ACTOPAN
Difficulty: Class 3+
Length: 9 miles (14.4 km)

Season: Lava springs
release water year-round
Character: Spring-fed,
runnable at source

◁ Rio Actopan

One might think those responsible for the sign identifying the put-in for the Rio Actopan as Descabezadero ("the beheaded") were trying to ward off boaters. The name more likely derives from use of the area for slaughter of animals or, who knows, perhaps the losing players in pre-Columbian ball games.

This macabre moniker could not be less apt. Descabezadero is a beautiful put-in where layers of ancient lava flow release waterfalls of clear water. Here river runners launch into azure pools and 9 miles (14.4 km) of blissful boating.

To find the river, take the road to the center of the town of Actopan and find the take-out bridge. Boaters can ask for "carretera al rio" ("the road along the river") or even better, try English and ask for the "cement bridge." To get to the put-in, follow the road west to Jalapa (Xalapa) along the north side of the river and look for the Descabezadero sign after a small roadside chapel on the left. A small dirt road leads to a parking area and a short, steep carry to the river. Freefall buffs can run a 20-foot (6.1 m) waterfall off a small diversion structure into the pool, and at some levels lower launches are available. Most, however, carry down to the pool to check the springs that seem to gush from everywhere.

From here down the river has an overall gradient of about 50 fpm (9.7 mpk) but seems steepest at the top. After a paddle around the pool, boaters commit to the first drop and nonstop action. The river is narrow, sometimes hidden and peppered with lava rocks. The crystal current moves swiftly through tropical scenery, with small eddies allowing boaters to gaze in wonder as even more waterfalls tumble in along the way.

The action slows after Villa Nueva, a small settlement about a third of the way down, where road access is available. Parking, camping, and food are available to the right of the steel bridge at "El Zital." Below here the scenery changes to small farms and chayote vines suspended on wire trellises. The rapids are well spaced, with an occasional steep stretch or boulder puzzle. Paddlers have time to take in the splendor and wave to the locals working their crops or bathing in the river.

At low flows a few primitive log bridges appear on the lower half of the river and may require an easy portage. The water only clouds slightly by the time it reaches the take-out. The biggest drop is just above the take-out bridge. The children of Actopan will likely be waiting to help carry kayaks, fold inflatables, load gear, and relieve boaters of a few pesos.

To most travelers, Actopan is best known as the site of one of the best-preserved sixteenth-century Augustinian monasteries in the New World, a sight worth taking in near the take-out.

(River specifications on following page)

◁ Rio Filo–Bobos

The Filo-Bobos river system drains the east slope of the Sierra Madre Orientals near the quaint town of Tlapacoyan. Set in a beautiful jungle area with good whitewater and pre-

Columbian ruins along its banks, it is quickly becoming one of the most popular rivers in Mexico. For all this, the names of the rivers still seem unsettled. Topographical maps show the Filo as the Bobos and the Bobos as the Tomata. Even local usage in the white-water community is disputed. One must accept these things in Veracruz where even the state capital has two spellings (Jalapa and Xalapa).

The river has three distinct runs. The upper Filo runs through a tight, boulder-congested canyon, making the run quite technical. It has a slightly shorter season than the downstream runs. Boaters must also carry about a mile (1.6 km) down a spectacular and steep trail near Zapotitlan to put in. The action starts quickly with a series of four Class 4 rapids. Boaters can also put in about 3 miles (4.8 km) farther upstream at an old bridge near Tatempa. This scenic run is nonstop Class 4 and includes a 12-foot (3.7 m) falls.

A bridge crossing the river between Tlapacoyan and Plan de Arroyos marks the take-out for the upper Filo run and the put-in for the popular main Filo run. Although easier than the upstream run, the main Filo run is still technical, with boulder-filled rapids punctuating calm stretches. The gradient on this run, as well as the downstream Bobos, is about 40–50 fpm (7.7–9.7 mpk) overall.

The river has some good side attractions. On the sedimentary slabs downstream of the first rapid on the right are some fine fossilized nautiloids. A bigger attraction is the ruins, just recently restored and promoted for tourist access. The first site is at the end of a narrow stretch against a long cliff wall on the right where a small trail leads to the larger of the two ruins. This pre-Aztec Totanaca Indian site features pyramids, a central plaza, a ball court, and explanatory signs in three languages.

UPPER FILO, ZAPITITLAN TO TLAPACOYAN BRIDGE
Difficulty: Class 4
Length: 4 miles (6.4 km)

TLAPACOYAN BRIDGE ON THE FILO TO LA PALMILLA ON THE BOBOS
Difficulty: Class 3
Length: 15 miles (24 km)

Season: June through December, often too low other months
Character: Good scenery, pre-Columbian ruins

Filo-Bobos river system (Mexico)

Downstream of here a cliff ridge appears on the left and eventually grows to imposing proportions with bromeliads and delicate waterfalls raining down to the river. The ridge holds back the Rio Bobos until it finally cuts through downstream at El Encanto.

As the towers of the El Encanto power plant appear atop the cliff on the left, a second, smaller set of ruins can be found on the right. A recent flood moved the river's course a short walk away from the site and almost buried a large pyramid. Just downstream of these ruins, and about 1¼ miles (2 km) from the confluence with the Bobos, is a trailhead on the left near a small stream. The trail leads over a low ridge that forms the tongue of land between the Filo and Bobos rivers and is a popular camping area. From here boaters can paddle/carry ½ mile (0.8 km) upstream and into a narrow cataract next to the outflow of the El Encanto power plant. This leads to a spectacular 80-foot (15.5 m) waterfall and pool almost completely encased between cathedral-like stone walls.

This begins the third run of the trip, the Bobos section. After a short float downstream about ¾ mile (1.2 km) the Filo and Bobos join and good rapids continue down to La Palmilla, a village set back from the river on the left. Although the water from the Bobos is sometimes quite clear, it is seasonally defiled with coffee bean shells from upstream processing plants. Apparently the harvest in late fall coincides with the boating season. Such is apparently the environmental toll of affordable coffee.

The largest rapid on the Bobos, El Embudo ("The Funnel"), is about halfway down the river to the take-out. Boaters can also continue another easy 3 miles (4.8 km) to Javier Rojo Gomez.

Chiapas Region

Chiapas is sometimes called the Estado de los Rios ("State of the Rivers"). It boasts the most plentiful and spectacular whitewater in southern Mexico. High precipitation and low latitudes combine for a multitude of little-known off-season runs, with rainforests and travertine the big attractions. This is part of the North American Rainforest, an area that receives 100 inches of rain annually along with snowmelt from 18,000-foot (3,474 m) peaks. Its canyons, jungles, and rivers hold a wealth of whitewater.

Sadly, this wealth has not translated into prosperity for the locals. Chiapas is one of the poorest rural states in Mexico, and poverty was a significant factor in the Zapatista uprising centered near the town of San Cristobal de la Casas in 1994. The threat of armed conflict slowed recreational development of the area's rivers and effectively closed the Jatate for three seasons. There is still a significant military presence in the area, but soldiers are generally helpful and friendly to tourists. Outfitters continue to run trips without problems, but visitors should do their own research, talk to ejido (local commune) chiefs, and be considerate of local customs. It is hoped that stability will return to the region, although, as of early 1998, sporadic violence in the area reminds that this time has not yet come. Stability may also come at a price, as an infusion of government spending to better economic conditions may go to pay for dams to drown some of these great whitewater runs.

Although the Usumacinta was unaffected by the uprising, since 1995 it has suffered its own plague. A band of banditos related to the drug trade prey on boaters in the lower reaches, effectively closing that part of the river.

As in other parts of Mexico, some of the language here descends from the Mayans and often results in two or more spellings for the same river or geographical feature. Suffixes -ja, -xa, and -ha mean "water" and are sometimes used interchangeably. The river on which Agua Azul National Park is set can be referred to as the Yash-ja or Paxil-ha as it goes through the park. This flows into the Shumulja or Shumulha or Xumulja and eventually the Gulf of Mexico. Got it?

Rio Usumacinta (Mexico, Guatemala) ➢

FRONTERA COROZA TO ROUTE 203 BRIDGE AT BOCA DEL CERRO, UPSTREAM OF TENOSIQUE

Difficulty: Class 1+ to Rio Chancala confluence, Class 3– thereafter
Length: 90 miles (144 km)

Season: All year, best January through March
Character: Multi-day jungle-and-archaeology adventure

Translated from Mayan as "River of the Sacred Monkey," the Rio Usumacinta is the largest river in Central America. Along much of its length it marks the border between Mexico and Guatemala. Draining a large area and flowing north, the "Usu" provides a pathway into the heart of La Selva Lacondona, the second largest rainforest in the world. Here a panoply of rainforest trappings awaits boaters under the jungle canopy including mahogany trees, ceibas, unusual palms, and multicolored flowers as well as howler monkeys, jaguars, tapirs, blue herons, toucans, macaws, and parrots. Waterfalls are abundant along the river.

The Usumacinta is also a pathway to a wondrous past, with several ancient Mayan ruins, both on the river at Yaxchilan and Piedras Negras or within easy reach at nearby Palenque and Bonampak. From 200 A.D. to 900 A.D. the river served as the highway connecting the great cities of the Mayans. About three hundred Mayan descendants, the Lacandones, are scattered along the river. "Discovered" only in the 1930s, they live much the way they did a thousand years ago, speaking their native tongue and preserving the Mayan heritage of textile weaving.

The Usumacinta is a big-volume river much of the year. High flows from October to mid-December can reach 200,000 cfs (5,660 cumecs), with low flows in April and May still at least 10,000 cfs (283 cumecs). The off-season flows make for a good winter escape from cold northern climates. It usually takes four to six days to run, and boaters often leave an entire day or more to explore the ruins. Most of the river is an easy float, but don't take this trip lightly, especially at higher water when the rapids of the Gran Canon de San Jose earn special respect and massive whirlpools can appear anywhere.

Access is from the Mexican side, which has the only good road that meets the river. Visitors can fly into Villahermosa, Mexico, and visit the ruins at Palenque on the way to the river. The put-in is at the town of Frontera Corozal, sometimes called Frontera Echeverria. The first 65 miles (104 km) are mostly flatwater, with the rainforests, scenery, and the ruins being the main attractions. The upstream ruins at Yaxchilan on the Mexican side have been restored and are among the most beautiful in Mexico. The downstream ruins, Piedras Negras, on the Guatemalan side are yet to be restored but include unique depictions of human sacrifices. Downstream of Piedras Negras is the most striking falls on the river where the travertine sidestream Bushilja or Bus'ilha ("Smoking Waters") enters.

At about 65 miles (104 km) downstream of the put-in, the Rio Chancala enters on the left and the Usumacinta leaves Guatemala behind and forms the border between the Mexican states of Chiapas and Tabasco. The river drops into the 1,000-foot-deep (305 m) Gran Canon de San Jose, a cataract the Mayans considered the entrance to their underworld. The canyon holds the best whitewater on the river. Boaters should get an early start on this stretch as camping sites are hard to find, especially at high water.

Rio Usumacinta (Mexico, Guatemala)

Those interested in rapids and not ruins have the option of coming into the Usumacinta via the Chancala. It's 22 miles (35.2 km) from the town of Rio Chancala to the confluence with the Usumacinta, with several Class 4 rapids. As one goes downstream the river leaves the open country and slips into the rainforest. The Chancala is a small river and is often too low to run after extended dry periods that are common in February and March.

The canyon opens up just before the take-out at the Route 203 bridge at Boca del Cerro. The Usu eventually flows to the Bay of Campeche in the Gulf of Mexico.

The Usumacinta has withstood the onslaught of human development in the ancient past. More recently, in the late 1980s, an international outcry forced both countries to shelve plans to dam the river. Growth and the need to better economic conditions, however, may bring the dam builders back to the Usumacinta.

Special Note: As of this writing, the Usumacinta cannot be safely run below Yaxchilan. Since 1995, a roving gang of bandits, whose repertoire includes river holdups, has plagued the area, taking advantage of the proximity to the border to avoid arrest. It is hoped that renewed stability in Guatemala and Chiapas will foster a cooperative government effort to eradicate this menace.

Rio Jatate ➤

The Jatate is a travertine-filled tributary of the Lacantun, which is, in turn, a tributary of the Usumacinta. The river begins as a resurgence from a cave system in the mountains near San Cristobal de la Casas. Here we feature the Jatate winding through many small valleys and gorges for some 80 miles (128 km). Its brilliant blue waters swirl through intense jungle and three different canyons, all in the heart of the land of the ancient Mayans.

The first two canyons are flush with travertine as dissolved limestone deposits beget magical blue-green pools that are similar to those of Havasu Creek on the Grand Canyon of the Colorado; here, however, boatable stretches of travertine extend through miles of exotic jungle.

The first canyon of the Jatate is for plucky expert kayakers only. Most boaters take two or three days to allow for a difficult hour-plus portage near the end that combines rock climbing, acrobatics, and a little bit of good fortune. Just downstream is another big drop, Last Hole, which may also be portaged.

After a long flatwater section the second canyon builds enough volume to allow rafts through. The lack of beaches has earned it the name "Canon sin Playas," but it does have plenty of travertine. This stretch is usually also a two- to three-day venture. Leave some time for playing in rapids, taking photos, and hunting for rare campsites.

The third canyon is below La Sultana and the Rio Tezconeja on the right. The travertine is lost here due to dilution from the Tezconeja. It has some very good whitewater but also has a tough portage around a long Class 6 that causes some to pass on this section. Kayakers generally run the first and second canyon and pass on the third below La Sultana. Rafters unable to run the first canyon often combine the second and third canyons for a multi-day run. Boaters can also continue down the Jatate through open country to San Quintin to explore the exotic Laguna Miramar, a 6¼-mile (10 km) hike to a remote tropical paradise.

Below San Quintin is Canon Colorado, a narrow Class 3 cataract with rapids at the entrance and exit and strong hydraulics in between. Below the Canon Colorado the Rio Santo Domingo enters on the right and the river becomes the Lacantun.

A word of caution is appropriate here: The Zapatista uprising interrupted river running on the Jatate from 1994 to 1997, but outfitters such as Ceiba Adventures have resumed exploration and river trips. Turmoil is not the only obstacle. Mexican maps are often inconsistent and confusing. Boaters on the Jatate use different access points, and visitors may wish to hire a competent outfitter or local shuttle driver just to help with logistics. Generally the put-in and take-out are both reached by driving out the road past Jatate Park. The upper canyon put-in is at the Pipe Bridge near Santa Rita or Rancho Zapote. The rafters' put-in, 10 miles (16 km) farther down, is known as either Puente Real

PIPE BRIDGE NEAR SANTA RITA TO SAN QUINTIN
Difficulty: Upper canyon, Class 5+, 4+; lower canyon, Class 4p; Class 2+ thereafter
Length: 80 miles (128 km)

Season: December through April
Character: Exotic travertine river in rainforest; verify information locally

or Puente Santa Cruz. The take-out/put-in between the second and third canyons is the bridge at La Sultana.

⊲ Agua Azul and Shumulja

The Agua Azul ("blue water"), on the Yash-ja river, is likely the most intense and concentrated travertine formation on the planet, with innumerable pools forming a maze of routes and waterfalls ranging in size from small drops to thundering cascades. This 3-mile epiphany of azure colors, fascinating channels, and almost iridescent beauty is set in a jungle-like background of hanging bromilades, palms, and ferns. It has mesmerized sightseers for years and is treated as a national park, although it is technically privately owned by the indigenous Chol Indian ejido cooperative. While nature lovers were dazzled by its almost surrealistic beauty, river runners saw the ultimate challenge, an opportunity to run waterfalls through beautifully sculpted limestone formations. The river eventually falls dramatically into the Shumulja where boaters can enjoy another fine one-day run.

Draining the windward side of the mountains and located at the base of the Yucatan Peninsula, the Yash-ja river begins as an ordinary jungle stream high in the surrounding peaks. The area receives huge amounts of rainfall due to the prevailing winds from the Caribbean, and the river is never short of water even during the dry season. Above the Agua Azul is an underground tributary rising from a limestone-rich cave system where travertine mixes with the waters and then precipitates. Over time it resolidifies over rocks, trees, or anything else it can grab onto. In a steep streambed, it forms magnificent channels, dams, and falls.

For vertically inclined boaters there are literally hundreds of opportunities with several drops over 20 feet (6 m), all but the tallest drop at 80 feet (24.4 m) having been run. Getting to the drops is half the fun, as the travertine formations allow boaters to surf through a maze of channel choices. For the last mile (1.6 km) all the routes converge for a tremendous set of six huge river-wide falls as the river leaves the park. The fifth is the unrunnable falls, and the sixth a 30-foot (9.2 m) plunge directly into the Shumulja.

For those into more restrained exploration of the best travertine in the world, a float down the Shumulja is an option. Nestled in a valley surrounded by mountains and populated by Indians and exotic birds, the Shumulja passes through three short canyons as various tributaries change the color of the water again and again. Eight miles (12.8 km) upstream of Agua Clara, boaters can take in the dazzling spectacle of the Agua Azul (the Yash-ja river) tumbling into the Shumulja river as the falls, sometimes called Balon Ahau (Mayan for "Lord Jaguar"), plunge over the last three drops. Each of the falls are between 40 and 80 feet high and perhaps 200 yards (183 m) across, turning the Shumulja an intense blue-green. Boaters generally spend some time exploring a maze of channels, dikes, and caves and staring in wonderment at the roaring falls and thick mist. Other limestone wonders are found elsewhere along the Shumulja including other spectacular caves, some of which can be explored by kayak.

Agua Azul National Park is located just off the road to the Jatate (Route 199), going south about 40 miles (64 km) from Palenque. The take-out for the Shumulja is at Agua Clara, 36 miles (58 km) south of Palenque on Route 199 and then west half a mile (1 km).

CENTRAL AMERICA

Guatemala

*I*n addition to the Usumacinta, which runs along the border between Mexico and Guatemala (see pages 155–57), Guatemala's wet central highlands hold numerous whitewater runs, but an unstable political situation has kept exploration and development to a minimum. In December 1996 the parties signed a formal peace and amnesty agreement ending thirty-six years of civil war. Some mistrust of the government lingers, and there is a lack of government control in some areas; however, continued peace could mean the rivers of Guatemala will more regularly play host to whitewater adventurers.

Honduras (covered in the following chapter) also has a wet central highland area and plenty of precipitation. Although the military plays a significant role in politics, the government is under civilian rule and moving toward stability. The spirit of exploration causes boaters to wonder if Honduras will eventually offer opportunities similar to Costa Rica. Although it is unlikely that Honduras will match Costa Rica's attention to tourism and preservation of its resources, river pioneers have found many good whitewater runs in the northern as well the western regions of the country. The most notable is the Cangrejal, which is described here.

Rio Cahabon ➤

LANQUIN CAVES TO MAIN HIGHWAY WEST OF EL ESTOR (NEAR CAHABONCITO)
Difficulty: Class 4
Length: 40 miles (64 km)

Season: All year, but best December through April
Character: Lush, tropical

The Cahabon (ka-a-BON) begins in the misty highlands of the rugged Alta Verapez region in Guatemala where much of its flow arises from vast underground springs. Among the inhabitants of these mystical headwaters is the quetzal bird. The iridescent green red-breasted quetzal would be only the size of a robin but for its beautiful, 3-foot (0.9 m) tail feathers. It is not only Guatemala's national symbol but it is the name given to this country's currency. Indian legend has it that in 1524 Tecun Uman, a leader of the Quiche Indians, took on the Spanish at the battle of Llanos del Pinal. Seeing Tecun Uman fall mortally wounded to the ground, a quetzal took pity and lifted the fallen hero from the battlefield, bloodying its breast. From this act the quetzal forever wears the blood of Tecun Uman on its distinctive red breast. The bird is considered by the Indians to be the symbol of heaven's protection.

The waters of the Cahabon usually run crystal clear and green, only getting muddy after the first rains of the season. They tumble through a steep canyon into the heart of Guatemala's cloudforest jungle. Later they emerge to the east in the remote Polochic Valley and empty into scenic Lago Izabal. As in many remote jungle areas, the roads are sometimes in bad condition and shuttles can be very difficult.

Put in on the Rio Lanquin about 4½ miles (7 km) from the town of Lanquin on the road to Coba. The put-in is just downstream from the Cuevas de Lanquin, the caves that are the source of the Lanquin's turquoise waters. The caves are considered by the Indians a sacred entry to the underworld. Most boaters put in below a tough rapid on the Lanquin and enjoy about a 7-mile (11.2 km) float to the confluence with the main Cahabon.

After the first 3 miles (4.8 km) on the Rio Lanquin, the road leaves the river and there are no villages. Native Indians live along the river much as they have for centuries. These descendants of the Mayas speak Keck'chi, one of several Guatemalan tribal languages that predate the arrival of the Spanish.

Several miles upstream on the main Cahabon is Semuc Champey, where the entire river passes through an underground cave rich in travertine. Below the outlet boaters can play on the travertine pools but should avoid the stretch from here to the Lanquin confluence where the river is laced with dangerous falls, undercuts, and sieves.

Downstream from the Lanquin confluence the canyon walls begin to close in and the Cahabon drops into a deep, verdant gorge. The rapids are initially easy, with lots of big waves at most flows and technical water at low flows. However, at about mile 5 (8 km) the Class 4 action picks up in a hurry with technical boulder-laden rapids, often in quick succession, including Rock 'n Roll, Y Entonces, Wrap Rock, and Sacacacca—the latter named by Guatemalan tourists whose backsides had bumped over too many rocks at low water. Just downstream of these rapids is a hot springs called Paraiso (not to be confused with the much larger springs on nearby Lake Izabal). At about mile 15 (24 km) the river passes under a road bridge to the city of Cahabon to the north.

About two-thirds of the way down is Chulac Falls, a 12- to 15-foot drop and a difficult hour-plus portage over a potentially dangerous boulder spree on the right bank. Many boaters arrange a vehicle portage around the falls. The portage road and some diversion tunnels are the remnants of the Chulac Falls hydroelectric project. The project, once stalled by funding and seismic concerns, is now slated to reappear upstream. Beware of the remains of the washed-out bridge at Chulac Falls; it is lodged in rapids just after the canyon entrance, and potentially dangerous at low water.

Below the falls the river drops into another beautiful canyon. Exploration of this lush area can be rewarding. About ½ mile (0.8 km) downstream of Chulac Falls is an incredibly deep cave with a small stream coming out and fine limestone formations. About 1 mile (1.6 km) downstream of the falls on the left is a hot springs and waterfall. The canyon opens up, and the main highway west of El Estor crosses the river about 7 miles (11.2 km) below the falls. Take out here and catch a bus or taxi pickup from Cahaboncita to El Estor. Some cross by motorboat to the north shore of Lake Izabal east of El Estor to enjoy a hot-water waterfall and cave system at El Paraiso farm.

Honduras

Rio Cangrejal ➢

The Cangrejal is set beneath the rugged mountains and spectacular waterfalls of Pico Bonito National Park where Pico Bonita peak rises some 8,000 feet (2440 m) in the Cordillera Nombre de Dios, "Range of the Gods." The river drops from high in the mountains to the beaches of the Caribbean in just about 20 miles (32 km), providing excellent whitewater boating in the lower reaches, arriving at the north-coast oceanside city of La Ceiba.

The river is set in a steep valley with no significant stretches of flatwater between the runs. The water temperature can be downright warm. At most runnable flows it provides constant pool-and-drop action, requiring river runners to negotiate narrow chutes as they weave between granite bedrock boulders. An unobtrusive dirt road follows the river, making shuttles easy. Although rain can cause the levels to fluctuate wildly, the runs are short, so emergency access is never too far away. Thanks to protection of the Cangrejal valley, the slash-and-burn deforestation that plagues much of the region is prohibited here.

Locals divide the river into five runs, referred to as the top, upper, middle, lower, and bottom. We have combined the short top and upper runs. We omit the bottom run which is little more than an alternate flatwater paddle route back to the beaches and hotels of La Ceiba that gets polluted as it reaches town. La Ceiba offers beachfront location and the availability of decent accommodations. It also has an airport, but most boaters arrive at San Pedro Sula to the west and travel by road to La Ceiba.

To get to the river from La Ceiba, take the CA-13 highway east toward Trujillo. The highway crosses the river at Puente Cangrejal about a mile (1.6 km) from town. Turn right (upstream) on the first road after crossing the bridge. The road follows the river and crosses from river left to river right about 8 miles (12.8 km) upstream. About 5½ miles (8.8 km) farther upstream the scenery opens up and the river splits into several tributaries.

The put-in for the top or upper section is the Puente Rio Viejo where the road again crosses the river from left to right about 13.5 miles (21.6 km) upstream of the highway bridge. The top section is tough and steep, with some big drops and possible portages around the many boulder-congested drops. The river drops into a small canyon at the top which gives way to a lush valley. An access point at a soccer field surrounded by thatch huts in the village of El Patal marks the transition to the upper section. Take out just above Puente Las Manges at a small trail at mile 8½ (13.5 km) above the highway bridge. Although the river is a little easier below El Patal, the moves are still tight and paddle routes are often blind.

Below Puente Las Manges is the middle section. The rapids here are even more congested than the upstream sections and eddy hopping becomes even more crucial. The first big rapid is Taco, which has a severe undercut and is often portaged. Farther downstream a 10-foot (3 m) drop announces Subway. Below the drop the river splits into two

PUENTE RIO VIEJO TO PUENTE LAS MANGES (TOP/UPPER SECTION)
Difficulty: Class 5p
Length: 3 miles (4.8 km)

PUENTE LAS MANGES TO BELOW EL NARANJAL (MIDDLE SECTION)
Difficulty: Class 4
Length: 3 miles (4.8 km)

EL NARANJAL TO 2 MILES ABOVE HIGHWAY BRIDGE (LOWER SECTION)
Difficulty: Class 3–
Length: 3.5 miles (5.6 km)

Season: All year; best November through April
Character: Lush, road near, several choices

channels, each with serious undercut hazards. Take out at the access point just downstream from the community of El Naranjal, the put-in for the lower run.

The lower Cangrejal is perhaps the most beautiful stretch as the river drops around huge, rounded boulders. The lower run is the most popular and the only section used for commercial rafting, though it still has several narrow technical drops, mostly at the top of the run. Kayakers here will find much with which to entertain themselves, including surf waves and at least one good ender hole. Take out 2 miles (3.2 km) above the highway bridge.

In November 1998, hurricane Mitch brought unprecedented flooding to the Cangrejal and widespread destruction to the La Ceiba area. River runners should check for resulting changes to access points and to the river itself.

Costa Rica

Costa Rica is sometimes called a "tropical utopia." Off-season river running took hold here in the mid-1980s, and it is now by far the most developed paddling center in the Western Hemisphere south of the United States. The rivers are generally rain-fed, which is no problem in a country where annual precipitation averages between 30 and 70 inches (76 to 178 cm) a year. Though good whitewater can be found on both sides of the country, most of the rivers are on the slightly wetter Atlantic side. Most rivers are run below 2,000 feet (610 m).

Geology plays a part as well. The Isthmus of Panama includes what is now Costa Rica and is only 11 millon years old, mere infancy in geologic terms. Tectonic movement created by subduction of the Cocos Plate beneath the Caribbean Plate has generated mountains up to 12,000 feet (3,660 m) high in four ranges, though most of the runs are set below 200 feet (610 m). The varied terrain and elevation gives Costa Rica several distinct ecosystems. Most of the population is concentrated in the central highlands in the center of the country.

The country has been democratic for generations, with the highest standards of living in Latin America. Unlike most Latin American countries, it lacks the large gap between the rich and the poor. It has no standing army and tries to remain neutral in all international conflicts. It is often referred to as the Switzerland of the Western Hemisphere, though it is not nearly so heavily defended.

Costa Rica looks to ecotourism as a means to supplement its economy, and the country also boasts of an array of national parks and biological reserves which occupy a greater percentage of the nation's land than just about any other country. The government began setting aside land in perpetuity for environmental preservation as long ago as 1862. In spite of this, the economic pressures of development are real and pose the same threat to rivers here as they do elsewhere in Latin America.

Rio Reventazon ➤

The Reventazon (ruh-ven-ta-ZOHN) is easily the most popular river in Central America. This dam-controlled river runs through a valley filled with sugar and coffee plantations and dotted with moss-covered trees. Set beneath the Turrialba and Irazu volcanoes to the north, it is about a two-hour drive from San Jose, Costa Rica's largest city and capital. Its name is Spanish for "bursting," reflecting the river's power as it usually runs at big flows.

Much of the Reventazon runs through a cliff-lined gorge, with gradients for the different sections averaging 80 fpm (15.4 mpk) on the Powerhouse run, 50 fpm (9.7 mpk) on the Tucurrique run, 75 fpm (14.5 mpk) on the Peralta run, and 50 fpm (9.7 mpk) on the Pascua run.

The action on the Powerhouse run begins immediately, with good rapids and tricky maneuvers required at the top. Continuous rapids follow in succession, powered by a steady gradient. Long stretches have been described as simply "one rapid."

POWERHOUSE TO TURRIQUE
(POWERHOUSE RUN)
Difficulty: Class 4–
Length: 5 miles (8 km)

TUCURRIQUE TO ANGOSTURA
(TUCURRIQUE RUN)
Difficulty: Class 3–
Length: 12 miles (19.2 km)

ANGOSTURA TO PERALTA
(PERALTA RUN)
Difficulty: Class 5–
Length: 9 miles (14.4 km)

(continued on following page)

PERALTA TO HIGHWAY BRIDGE
(PASCUA RUN)
Difficulty: Class 4
Length: 12 miles (19.2 km)

Season: All year
Character: Popular,
tropical, dam-controlled,
with many choices

The Powerhouse and Tucurrique runs are sometimes combined, and commercial rafting trips often begin at Tucurrique. The Tucurrique run is easier, with continuous, forgiving rapids and plenty of playspots for hard-boaters. The Rio Pejibaye, which enters from the right, is a popular tributary, especially when the Reventazon is too high.

The river's most challenging section is the Peralta run from Angostura to Peralta. On this reach, convoluted big-water rapids cause most boaters to scout the bigger drops. The rapid with the biggest reputation is El Horrendo, but there are several nearly as long and difficult. This section is considerably more difficult and dangerous at high flows. It is possible to exit partway down on the left at Turrialba and carry gear a short way out. The take-out is near Angostura under a bridge in the middle of a rapid called The Land of a Thousand Holes. Floods and earthquakes have played havoc on the access roads here, and it is probably best to hire a shuttle truck to pick you up at the bottom.

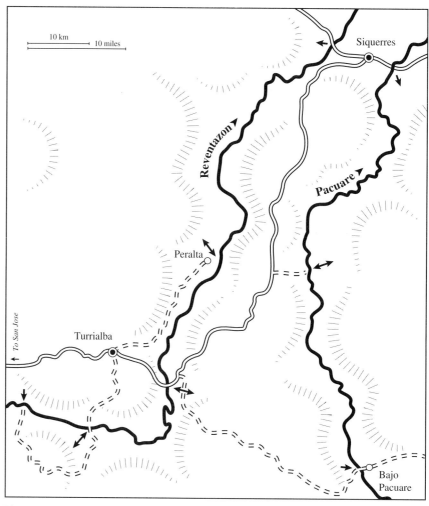

Rio Reventazon and Rio Pacuare (Costa Rica)

The usual put-in for the Pascua run is on the right, a few river miles downstream of the town of Peralta on the left. However, it is many road miles between these points and the roads are poor, so few paddle this stretch. The Pascua run is more continuous and quite challenging. The final take-out at Pascua is not far from the take-out for the Pacuare as the mountains open up to the lowlands.

Upstream from the Powerhouse is a difficult run beginning just below Cachi Reservoir. This experts-only stretch is usually dewatered and rarely run. Water quality on the described runs has suffered in recent years, but the biggest threat to the river is yet to come. The ICE, a national utility, has proposed a dam, the exact configuration of which has not been made clear but which would surely put most of the river under water. Resistance from river runners and other groups and lack of funding have slowed the project, but a questionable environmental study has been approved. Sadly, the ICE seems committed to the project.

Rio Pacuare ➤

Just to the south of the Reventazon is a river with a much different character. The Pacuare (pa-KWA-ray) is a pristine, exotic, and remote tropical river that combines great whitewater, fine jungle scenery, and a profusion of birds and other wildlife.

The Pacuare's headwaters are high in the Cordillera de Talamanca, and the river usually stays clear and runnable year-round. Although either of the runs featured here can be done in one day, camping allows boaters to extend the experience and enjoy the surrounding jungle. Birds abound, including toucans, parakeets, herons, and egrets. Equally spectacular is the giant blue morpho butterfly. Monkeys and sloths may be seen lurking around the banks. The rapids are pool-and-drop and generally formed by ledges or boulders. Logs and strainers can be a hazard. The Pacuare, along with sections of the Apurimac and the Colca, was first descended by the Polish group Canoandes in 1980.

The upper run is long, isolated, and very challenging with a gradient of about 90 fpm (17.4 mpk). It gets much less use than the lower run, although it has much to offer. The run consists of three difficult, constricted canyons filled with ledges and boulder-strewn rapids. The put-in is at a road crossing the river at Bajo Pacuare, which is not to be confused with the village of the same name located at a bridge downstream between the first and second canyons. In the second canyon the biggest drop is called Jumping Bobos Falls for the spawning fish sometimes seen attempting to ascend the falls. A 1¾-mile (2.7 km) oxcart trail at San Martin has been improved for two-wheel vehicle traffic. Check locally at Tres Equis for alternate road access nearby. These are the put-in options for the lower run also.

The river in the more popular lower run is set in a deep gorge and has a gradient of around 50 fpm (9.7 mpk). Commercial rafting trips are common here, and kayakers find plenty of playspots. About a mile (1.6 km) inside the gorge on the left is Terciopelo ("velvet") Creek, which makes a good side hike and climb up to a falls and plunge pool. About two-thirds of the way down is Upper Huacas Rapid, just before Huacas Falls where a side creek drops some 150 feet (46 m) into the river. Just downstream is Lower Huacas (Class 4–), the toughest rapid on this stretch. After the canyon opens up, farms and villages appear. Downstream the river enters the narrow Dos Montanas Canyon.

Bajo Pacuare to San Martin, near Tres Equis (upper run)
Difficulty: Class 5
Length: 15 miles (24 km)

San Martin, near Tres Equis, to highway bridge east of Siquirres (lower run)
Difficulty: Class 4–
Length: 17 miles (27.2 km)

Season: All year; can get very low during the dry season (January through April)
Character: Free-flowing, exotic tropical river

Huacas Waterfalls on Rio Pacuare, Costa Rica. *(Aventuras Naturales)*

The Pacuare is the first Central American river to be accorded "wild and scenic" status; however, this designation does not necessarily assure protection from previously enacted rights of the national utility to tap hydro power. In spite of conservation efforts, a massive dam project proposed for Dos Montanas Canyon could drown most of the river. As with the dam on the Raventazon, opposition groups and lack of funding stand in the way of the project. Clear-cutting of the rainforest upstream also continues to threaten the river environment.

◁ Rio General

CHILES TO PAN AMERICAN
HIGHWAY NEAR SAN ISIDRO
Difficulty: Class 4–
Length: 8 miles (12.8 km)

PAN AMERICAN HIGHWAY NEAR
SAN ISIDRO TO PAN
AMERICAN HIGHWAY NEAR EL
BRUJO
Difficulty: Class 3+
Length: 42 miles (67.2 km)

Season: May through
December, other months
after rains
Character: Tropical; wide
flow fluctuations

The Rio General (HEN-ur-AL) is sometimes called by its upstream name, the Chirripo. This tropical multi-day run is considered to be one of the world's great big-water surfing rivers. The river has its headwaters in the rainforests of Mount Chirripo, Costa Rica's highest mountain at 12,529 feet (3,820 m). It drains the Pacific side of the mountains, and much of the drainage has been cleared for agriculture. Perhaps because the area is more developed than that of the Pacuare, the flows fluctuate quickly and drop to unrunnable levels more frequently. Though the forests have mostly been cleared, farms dot the riverside, as do local cowboys, ceiba trees, iguanas and other exotic wildlife. In the last few years agricultural runoff from livestock has adversely affected water quality, causing some commercial companies to go elsewhere.

The first section, consisting of the 8 miles (12.8 km) from Chiles to the Pan American Highway, is more continuous, though not really more difficult than the lower run, and can be run in a day by itself or as part of a trip with the lower run. Halfway down the run, a midstream island creates an interesting rapid often obscured with reeds and trees. Downstream of here the rapids slacken somewhat, and farms and houses are more noticeable.

The lower section usually takes a few days. About 2 miles (3.2 km) below the Pan American Highway, the Rio Pacuare enters from the right, nearly doubling the flow. Other tributaries further augment the flow along the run. The river occasionally drops into gorges, with nice side falls. The rapids are usually well spaced and forgiving, but in some stretches the whitewater is continuous. The overall gradient averages about 40 fmp (7.7 mpk).

The lower section of the General is famous for its surfing rapids, including Chacalacca. The last 10 miles (16 km) are easier and offer a chance to enjoy the scenery.

Rio Sarapiqui ➤

The Sarapiqui is located north of San Jose and drains a very wet, volcanic area. The drive to the river from the capital takes visitors through a land of volcanoes, lakes, and waterfalls as the road scales mountains and passes through national parklands. A highway follows the river, so many river access points are available.

The river will not disappoint. Its waters are usually clear, and the lower elevation gives the area a true jungle feel. Though much of the Sarapiqui runs through dense jungle, scenery is secondary to challenging, boulder-garden-variety rapids on all but the lower stretch.

The upper run, from San Miguel to La Virgen, is mostly run by expert kayakers, with the gradient about 90 fpm (17.4 mpk). The action is nearly continuous, especially at the beginning, with many rapids ending in big drops. Keep an eye out for logs and strainers.

The middle section, from La Virgen to Chilamate, is a popular rafting trip, and the gradient drops to about 55 fpm (10.6 mpk). In places the river leaves the tropical forest for farmland.

In the bottom section, Chilamate to Puerto Viejo, the river returns to dense jungle for a very exotic float teeming with tropical birds of nearly every description as well as river otters and other exotic mammals. The river is sometimes channelized, and boaters must choose routes as well as share the river with natives in dugout canoes and small craft.

Near the Sarapiqui are the popular tourist towns of La Fortuna and Volcan Arenal, where the volcano is still quite active. Another whitewater river, even closer to La Fortuna, that has been getting a lot of use recently is the Penas Blancas.

SAN MIGUEL TO LA VIRGEN
   (UPPER RUN)
Difficulty: Class 4+
Length: 7 miles (11.2 km)

LA VIRGEN TO CHILAMATE
   (MIDDLE RUN)
Difficulty: Class 3
Length: 7 miles (11.2 km)

CHILAMATE TO PUERTO VIEJO
Difficulty: Class 1+
Length: 7 miles (11.2 km)

Season: June through
   December; longer as you
   go downstream
Character: Tropical; several
   varied sections to choose
   from

Rio Corobici ➤

The Rio Corobici is located in the northern, drier part of Costa Rica on the western shoulder of the mountains and flows to the Pacific. It runs adjacent to Palo Verde National Park in a region known as the Guanacaste, and supports different flora and fauna than the rain-soaked jungles on the Atlantic drainage. The lack of water elsewhere in the Guanacaste makes the river a natural draw for birds and wildlife in need of food, water, and shelter. The river corridor supports an abundance of exotic animals, including howler monkeys and armadillos as well as hundreds of species of tropical and migratory birds and exotic vegetation.

The river gets trans-divide diversions from a hydroelectric project on the Arenal River, allowing for year-round boatable flows. Partway down it is joined by the Rio

ROUTE 1 BRIDGE TO BEBEDERO
Difficulty: Class 2–
Length: 13 miles (20.8 km)

Season: All year
Character: Mild, tropical

Tenorio and takes that name downstream. The first two-thirds of the run are mostly wild with few signs of civilization. Some farms and ranches appear in the lower reaches. Don't be lulled by the mellow rapids; islands and strainers often require some attentive maneuvering.

Boaters can also put in upstream on the Rio Magdalena at Sandillal for a pleasant 3-mile (4.8 km), Class 2+ run down to Route 1 and the town of Corobici.

SOUTH AMERICA

*T*he story of South American whitewater begins some 70 million years ago, when, geologists tell us, the west coast of the continent began riding up on the Nazca Plate. Perhaps nowhere else on the globe have plate tectonics had such a marked and immense effect. The abduction zone created the Andes and the subduction zone formed the Peru-Chile Trench, as deep as or deeper than the Andes are high, resulting in a spectacular disparity of some 40,000 feet (12,200 m) in land elevation within only 100 miles. Igneous upwellings erupted as volcanoes that riddle the Andes; these sentinels are the world's highest and run along the spine of the continent from one tip to the other. Erosion eventually exposed the extraordinary crystalline ranges of the Cordillera's Blanca, Vilcanota, and Vilcabama mountains of central Peru. Further intense pressures folded and faulted the area on a grand scale during the Oligocene period 35 million years ago, and the effects can still be seen in most of the deep river canyons described here. More recent eruptions from 30 to 2 million years ago left layers of volcanic and sedimentary rock. Glaciers later carved the mountains and canyons of the Andes into their present form.

The scale of the Andes is remarkable. If laid across North America, they would stretch from Havana to Juneau, some 4,500 miles (7,200 km). They feature peaks of over 20,000 feet (6,100 m) for much of their length from the equator to 35° south latitude, including the highest peak, Cerro Aconaugua, at over 23,000 feet (7,015 m). Only the Himalayas are higher. All this geological activity has created a wonderland of rocky peaks, snow-capped volcanoes, broad river valleys and deep canyons, waterless deserts, icy fjords, deep blue glaciers, turquoise lakes, and sandy beaches.

The return of relatively stable democracies in Chile and Peru have helped focus the world's attention on the many great rivers of this range. While road conditions may be more difficult than in more developed areas, access is usually available and the climactic diversity and friendly people make the effort worthwhile.

South America

Chile

*I*n many ways Chile mirrors the Pacific Coast of North America. Northern Chile bears similarities to Mexico. Sometimes called Norte Grande, it is dominated by the Atacama Desert. Only one river regularly reaches the sea, and some weather stations have *never* recorded rainfall. Perhaps early river runners arriving in Arica in northernmost Chile noticed that many of the houses had no roofs, always a bad omen for those looking for big water. The area around Santiago is much like central California, with most of the country's population and agriculture set in a warm Mediterranean climate. The lake region in the south resembles British Columbia with changeable summer weather, cool damp winters, and sparse population. Chile does not have large tracts of truly pristine wilderness; it has lots of lightly populated, underdeveloped backcountry. The Andes gradually get smaller and wetter as one moves south, and most of the good rivers are found well south of Santiago.

Chile and great whitewater boating have been synonymous for the last two decades, a veritable international mecca of whitewater south of the equator. Unless trends change dramatically, this distinction will be very short-lived. The legend of Chilean whitewater began with the Rio Bio-Bio in the 1980s. In early 1997, just eighteen years after the discovery of this paradise, most of its great rapids were drowned under the reservoir formed by the Pangue Dam. Its upper reaches are slated for a similar fate.

With the rejection of General Augusto Pinochet in 1989, Chile celebrated the return of democratic government and a general economic revival. Sadly, the reactionary element remains, and the new government does not consider the environment a priority. Lack of environmental controls are even extolled as an inducement for international investment. New dam projects are contemplated for some of Chile's finest whitewater. Although there is a small, enthusiastic boating community, most Chileans have little income or time for river running; understandably, they sense that the economic boom gives them a rare opportunity to participate in economic betterment for themselves, a view recently reinforced by an elaborate media campaign touting the benefits of hydro power for all Chileans. This is a challenging climate for environmental activism.

With the loss of the Bio-Bio, the focus shifts to other equally spectacular threatened rivers, including the Futaleufu and the Fui. Ironically, the economic benefits of what could be a profitable and enduring tourism industry for the country may be lost to these more marginal projects.

We have picked six rivers in Chile, but the descriptions given should give an idea of the dozens of other runs. Those interested may wish to read *The Rivers of Chile* by Lars Holbeck (AWA, 1992) or wait for the posthumous release of John Foss's *The Whitewater Rivers of Chile: A Rafting and Kayaking Guide*.

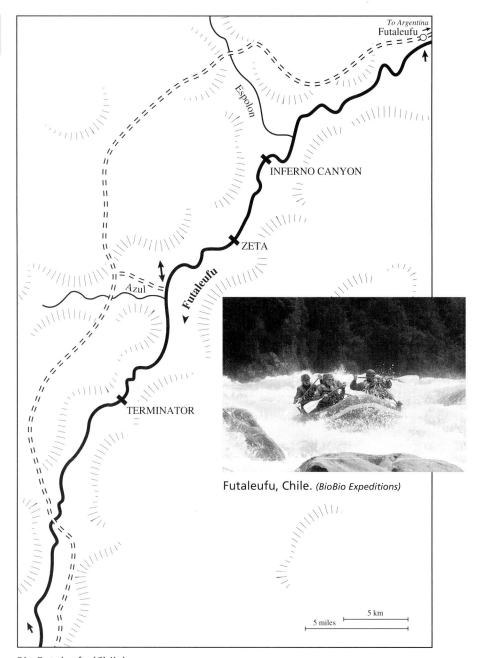

To Argentina
Futaleufu

INFERNO CANYON

ZETA

Espolon

Azul

Futaleufu

TERMINATOR

Futaleufu, Chile. *(BioBio Expeditions)*

5 km
5 miles

Rio Futaleufu (Chile)

Rio Futaleufu ➤

Discussions of the world's greatest whitewater rivers often start with and hopefully will always include the Futaleufu. With more than a dozen big-water rapids, a dramatic landscape, friendly locals, and unimaginably azure water, the "Fu" is one of the few rivers that could make the long and difficult trek to this corner of the planet worthwhile. Its location keeps it uncrowded, but, ironically, well-documented usage and the economic viability of boating-supported commerce may be needed to help keep this crown jewel of the world's rivers running free. Should its waters fall prey to huge hydroelectric dams, as did those of the Bio-Bio, Chile will no longer hold its status as the major international paddling destination.

Futaleufu (foo-tah-LAY-ah-foo) means "Big River" or "Grand Waters" in the language of the Araucanian Indians, who have carved out a living along its banks for hundreds of years. The Futaleufu begins in Argentina where lakes clear the glacial silt and release only the upper thermocline of relatively warm water across the border near the town of Futaleufu. The waters then careen through several granite canyons in a beautiful valley beneath glacier-laden peaks. The rapids along the way are filled with seemingly endless huge waves, effervescent, transparent boils, and frothy whirlpools.

The beauty of the Futaleufu and much of the reason it did not receive the earlier fanfare of the Bio-Bio is its remoteness in southern Chile. Route 5, the only major highway in Chile, ends well before it reaches the Futaleufu. Several challenging travel options are available from the southern terminus of Route 5, the bustling port town of Puerto Montt. There are three ferry-service routes to Chaiten which can carry vehicles and gear; be sure to book reservations in advance. A few commuter planes go direct but will not carry much gear. Another possibility is a scenic drive across the border into Argentina and then heading south to Esquel on the Carretera Austral, returning back into Chile at

INFERNO CANYON, TOWN OF FUTALEUFU TO SUSPENSION BRIDGE ABOVE RIO AZUL CONFLUENCE
Difficulty: Class 5
Length: 12 miles (19.2 km)

RIO AZUL CONFLUENCE TO BELOW CASA DE PIEDRAS
Difficulty: Class 5
Length: 11 miles (17.6)

Season: December through April
Character: Clear blue water, beautiful canyons and countryside

Zeta Rapid, Futaleufu (Chile). *(BioBio Expeditions Worldwide)*

the town of Futaleufu. Unfortunately, as of this writing rental cars are not allowed to cross the border into Argentina. Each of the routes is its own adventure.

Although beautiful, the waters of the Fu are not to be taken lightly. This is a pool-and-drop river, with an overall gradient of 25 to 50 fpm (4.8 to 9.7 mpk), but the pools are long and the drops are big. Low flows run from 5,000 to 12,000 cfs (141.5 to 339.6 cumecs) and higher, making for big water with big hydraulics. Even pursuing easier routes along the sides leads to confrontations with eddy fences and surges which push boats back into the maelstrom. Solid paddling skills and a reliable roll are minimum

First Descent of Staircase

The trip to Chile was part of that awkward transition time: me and the boys on a road trip accompanied by my future wife promising to be a "trouper." Some things were just a little different than before. One night in the pitch dark I asked for the toothpaste. I found myself brushing my teeth with something called make-up foundation. Hmmmm. Flesh-colored teeth.

We camped out at various rivers along the length of Chile for more than two weeks, but this finally came to an end at the Futaleufu. Facing another night in a "rustic" camp that could have been home to the Joad family in another era, I was told it was time to find a dry room with plumbing.

Let me explain that the entire Futaleufu area has a certain feeling of genuineness to it that is hard to describe. The river is awesome, brash, and easy to access. The locals are approachable, but the entire area for good reason feels a little disconnected from Chile or, for that matter, conventional reality. The town of Futaleufu could easily be the setting for a Chilean version of "Northern Exposure."

To this strange place we came to find a hotel. It is only appropriate that it should be a little disconnected as well. Cruising around the streets of the town, passing the strangely lit shops and strangely built structures, we soon found ourselves in front of the Hotel Continental, the pride of its motherly proprietor, Raquel.

The Continental seemed to be a hundred years old—so old, in fact, the ceilings were barely 6 feet, making life an adventure for taller folk. Much of the hotel was hardwood, finely polished to a slickness that could only have been achieved by decades of polishing inflicted by Raquel and her predecessors. I made this discovery upon first walking in to negotiate our lodging, when I slipped and almost fell as the mat came out from under me. For good measure I did the same thing on the way out. It was apparent the wool or cloth on the floor reduced the friction coefficient to nil. In my best, awful Spanish I told Raquel the footing was "muy malo." She agreed but probably figured another polishing job would remedy the floor's condition.

Early the next morning I awoke to an awful crashing noise. Ken, our most fearless water-fall jumper, was so excited about hitting the rapids, he decided to take on the hotel's long, twisting wooden staircase in his woolen socks. I found him lying battered and beaten at the bottom. That night I'm sure Raquel polished those stairs again for good measure.

—Dan Dunlap

kayak requirements. Outfitters use rafts of 18 feet and longer, as small rafts or inflatable kayaks are no match for the bigger rapids.

The river is generally divided into two sections. Although both are solid Class 5, the upstream run, Inferno Canyon (locally known as Canon Inferno), is more remote and access is difficult to impossible at some points. The action is more extreme here, with long stretches of calm water between huge rapids. Unlike the lower canyon where the biggest rapids are more easily portaged, the steep walls of Inferno Canyon make it difficult to impossible to portage, and a swim here likely will include an epic and unwanted tour of the closely spaced rapids just downstream. At high water it is often good judgment to paddle elsewhere. Even at lower flows, experienced boaters and outfitters usually elect to do the lower canyon first to measure themselves for the upper canyon.

The put-in for the upper canyon is only 3 miles (4.8 km) from the border, just upstream of the town of Futaleufu. Put in at Jelves Bridge which crosses a mini-canyon just above town. A boat ramp is available for rafts. Kayakers can put in above on the right and run the extra rapid. Downstream boaters take in a few easy rapids and short gorges before the Rio Espolon joins on the right and adds to the flow. Another option is to put in on the Rio Espolon road bridge just west of town. Shortly after the Rio Espolon confluence the river drops into the constricted Inferno Canyon. While it might be possible to paddle a kayak back upstream and exit on private land at low flows, generally from here boaters are committed to taking on the assemblage of raucous hydraulics, immense waves, fierce keeper holes, and eddy fences below. The first big drop, the Inferno ("Hell"), is a hole-laden monstrosity that signals the most challenging series of rapids. Portaging is not an option here, and the swift current will likely take a swimmer through an ominous Dante-esque ordeal including two more downstream rapids, Purgatorio ("Purgatory") and Danza de Los Angles ("Dance of the Angels"). Just below is another major rapid, Escala de Jacobo ("Jacob's Ladder").

Downstream of Inferno Canyon the walls open to Las Escalas Valley. Boaters willing to hire an oxcart could access the river at this point and put in on the left. Do not disturb the fishing lodge. After a long, mellow float the river approaches the next major rapid, Zeta (Z Drop). Be careful here. If Zeta seemed too easy, you may have paddled False Zeta and are now heading for the real thing. As the name implies, the river angles off obliquely against massive boulders. The rapid is deceptively dangerous, especially at high levels. This is a mandatory scout, and most boaters elect to carry on the right to avoid the dangerous undercut wall at the bottom and an ominous whirlpool on the left. Zeta is the site of an Earth River camp and an excellent place for photos.

About 4 miles (6.4 km) above the midway access is the final major rapid, Salto Feo, also known as Throne Room, where the center current eventually pushes boaters into a keeper hole. Kayakers have sustained good surfs off a huge cushion provided by a massive boulder called the Throne. However, this rapid has humbled some of the planet's best paddlers. Dan Gavere's tortured run memorialized in the film *Paddle Quest* serves as a reminder that the literal translation of Salto Feo is "Ugly Jump Falls." Some comfort is provided by a large recovery pool or the easy portage on the left. Rapids and pools continue to the midway access at a suspension bridge.

The midway access is a few hundred meters above the confluence with the Rio Azul, approximately 14¼ miles (23 km) southwest of the town of Futaleufu. The striking 7,000-foot (2,135 m) Tres Monjas ("Three Nuns") Peak rises above the river here on the left. Just downstream on the right near the Rio Clara confluence is the Expediciones Chile camp, operated by Chris Spelius.

Most boaters favor the lower section, especially for their first day on the river. This is not to say it's easy. The full run holds several long, difficult Class 5 rapids, but they are spaced between numerous and consistent easier drops. The lower section is closer to road access and, unlike the upper run, can be run twice in a day. At most flows kayakers will find waves, holes, and endospots in virtually every rapid. Those wishing to get the feel of the river can first run a shortened section from the swinging bridge at Zapata to the concrete bridge, Puente Futaleufu, with mostly Class 4 action.

Probably the most difficult rapid on the lower section is the ominously named Terminator, a long, broad, complex Class 5 rapid with massive holes arranged on the center and right. The largest hole, about two-thirds of the way down, also takes the name Terminator, perhaps because an exploratory first raft descent ended here in 1985 after a reported half-hour surf. The right side of this monster is backed by a downstream boulder. Most boaters look for difficult "sneak routes" or carry around.

Terminator marks the beginning of the most continuous whitewater section on the lower run, including two rapids—Kybers Pass (Class 5–), with another nasty hole, and Himalayas (Class 5–)—following in brisk succession.

Alternate access is available at the swinging bridge at Zapata, easily visible from the road. From here it is a constant stream of Class 4 and 4+ rapids to the next bridge, Puente Futaleufu (also known as "the concrete bridge"). The most difficult rapid in this stretch is Mondaca (Class 5–) where a massive center flume directs boaters towards an immense downstream hole. The action picks up again below the concrete bridge access point with Mas y Menos (Class 5–) and Casa de Piedra (Class 5). At Casa de Piedra the river is blocked with several boulders, the largest being one the size of a house in mid-current. Eddies help boaters pick among several routes, none of them clean. Take out 650 feet (200 m) downstream of Casa de Piedra on river left. The name, meaning "House of Stone," derives from bygone days when local cowboys ("Huasos") camped here. Boaters may also continue downstream through more forgiving rapids and splendid scenery all the way to Lake Yelcho.

Although there is much reason to hope the Futaleufu will be spared, the plans are to build several hydroelectric dams along its length. These include one midway through the lower section, which will drown all of the river's good whitewater as well as local farmland and the Espolon and Azul rivers. Most of the energy would be exported to Argentina, and access roads between the countries would be inundated. Outfitters are backing local groups and the internationally based Futa Fund in hopes that this elegant gem will endure for future generations of river runners.

Balsedero Caracoles to Rio Quepuca confluence
Difficulty: Class 3
Length: 30 miles (48 km))

Nirreco Canyon, Rio Quepuca confluence to Heartbreak Hotel
Difficulty: Class 5
Length: 7 miles (11.2 km)

◁ Rio Bio-Bio

Americans have come full circle with respect to environmental issues, a level of consciousness not achieved by the Chileans who, understandably, want to partake in the wealth and comfort accompanying technological growth. Most Chileans are neither whitewater enthusiasts nor eco-tourists and find it difficult to accept arguments from boaters and industrialized countries that they should not develop their resources as others have done.
—John Foss

Mornings in Chile are usually filled with wondrous songs of its native birds. The nation of Chile draws its name from the chant of a native songbird, as does the name Bio-Bio which some say derives from the song of a local flycatcher. Others say the name is the local dialect for "very wide." In any event, the short-lived beauty of a songbird is a fitting metaphor for the brief life of what was surely one of the world's greatest whitewater rivers.

Boaters' talk of the great Bio-Bio began to take on the tone of an obituary in early 1997, when the Pangue Dam was completed and filled. The reservoir, some 9 miles (14 km) in length, drowned the legendary Royal Flush and Cien Saltos ("One Hundred Waterfalls") canyons, some of Chile's greatest whitewater. The Pangue is only the first of as many as six projects that may ultimately silence nearly all of the mighty river's rapids. As of this writing, there is still much good whitewater to be run on the upper sections of the river, but those interested should not delay: the Bio-Bio is on a timetable of destruction. Because the dam projects are set to continue during the shelf life of this guide, those interested should check beforehand on the status of the remaining runnable sections. We describe the river in unabridged—or rather undammed—fashion as a record of what is being lost.

Beginning from Lake Galletue and Laguna Icalma in the high Andes, the transparent green waters of the Bio-Bio journey to the north and west through several gorges, powerful big-water rapids, resplendent scenery, and innumerable side waterfalls. The headwaters even afford some great trout fishing. The geology is highly volcanic, and the smoking, snow-covered 10,000-foot (3,164 m) volcanic cone of Callaqui oversees much of the river. The Bio-Bio is a classic multi-day trip with numerous soft sand beaches along its length. Shorter runs are possible, as a shuttle road follows the river except in the canyons. Some companies run a series of day trips along the river, maintaining one base camp. The river has an overall gradient of 34 fpm (6.6 mpk).

Our put-in is where the road from Lonquimay meets the river, just upstream from Balsedero Caracoles. The upstream stretch from Lake Galletue to this point is an easy float; considering the spectacular action downstream, it really gets little use unless the flows are too high to run the lower section. Flows on the Bio-Bio are higher and more pushy in December when snowmelt raises river levels, and lower toward February. If the flows from Lago Galletue are skimpy, don't worry—they will triple to between 3,000 and 20,000 cfs (84.9 and 566 cumecs) at the take-out.

The first featured run from Lonquimay to Nirreco Canyon passes through scenic foothills reminiscent of California's Sierra Nevada. Deciduous forests and exotic flora blanket this realm, including cedars, Lombardy poplars, and cypress. Of particular interest is the araucaria araucaana, the prehistoric giant tree of the region. The tree has been around at least two million years, and individual trees may be two thousand years old. Hiking and camping opportunities are plentiful here. Interaction with the friendly local farmers, cowboys, and indigenous Mapuche Pehuenche Indians can be a delight. The Pehuenche are particularly engaging and inquisitive. Years ago they stubbornly resisted Spanish conquest. They even remained outside Chilean authority until as late as 1882. They have just as stubbornly resisted efforts of dam builders and the government to relocate them from their native soil, and with good reason: there is no comparable area for relocation that fits their traditional lifestyle. The araucaria araucaana seed is the most important staple of their diet, and they consider the tree sacred.

Along this first section of river an unobtrusive dirt road parallels the river and eventually crosses to river right, continuing to Rio Lomin at about mile 25 (40 km). A few

Bio-Bio River, Chile.
(BioBio Expeditions Worldwide)

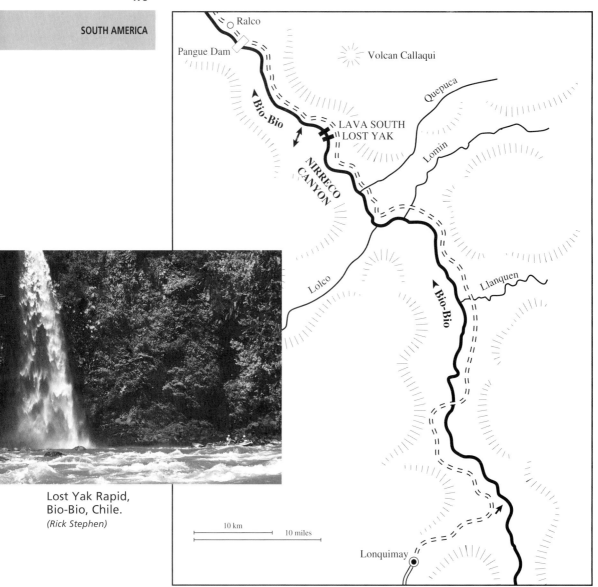

Lost Yak Rapid,
Bio-Bio, Chile.
(Rick Stephen)

Rio Bio-Bio (Chile)

miles above this point Volcan Callaqui first comes into view and is often visible above the canyon walls as the river circles it to the take-out.

Where the Rio Lomin joins from the right is a popular stop, and a short hike up the Rio Lomin leads to a hot springs. The springs are on private land and lately access has been denied; inquire locally. The Rio Quepuca joins at about mile 30 (48 km) from the right and provides the usual access for those just doing Nirreco Canyon as well as a take-out for the first run. The biggest rapid above Nirreco Canyon is Island (Class 4), about two-thirds of the way down.

The landscape changes abruptly as the Bio-Bio pours into Nirreco Canyon. Here metamorphic and granite formations channel the flow as the river gushes over the more than one hundred rapids that give the Bio-Bio much of its reputation. Few would argue that Nirreco Canyon is one of the world's classic big-water runs, with such big drops as Jugbuster and Milky Way (both Class 4+), Lost Yak and Lava South (both Class 5), Cyclops and Last Laugh (both Class 4+).

Jugbuster is below a suspension bridge and a few hundred yards above the proposed Ralco Dam site. It is a short, difficult drop with routes dictated by the flow, none of them easy. Milky Way is a long series of holes and breaking waves above a large recovery pool. The rapid is named for the white glacial rock flour of the Rio Malla which enters halfway down.

The splendid 120-foot (37 m) Rio Nirreco waterfall jets in from the vertical canyon wall on the right, signaling the beginning of one of the most difficult and at the same time visually stunning stretches of river anywhere, the Lost Yak and Lava South rapids. Constant action between the two rapids, especially at high water, gives this stretch its Class 5 rating. This reach is particularly perilous for rafts in light of the possibility of a long swim. There are only a few hundred yards to recover before Cyclops where the entire river piles into the wall in an abrupt right turn. The rapids continue to Last Laugh, only slightly less difficult, where boaters must avoid a huge pourover in the center of the river. More forgiving rapids continue to Heartbreak Hotel—also known as Jose's Pasture—at about mile 37 (59.2 km). Marked by a huge basalt outcropping on the right, this is indeed a real pasture. In full swing the pasture is a crowded mix of fiestas and squealing pigs overseen by Jose, who, as a true Chilean, loves his vino tinto. Some river runners who prefer to pass on the merry-making and commotion may wish to camp downstream. The Pasture is also a good access point for hot springs and treks to Volcan Callaqui, a tough day-and-a-half hike from the river. It is approximately a four-hour hike to the Araucaria Forest of the upper Rio Malla drainage, a base camp for the climb.

Downstream is the beginning of the Cien Saltos ("One Hundred Waterfalls") Canyon run, most of which is now covered by the reservoir above the Pangue Dam. Boaters can still continue from Jose's Pasture to Termas de Avellanos.

The Pangue is a tragic monument to the demise of the Bio-Bio. Below these waters lie much of Cien Saltos, one of the most striking canyons in the world where countless waterfalls cascaded into the river from dense deciduous forests. Under the reservoir and in fact below the dam itself are the remains of the rapids of the legendary Royal Flush Canyon, a series of classic rapids named after a poker hand including Ace, Suicide King, Queen of Hearts, One-Eyed Jack, Ten, and the Joker.

The featured runs are slated to be drowned and dewatered by the Llanquen Dam, to be built 2 miles (3.2 km) downstream from the confluence with Rio Llanquen, which enters on the right at about mile 18 (28.8 km), and Ralco Dam downstream, both of which will serve to store water for the Pangue Dam. When built, the Ralco Dam will flood the largest area within the Bio-Bio watershed and divert most of the flow through a tunnel, in turn dewatering the downstream stretch, including Nirreco Canyon all the way to Heartbreak Hotel.

Downstream of the Pangue Dam is an additional 25-mile (40 km), Class 3 river trip from Rio Queuco to Puente Cuileco, just upstream from Santa Barbara. Sadly, two proposed dams are slated for this run.

Puente El Yeso to Puente San
	Alfonso (upper run)
Difficulty: Class 4+
Length: 6 miles (9.5 km)

Puente San Alfonso to Puente
	El Toyo
Difficulty: Class 3+
Length: 5 miles (8 km)

Season: November through
	March
Character: Continuous
	gradient, glacial runoff,
	road nearby

◅ Rio Maipo

The Maipo is just 40 miles south of Santiago, and it is a favorite of boaters from the capital city. It is often the first run for visitors just arriving in Chile, as boaters landing in Santiago in the morning can be on the water by the afternoon. Newcomers expecting clear azure cascades will be a little disappointed with the brownish glacial runoff, but the flows are plenty big enough to hone skills for the Bio-Bio or the Futaleufu. The river is set between steep canyon walls of sedimentary rock that are particularly impressive in the upper reaches. The area is dry, with stands of poplar, aspen, and eucalyptus scattered among brush and cactus. Shuttles are a breeze as the road follows the river the entire distance.

Although the nearby road provides many access points and options, the river is generally divided into two runs. Both have continuous big-water rapids along most of their length. Put in for the upper run at the bridge over the Rio Yeso. The Yeso is clear, steep, and cluttered with boulders for the short stretch before it meets the Maipo which has just emerged from an unrunnable cataract. The upper Maipo is filled with continuous Class 4 drops, and kayakers will find an abundance of playholes and surf waves. The gradient of 80 fpm (15.4 mpk) here attests to nonstop action. At high flows it is as much as a full class higher due to the lack of eddies and the possibility of a long swim. Boaters should be wary of the many undercut rocks along the river. The toughest stretch is La Curva del Frances ("Frenchman's Curve"), named for a foreign boater who deemed scouting the rapid to be beneath him. He was soon taught the error of his ways. It is a long, arching S-curve near the road just upstream of where the road narrows next to a tunnel covered with graffiti. This tough rapid continues downstream through a blind right-hand bend with a big drop. A popular take-out is Puente San Alfonso just upstream of the town, although this area was recently posted as closed for construction of a new bridge. Hiking and rock climbing are also popular in the upper canyon.

Puente San Alfonso is the usual put-in for the lower run. San Alfonso has its own kayak school (Cascade Expeditiones), and river folk can always be found there during peak season. Its most famous (or infamous) resident is retired dictator Augusto Pinochet, who lives about 3 miles downstream at Melocotine.

The lower section is more forgiving and a good training ground for novice boaters. The biggest rapids on the run are in a small bedrock canyon near the former dictator's well-guarded home on the right. As the sound of barking guard dogs fades, a series of rapids and holes keep boaters on their toes. The largest is Pinochet's Hole, a river-wide drop which used to be more difficult before floods changed it in 1993. Perhaps those that stray too far left—currents, political figures—may disappear. In 1986 the shuttle road was the site of an unsuccessful assassination attempt.

Several places—including some private campgrounds—can be used as a take-out, or boaters can continue on to Puente El Toyo, a large bridge spanning the river 5 miles downstream of the put-in.

*(River specifications on following
	page)*

◅ Rio Trancura (Pucon)

The most popular river in Chile in terms of user-days is not the Bio-Bio or the Futaleufu, but the Trancura, also known as the Pucon. Its traffic is mostly paddle rafts filled with vacationers from Pucon, the summer resort town just to the west of the river. The whitewater is just part of the scene in Pucon and Villarrica. The area sits under the visage of Volcan Villarrica (2,840 m), a major active volcano, which belches black smoke and occasionally lava and flames. The volcano also provides for beautiful black sand beaches on Lago Villarrica. During the summer the area draws Chile's and Argentina's young, as well as a wealthy parent or two, and can be quite a scene. Pucon supports at least three rafting companies, and competition is fierce. A half-day trip on the lower section is hard to beat at $10 U.S.

The Trancura flows through an area of mixed woods and pastures and offers a little something for everyone. The upper reach draws expert kayakers as well as the more adventurous rafting customers. The lower section has good intermediate whitewater for kayakers and those interested in a more gentle rafting outing. Puente ("bridge") Metrenehue separates the challenging upper section from the more popular lower section. Both runs are accessible by road from town.

The upper run begins about 4¼ miles (7 km) upstream of Puente Metrenehue along a road on the right side of the river. Put in at an opening in the fence at a small bluff over a calm stretch of the river. On a clear day, great views of Volcan Villarrica appear upstream at various points on the river. The rapids consist of a series of basalt ledge drops signaled by mist rising from horizon lines. The first drop is straightforward. The second drop must be run on the right and cannot be run on the left where the river empties into a spectacular wall of sieves and waterfalls. Downstream of the third ledge a large rock formation announces a Class 6 waterfall, Salto de Mariman. A well-defined portage trail on the left provides some fine views of the river and leads past the 30-foot (9 m) falls and a complex Class 5 rapid just below. Kayakers have run the falls, but most carry, especially at higher flows. Some boaters are able to line boats over the smaller falls on the left and put in an eddy just below. After this stretch, the rapids ease considerably.

The section below Puente Metrenehue—the lower run—is the most heavily used stretch of river in Chile, as paddle boats laden with young partygoers splash down its well-spaced, forgiving drops. Most of the rapids are formed by river-wide boulder gardens which generate big waves at high flows. The biggest rapid, Pescadero, is a basalt ledge marked by a huge stone formation on the left. Take out at Puente Quelhue, a miniature version of the Golden Gate Bridge off a road 1 mile (1.6 km) east of Pucon. Downstream the river flows into Lago Villarrica and back to the party. Peak paddle-raft season is late December through February.

Expert kayakers can have a go at the highly touted Class 5+ run farther upstream, starting at Puente Puesco, or other expert runs nearby such as the Maichen or the big waterfalls of the Palguin.

Rio Fui ➤

This is steep-creekin', Chilean style. Here countless waterfalls provide curtains of clear, warm falling water and plenty of soft air and pools to land in. The Fui (sometimes spelled Fuy) begins at the diminutive Lago Pirehueico in Chile's Lake District. The waters tumble down a magnificent, staircase-like streambed through a jungle of bamboo, colored with blackberries and fuchsia. At lower flows it is not unusual to see local anglers along the banks with bamboo poles and tin-can reels landing big rainbows. Active volcanoes such as nearby Choshuenco, 7,915 feet (2,415 m), overlook the scene.

The upper section is a world-class run featuring nonstop pool-and-drop rapids and waterfalls, at least three of which are in the 20- to 30-foot (6 to 9 m) range. All can be either run or portaged. The action starts after a good warm-up and reaches a high point

---

BALSEO LLAFENCO TO PUENTE METRENEHUE (UPPER RUN)
Difficulty: Class 4+p
Length: 6 miles (9.6 km)

PUENTE METRENEHUE TO PUENTE QUELQUE, UPSTREAM OF PUCON (LOWER RUN)
Difficulty: Class 3
Length: 5 miles (8 km)

Season: October through April
Character: Great scenery of the Chilean lake district, volcanoes

LAGO PIREHUEICO (PUERTO FUI) TO ABOVE NELTUME (UPPER RUN)
Difficulty: Class 5
Length: 4 miles (6.4 km)

PUENTE HUILO-HUILO TO LAGO PANGUIPULLI (LOWER FUI)
Difficulty: Class 4
Length: 3 miles (4.8 km)

Season: December through March
Character: Beautiful wilderness, waterfalls

at a 30-foot (9 m) waterfall, Salto Las Leones. Smaller drops follow another 30-foot (9 m) drop and then the road again meets the river. (The falls are accessible by an unmarked trail from the road, but the several trails through the bamboo are confusing.)

Avoid the temptation to continue on downstream into the Huilo-Huilo Gorge. The gorge has even more falls, including Huilo-Huilo at over 100 feet (30 m) which is the focus for a small roadside attraction on the road along the river. Easy drops downstream lead to brutal portages through walls of bamboo which most boaters consider not worth the trouble. Some locals call the river here the Huilo-Huilo, although this is actually the name of a side stream near the falls.

Below the Huilo-Huilo Gorge the river opens up with a continuous gradient for both rafts and kayaks as paddlers negotiate either boulder gardens at low flows or big pushy rapids in high water. The put-in for what is called the middle Fui is at Puente ("bridge") Huilo-Huilo on the main road. (Boaters ready for a short hike can put in at a trail through a pasture about a mile upstream and run some bigger drops.) Take out at the first concrete bridge, or continue the run farther downstream to some easier rapids and good playspots, taking out at a wooden bridge or Lago Panguipulli. The smoking visage of Volcan Choshuenco sits above the river, and colder water from its upper reaches joins the Fui here, making it cooler than the upper section.

Downstream is an even easier big-water run between the two glacial lakes, Lago Panguipulli and Lago Ranihue. In this scenic stretch the river is known as the Rio Enco. The nearby town of Panguipulli, all of its downtown streets lined with roses, is worth a visit.

The Fui, Chile Waterfall Kayak.
(BioBio Expeditions Worldwide)

PARQUE NACIONAL INGLES, NEAR MOLINA
Difficulty: Class 4
Length: 1/3 mile (0.5 km)

◁ Seven Teacups (Las Siete Tazas)

No description of free-fall kayaking in Chile would be complete without mentioning the Seven Teacups (Las Siete Tazas) section of the Rio Claro in the Parque Nacional Ingles near Molina. Although far north of the Rio Fui, The Seven Teacups provide a similar opportunity to practice big jumps. The "teacups" are pools between runnable waterfalls pouring over carved basalt ledges in a tight canyon. For anyone so inclined, this is nothing short of the ultimate playground, with at least three of the drops in the 20- to 30-foot (6 to 9 m) range. The first drop and the last drop before the take-out are the biggest, but there are several good smaller ones in between as plunge follows plunge. The surroundings couldn't be better. Imagine crystalline water flowing through a series of intimate, shadowy grottoes above a bed of multicolored pebbles.

The whole run is barely 1/2 mile (0.3 km) in length, and there is no shuttle road. Boaters must carry their boats up a poorly marked trail and lower them on ropes to the put-in. A fixed line assists the hoist/carry up from the take-out to a developed trail. Bring ropes and carabiners. Avoid the last drop near the trail, unless you have a plan to extricate yourself from the pool below. Farther downstream is Salto Leona, a spectacular 70-foot (21 m) drop made inaccessible by an unrunnable cataract just upstream.

Recently the park authorities have taken up charging kayakers 5,000 pesos (about $12 U.S.) per day for using the run, and this does not include a shuttle on their motorcycle. Camping is available in the park.

Ambitious experts still looking to drain their adrenal glands can head farther upstream to the Vientidos Saltos ("Twenty-Two Waterfalls"), the steepest runnable creek in Chile. This stretch has been negotiated at extremely low levels. Boaters must deal with logjams and undercut walls. Neither section should be run at any but very low flows.

Argentina

*A*rgentina is graced with natural beauty comparable to that of Chile and the tallest peak in the Western Hemisphere; but, it does not share in the Andes' bounty of white-water. The eastern slopes are not as steep as Chile's, and the mountains block the Pacific precipitation fronts, making the eastern climate drier and the east-flowing rivers less pristine. The Rio Mendoza, for instance, is often turbid. But don't cry for Argentina's paddlers. Because the border between the countries wanders on both sides of the water-shed divide, some Argentinean rivers, like the Rio Manso, flow west with the clear azure hue of the great Chilean rivers. Chile is a short drive, and Argentina controls the only road access to the Rio Futaleufu.

Rio Mendoza ➤

USPALLATA TO POTRERILLOS
(COMMERCIAL SECTION)
Difficulty: Class 4–
Length: 31 miles (50 km)

Season: November through March
Character: Dry area, continuous gradient

Cerro Aconcagua, at about 23,000 feet (7,000 m), is the highest peak in the Western Hemisphere and forms part of the Andean ridge, which shelters the eastern slope from most of the Pacific moisture and limits the whitewater choices in Argentina. The Rio Mendoza drains the glaciers of Aconcagua and is one of the few whitewater runs on the eastern slopes of the Andes.

Although its waters are not of the transparent quality of the great runs of Chile, the Mendoza has much to be said for it. The rapids are challenging and consistent while not being life-threatening. The Argentinean wine country is a fine setting for whitewater boating, with wine-tasting optional. The river runs along the main highway between Santiago, Chile, and the populated areas of Argentina, making the shuttle easy by South American standards. Commercial outfitters are readily available, and trips or shuttles are easily arranged out of the city of Mendoza.

It is possible to put in upstream for a Class 2 run in Punta de Vacas. However, the scenery and whitewater are not as good.

Downstream on the Mendoza, the Canon de Cacheuta offers more challenging whitewater (Class 4+) and good scenery. Known as the 3-mile (4.8 km) "canyon run," it begins about 7½ miles (12 km) below the take-out for the featured run.

For those looking for a more pristine run in Argentina, check out the Rio Manso, located in a remote area in the heart of the Argentinean Lake District, much farther south. The clear-flowing waters of the Manso begin at the outflow of a lake in the Nahuel Huapi National Park, providing Class 5 wilderness action to Lago Steffan. The Manso passes through a remote canyon with numerous advanced and expert technical rapids, waterfalls, and portages. The river flows along the border of the park, providing great views of Volcan Tronador, south of Bariloche. Downstream the Manso flows into Chile and some even more difficult rapids. Boaters driving through Argentina to the Futaleufu with some time on their hands may want to take on this tough one-day run.

Peru

*I*t is hoped that the current democratic government will continue to bring renewed political and economic stability to Peru. While recent setbacks show that true peace can be elusive, the situation has improved so as to open the doors for river runners to explore some of the fine rivers of this startlingly beautiful country. Much of the whitewater is near Cuzco, the historical capital of the Inca civilization; other rivers are on the drier eastern side of the Andes. Among the jewels is the headwaters of the greatest of all rivers, the Amazon, a river of incomprehensible dimensions. It has been estimated that one-fifth of the freshwater runoff of the globe returns to the sea through its mouth. At its headwaters in a semi-dry area of 20,000-foot (6,100 m) Andean peaks, flows are much lower. As one moves to the east, the climate becomes continually wetter, creating the Amazon rainforest. Outfitters in the capital city of Lima promote popular day trips, but serious river runners will want to partake of some of the best multi-day whitewater trips to be found a little farther from civilization.

The Peruvian rivers carve through an unparalleled spectrum of geography—glaciers, grassland, villages, agricultural valleys, desert canyons. The variations are so great that the same river will often have several different names among the locals, each section offering its own distinctive look and feel.

◁ Rio Colca

COLCA CANYON, HACIENDA CANCO TO END OF THE CANYON
Difficulty: Class 5+p
Length: 35 miles (56 km)

Season: Dry season, June through November; too high during the wet season
Character: Deep, dry, isolated canyon

For those ready to take on an arduous descent to the put-in, run numerous Class 5 rapids over several days, and brave myriad other risks, there is the Colca. Perhaps more so than any run in this book, descending the Rio Colca is an odyssey. The experience is a physical and mental ordeal providing its own spiritual reward, a bit like climbing Mount Everest.

The Colca carves an uninhabitable valley in its upper reaches, then dives to sea level, changing its name five times—from Paco to Chilamayo, Colca, Majes, and finally Camana—by the time it reaches the sea. With canyon walls that reach 13,000 feet (3,965 m) above the river on one side and more than 10,000 feet (3,050 km) on the other, the Colca is probably the deepest canyon in the Western Hemisphere. It is twice as deep as the Grand Canyon, and no less dramatic. The river cuts through half a billion years' worth of sandstone, limestone, slate, and quartzite sitting beneath layers of volcanic eruption. Active volcanoes, often visible from the canyon, still send forth plumes of smoke. The headwaters of the Amazon on the Apurimac are only 12 miles (20 km) away on Monte Misme.

Although the canyon was first "discovered" by two American airmen in 1929, parts of it had at one time been a thriving Inca agricultural area laced with a network of irrigation channels, terraces, and stairways. Colca Canyon was first descended in 1981 by Canoandes, an improbable and ill-equipped group of expatriates from Poland. This feat of bravery and faith is reminiscent of John Wesley Powell's exploration of the Grand Canyon, especially when one considers that they not only ran the section described here but the even more difficult and desolate stretch just upstream. Just above the put-in for this run is Pope John Paul II Falls, named by the Poles in honor of the pontiff from their hometown of Krakow.

The burro-assisted hike to the put-in generally takes all day. Those running the Colca can arrange to rent burros and porters at Huambo to make the descent to Hacienda Canco ("chocolate"), a tiny village at the canyon floor and home to five or six native families. The residents are self-sufficient by necessity and harvest everything from potatoes and red chile peppers to bananas and turkeys. Although the trail is in generally good condition, rock throughout the canyon can be unstable and a misstep can be fatal. Once at the bottom, boaters must avoid being a target for rocks that may plummet down from the canyon walls without warning.

The canyon poses other challenges. Extreme seasonal flooding usually rearranges the fragile rock underlying the rapids, so each trip is a little different. Be prepared for cold, due to limited sunlight in parts of the canyon. Early-morning starts help to avoid strong afternoon winds and the biting flies that can be a problem during the day, especially late in the season. Full-coverage clothing and chemical repellents are advised.

Although the extreme geology, dry climate, and limited sunlight leave the canyon barren of most plant life, it is not lifeless. Otters and black salmon are at home here, and boaters have supplemented their rations on the good fishing. Overhead are condors with wingspans up to 10 feet as well as black-chested eagles and osprey. The canyon has achieved national sanctuary status for protection of these birds. Waterfalls upwards of 1,000 feet can be found along the river, and there are many caves.

Boaters should be informed and careful. Upstream diversions can reduce the flow at the put-in by two-thirds, as an irrigation project drains water from the Colca to the previously barren Majes Valley. Flows should be low at the put-in, preferably from 400 to 700 cfs (11 to 19.8 cumecs). A few miles downstream the clear water of the Rio Mamacocha enters on the right and nearly doubles the flow. Flows above 1,500 cfs (42.5 cumecs) just below the confluence mean the river is probably too high to run. If so, a difficult hike out is possible along the Rio Mamacocha, one of the many spectacular side hikes in the canyon.

Although the Colca has many tough rapids, the toughest are divided into three sections. The first section, after the Rio Mamacocha confluence, includes the Gutter where the river squeezes through one massive chute, followed by the aptly named Landslide. Next is a series of the three really difficult rapids beginning with Canoandes, a series of two waterfalls with over 20 feet of vertical drop. Downstream is Chocolate Canyon, about 16 to 19 miles (26 to 30 km) from Canco, with slightly easier rapids and walls the color of every variety of chocolate.

The second section is the very difficult Reparaz Canyon, about 2 miles (3.2 km) downstream of Chocolate Canyon. Named for a Peruvian geologist and college professor, Gonzalo de Reparaz, who explored and mapped the canyon in the 1970s, the canyon includes a long, complicated rapid that is almost impossible to scout.

The third section is just downstream of Reparaz Canyon. This features a minimum two-hour mandatory portage on the right through Poles Canyon, a narrow, thunderous maze of undercut rocks and crisscrossing currents. The portage takes boaters only two-thirds of the way down, and boaters must negotiate the rapid's last drops.

Below this the canyon opens up, and the take-out is a couple of hours downstream where a road meets the river from the right.

Difficulty: Class 2+ to 4
Length: 50 miles (80 km)

Season: All year
Character: Very scenic,
with good whitewater

◁ Rio Urubamba

Flowing north through the "Sacred Valley of the Incas" is the divine river of the Incas, the Urubamba, sometimes known as Rio Vilcanota or Vilcamayo. Located only forty minutes' drive east of the ancient Incan capital of Cuzco, the Urubamba leads to the Inca trail and Machu Picchu, the continent's most spectacular archaeological site. Were it not for its setting at the heart of the Inca empire with splendid ruins scattered along its banks, the Urubamba would still rate inclusion in this book. The river and environs offer ample natural beauty, great whitewater, and centuries of tradition reflected in the customs and dress of the local peasants.

For all its greatness, the Inca empire lasted for barely a century. Prior to 1430, Incan rule was confined to the valley around Cuzco. However, a string of military victories over neighboring tribes beginning in 1430 marked a remarkable expansion of rule and influence. When the conquistadors arrived in 1532, the entire area from southern Colombia to central Chile was dominated by the Incas. Cuzco is now the oldest continually inhab-

Urubamba, Peru. *(BioBio Expeditions Worldwide)*

ited city in the Western Hemisphere and worth the time to explore. The name means "naval" in the Quechua language spoken by the Incas.

The "Sacred Valley" section of the river from Huambutio to Pisac is often run in one day (Class 2 and 3), passing through a majestic red sandstone gorge anointed with Spanish moss and small farms with walls dating back to Incan times. At Pisac, boaters can visit the most spectacular sun temples of the Inca empire. Other, more difficult stretches downstream include Pisac to Kalca, an 11-mile (17.6 km) stretch; Kalca to Urubamba (Class 3 and 4), also called the Huaran-Sapo section; and Urubamba to Ollantaytimbo, where boaters may choose shorter runs, including Ollantay Rapids, from the road access along the river. The Incan culture comes into focus near Ollantaytimbo. Here are several sections of well-preserved terraces, a lookout post, the foundations of a bridge, and even a quarry where ancient workers moved rocks weighing up to a hundred tons across the river and into place on citadels. Some "weary" stones are still in place on the trail.

Below Ollantaytimbo the road veers away and railroad tracks accompany the river en route to Machu Picchu. For the next 60 miles (96 km) the river tumbles down several spectacular cascades best admired from the train, although some reaches have been run by expert kayakers. There is a hydroelectric dam just upstream of the trailhead to Machu Picchu.

Downstream from Machu Picchu to Quillabamba is a challenging stretch of Class 4 water. Since put-in access is only available by train, this section gets little use. Here the surrounding area becomes verdant and deeply forested as the Urubamba approaches the Amazon rainforest. The sections downstream of Machu Picchu include the reach from Challey, where the railroad ends, to Quillabamba (Class 3 and 4), and from Quillabamba to Escarte (3+). Here the water warms as the elevation drops through the La Convencion Valley. Below Escarte the Urubamba's metamorphosis from high Andean cascade to meandering rainforest river is complete as the river disappears into the jungle.

Rio Apurimac ➤

HUAPACHACA BRIDGE (NEAR CHINCHAYPUJIO) TO CUNYOC BRIDGE

Difficulty: Class 5
Length: 40 miles (64 km)

Season: May through October (during dry season)
Character: Deep granite canyon, isolated multiday classic

For all the attention given to identifying the source of the Nile, the source of the Amazon was still in controversy until fairly recently. It is now believed to be just to the north of Colca Canyon at the top of the Andes at more than 20,000 feet (6100 m) where it is only a small, glacier-fed stream. From this most distant point, barely 100 miles (160 km) from the Pacific Ocean, the world's largest river drainage begins. On the way it changes its name from the Carhuasanta to the Challamayo, the Hornillas, and then Apurimac before becoming the Amazon. By the time it reaches the Atlantic, almost 4,000 miles (6,400 km) from its source, it is by far the largest river on Earth. Although the Nile is slightly longer, the Amazon dwarfs it in sheer size. It is estimated that one-fifth of the fresh water returning to the Earth's oceans passes through its mouth, creating a freshwater pocket extending as much as 100 miles (160 km) out into the Atlantic.

While the Amazon spends most of its time meandering slowly through the world's largest rainforest, river runners look to its origins, where spectacular whitewater rushes through an array of deep, beautiful canyons. Here it is called the Apurimac, or sometimes just "Apu." Apurimac comes from the Inca words *apus* ("lords") and *rimac* ("a single voice"). To the Quechua Indians who presently inhabit the area, and to the Incas from whom they descended, the river is the "great speaker" or "lord oracle."

The period of the greatest Inca conquest was under the empire's ninth ruler, Pachaucuti, "Overturner of the World," and resulted in extraordinary expansion. With no knowledge of the wheel or the arch and with no written system of language or math, the Incas constructed remarkable cities, irrigation systems, and networks of roads and bridges linking an empire of some 3,000 miles (4,800 km). Runners stationed every few miles transmitted messages swiftly throughout the empire.

This growth was almost checked by the Apurimac. The Incas were not river runners; in fact, few, if any, swam. Such was their respect for the river that for decades the Apurimac separated the Incas' developing empire from cultures to the north. Ultimately, tenacity resulted in a suspension bridge woven of native grasses spanning the river. The site of this bridge, just downstream of the whitewater run featured here, was maintained for more than three centuries by the villagers of Carahuasi. The bridge's collapse in the 1890s provided the drama of Thornton Wilder's 1929 book *The Bridge of San Luis Rey*. To this day, the townsfolk weave grasses into bridges across the river.

At the put-in for this section, the river has already dropped to an elevation of about 7,000 feet (2,135 m) and has grown to major proportions, flexing its might by carving deep canyons in its path. Boating is strictly a dry-season activity when the flows drop to runnable levels.

The put-in is the Hualpachaca Bridge, sometimes called Puente Militar, about a five- to six-hour drive or bus ride northwest from Cuzco. Boaters generally take four days to run this stretch, taking out just upstream from the Cunyoc Bridge on the road from Cuzco to Lima.

Below the Hualpachaca Bridge are several Class 3 and 4 warm-up rapids. The pool-and-drop rapids gradually become bigger and closer and eddies smaller as the river drops between 1,000-foot (305 m) granite walls. The most spectacular scenery is in a sculptured

I met John Foss in 1987. What I initially interpreted as an overearnest familiarity I came to appreciate over the years as a childlike enthusiasm for rivers, the canyons they flowed through, geology, and history. John was part of a dying breed of kayaker known as the expedition paddler. His great love was loading up his boat with camping gear and setting off into wild, intriguing, and often very remote river canyons. Between trips he could be found poring over books and maps while scheming his next adventure.

Throughout the remainder of the 1980s and into the 1990s we frequently paddled together in Chile, Peru, and California, seeking out new runs and enjoying the beauty of the classic runs. But there is one incident in particular that stands out in my mind.

In 1995 I was leading a commercial raft descent down the Acabamba Abyss of the Apurimac River in Peru. None of us had been there before, and our knowledge of the canyon was limited to some rudimentary notes scribbled by one of the infamous Poles of the Canoandes group who did the first descent, a chapter out of Joe Kane's Running the Amazon, *and some horribly inadequate maps. This is one of the most fantastic sections of river anywhere in the world for a team of solid Class 5 kayakers who want to spend a week running beautiful whitewater surrounded by granite in a deep and remote canyon. Though I longed to be in a creek boat responsible only for myself, instead I carried with me the responsibility of peoples' lives and food for eight days on the* (continued next page) granite gorge within the main gorge that continues a few miles past the Rio Picaro confluence.

The canyon gorge opens up a few miles below the Picaro where the locals work terraced farms on top of gently rounded hills. The whitewater remains unabated through this section. Major rapids may require portaging at Oracle Falls, Space Odyssey, and Molar de Muelas (Sore Molar), a long and technical Class 5 and the most difficult on the run. The overall gradient is 36 fpm (7 mpk).

Gold miners work the lower stretches of the river. These bedraggled throwbacks to the nineteenth century are friendly and may give boaters a hand with their portage in exchange for some food. The lush landscape in the lower section includes orchids, bromeliads, and huge overhanging ferns.

Boaters running the Apu should be prepared to deal with biting flies the locals call "mosquitos." Keep an eye out for scorpions, snakes, and other biting fiends as well. The sand flies are day feeders and do not venture over water; accordingly, it's wise to boat from dawn till dusk and bring full-coverage clothing and/or repellent.

Exploration beginning in the 1970s brought details of other runs both above and below this section. Upstream is Black Canyon, and below is the Acobamba Abyss. These runs are only suited for those into expedition boating and gear, and comfortable at the extreme end of navigability. One particular stretch of note is downstream of the take-out at the Cunyoc bridge, the extremely difficult Acobamba Abyss. This reach begins with 7 placid miles (11.2 km) until huge polished boulders begin to constrict the river to progressively smaller routes, at times only a few feet wide. As the gradient mounts, the rapids become very imposing, and at one point there are five major portages in less than a mile (1.6 km).

river. We encountered tremendously difficult whitewater at every turn, and maintained a foreboding sense that the take-out was a long way away.

John kayaked along with us and carried with him photocopies from a book he had read about the Incas. His loose-leaf chapter hinted that the lost Incan city of Vilcabamba was in the mountains about the river, and he was literally ready to start hiking. In fact, he tried to convince me that we should abort the trip and head for the hills in search of what had eluded explorers for almost a century. I was incredulous. How could I! I was responsible for the lives of an obstetrician who had babies to deliver, a computer businessman with 2,000 employees, an Indian Chief with a tribe to look out for, and everyone else on the trip!

We ended up moving downstream at the turtle's pace that rafters can be so competent at maintaining. We were two and a half days late to the take-out, and we never went off in search of Vilcabamba. But John's enthusiasm for heading off into the forest in the face of such responsibility is a tribute to his childlike attitude. John Foss was really an eight-year-old in the body of a grown man.

—Beth Rypins

Note: On July 5, 1998, John Foss drowned while kayaking the first descent of the Rio Huallabamba in northern Peru.

Santa Ana put-in at Putina Punku (near San Juan del Oro) to Tambopata National Reserve (near Puerto Maldonado)
Difficulty: Class 4
Length: 120 miles (192 km)

Season: May through October (during the dry season; usually to high in the rainy season)
Character: Lush, isolated river with bird and wildlife viewing

◁ Rio Tambopata

Descending the east face of the Andes from high-country alpine forests all the way down to the jungle floor, the Tambopata is an epic boating journey. The run combines several days of challenging whitewater in the upper reaches with an unforgettable voyage through pristine and dazzling rainforest and game reserves in the lower reaches. Isolation, good fortune, and human wisdom have so far preserved this area, which may hold the greatest biological diversity of any preserved area in the world. The efforts continue, as several national parks have been proposed. A raft or kayak is without a doubt the best vehicle from which to appreciate this beauty.

Located just north of Lake Titicaca on the Peruvian border, the Tambopata flows north and forms the border with Bolivia for a few miles below the put-in near the old gold-mining town of San Juan del Oro. The rapids on the upper reaches are not only technical, but they are always exciting. Beginning as rock gardens, they swell to roller-coasters as the flow builds, moving from Class 3 to solid Class 4 a few days down the river. The many sandy beaches offer good camping, and there are opportunities for several short side hikes. Exploring the tributaries for waterfalls can be rewarding, as can be fishing in the nearby lakes.

The second half of the trip is a chance to take in the pristine beauty and observe the wildlife of the tropical rainforest. Along these calm waters are numerous monkey species including the howler and emperor tamarin, as well as otter, capybara, tapir, ocelot, miniature red deer, and even the elusive jaguar. Tree frogs, butterflies, and orchids add brilliant color. Enormous bird-eating spiders live here, and 100-pound (45 kg) catfish can be found in the river. The jungle canopy, which includes mahoganies, kaypocs, coral bean trees, and rubber trees, rises 120 to 180 feet (37 to 55 m) above the jungle floor.

The impetus for preservation, however, is provided by the more the 1,000 species of native birds. Parrots, toucans, herons, kingfishers, king vultures, eagles, hawks, and kites nest in the area. Eight species of macaw, the largest of the parrot family, are still abundant in southeastern Peru. A visit to the "macaw lick," called the Colpa, on river left near the Colpa Lodge, is an indelible study of color and sound. For reasons not fully understood, these inquisitive and entertaining winged entertainers gather to eat clay amid fits of squawking and tantrums of feather ruffling.

At the confluence with the Rio Madre de Dios, the current slackens, and most rafts use motorized canoes to assist the float to a jungle lodge situated in the Tambopata Wildlife Preserve where day hikes are popular, and on to the gold-mining town of Puerto Maldonado. The Tambopata continues on to the Amazon.

The little town at the put-in had the disturbing practice of using the river as its latrine, which made for a rather ugly beginning, but soon after we shoved off several side streams entered the river, diluting the bad stuff. Things started looking up! The jungle towered over us as we quickly left civilization behind. A huge king vulture sailed 30 feet over our heads and observed us closely from his new perch. Rog and I had brought our own two-person inflatable kayak, which we paddled most of the trip. The paddling was easy Class 2 for the first couple of days, but as it continued to rain off and on, the river kept increasing in volume. By the time we got to the bigger rapids on day four, we had enough water to make them Class 3+, and pretty big and powerful. We had a wonderful time, but flipped three times in the big stuff before we got completely worn out and jumped into the bigger rafts with the other folks toward the end of the day.

Downstream the river mellowed out and we got to see lots of wildlife: capybara, spider monkeys, birds, and even a tapir, a strange animal that looks like a cross between a big pig and a small elephant. They are pretty rare now, so it was a real treat. It came down to the opposite bank of the river in the early morning while we were having breakfast at camp. Tapirs can't see well, so this one waded into the river and started swimming over toward us, got about halfway, became cautious as it caught our scent, and after a few minutes of indecision turned around and dashed for the jungle. Wow. We saw lots of other wildlife, including hundreds of macaws and other parrots at dawn on the day we passed the clay lick. It was an amazing spectacle.

After seven or eight days on the river, Rog and I got dropped off at a jungle resort where we spent the next four days walking around in the lowland jungle looking at birds and other animals. It was great. We even saw a jaguar on the river bank on our last day, on the way to Puerto Maldonado and the flight to Cuzco.

On the "down" side, there were times when the sand flies, chiggers, and no-see-ums were horrendous, and ever unscrupulous! We wore long-sleeved and long-legged clothes all the time, especially on the river and in the jungle, but you know there were some times when the pants had to come down, and then those little buggers zoomed right in. Talk about unfair tactics! I eventually learned to apply mosquito repellent to my bum before each such event, but not before I got a collection of bites that rivaled the constellations in a moonless sky. But the trip was well worth this "price." The Tambopata was one of the top wilderness experiences of my life.

—Audre Newman

Ecuador

$\mathcal{E}$cuador sits on the Pacific Coast of South America, astride the Earth's equator. The northern Andes cut through the center of the country with twenty-two peaks between 14,000 (4,267 m) and 20,696 feet (6,308 m), including the world's tallest active volcano, Cotopaxi at 19,614 feet (5,978 m), and the only snowfield in the world bisected by the equator. The Ecuadorians are accustomed to high elevation, as the capital city of Quito is at 9,000 feet (2,745 m) and much of the country's population is located in the central highlands region. Until recently Ecuador's main product was the export of bananas, but a growing tourist trade provides a growing source of income. Most Indians speak Quechua, with Spanish as a second language.

Much of Ecuador holds lush forests and remote canyons, with plenty of precipitation and excellent whitewater potential. Most of these rivers are just being explored, and the concept of "paddling Ecuador" is just starting to become popular. We cover two rivers, the Toachi and the Quijos, but Ecuador has several other runs, from big-volume rivers to steep creeks. Another new run that is being promoted is the Rio Upano, also known as the "River of Sacred Waterfalls," an east-slope river farther south in Ecuador.

◀ Rio Toachi

ALLURIQUIN TO NEAR SANTO DOMINGO
Difficulty: Class 3
Length: 12 miles (19 km)

NEAR SANTO DOMINGO TO BELOW THE CONFLUENCE ON THE RIO BLANCO AT VALLE HERMOSA
Difficulty: Class 4–
Length: 12 miles (19 km)

RIO BLANCO, VALLE HERMOSA TO LA CONCORDIA
Difficulty: Class 3–
Length: 13 miles (21 km)

Season: All year, except in July to September (dry season) when flows may be too low; extreme high flows should be avoided
Character: Widely fluctuating, west-slope river

West of the Ecuadorian capital of Quito, flowing northwest from the cloudforests of the high Andes down to the tropical rainforests of the Ecuadorian coast, is the Rio Toachi, which joins and becomes the Rio Blanco for the last of the three sections described here. Each section can be run separately or combined for a trip of approximately 37 miles (59 km). As of 1995, the Toachi was the river getting most of the whitewater usage in Ecuador.

We are dividing the Toachi into three sections: Alluriquin to near Santo Domingo; near Santo Domingo to below the confluence on the Rio Blanco at Valle Hermosa; and on the Rio Blanco, Valle Hermosa to La Concordia. Each is a study in the beauty of nature and biodiversity, with countless species of exotic orchids, birds, and butterflies. The rare southern river otter is found in these waters. Just upstream of the Toachi is a panorama of earthquake faults and active volcanoes, including Cotopaxi, Ecuador's largest active volcano and the setting for a national park.

The most challenging and popular whitewater is in the second section, downstream of the city of Santo Domingo, where river runners take on continuous Class 4 rapids in the exquisite and uninhabited Sapos Gorge. The river takes you near the isolated villages of the Colorado Indians and the aptly named Valle Hermosa ("Beautiful Valley").

A good 24-mile (38 km) Class 3 stretch of the Rio Blanco can also be run, beginning at San Miguel de Los Bancos upstream of the Toachi confluence and ending at Valle Hermosa or continuing on to La Concordia.

Rio Quijos ➤

COSANGA TO UPSTREAM OF SAN
  RAFAEL FALLS
Difficulty: Class 4
Length: 50 miles (80 km)

Season: All year possible,
  but usually too high in
  rainy season
Character: Big river in wet
  environment

Over the spine of the Andes east of the Ecuadorian capital of Quito is the Rio Quijos, first run by the Polish group Canoandes in 1983. In 1987 a major earthquake rocked this valley, killing some 2,000 people including a group of engineers studying the feasibility of building a dam on the river. The plans for a dam died, and landslides from the quake destroyed the main road and filled the river with silt, altering many rapids.

The weather pattern on the east slope of Ecuador generates tremendous amounts of rain—about 70 inches a year—making the waters of the Quijos big and wild most of the year. No boater should consider taking on these raging rapids except during the driest months from December to March. Flash floods on the main river or side streams are always a possibility.

The Quijos is big and wide as it flows northwest here near the city of Baeza. A few miles below the take-out is the spectacular San Rafael Falls, at about 500 feet (153 m) the highest in Ecuador. The falls can be viewed after a short trek from the road leading to the village of Reventador, which shares its name with a nearby volcano. Downstream the Quijos flows east where it joins the Napo and eventually the Amazon.

Excellent river running is also available on an upstream tributary, the Rio Cosanga, as well as on the Quijos above its confluence with the Cosanga. To the south is the "River of Sacred Waterfalls," the Rio Upano, an increasingly popular paddling destination.

AFRICA

*S*ince the Leakey excavations in East Africa in the 1950s and '60s, Africa has been recognized as the birthplace of the human race and the cradle of modern civilization. Yet modern civilization here is in many respects still in its infancy. As Africa emerges from a long history of colonialism, it sometimes seems the only constant is change, while social and political stability proves elusive.

In spite of Africa's troubles, travelers can still experience much of the exotic diversity that drew European explorers and adventurers. Africa is home to the world's largest game reserves, the largest desert, and some of the largest rainforests. Mount Kilimanjaro still rises above the East African plateau, and the Rift Valley is still one of the planet's great geologic and scenic attractions. No less fascinating are the many thousands of tribal peoples who have made this their home here since the dawn of time.

Although Africa has a few great rivers, from a whitewater paddler's point of view the climate and topography have some shortcomings. The Sahara, the world's largest desert, dominates the northern one-third of the continent. The west-central region gets plenty of rain but is mostly flat. The southwest is mostly desert. The east-central and southeastern regions have the greatest geographical promise, with significant mountains and seasonal rainfall. The Republic of South Africa, covering the southernmost part of the continent, is home to several fine, easily accessed whitewater runs and is also the home of an active river-running community that has produced some world-class paddlers.

Foremost and easily the most popular among Africa's rivers is the Zambezi, with up to 50,000 users annually. The fourth largest river on the continent, it divides Zambia and Zimbabwe where it provides the world's most spectacular one-day river trip, just below Victoria Falls.

Ethiopia, Kenya, and Tanzania, in the central eastern part of the continent, have some good whitewater rivers which also provide great game viewing. Renewed political stability in certain areas fosters more exploration, and new runs are still being discovered here.

The White Nile in Uganda was just recently opened to commercial rafting by Adrift of New Zealand and features big-water flows on the scale of the Zambezi. On the other

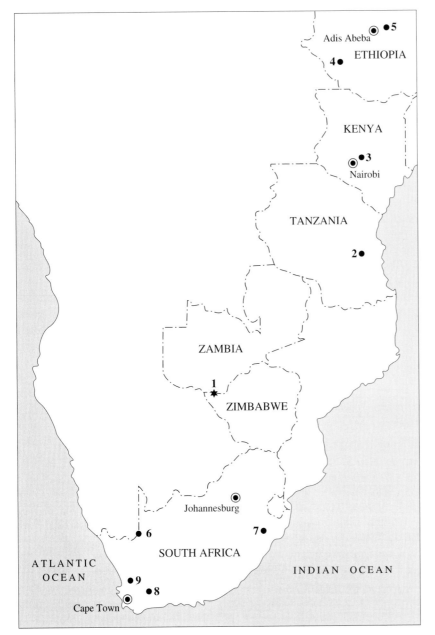

Africa

1 Zambezi River (see page 197)
2 Rufiji River
3 Tana River
4 Omo River
5 Awash River
6 Orange (Senqu) River
7 Tugela River
8 Breede River
9 Doring River

end of the river spectrum, Reunion Island, east of Madagascar in the Indian Ocean, reportedly holds rain-fed creeks reminiscent of those of Corsica but even steeper.

All of this is not to say that river running in Africa is as simple and carefree as in highly developed countries, because it isn't. Although the infrastructure and availability of vehicles and gear in South Africa is good, boaters in other countries may have trouble without the help of outfitters. Keep in mind that everything takes longer in Africa, so allow lots of time and be prepared to be very patient.

Nearly all Africans are very poor, and high population growth, recurrent droughts, and poor infrastructure all exacerbate hardship. Visitor warnings must be taken seriously. Travelers must be informed and keep their wits about them, as well as maintaining an open, respectful attitude toward the locals. Those willing to travel under these conditions are rarely disappointed.

No discussion of Africa is complete without mention of the continent's amazing wild creatures, both great and small. Floating on a raft or kayak provides an almost ideal platform to observe them in their native setting. It could only be better if boaters were assured they are at the top of the food chain. Flat-water sections of some rivers are the domain of the hungry crocodile and the often testy hippopotamus. Both are dangerous and require the assistance of experienced personnel to spot and avoid them. Some dangers are even more unusual. Zambezi sharks are known to swim up to 400 miles (640 km) upstream from the ocean and attack boaters. Few who spend much time in Africa return without a story or two about the strange insects. Boaters should make note of and take precautions for the stinging or biting insects resident in the areas they will visit.

Zimbabwe and Zambia

BAKOTA GORGE, BOILING POT
  BELOW VICTORIA FALLS TO
  BELOW RAPID NUMBER 18
  (USUAL TAKE-OUT AT LOW
  WATER; ABOVE NUMBER 11
  TO BELOW NUMBER 23 AT
  HIGH WATER)
Difficulty: Class 5–$_p$
Length: 14 miles (22.4 km),
  a one-day run

NUMBER 18 TO MATETSI RIVER
  (CONTINUATION, AT LOW
  WATER; FROM BELOW
  NUMBER 23 AT HIGH WATER)
Difficulty: Class 4$_p$
Length: 61 miles (97.6 km)

Season: Rapids 1 through
  10, August through
  December; all year below
  Number 10, unless heavy
  rain year
Character: Big, warm water
  in sheer-walled basalt
  gorge; dazzling waterfalls

◁ Zambezi River

In 1855 missionary and explorer Dr. David Livingstone came upon Victoria Falls, known locally as Mosi-oa-Tunya ("the smoke that thunders"), on an overland crossing of Africa in search of a natural highway across the continent. He crawled near to the edge and peered over. Although his dreams of an easy water transport across the continent were crushed, some of the most inspired passages of his journal describe his experience of the falls. He spent time exploring and attempted to measure them, then named them after Queen Victoria and resumed his journey to the coast.

Later the mile-wide, 300-foot-tall (1,700 m x 110 m) falls were declared one of the seven natural wonders of the world, as droves of tourists came to stare in wonderment. In the 1970s civil war rocked the area, stalling exploration. However, Richard Bangs of Sobek recognized the Zambezi below the falls as one of the world's greatest big-water runs and in 1981 organized the first descent. River running was followed by other diversions, and Victoria Falls is again a major tourist destination. The area is now a hotbed for adventure sports devotees partaking in bungee-jumping, ultralights, and riverboarding, as well as boating.

The Zambezi below the falls is like no other river. With sheer, spray-soaked canyon walls, thundering falls, and mist rising a third of a mile (half a kilometer), there is certainly no more impressive river put-in anywhere. The immense, warm, jade green flows and the enormous, well-spaced rapids make the Zambezi one of the world's finest white-water experiences.

Zambezi River, Zambia and Zimbabwe. *(BioBio Expeditions Worldwide)*

The river scene is world-class, too. Local porters, often barefoot, labor mightily carrying gear up and down the canyon in the intense heat. Massive rapids, most of which are known only by their sequential number, often catch and flip the big commercial rafts. The more adventurous customers are disappointed if the trip does not include a flip and swim in the bathtub-warm water. Some commercial companies oblige with an intentional but unannounced flip in Number 18 (also known as Oblivion).

From its headwaters in western Zambia, Angola, and Zaire to the Indian Ocean, the Zambezi passes through and forms the border of four south-central African countries for nearly 1,674 miles (2,678 km). The falls and the river on this run mark the border between Zambia to the north on river left, and Zimbabwe on the right.

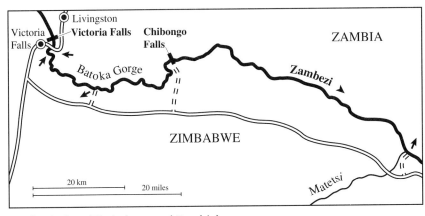

Zambezi River (Zimbabwe and Zambia)

The giant baobab tree dominates vegetation in the area. Local legend has it that a mischievous baboon took the seeds from the creator and planted them upside down, causing its roots to appear to grow upward. Birds include kingfishers, fish eagles, black eagles, hornbilled trumpeters, cormorants, and the very rare Taita falcon. Monkeys, baboons, klipspingers, and the rock hyrax are common along the shore. Hippos and crocodiles lurk in the calm-water sections, as neither care for whitewater. The deadly black mamba snake is rare but always a show-stopper when it appears. Scorpions and the dung beetle are common as are huge termite mounds. As the river makes its way downstream from the top of the rainforest environment over the falls and down to the drier lower lands of the Matetsi Valley, the wildlife, vegetation, and climate change.

Above Victoria Falls the river is a very wide streambed supporting easy wildlife-viewing canoe trips as wildlife reserves can be found on either bank. Game floats are also run below Kariba Dam.

Batoka Gorge is a study in back-cutting. The falls were originally some miles downstream but gradually carved upstream through the massive basalt plateau to the present site. This cutting phenomenon often followed faults perpendicular to the river path, leaving a distinctive zigzag assemblage of gorges, readily seen from the air.

Flows on the Zambezi usually range from 10,000 to 60,000 cfs (283 to 1,698 cumecs). Starting in July, the dry season takes hold, and the river drops from its rainy-season maximum. In November or so, the rains start again, and the river starts to rise.

The 6-mile (9.6 km) section of the river from just below the falls to Number 10 cannot be run at high flows, because of the difficulty of Numbers 7 and 9. Every boater planning a multi-day trip will want to run this section, so to be sure you are on the river

Zambezi River, Zambia and Zimbabwe. *(BioBio Expeditions Worldwide)*

during the Boiling Pot season, you may want to plan to run the river between August and late October.

Most trips are one-day excursions through Batoka Gorge, and particularly the upper canyon which contains the most concentrated section of rapids. The pool-and-drop character of the river makes for very distinct rapids. Described here are what are traditionally considered the more difficult rapids.

The more desirable put-in has been from the Zambian side, right below Victoria Falls, because it allows one to explore beneath the falls, and, if you dare, to carry up a ways and run the "negative rapids," a series of three monstrous cataracts that emerge from the mist-shrouded base of the falls. This is the sole domain of the most intrepid expert kayakers. The put-in from the Zimbabwian side usually starts at Number 4, beyond the view of the falls. However, since many take-outs are in Zimbabwe, this gives the advantage of avoiding some strenuous and time-consuming pre-launch logistics called the "Border Shuffle." It is reported that one operator (the New Zealand–based Adrift) has recently been granted approval to launch at Number 1 on the Zimbabwe side.

At low water the usual day run ends below Number 18, taking out on the Zimbabwe side. At high water the run is from above Number 11 to below Number 23, with put-in and take-out access on the Zambian side. From either take-out, the hike out of the gorge is strenuous.

Only the most notable rapids (all either Class 4 or Class 5) are described here:

Number 1 is set beneath the spectacular bridge that links the two countries. The rapid begins with the Boiling Pot, a sticky eddy on river left, which should be avoided.

Number 3 is a steep drop with a somewhat blind entrance and a strong reversal on the left wall.

Number 4 (Morning Glory) is the first major rapid and usually run on the left. In high water it is only scoutable on the right, requiring boaters to execute a tough ferry.

Number 5 (Stairway to Heaven) is possibly the biggest and one of the best commercially run rapids in the world. Most boaters run down the center to the left of the large pourover and then into the infamous Catcher's Mitt. Lateral waves on either side can stand even the largest raft on its side tubes.

Number 6 (Devil's Toilet Bowl) is a narrow constriction with powerful hydraulics.

Number 7 (Gulliver's Travels), the third difficult rapid, should be scouted by catching the large eddy on the right well above the rapid and walking all the way to the bottom to view the entrance from below. This is probably the most technically demanding rapid on the river. Most boaters plot a route through the boulders and ledges to the right. A river-wide ledge halfway down is called The Crease. The massive waves below earn the name Land of the Giants. At high flows both Numbers 7 and 9 become far too large to run. Number 8 offers route options; the more daring runs, in the center and left, often result in flips.

Number 9 (Commercial Suicide) is usually portaged on the right. Boaters should plot their next stop from Number 8 so as not to get swept into this rapid by the uninterrupted flow. It has been run at optimum levels on the right.

Number 11 (Terminator) is more difficult at low flows. Only a narrow line is available to run. Commercial trips during the shoulder season put in here from the Zambian side unless flows are high enough to form a whirlpool above Number 14.

Number 13 is a big series of waves which become more difficult at high levels. Just downstream and around the corner above Number 14 is Number 15 (Are You Experienced?). A dangerous whirlpool forms here at extreme high flows, halting all commercial boating in the canyon.

Number 16 has, at high flows, some of the biggest waves on the river. Scout on the right.

Number 18 (Oblivion) has, at lower flows, a powerful hole that stops rafts dead in their tracks and can result in some spectacular extended surfs and violent flips. Some commercial groups shun cheat routes on either side and give their guests the chance to join the warm-water carnage.

The numbered rapids end at 23, but tough rapids are still to be run; also, below Number 23 crocodiles are more common and hippos may be present, and kayakers especially should be careful. At about $18\frac{1}{2}$ miles (30 km) are Closed Season and Open Season, both very technical at low flows. At mile 28 (km 45) is Chimamba, a difficult drop at higher flows. Scout and possibly portage on the right.

Just downstream from Chimamba is Upper Mweemba, sometimes spelled Moemba (also known as Ragdoll). Here boaters must negotiate a blind left-turn entrance into a series of big waves and holes. About 300 yards (275 m) downstream is Lower Mweemba, a mandatory portage, though kayakers have run the big falls.

At mile 31 (km 50) the Chibongo River, the site for a proposed hydroelectric dam, signals a mandatory portage of Chibongo Falls on the right. Put back in near some sloping ledges about 50 yards (46 m) below the last falls.

Downstream is Son of Ghostrider, followed by the much more impressive Ghostrider. Boaters should identify the small eddy on the left below Son of Ghostwriter before entering the rapid; you will need to eddy out here to scout Ghostrider. Ghostrider holds the biggest waves on the river and a powerful eddy. Just below Ghostrider, after the long pool and a left turn, is Deep Throat, generally portaged on the left.

About 40 miles (64 km) from the put-in is the Kalamba confluence, about $1\frac{1}{4}$ miles (2 km) below which the river turns left. Two-thirds of a mile (1 km) below this turn is Asleep at the Wheel. You must stop and scout well above this rapid; definitely above the split in the river, where the much smaller left channel heads off at almost a right angle. If you are "Asleep at the Wheel" and miss the left channel, you will be committed to running the much tougher right side without the benefit of a scout.

From here the canyon opens up, and hippos and crocodiles become more common. Relatively easy boating awaits for another $38\frac{1}{2}$ miles (62 km) to the take-out at the Matetsi River confluence, at about mile 78 (km 126).

For all the Zambezi's wonders, it is in serious danger. A hydroelectric power dam nearly 200 meters high has been proposed near Chibongo Falls, approximately 31 miles (50 km) downstream from Victoria Falls. The proposed dam would inundate the river to $1\frac{1}{2}$ miles (2 km) below the falls, drowning all of the major upstream rapids. It is hoped that the significant tourist industry surrounding the falls and the Batoka Gorge will cause this project to be reexamined.

Tanzania

Rufiji River ➤

The Rufiji River sojourns through Tanzania's magnificent Selous Game Reserve, which, at over 18,000 square miles (46,620 sq km), is the largest reserve in Africa. This is one of the wildest places on the continent, with virtually no roads, just a network of trails that get little use. Signs of development can be found only at the park's edges, leaving rafts as the ideal vehicle for a safari, not unlike those taken by Africa's first explorers. The landscape is impressive, beginning with the spectacular chutes and misty cataracts of Shiguri Falls and continuing with vast grasslands, baobab trees, wild figs, and the fine sandstone formations and rapids of Stiegler's Gorge. In fact, even getting to the river is a bit of an adventure. Some use the Chinese-built Tazara Railway, which cuts through the north part of the Selous Game Reserve and gives a good preview of the game viewing. The road to the put-in is 96 miles (155 km) long, primitive, and often impassible. A fee of approximately $60 U.S. is charged to run the river.

Some of the best action on the Rufiji is the wildlife. Lions, wildebeests, fish eagles, ibises, and countless other species live much as they have for ages with virtually no pressure from civilization. Hippos, and less frequently crocodiles, can be found all along the river, causing both wonder and concern; in fact, hippos are such a concern that local authorities require groups to hire professional, armed game scouts to accompany all trips.

From the put-in, it is an easy +50-mile (80+ km) float down to the mouth of the Ruaha River on the left which warns boaters that they are about to enter the sheer-walled Stiegler's Gorge (Class 3). The gorge is less than 10 miles (16 km) long but has some good

CONFLUENCE OF LAWEGA AND KILOMBRO RIVERS (BELOW SHIGURI FALLS) TO STIEGLER'S GORGE
Difficulty: Class 1+
Length: 55 miles (88 km)

STIEGLER'S GORGE TO RUFIJI RIVER CAMP
Difficulty: Class 3
Length: 25 miles (40 km)

Season: All year (wet season starts in January)
Character: Exotic wildlife trip

The Selous is the largest uninhabited game reserve in the world. In the Selous, one doesn't catch a safari bus to the corner of Giraffe and Warthog. To see the Selous, one hikes and one paddles. And when an aggravated hippopotamus is charging one's rubber raft, one paddles very hard, indeed.

When I announced to family and friends that I was going hiking and river-rafting through a vast patch of African cabbage, they didn't ask why. They must have realized that after three years bent over an idling and backfiring novel, skinning my knuckles on every bolt and wrench in the literary toolbox, I needed to blow a little carbon out of my own exhaust. Perhaps they also sensed that after my recent dealings with editors, agents, lawyers, producers, and reviewers, I might be primed for the company of crocodiles.

Nobody was particularly concerned that I was off to walk with the animals, talk with the animals, squawk with the animals. After all, I once turned down an offer of zebra steak in a weird restaurant in Hawaii, and have made it a lifelong practice never to date women who wear leopard-skin pillbox hats. My beast karma was pretty good.

—Tom Robbins, from Paths Less Traveled

rapids, especially near the top. The easily scouted and/or portaged drops are the only whitewater on the river. Below them the canyon opens to a spectacular wildlife area known as the Great Ruaha. Boaters often take layover days, using the time for long walks into the bush accompanied by scouts. The lower section of the river changed its course in the early 1970s and now follows a braided course into Lake Tagalala.

A popular alternative is to put in at Stiegler's Gorge, which allows for a shorter run of about 25 miles (40 km). Another possibility is putting in upstream of the Rufiji and the Great Ruaha River where good whitewater has been scouted, as have numerous hippos stationed after the drops. This stretch apparently waits to be run.

Kenya

Tana River ➤

Born in the snowy, southern slopes of equatorial Mount Kenya at over 17,000 feet, the Tana is Kenya's largest river. It wanders in a meandering arc northeast through the dry East African eastern scrubland and finally runs almost due south to the Indian Ocean. The described sections are just north of Nairobi, and the put-in is just north of Sangana.

The Tana is a good combination of wildlife, scenery, and whitewater. Among the attractions along the river is abundant birdlife, including herons, hammerkop, ibises, kingfishers, weaver birds, fish eagles, Egyptian geese, and paradise flycatchers. Trees include wild fig, eucalyptus, and camphor.

Most of the rapids near the top are Class 3 for the first 2 miles (3.2 km), followed by a calm middle stretch with good sightseeing. Downstream the whitewater picks up again, with two Class 4 rapids in the final 4-mile stretch. The names of the rapids are Dog's Back, Can of Worms, Captain's Folly, Fish Eye, Spasms, Sphincter-Flexor. The rapids are tougher at high water but are not continuous. At the last Class 4 rapid is a 25-foot (7.6 m) waterfall that kayaks occasionally run. This area is an excellent place to relax and jump in the falls.

To get to the put-in from Nairobi, turn left at the "T" after entering the Sangana town limits and go through town, across the railroad tracks, and over a bridge which crosses the river just downstream of the bridge. Alternatively, turn right at a dirt

NEAR SANGANA
Difficulty: Class 4
Length: 9½ miles (15 km)

Season: Year-round; sometimes too low in February, March, September, or October
Character: Rural, exotic birdlife

Bogart: *How'd you like it?*

Hepburn: *Like it?*

Bogart: *Whitewater rapids?*

Hepburn: *Kind of a dream.*

Bogart: *I don't blame you for being scared, Miss, not one little bit. Ain't no person in their right mind ain't scared of whitewater.*

Hepburn: *I never dreamed that any mere physical experience could be so stimulating.*

Bogart: *How's that, Miss?*

Hepburn: *I've only known such excitement a few times before, but usually in my dear brother's sermon when the spirit was really upon him.*

Bogart: *You mean you want to go on?*

Hepburn: *Naturally.*

Bogart: *Miss, you're crazy.*

The African Queen

trail just before the bridge and follow it along the river for about a mile, crossing a small bridge over a stream, and putting in below a 6-foot falls. This adds a mile to the run and some good Class 3 rapids. Watch out for the undercut on the left on the first rapid, Dog's Back.

Much of the land along the river is privately owned farmland, and care should be taken when scouting not to trample hand-tilled plots.

If you ever find yourself looking for whitewater in East Africa, don't spend too much time looking for the Ulanga and Bora rivers, where the action in *The African Queen* takes place. The rivers, which Bogart's character claims hold 100 miles of whitewater between Fort Shona and Lake Victoria, aren't on the map. Too bad.

Ethiopia

Omo River ➢

The Omo River is considered one of the most remarkable multi-day trips in the world. This is one of the early pioneering trips by Sobek in the 1970s, and it is now run regularly by several other international outfitters. The drainage is very isolated, with only two roads reaching the river. Boaters are some of the few outsiders seen by the local people. The put-in is at Gibe Bridge, about 110 miles (176 km) southwest of Ethiopia's capital city, Adis Abeba (Addis Ababa), one of Africa's most intriguing metropolises. It drops into deep canyons and dramatic gorges, with scenery and ecosystems changing constantly. Most river runners encounter whitewater every day for the first two weeks of the trip. Waterfalls, hot springs, and excellent side hikes are among the attractions. Wildlife is abundant, especially in the second half of the trip. Exotic birds, antelopes, warthogs, colobus monkeys, baboons, and even lions visit the river. Hippos can be often counted by the hundreds, and rafts have taken hippo and crocodile bites in the past. Welcome to the food chain!

As fascinating as the wildlife is, it is matched by the diversity of isolated human cultures, more evident in the second half of the trip. From here down at least eight separate cultural groups make their home, including the near-stone-age Kwegu, Bodi, and Mursi tribes. They often hail boaters from the shore to interact. These are Africa's native peoples as they have been for centuries, each with their own distinctive dress and decoration: hairdos, lip plates, ear plugs, and bark cloth or leather skirts.

The canyon climbs almost a mile deep, and most of the whitewater is upstream of midway access at Bele Bridge near the town of Sodo. The whitewater is less intense below Sodo, and the area is more open with great views of farmlands and mountains in the distance.

Although the Omo has a large streambed, rainy-season flows usually are too high to run safely and too rocky during the heart of the dry season. A short rainy season in March and April is followed by the major rainy season from May through September. Recommended flows at the put-in are between 1,000 and 4,000 cfs (28 and 113 cumecs), and the flows are usually several times larger at the take-out.

Birdlife and hippos are more prevalent in the lower run. Tsetse flies can be a problem and river runners usually employ full coverage, which is more effective than repellents. Malaria prophylaxis is recommended.

Ethiopia also offers other outfitted trips, including the Tekeze, a deep river canyon to the north of the Omo in a drier drainage.

GIBE BRIDGE NEAR ABELTI TO OMO NATIONAL PARK NEAR THE MUI RIVER CONFLUENCE

Difficulty: Class 4– to Bele Bridge near Sodo, Class 2 below the bridge

Length: 330 miles (528 km)

Season: September through November, April and May

Character: Whitewater canyon for the first 100 miles (160 km); exotic culture and wildlife

Difficulty: Class 4–
Length: 60 miles (96 km)

Season: All year
Character: Shorter than
other East African
classics

◁ Awash River

Located about 140 miles east of Adis Abeba (Addis Ababa) and set about 9° north latitude, the Awash is a popular day or overnight trip. The put-in is just downstream from the park headquarters, where the river drops dramatically into a deep gorge just below Awash Falls. Good read-and-run rapids follow for the first few miles.

Though technically runnable all year, very high flows in the wet season (summer, north latitude) are not recommended, and flows are sometimes too low during the dry season from September to March. The river is still quite silty for this run in spite of upstream dams. It marks the border of Awash National Park, the left bank being within the park; there is a small fee for park entry. Good wildlife spotting includes crocodiles, kudu, dik-dik, baboons, and a variety of birdlife. The first 28 miles (44.8 km) in park are the most popular; sometimes this stretch is run as a weekend trip.

The area is an important archaeological region, with findings of skeletal remains of early man.

South Africa

Located at the southernmost tip of the African continent, the Republic of South Africa (RSA) is the traditional home of the bushmen, Zulus, and other native peoples. Centuries of European colonization and development based on mining, industry, and commerce turned South Africa into the wealthiest and most diverse country in Africa. South Africa parted from the British Commonwealth in 1961, but retained the racial system of apartheid. The system collapsed under the weight of international isolation in 1994 when the country had its first democratic all-race elections.

While politics in South Africa stole headlines, a generation of boaters grew up in South Africa keen on competitive and recreational paddling. International sanctions reinforced isolation, forcing South African river runners to be resourceful and self-reliant. Difficulty in importing boats led to many home-grown designs and ultimately influential innovations. The Corsica S derives from a South African original, and many cutting-edge rodeo boats draw inspiration from South African prototypes. Small groups explored the region's rivers, developing the tough-mindedness needed to brave not only the rugged country but some rather unique dangers as well. As a result South Africa has produced some great paddlers including Corran Addison, Jerome Truran, and Stan Ricketts. With apartheid and international sanctions now part of history, the path is paved for visitors to enjoy South Africa's great rivers, modern amenities, and natural beauty.

A special thanks to Graeme Addison and the South African Rivers Association for their generous contribution to this chapter.

Orange River (Senqu) ➤

The Orange River was known to the original inhabitants of western South Africa, the San and the Khoikhoi, as !Gariep— "the Great River." It was renamed in the eighteenth century after William of Orange, who later became the King of England.

By far the largest and longest river in South Africa, the Orange, also known as the Senqu in its upper reaches, has its headwaters in the Drakensberg Mountains in the landlocked county of Lesotho, not far from the Indian Ocean. It does not flow to the Indian Ocean, however; it sojourns west to the Atlantic, a distance some four times as great. The river passes from snow-clad highlands to temperate grasslands. Throughout its middle course the Orange flows through irrigated farmlands, with a growing wine industry in the vineyards that begin to appear from the confluence with the Vaal onwards. The Vaal itself has reliable flows and is popular with river runners from the Johannesburg area. The Orange then passes through the semideserts of Bushmanland and the Kalahari before entering one of the world's driest deserts, the Namib. On the way it meanders through several game reserves. The slow-moving lower reaches form much of the border with Namibia. The more popular sections described here provide the best whitewater and most enjoyable scenery.

The Upper Senqu, in Lesotho, can be paddled in the warmer summer months from September through April. This semiarid area features some easy Class 2+ paddling

ABOVE HOPETOWN TO DOUGLAS (THUNDER ALLEY)
Difficulty: Class 3+$_4$
Length: 50 miles (80 km)

GORGE BELOW AUGRABIES FALLS
Difficulty: Class 4+$_p$
Length: 5 miles (8 km)

ONSEEPKANS (ORANJE) GORGE, ABOUT 2½ MILES BELOW ONSEEPKANS TO ONSEEP FARM
Difficulty: Class 3
Length: 11 miles (18 km)

PELLA MISSION TO VIOOLSDRIFT
Difficulty: Class 2 to 3
Length: 90 miles (144 km)

(continued on following page)

Difficulty: Class 1+
Length: 70 miles (112 km)

Season: All year from
Thunder Alley
downstream; summer
only in Lesotho

Character: A big river
through a dry area;
varies, but very flat most
of the way; many trip
options; verify
information locally

through scenic sandstone gorges. Even better scenery can be found on the river's major tributary, the Sinqunyane.

The most popular section for commercial rafting on the Orange is Thunder Alley near the town of Kimberley, a historic diamond mining town where a massive "Big Hole" is all that remains of one of the world's largest diamond mines. This section is above the confluence with the Vaal and, like most of the Orange, is flat, but it does contain the Shake, Rattle 'n Roll series of rapids about $18\frac{3}{4}$ miles (30 km) above the village of Hopetown. It is here that the first diamonds were discovered in the last century. Below Hopetown for about 25 miles (40 km) the river runs in a fast channel known as Thunder Alley. The most difficult and dangerous cataract is Hell's Gate (Class 4), sometimes portaged at high flows. Downstream of the Ural confluence, the Orange wanders for about 100 miles (160 km) through less scenic and drier landscape to the Augrabies Falls area. The river slows, with occasional drops and one more series of cataracts near Keimoes. Watch for fallen-tree and log hazards.

About 74 miles (120 km) west of Upington is Augrabies Falls where the river drops some 262 feet (80 m) into a spectacular stone trough and over a dramatic sequence of rapids and cascades in a desert setting. Augrabies Falls is a national park and a major tourist attraction in its own right, especially at high water when the current pours over and around strange rock formations that line the sides of the canyon. According to speculation, a fortune in diamonds has accumulated at the bottom of the falls waiting for the river to dry up to be mined, but no one is holding their breath.

A 6-mile (10 km) Class 3 section above the falls is commercially rafted, but one of the finest advanced runs in the subcontinent can be found in the Class 4+ gorge beginning near the foot of the falls. To run the gorge requires permission from the Augrabies Park warden. Permission can be obtained by contacting the SA Rivers Association in ad-

Sand Beach on Orange River, South Africa.

vance, or arriving at the warden's door with convincing evidence of your skills. Watch flows carefully, as the run is considerably more difficult and dangerous at high flows. Sieves caused by fallen boulders are a particular risk, even at low to medium flows. Expect three or four possible portages on the main 5-mile (8 km) run. All rapids should be scouted, and river runners should assess the run and their skills carefully, as climbing out is extremely difficult. Take out at Echo Corner.

From about 18½ miles (30 km) below Augrabies Falls the river begins to form the border with Namibia. This area is commercially canoed, offering a unique "two-ships" trail involving two days on the water and two days of camel-riding in the flanking desert. Farther downstream is the Oranje or Ontseepkans Gorge, a Class 4– run near Pofadder. About 2½ miles (4 km) below the palm-fringed oasis of Onseepkans, the Orange splits into a Class 3 route on the right and a main gorge route on the left. If uncertain, take the right route which begins opposite the mission church steeple. View the unrunnable !Gariep Falls (also known as Orange Falls) from the end of the chicken run, then paddle back up the long series of pools to a side-entry into the main gorge. Watch out for fallen boulders causing unseen and powerful sieves, especially at low to medium flows, making scouting essential, especially at lower flows. At high flows most of the rocks disappear, and the serious risk is at the foot of the falls entering at right, where the current pushes boaters towards an underwater cave on the opposite side. Take out at the Onseep Farm on the left. The whole run from Onseepkans is 11 miles (18 km) and takes at least a day. Farther downstream is a Class 2–3 run from Pella Mission to Vioolsdrif, featuring Ghoum-Ghoum Falls. Temperatures of 125° F (52° C) in the shade have been recorded in nearby Goodhouse, making this reputedly the hottest place in Southern Hemisphere.

As the river approaches the Atlantic, it winds its way through the wildly contorted and folded mountains of the Richtersveld National Park. Paddling is not advised in the hot months from December through February. A popular run here is from Vioolsdrif (or Noordoewer, the main road crossing from South Africa into Namibia) to the confluence with the Fish River (also known as Vis River). Canoes are a good choice for this quiet-water float where boaters can view magnificent Namib scenery and wilderness with Goliath herons, lovebirds, and fish eagles. Flatwater, grit-laden headwinds off the Atlantic, and permit requirements related to diamond mining make the section below Fish River less appealing.

Tugela River ➢

The Tugela is one of the many warm-water rivers in Zululand and Natal coming off the Drakensberg. Natal is the wettest area of South Africa, receiving regular summer rains from the Indian Ocean between November and March, the best boating being in February and March. The Tugela is known for excellent camping and good surfing at high water. This is a summer-rainfall river (October through April) but never reliable except in its lowest reaches. It can flood or dry up. At good levels it is big, boisterous, brown, and steep.

The Tugela is Zululand's river, and its name means "the startling one." Traditionally clad Zulu peoples are still seen along the banks, though they are more likely to be carrying home-made pipe guns than spears. Visitors are welcome if you observe the tribal niceties—paying respects to chiefs and not walking across graveyards. Most Zulus consider paddlers crazy anyway because they believe the "water spirit" will eventually

TUGELA CANYON, COLENSO TO
  CAUSEWAY BRIDGE
Difficulty: Class 4ₚ
Length: 40 miles (64 km)

TUGELA RED RAVINE, CAUSEWAY
  BRIDGE TO ABOVE WEIR AT
  NQUBEVU STORE
Difficulty: Class 3–4
Length: 30 miles (48 km)

TUGELA GORGE, NQUBEVU STORE
  TO JAMESON'S DRIFT
Difficulty: Class 3–4
Length: 43 miles (70 km)

(continued on following page)

Lower Tugela Gorge,
Jameson's Drift to
Mandini Drift
Difficulty: Class 3
Length: 50 miles (80 km)

Season: October through
April
Character: Popular
wilderness run in eastern
South Africa

steal your soul and drown you. One irritant along the Tugela is theft and stoning by village thugs. The best way of dealing with this is to camp near traditional dwellings and visit the local headman, drink some beer with him, get his permission to stay overnight and pay his nominated guard. Do not leave cars parked anywhere except inside the compound of a police station or business.

The Tugela River arises in virtually the same montane wetland as the Orange (or Senqu) River in Lesotho. The height of this swamp is around 10,000 feet (3,050 m). The Tugela then falls off the Drakensberg amphitheater as the spectacular Tugela Falls, a drop of nearly 2,000 feet (610 m); only Angel Falls in Venezuela has a greater single drop.

Then for many miles the Tugela is rather flat, flowing through the Natal midlands. It is dammed at Speionkop and much of the water pumped back over the Drakensberg to keep the industries of Johannesburg running. Fortunately, there are still many undammed tributaries, so below Speionkop ("Spy Hill"—a Boer War battlefield) the river picks up volume again. At Colenso is a weir, and from here commence the four gorges of the Tugela. The countryside is truly spectacular, with the deepest parts of the Tugela Gorge being as deep as the Grand Canyon but looking more like the jungle mountains of middle Peru. Marijuana is grown in these hills, mostly for export to the outer world. Drug lords and Zulu warrior clans coexist in a truly wild African setting.

The Tugela Canyon run begins below the weir at Colenso. After negotiating a drop with a sticky hole near the weir, beware—three major falls lurk downstream: Hart's Hill Falls, 36 feet (11 m); Little Augrabies, 82 feet (25 m) in cascades; and Colenso Falls, 130–64 feet (40–50 m). These drops have little upstream signature, and failing to recognize them has proven fatal in at least one instance. The route between is interspersed with Class 3 and 4 rapids, plenty of wave trains, and stoppers for playing in. After the Colenso Falls you enter the canyon proper, and it's a good 50 miles (80 km) to the next take-out. There are playholes aplenty including some big Class 4 rapids with colorful local names. A popular side hike is upstream to Little Niagara Falls on the Klip River. Below Zingela Game Farm safari camp, there are more Class 3–4 rapids. Take out at the Causeway Bridge at Tugela Ferry, which marks the end of the canyon.

Tugela Red Ravine, a laid-back route after the canyon, nevertheless offers riverwide surfing waves. People have been put off going here in recent years by a spate of car break-ins and stonings. Look out for flying rocks hurled by villagers on the heights. Also look out for hungry crocs in the pool below 13-foot (4 m) Mashunka Falls. The area has been unsettled by faction-fighting between different clans of Zulus. Watch out for the big weir at the take-out, which is dangerous at high water. Two big tributaries enhance the flow: the Bushmans and Sundays rivers; both offer good creek-boating when flows allow. The Red Ravine gets its name from a spectacular volcanic ridge that glows in the afternoon sun.

The most popular run is through the Tugela Gorge, a secluded gorge with lush vegetation and white sand beaches. From Nqubevu store to Jameson's Drift is about 43 miles (70 km). The river is fed by several big tributaries, including the Mooi and Buffalo rivers. There is a big commercial rafting camp at Mfongosi, and upstream on the Mfongosi is a popular set of waterfalls. The place is very wild, and it is not uncommon to meet a local chieftain (in a suit and a Mercedes) guarded by thugs with AK47s. Below Mfongosi the gorge proper begins, dotted with big Class 4 rapids known as Skull, Pearly Gates,

Drunkards, Horrible Horace, Desperate Doris, Unicorn, Four Man Hole, Bus Stop, Corner, Souse Hole, and Irish Hole. Take out at Jameson's Drift bridge. Downstream from here to the Mandini bridge is the Lower Tugela Gorge. With only a few smallish Class 3 rapids, it is usually only run when the upstream runs are too low. Watch out for the rapid below Mandini bridge and the Zambezi sharks in the lagoon below as the river nears the Indian Ocean.

Pietermaritzberg is the local boaters' hangout. Paul Simon's backup vocal group on the *Graceland* album, Ladysmith Black Mambazo, is from nearby Ladysmith where the Klip River, another tributary of the Tugela, is runnable after moderate rain. Watch out for the falls below Ladysmith, aptly named Little Niagara. Other fine rivers in the area include the Umgeni and the Umzimkulu, as well as the popular Umkomaas.

Breede River ➤

Rising in the Hex River Mountains of the Boland and flowing through rolling country hills, the creeks leading into the Breede offer very tight and steep boating for expert kayakers. As the valley flattens out, the main Breede meanders through vineyards and pretty gorges before emptying into the Indian Ocean at Witsand. Much of the popularity of the river is due to its location, just two hours east of Cape Town in the heart of South Africa's wine country.

The Breede features three distinct types of run described here. The creeks in the Du Toit's Kloof and Bain's Kloof mountains are the Breede's headwaters and tend to be kayakable only after several days of rain and snow. They are all steep, with waterfalls up to 30 feet (9 m), wild cascades, and staircase rapids. All are accessible from nearby roads or farm tracks. It is advisable to contact the SA Rivers Association for directions and connections with local paddlers.

The upper run, sometimes called the wine-country run, is reached via Route NJ, about 62 miles (100 km) northeast of Cape Town near Worcester. Usually floated in two leisurely days, the run features the pristine beauty of the foothills, fine birdwatching, and good camping on white sandy beaches.

The whitewater run is located about 124 miles (200 km) east of Cape Town via Route N2 just downstream of Bontebok National Park, 4½ miles (7 km) southeast of Swellendam, in a more isolated stretch of the river. The put-in is accessed at a campground in Bontebok National Park (small entrance fee); beware of metal "buffalo spikes" just below the put-in, designed to keep Cape buffalo in the park (hopefully the spikes are to be removed, since the buffalo are long gone). The park is a preserve for antelope, bontebok, and other animals in an environment reminiscent of the Cape before the coming of agriculture. Access to the park by river is not permitted.

The rapids are playful, but at Waterfall (Class 2+) the bed is shallow and the rocks are sharp. Take out at a bridge accessed from a road on the left side of the river.

The Cape also supports several other creeks popular with urban kayakers and close to Cape Town. These include the Palmiet, Riversonderend and the Upper Berg, and the Upper Olifants.

UPPER BREEDE, NEAR ROBERTSON DAM (UPPER, OR WINE-COUNTRY RUN)
Difficulty: Class 1
Length: 16 miles (25.6 km)

LOWER BREEDE, NEAR SWELLENDAM (WHITEWATER RUN)
Difficulty: Class 2
Length: 8 miles (12.8 km)

Season: April through November except after extended dry periods
Character: Scenic and mostly flat

Doringbos to Klawer Bridge
Difficulty: Class 3+
Length: 37 miles (59.2 km)

Season: June through
September
Character: Remote and
scenic canyon

◁ Doring River

The Doring River flows west through the Cedarberg Swartruggens Mountain Range, where it joins the Olifants River before reaching the Atlantic. About a three-hour drive north of Cape Town, the Doring features a couple of two-day wilderness runs; these are combined in the one-to-three-day trip recommended here, from Doringbos to Klawer. Eagles, baboons, otters, and rhebok may be seen along the river, as can paintings by bushmen. The Doring valley is virtually free of human habitation.

Access is from Clanwilliam on well-marked gravel roads leading to the commercial put-in. Talk to local farmers on the access roads for permission to enter. Camping is possible on the many white beaches overlooked by caves, but commercial companies tend to claim the best camping spots. Heavy rain and even sleet are common during the winter months, so equip accordingly.

Corran Remembers

Corran Addison and his father, Graeme, found themselves leading a group down the Tugela. It included a contingent of the AWB, a South African right-wing group who required a raft laden with beer for provisions. They awakened one morning to the frantic grunts of a cow being washed downriver: heavy rains had resulted in a massive flood. They continued.

In a two-man crocodile (inflatable canoe) were three very large, noisy Afrikaners. They were drinking out of bike bottles, and yelling "AWB." One was paddling furiously, spinning the boat as the others yelled : "War's die foeljie, waaaar's die foeljie?" (where's the birdie?). My father beckoned me to take care of them.

The bottles they were sucking at were filled with something other than water and had them drunk as a skunk. The stern man stood up, yelled "War's die foeljie?" and sat back down defiantly. It was amusing, but what was that roar? I looked downstream. Where were we? By all accounts, there shouldn't be anything of size for miles. Not until the falls. The falls!

Aaaaagh! In a flash of terror I realized where we were.

Frantically, I looked for a beach to land the drunken trio. "Paddle, paddle!" I yelled. All three began stroked half-heartedly on the right as the boat spun faster. Looking up I could see the billowing mist, hear the roar and the thundering air. I turned to the three oafs. "You're all going to die," I yelled. I paddled for the bank. No matter how hard I paddled, the water was moving faster. For an instant I thought all was lost. Ten feet above the falls was a small, lone eddy. Safely there, I spun to look for the crocodile. Nothing. They were surely over the falls.

Then from behind me I heard, "Jirra, man, but that was close." I spun around to see three very sober, humbled, ashen Boers sitting in the eddy, neatly parked. How they made it there is beyond me.

We clambered up the dam and looked into the abyss below. Before us was a river wide hole at the base of the most impressive falls I had ever seen. Entire trees, dead animals, and debris pounded each other. No sooner would a new tree, 40 or 50 feet long, fall into the hole, than it would snap like a toothpick. Nothing survived. The river downstream was clear of debris, the hole acting as a perfect sieve.

EUROPE

$\mathcal{T}$he best rivers in Europe tumble down the jagged valleys of the Alps, through carefully maintained forests, farmland, and quaint villages. The Alps' formidable height and many glaciers combined with good precipitation levels provide some great flows. The rivers are usually easily accessed through the continent's advanced highway and railroad infrastructure. The trade-off is the lack of wilderness runs and the all-too-common alteration of the rivers for power, irrigation, and flood control. All of the alpine rivers featured are followed by both a road and a railroad except the Grand Canyon of the Verdon, which has neither, and the Vorderrhein (Upper Rhine) which is followed by a railroad. This does make for some convenient shuttles, and on many runs, such as the Vorderrhein, boaters can simply catch the train. At least one run, the Isar, can only be accessed by taxi service. As for wilderness, you will have to be content with unspeakably beautiful mountains towering over medieval villages, each adorned with antique church steeples. It's a bit like paddling through a postcard.

The Alps are the result of tremendous buckling and deformity caused by the horizontal forces of colliding continents as the African and Eurasian plates began to collide about seven billion years ago. Some of the monoliths that form the highest peaks in Switzerland have been moved more than 60 miles from their source. The result is a spectacular and complex combination of igneous, metamorphic, and sedimentary rock thrust to its present elevation only about five million years ago and carved to its present-day form by glaciers in the Pleistocene era.

This range of stunning granite peaks and glacial valleys that dominate the landscape of Europe have over the years posed an imposing barrier to marching armies as well as human migration. The Alps were the first large mountainous area to be heavily developed and populated. Yet, in spite of this, they retain most of their natural beauty. The inhabitants of the mountains developed their own alpine culture, architecture, and folklore, and to their credit they have preserved their forests. This is in no small part due to a love of the outdoors and sport that developed here and continues year-round. Fortunately, the ruggedness of the mountains and lack of heavy industry here largely spared the Alps from the destruction that befell most of Europe during the world wars.

1   Durance River (see page 217)
2   Guil River (see page 217)
3   Ubaye River (see page 217)
4   Verdon River (see page 220)
5   Var River
6   Isere River
7   Drac River
8   Veneon River
9   Dranse River
10 Ardeche River
11 Rio Noguera Pallaresa
12 Dora Baltea River (see page 226)
13 Noce River
14 Inn River (see page 229)
15 Saane River
16 Simme River
17 Aare River
18 Vorderrhein River
19 Reuss River
20 Loisach River
21 Oetz River (see page 229)
22 Salza River
23 Tavignano River (see page 238)
24 Vecchio River (see page 238)
25 Rizzanese River (see page 238)
26 Sjoa River (see page 240)
27 Jori River
28 Driva River
29 Dagali River
30 Spey River
31 Tryweryn River

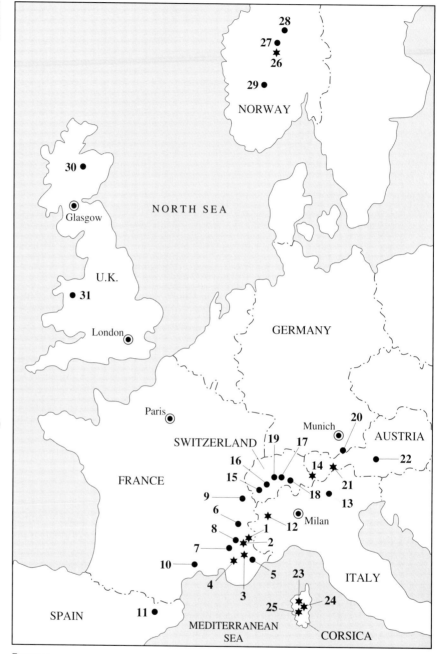

Europe

The Alps cover most of Switzerland and Austria, and parts of eastern France, northern Italy, southern Germany, and northwest Slovenia. The end of Soviet domination to the east has opened rivers like the Soca in Slovenia. One must hold out hope that a benevolent "new world order" will continue to open boating opportunities throughout the Eastern Bloc.

The pioneer sportsmen of the Alps are credited with adapting the flatwater kayak to the sport of whitewater early in the twentieth century, paddling Klepper folding kayaks, which were originally meant for flatwater, in the fast-moving rivers. The Europeans also first developed the fiberglass kayak. Kayaking remains quite popular throughout Europe, both for competition and recreation, and the Europeans have developed innumerable design and manufacturing innovations for plastic kayaks, including stub-nosed kayaks to avoid pins in the shallow, rocky alpine creeks. Rafts and inflatable kayaks arrived from the West in the mid-1980s and are generally confined to commercial outfitters. Riverboarding, locally called hydrospeeding, is well established.

Europeans also pioneered the construction of artificial whitewater courses, as noted in descriptions of some of the featured rivers. Such courses are gaining popularity elsewhere, particularly in the eastern United States, and it is likely the trend will continue.

The Alps are not cheap. Prices, particularly in Switzerland and Austria, can be a real eye-opener for cost-conscious boaters relying on weaker currency. Fortunately, hiking and car-camping are respected European traditions, and reasonably priced, well-appointed campgrounds are plentiful and generally the only place to camp legally. Certain camps attract whitewater boaters, and are ideal spots to find boating buddies and make friends.

Note that in most of the Austrian Alps private rafting is outlawed in all commercially run rivers unless accompanied by a licensed guide. The ostensible purpose is for safety reasons, but regulation also reflects protection of local commercial rafting companies and the scarcity of private rafters in Europe.

The Alps are not the last word in European whitewater. Scandinavian countries, particularly Norway, have numerous less-explored and less-developed rivers, allowing for some beautiful multi-day runs. Most of Norway is mountainous, with peaks reaching over 8,000 feet, but the northern latitude shortens the season.

Corsica's steep creeks are legendary. If your skills are up to some serious hair-boating, catch the ferry to this Mediterranean island where 9,000-foot (2,727 m) mountains drop almost vertically to sea level, making for some great waterfall runs from late March to mid-May.

Although the British Isles get plenty of rain and access roads are everywhere, the low altitude (4,000 feet in Scotland and 3,000 feet in Wales) and widespread development limit the opportunities. Britain does generate innumerable, enthusiastic kayakers, who learn the art as members of school and local clubs and polish their skills in competitions. They get by on certain well-traveled rivers in England, Scotland, and Wales, but the lack of outstanding rivers and legal restrictions on access make paddling in Britain an upstream battle at times. Smaller rivers are deemed private, and passage is sometimes governed by access agreements negotiated with landowners and fishing guides by the governing paddle associations. The laws in Scotland are similar to those in England, but the Scots are independent-minded and access is more relaxed. Inquire locally of the British Canoe Union or the Scottish Canoe Union if you wish to paddle privately. Road trips to the Alps are popular with English paddlers. It is easy to understand why.

It is hard to imagine going to Europe just to run rivers, and most enthusiasts will want to mix a bit of sightseeing and other adventures into their trip. With that in mind, we'll begin this section with some of the more popular runs in the mountains of south-central France and the Pyrenees along the French-Spanish border.

France

MIDDLE DURANCE, L'ARGENTIERE
TO SAINT-CLEMENT
Difficulty: Class 2
Length: 11 miles (18 km)

LOWER DURANCE, SAINT-
CLEMENT TO EMBRUN
Difficulty: Class 3
Length: 10 miles (16 km)

Season: April through
October
Character: Popular
Southern Alps river,
center of river-running
area

◁ Durance River

The Durance is one of the main paddling centers in the world. River runners interested in meeting fellow paddlers, exploring a wide range of rivers, learning the arts of kayaking, rafting, and rescue, or just ready to spend some time in a fun French town will be at home here. Its big, greenish, silty waters, its many runnable tributaries, and its setting on the quaint French towns of Embrun and Briancon have drawn whitewater boaters since long before the modern sport of river running. In fact, the Association des Radeliers de la Durance occasionally reconstructs historical wooden rafts and descends the river in garb from earlier periods. Today the various campgrounds along the Durance, especially at Rabioux and L'Argentiere, are a melting pot of boaters from around Europe and elsewhere. Most spend time on the main river in preparation for the more challenging tributaries of the Guil and Ubaye (discussed in their own essays) or other runnable tributaries such as the Guisane, Claryee, Gyr, Onde, Gyronde, Fournel, Biaisse, Rabioux, Crevous, and Vacheres. The artificial slalom course at L'Argentiere gets plenty of use.

Much of the drainage of the Durance is near the Ecrins National Park, an area filled with spectacular glaciers, lakes, and mountain forests. Farther downstream the river is laced with dams and weirs, the largest being downstream of Briancon at Prelles, where most of the water is diverted. However, in spite of diversions, much of the river usually maintains a big-water flow.

The featured sections of the Durance are sometimes called the Middle Durance between L'Argentiere and Saint-Clement, and the Lower Durance between Saint-Clement and Embrun where the river is impounded by Lac d'Serre-Poncon reservoir. Boaters can put in below the artificial slalom course at L'Argentiere for the middle run. The put-in for the more popular lower run is on the left above the bridge in Saint-Clement, although other put-ins are available. Access can be found at the Rabioux campground near Chateauroux, where the Rabioux enters on the right. This is a river-runner hangout and the site of Rabioux Rapid, the most difficult on the run at Class 3+ and probably the most famous rapid in Europe. Much of the development of European river running was tested here, and pioneers suffered many a mishap, as the river narrows into some big waves with tricky eddies on either side. Modern equipment and skills have tamed it, but hard-boaters can still get a good surf, ender, and, at certain levels, even a cartwheel here. The campground is one of the great meeting places for paddlers, and the peak-season atmosphere is amazing, with floodlights allowing night surfing until midnight complete with spectators and vendors. The remains of a miniature golf course, with canoes decorating some holes, can be seen here.

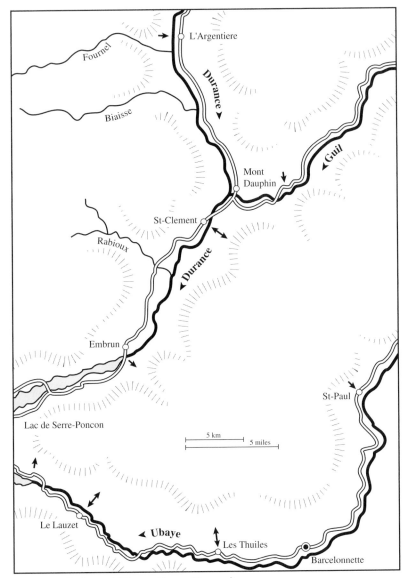

Durance, Guil, and Ubaye Rivers (France)

Below Rabioux the valley opens up to scenic farmland down to Embrun. Embrun is a quaint vacation town with chateaus and church steeples nestled under the mountains of the Haute (High) Alps. Commercial rafting outfits use Embrun as a base. There are several take-out options at Embrun, including one near the N94 bridge.

The easier Class 2 section from L'Argentiere to Saint-Clement is a good warm-up for the lower section and a nice place to practice technical paddling or enjoy the scenery. The Durance also has some tough sections, mostly found in two difficult gorges, one upstream of Briancon and the other just below the Prelles Dam. The upstream Class 4+ Briancon Gorge between La Vachette and Briancon marks the transition of the Claree to the

Durance. This steep, technical run, sometimes called the Ravin de Malafosse ("Bad-Hole Ravine") is run annually with boaters donning full protective gear. Upstream the Claree offers good Class 4– paddling from Nevache to Plampinet and Class 2+ from Plampinet to La Vachette. Downstream of the Prelles Dam, the Durance Gorge is a similar but more difficult run, with Class 4+ whitewater to L'Argentiere. Runnable flows here require good timing. The run has limited access and at least one tough portage. The Durance is largely dewatered between Briancon and the Prelles Dam.

◁ Guil River

The Guil is another eastern tributary of the Durance, joining the river just upstream of Saint-Clement near the towns of Guillestere and Mont Dauphin. Like the Ubaye, the Guil flows from its headwaters at a little over 11,000 feet into a spectacular cataract before meeting the Durance.

The Guil Gorge is typical of the beauty of the canyons of the French Alps, with vertical stained and painted yellowish walls several hundred feet tall in most places. It is also a study in the historical use of rivers. In the upper gorge the Guil wraps around a massive rock outcropping and serves as a moat for the fortress-castle of Chateau Queyras; this area is part of Parc Natural Regional Queyras. Just downstream one can find a less quaint usage, as a dam at La Maison du Roi usually dewaters the stretch below. Through no small feat of construction, a road was carved on and tunneled through the canyon walls, providing some great views.

The first run, Chateau Queyras Gorge, is less than a mile long but is included as much for its beautiful setting as for its whitewater. This run through a steep gorge is part of the natural moat protecting Chateau Queyras, which sits high above the river. A small road on the left allows scouting and a take-out at a bridge. The river is also runnable above and below here, but boaters should be wary of weirs. Below here the river drops into another Class 4+ gorge called L'Ange Gardien (Guardian Angel Gorge), named for a large rock formation towering overhead. This run is slower-going than the Chateau Queyras Gorge and includes several big drops and some recommended portages. The take-out is about 1½ miles (2.4 km) below the take-out for the Chateau Queyras run.

The put-in for the Middle Guil is at the bridge near Montbardon; this allows a nice warm-up paddle before the action begins. Another option is to put in about half a mile upstream above or below Triple Step rapid. This is near the road and adds several rapids to the run. Scout Triple Step carefully with an eye to a concealed and potentially dangerous cavern on the right bank. The run is consistent and technical, with a gradient of about 100 fpm (19.3 mpk). The toughest rapids are the Guil Staircase and a narrow chute partly under a huge boulder called the Letter Box. This last difficult rapid goes by the French name "L'Ex-Infran du Tunnel," indicating that it was once considered unrunnable. It is often portaged on the right. Take out where the river flows into the reservoir backwater at La Maison du Roi.

Downstream of the dam near the first tunnel is a very narrow, steep trail beginning right behind the appropriate "danger" sign. This leads to the most scenic and most treacherous section of the Guil, the Guil Gorge (Class 5p). This section is generally dewatered by the dam, but runnable flows allow for a very technical, tough run with at least one portage. The gradient here is about 125 fpm (24.13 mpk). Be very careful. High flows are dangerous, and sudden dam releases have proven fatal to kayakers caught unaware.

CHATEAU QUEYRAS GORGE
Difficulty: Class 4+
Length: 1 mile (1.6 km)

MIDDLE GUIL, MONTBARDON TO LA MAISON DU ROI
Difficulty: Class 4+
Length: 5 miles (8 km)

GUIL GORGE, BELOW DAM AT LA MAISON DU ROI TO EYGLIERS BRIDGE
Difficulty: Class 5p
Length: 3 miles (4.8 km)

LOWER GORGE, EYGLIERS BRIDGE TO BELOW MONT DAUPHIN
Difficulty: Class 3
Length: 4 miles (6.4 km)

Season: April to late summer
Character: Tributary of the Durance journeying through a tight, narrow gorge

The take-out for the Guil Gorge and the put-in for the less life-threatening Lower Guil is Eygliers bridge. Near the bridge, water from the upstream diversion reenters, providing good flows for the mostly Class 3 rapids on the downstream run. The river passes under the towering cliffs of the fortified town of Mont Dauphin. This stretch, with a gradient of 50 fpm (9.65 mpk), is popular with kayaks and rafts. Take out just downstream of Mont Dauphin, or continue on the Durance to Saint-Clement.

Ubaye River ➤

The free-flowing Ubaye drains a large area south of the Guil along the border with Italy where some of the peaks in these Haute (high) Alps climb over 10,000 feet (305 m). It is one of the most enjoyable rivers in the Durance area, and some consider the Ubaye Valley to be the most beautiful whitewater destination in the Alps. The Ubaye has plenty of water and much to offer river runners of most skill levels, including a slalom course. The Ubaye is runnable as a small alpine stream to big water in its lower reaches, with a gradient that varies from 40 to 100 fpm (7.72 to 19.3 mpk). It has escaped the dams that hinder the course of all the other major rivers in the southern Alps. Like the Drac Noir, black clay found along its banks darkens the river after rainstorms.

The upper section from Saint-Paul to Les Thuiles starts as an alpine stream, and a small one when compared to the lower reaches, but it has good intermediate action and some very cold water. Some put in at Lauziere to avoid paddling the less interesting upstream reaches. Putting in above Saint-Paul is prohibited. The river is set in a wooded canyon with a backdrop of alpine peaks, and the massive Fort de Tournoux is situated on the right bank. Tributaries increase the flow in the lower reaches, but the rapids are still intermediate to the take-out just upstream of Les Thuiles.

The section from Les Thuiles to Le Lauzet is bigger and gradually becomes much more challenging than the run upstream. Once the river reaches the bridge at Fresquiere, the rapids become technical boulder drops as the gradient steepens. This stretch is considerably more difficult and dangerous at high water when a long swim could be critical. The section downstream of Le Martinet is used for competitions and is sometimes referred to as the Race Course run. The action is constant Class 4 water, with 3- to 4-foot (0.9 to 1.2 m) waves and drops everywhere. The section is known for big holes that can propel unwary kayakers in any direction, including skyward. Most rapids lack clean routes, and precise maneuvering skills are needed. At the end of the run, the canyon walls close in and an old Roman bridge appears several hundred feet above the river. Take out at a campsite on the left after the Roman bridge.

The Royal Gorge (Ubaye Gorge) from Le Lauzet to the Lac d'Serre-Poncon Reservoir is an experts-only run in a deep cataract. It is very sensitive to flows and should be avoided at higher water. The difficult rapids begin just below a dramatic waterfall that comes into the gorge on the right. The first rapid, Moulinette (sometimes called Lions Den), begins with a narrow chute and ends with the current flowing into an undercut. It is generally portaged on the left and can be previewed by climbing down from the road. Just downstream is another very long, steep rapid with big boulders, drops, and holes. This scenario continues with the rapids slowly becoming easier. In places the canyon narrows to the length of a kayak paddle. With vertical rock cliffs on either side, the bigger rapids are bottlenecks with drops and holes in series. The river empties into the reservoir at Lac d'Serre-Poncon near the Roche Rousse Kayak Centre.

SAINT-PAUL TO LES THUILES
Difficulty: Class 3
Length: 16 miles (25.6 km)

LES THUILES TO LE LAUZET
Difficulty: Class 4
Length: 9 miles (14.4 km)

THE ROYAL GORGE, LE LAUZET
TO LAC D'SERRE-PONCON
RESERVOIR
Difficulty: Class 5+
Length: 3 miles (4.8 km)

Season: April through October

Character: Large tributary of the Durance to the south

Difficulty: Class 5
Length: 20 miles (32 km)

Season: May through
September
Character: Isolated,
difficult, dam-controlled
river in deep canyon

◅ Verdon River

What is in many ways the most spectacular run in Europe, the Grand Canyon of the Verdon, is also probably the continent's oldest and most interesting piece of geology. Unlike the Grand Canyon of the Colorado, where incessant erosion gradually cuts through the desert floor, geologists believe the Verdon was once an underground river cracked open by a rift, a canyon built from the bottom up. The tight, narrow limestone crevasse is flanked with sheer 1,000-foot walls and beige limestone formations that resemble those of an underground cavern. Bizarre geology begets bizarre hydrology. The main current often wanders underground and temporarily disappears in calm water, only to reappear downstream as it gushes out from underneath. The waters vary from incredible green to blue, and river runners can follow the river through a natural underground cavern.

The Grand Canyon of the Verdon is unique in one other respect: It is the only major whitewater run in the Alps that has no road or railroad along its banks. No towns, villages, or farms intrude into the river experience. Although the stretch is situated between artificial reservoirs, the difficult terrain limits access and emergency help, and rescue could be hard to reach by European standards. With this said, however, the journey is certainly worth the effort. The Verdon has earned its reputation for decades as the classic run of the Alps.

The run can be done in one day, although this would be an undertaking and a waste of an opportunity to savor the experience for someone new to the river. Most boaters approach it as a two-day expedition to fully appreciate the riverscape and to carefully scout the routes, which are narrow and often blind. Trails for portaging and scouting are often marked by painted crosses and signs. Flows are determined by releases from the dam at the Castillon Reservoir. Summer releases are less dependable than those in spring and fall. Recommended flows are between 175 and 900 cfs (5 and 25 cumecs). The average gradient is 25 fpm (4.83 mpk), and you should expect several portages. If you change your mind about running the Grand Canyon, there is difficult access several miles below

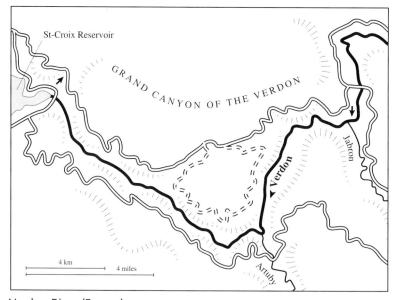

Verdon River (France)

the Jabron River put-in at Point Sublime. A major tributary, the Artuby, enters on the left about a third of the way down. Because of the difficulty in bringing gear down to the river, some boaters avail themselves of a trail on the right midway through the run, stow their gear, and hike for an hour to a camp on the north rim.

The underground section is about two-thirds of the way down the river. At a blind bend the river narrows, and boaters can touch both walls with outstretched hands. The cave has no rapids, nor is it completely dark. Once inside, boaters must execute a short portage over a limestone dike and paddle down to where the river stops against a wall and dives underground again. Here boaters carry through a 4-foot opening. Other passages require kayakers to lie back on the rear deck to squeeze through. These things are considered normal on the Verdon.

Boaters may wish to check out an easier, scenic Class 3 run upstream from the Castillon Reservoir from Colmars to Saint-Andre-les Alpes. The run is free-flowing and is followed by a road. Below the reservoir, but above the Grand Canyon, is a scenic Class 2+ stretch that also makes a good warm-up. Sadly, the Sainte-Croix reservoir drowned the very bottom of the Grand Canyon, a stretch noted for a beautiful natural stone bridge near the canyon exit.

Var River ➤

Running free from its headwaters at over 9,000 feet (2,745 m) in the Col de la Caylle, the emerald waters of the Var dance merrily down the southern French Alps (Alpes Maritimes) on their way to Nice where they meet the Mediterranean on the French coast. The high elevation of the headwaters fills the Var with snowmelt and whitewater.

The Var here runs through Gorges de Daluis, a vivid red bauxite gorge laced with good, tight, technical rapids and some beautiful side waterfalls. Put in on either side of the river as it leaves the village of Guillaumes. The toughest rapid is Rapide du Cantet, which comes up just after Le Cantet River enters on the right. After exiting the gorge, the river slows, and one can exit at Daluis or continue down Class 2 waters to the confluence with the Coulomp on the right.

Some expert kayakers have tried their hand at some of the more difficult upstream stretches.

GORGES DE DALUIS, GUILLAUMES
TO DALUIS
Difficulty: Class 3
Length: 5 miles (8 km)

Season: April through July
Character: A tight river gorge close to the French Riviera

Isere River ➤

The Isere drains the flanks of the glaciers of the French Alps north of the Durance area. Most of the river running on the Isere is on the section from Bourg Saint-Maurice to Centron. Kayaks and commercial rafts share the river with anglers, and order is preserved by closing the run during the best fishing hours in early morning and late evening.

Put in on the left below the slalom course at Bourg Saint-Maurice. River information is generally posted at the put-in. Flows can be big here. The slalom course has been wrecked by floods on more than one occasion and is sometimes out of commission. The course and the short stretch upstream, below a weir, are tougher than the rest of the run. The run is often divided at Gothard, and there are good rapids just upstream of Landry and Gothard named after the towns. A bike path on the left, built for the 1987 world championships, provides a handy bike-shuttle option.

A tributary, the Doron de Bozel, is a smaller, steeper glacier stream that enters the

BOURG SAINT-MAURICE TO
CENTRON
Difficulty: Class 4
Length: 14 miles (22.4 km)

Season: April through October
Character: Popular French Alps river, good access

Isere downstream at Moutiers. The last 5 miles (8 km) from Brides-les-Bains to the Isere is Class 4.

◁ Drac River

Formed by the confluence of the Drac Noir (Black Drac) and the Drac Blanc (White Drac), the Drac drains the west slope of the High Alps in southern France. The main stem of the Drac is popular with rafters and easily accessed. It runs through a broad valley, with the jagged peaks of the High Alps visible to the west. This is an agricultural and wooded area with several small towns nearby.

This stretch of the Drac has few midstream rocks but can be somewhat braided and gravelly. High flows are more interesting, although the river will be quite muddy after rains.

Pick one of several put-ins near the confluence with the Ancell River which enters from the south. To get to the take-out, take the road Glaizil from Le Motty. Access the river from the bridge or just upstream at the gravel yard on the right. Boaters should be careful not to continue past the bridge, as an unrunnable gorge lies between the bridge and Lac de Sautet.

The difficult but runnable upstream Drac Noir draws its name from the black clay along its banks which adds a dark hue to the waters after heavy rainstorms. The Drac Blanc, Drac Noir, Ancelle, Severaissette, and Severaisse are all runnable tributaries available to boaters in the area.

◁ Veneon River

The Veneon drains the glaciers of the Barre des Ecrins at over 13,000 feet (3,965 m). The river eventually meets the Romanche, which in turn runs through another very difficult gorge and flows into the Drac before joining the Isere at Grenoble.

The reach described here is really three sections separated by an unrunnable cataract at Champhorent about one-third of the way down and a weir which dewaters much of the river about two-thirds of the way down. There are several intermediate access points along the river.

The upper section gets progressively more difficult as one moves downstream, with two rapids which should be portaged. Boaters finishing the first run must catch a footpath to carry up from the gorge at Champhorent and take a short drive around the first cataract. The upper reach is generally run later in the season from August to October when flows are lower. In the second section all the big rapids have been run, but the river is riddled with nonstop powerful rapids, pourovers, and drops. The weir about two-thirds of the way down diverts much of the flow and thus allows downstream boating much earlier, usually starting in April. By the time flows in the upper section have dropped to runnable levels, this section is too low.

In any season the Veneon is a beautiful river, with deciduous forests and blue glacial water tumbling down the boulder-riddled streambed. The upper section in late season presents a invigorating autumn landscape with white birch trees and multicolored leaves. The bottom section also holds some fine scenery. The area also offers some good hiking around La Bararde. The river is unrunnable beyond Pont des Ougiers.

The whitewater on the Romanche is also difficult and challenging, and in many respects is similar to the Veneon to the north. The most popular run on the Romanche is downstream of the mountain resort of La Grave.

Dranse River ➤

This darling of the northern French Alps offers a full range of whitewater from steep creeks in the reaches above the runs described here to commercially popular scenic floats. The Dranse runs from south to north, draining a lower elevation area of the Alps, less than 8,000 feet (2,440 m). It ultimately empties into Lac Leman (Lake Geneva) at Thonan-les-Bains. The mountains and the lake provide part of the border between France and Switzerland.

The Dranse is formed by the confluence of the Dranse d'Abondance (eastern fork) and the Dranse Morzine (middle fork). Creek-boaters run either fork in the spring.

The featured runs begin at Boige, just downstream of the confluence. At Boige the Brevon also joins on the left. A very dangerous sieve, Le Syphon, is just downstream of the bridge at Pont de L'Eglise. Boaters wishing to avoid the difficult rapids downstream will take out at the bridge. Downstream of Le Syphon the river enters the very difficult Les Ex-Infrans, a section that has been run by top experts but has claimed the lives of several river runners. AN Rafting has an office on the river and provides a free, detailed English information sheet.

The intermediate access point at La Cassine marks the beginning of the easier Middle Dranse. This scenic run is a favorite of kayakers and rafting companies alike, with forgiving rapids and plenty of surf waves. Rapids include La Grille, Les Escaliers, and La Grotte. Take out near the highway bridge over the river upstream of Thonon les Bains as the canyon opens up and the river empties into the lake.

BOIGE TO LA CASSINE
Difficulty: Class 5
Length: 2 miles (3.2 km)

LA CASSINE TO PONTE DE LA DOUCEUR
Diffculty: Class 3+
Length: 4 miles (6.4 km)

Season: April through August
Character: French river near Swiss border and Geneva, close to road

Ardeche River ➤

The peaks of the Massif Central of south-central France are not in a league with the Alps, but they do reach about 5,000 feet (1,525 m), high enough to support a few good whitewater runs. The most prominent river in the region is the Ardeche, running southeast near the top of the Provence area of southern France. The passage featured here runs through a nature preserve and a spectacular limestone gorge. The canyon walls approach 1,000 feet (305 m), and a trail follows along the river. The Ardeche meets the Rhone, which in turn passes Avignon on its journey to the Mediterrean Sea.

Renting canoes and small rafts here is popular; however, water levels can fluctuate dramatically. Vendors will not rent boats to the public at high water.

The put-in at Pont-d'Arc epitomizes the graceful beauty of erosion in the gorge, as a splendid natural limestone arch spans the river. Along the run, routes of underground rivers and caves appear and the sculpted rocks and canyon walls offer some fine iridescent colors. A well-engineered road follows much of the river on the left, affording several sightseeing opportunities.

Near the top of the run is Ebbo Cave and downstream is the Dent Noire (Black Tooth) rapid, situated beneath the towering Saleyron Cliffs. Throughout the run rapids and calm passages alternate as the river passes other sights including Morsanne Needle on the left, and the jagged red and black spikes of Abeilleres Rock on the right. Downstream is the Madeleine Cave on the left upstream of the colossal Cathedral Rock. Downstream is Saint-Marcel Cave, below which the gorge begins to open and the Aigueze Tower announces the take-out near the bridge at Saint-Martin-d'Ardeche.

PONT-D'ARC TO SAINT-MARTIN D'ARDECHE
Difficulty: Class 2
Length: 18 miles (28.8 km)

Season: April through October
Character: Isolated, popular, mild

Spain

LLAVORSI TO PONT DE LA
FIGUERTA
Difficulty: Class 2 to 4+,
depending on section
Length: 22 miles (35.2 km)

Season: April through July
Character: Mountainous,
road nearby, heavy local
usage

◁ Rio Noguera Pallaresa

The Noguera Pallaresa drains the south side of Pyrenees in the northeastern corner of Spain about 155 miles (250 km) northwest of Barcelona. The river runs through the Pallars Sobria region, a high mountain basin and one of the most pleasing settings in Catalonia. Here medieval hamlets famous for their fine, old stone churches dot a series of small valleys and green mountains, all set beneath 10,000-foot (3,050 m) peaks. Local custom dictates that each town have an annual party on a different summer weekend, so something is always happening somewhere. This is a vacation center for all types of outdoor activity including trekking, biking, hang gliding, skiing, spelunking, and even jumping from bridges ("puenteing"). There is even a museum of rafting in nearby Pallars Jussa.

The run begins at the picturesque mountain village Llavorsi, a center of regional whitewater activity and the juncture of three valleys: Vall Farrera, Vall de Cardos, and Vall d' Aneu i Espot. Most boaters put in near the bridge at Llavorsi. Below here the river flows through a narrow valley for 8 miles (12.8 km) down to the town of Sort. The Pressa Central de Sort is a weir just upstream of the main part of town. It can be run at certain levels. The valley then opens up but gradually narrows again down to the town of Baro, about 5 miles (8 km) downstream of Sort, and then continues to where the valley opens up again about 2 miles (3.2 km) upstream of a major reservoir, Embalse de San Antonio. Downstream of Baro is Gerri de la Sal. Most boaters take out at Pont de la Figuerta, upstream of the reservoir.

There is an array of bridges along the river including foot bridges, old stone bridges, suspension bridges, as well as more modern spans. A road follows the river most of the way, crossing at Rialp. The river has several levels of difficulty, and paddlers can choose a stretch best suited to their abilities. All type of craft including kayaks, rafts, and riverboards (called hydrospeed) can be found on the river, as can commercial rafts filled with fun-loving Barcelonians. In early July the river hosts a major international whitewater competition with kayaking, rafting, and riverboarding.

Italy

Dora Baltea River ➢

Towering above of the Italian resort town of Courmayeur stands Mont Blanc in a group of jagged, glaciated peaks the Italians refer to as Groupo Monte Bianco. At over 15,000 feet, this is the roof of Europe, straddling the border with France and Switzerland. Tumbling down from the southern face of these mountains are the icy, almost opaque waters of the Dora Baltea. The drainage generates so much water that most of this river is at its best only in late summer when levels have dropped. The Dora Baltea provides some 29 miles (46.4 km) of spectacular boating from just downstream of Courmayeur to just upstream of Aosta, a modern city built around ancient Roman ruins. There are few rivers with such spectacular headwaters or scenery throughout.

Over two millennia of use has exacted its toll on the Dora Baltea. The construction of stone banks has left the river fast and eddyless in some stretches. Weirs, diversions, and other projects built and abandoned over the centuries require awareness, scouting, and occasional portaging. While Italy has been criticized for its shortcomings in whitewater preservation, it makes amends in other ways. The country has a different feel from Switzerland and Austria, with older, more varied architecture. The locals are friendly, the accommodations and camping are comparatively affordable, and the food is generally excellent.

The first section from Courmayeur to Pre-Saint-Didier begins at the bridge in Courmayeur, and the take-out is on river left where the main road leaves the river. This is an extremely demanding, late-season run for expert kayakers only. The steep gradient and lack of eddies as well as several weirs and bridges make this unrunnable at anything but the lowest flows. Even boaters with confidence in their skills should scout the river carefully beforehand with an eye to several portages and to surviving a swim in the event of a wipeout. The continuous Class 5 rapids ease somewhat after Champex, but demanding rapids continue to Pre-Saint-Didier. Most river runners will prefer to enjoy this section from the bank with the understanding that some of this glacial water has been frozen for decades or maybe even hundreds of years. With its regained freedom, can it be blamed for its reckless exuberance?

The second section, from Pre-Saint-Didier to near Derby, is more popular, with several bridges affording a pre-run scout. Although it is less extreme than the run above, the streambed is rocky, the flows are fast, and useful eddies are an exception rather than a rule. Several weirs require scouting and/or portaging. A solid roll, especially upstream of Morgex, is a prerequisite. A broken weir beneath the bridge at Morgex can be run in the middle, and a concrete bridge upstream of LaSalle marks the beginning of the reservoir above LaSalle. The reservoir has three weirs which may be runnable depending on the flow but must be scouted. An access point is at LaSalle behind the Meuble Bar Mirage with a short carry to the road.

From here downstream to Leverogue is a 6-mile (9.6 km) section of river that should be avoided.

COURMAYEUR TO
PRE-SAINT-DIDIER
Difficulty: Class 5p
Length: 5 miles (8 km)

PRE-SAINT-DIDIER TO DERBY
Difficulty: Class 4
Length: 9 miles (14.4 km)

LEVEROGUE TO NEAR VILLENEUVE
Difficulty: Class 4
Length: 4 miles (6.4 km)

VILLENEUVE TO SAARE
Difficulty: Class 3
Length: 2 miles (3.2 km)

Season: July through October
Character: A major river with varying seasonal options

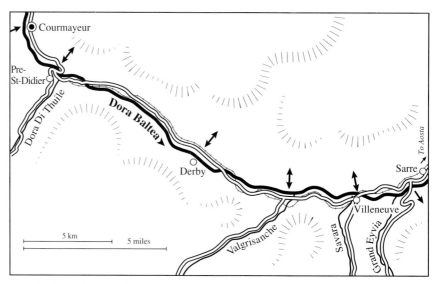

Dora Baltea River (Italy)

Below Leverogue is another difficult Class 4 section with at least one weir. A spectacular cascade bouncing diagonally down the mountainside on the right bank is just upstream of a riverside restaurant and bridge to Chambodey and La Perla. Just below the take-out near Villeneuve is an unrunnable weir. Boaters should cross the bridge and locate the best of several take-outs on river right and take out upstream of the weir.

The next stretch, from Villeneuve to Sarre, is a popular Class 3 stretch which includes the confluence with the Grand Eyvia River. At this point the Dora Baltea is assuredly a big river. While this stretch is commonly run by rafts and kayakers, it is not without its dangers. Stone-wall channeling has eliminated eddies, making it difficult to exit or even stop in some places, especially at high waters. The put-in is on the right just downstream of a bridge and small park downstream from Villeneuve. Avoid putting in on the bridge crossing the Dora di Rhemes, which is above a dangerous weir. This lower section is wide and filled with holes and waves. A weir is found where the Grand Eyvia enters. Take out at the bridge above the reservoir at Sarre.

The Dora Baltea boasts numerous runnable tributaries which can keep boaters busy in the area. These include the Dora Drhemes, the Grand Eyvia, the Urtier, the Savara, the Valnontey, and the Evancon. These vary in difficulty from moderate to extreme. Most flow through dramatic gorges, and all are glacier-fed.

◁ Noce River

Fed by glaciers in excess of 11,000 feet (3,355 m), the Noce bounces down the relatively remote and lush alpine Vale di Sole east of the Dora Baltea. Running beneath dramatic limestone walls through a valley of lush forests, vineyards, and orchards is some of Italy's finest whitewater. The azure-blue waters of the Noce are far enough away from population centers that they generate little commercial traffic, and the river remains unspoiled, uncrowded, and accessible to nearly all type of craft and skill levels. The river is medium-

COGOLO TO DIMARO
Difficulty: Class 5
Length: 3 miles (4.8 km)

MONCLASSICO TO PONTE STORI
Difficulty: Class 2
Length: 5 miles (8 km)

(continued on following page)

volume, but good glacial flows give it a bigger-volume feel. The good local cuisine and wine are an added attraction.

The first section from Cogolo is very difficult, but the rapids ease after a major tributary, the Vermigliana, enters on the right near Cusiano. The rapids remain friendly to DiMaro, a stretch which makes a good warm-up for the rest of the river. An alternate put-in is above the Vermigliana confluence where the main road crosses the river. Keep an eye out for weirs on this section.

At Mezzana is the Impianto slalom course. The stretch rates a Class 4 and is quite steep. This was the site of the 1993 Whitewater World Championships. It can get crowded and is sometimes closed for competitions. From here to DiMaro the action is nonstop, with continuous rapids and frequent rock obstructions. Some boaters elect to take out left below Mestriago to avoid portaging a weir and the section's most challenging rapid, the Sawmill Cataract, rated a Class 4+ and very tough at higher flows.

The next section, from Monclassico to Ponte Stori, also begins easily and ever so subtly grows into big rapids. Watch for a weir below a concrete bridge at Male. Below Male there is again big action at the confluence of the Rabbies on the left. The whitewater continues unabated, featuring the entire gambit of holes, waves, rocks, and eddies, until the Ponte Stori bridge.

Next is the experts-only Noce Gorge from the Ponte Stori bridge to Lago di Guistina where the Noce squeezes through a beautiful, tight cataract that is as wild as it is difficult and quite dangerous at high water. Boaters committing to this section will need to stop and scout often. A trail on the left at the top of the reservoir provides the take-out. When the reservoir is high, the very difficult rapids are covered.

The Vermigliana and the Rabbies are two options for expert boaters, as well as the somewhat easier Noce Bianco.

PONTE STORI TO MOSTIZZOLA
(LAGO DI GUISTINA)
Difficulty: Class 4
Length: 10 miles (16 km)

Season: April through October
Character: Popular Italian Alps river with good road access; many choices in the area

Switzerland

Season: April through
   October
Character: A glacial river
   with many options in
   both Switzerland and
   Austria

◁ Inn River

The Inn is called "the King of Alpine Rivers." Even more so than the Durance in France, this is the home of European river running, with the first sporting descents beginning almost a century ago. With its headwaters in the Bernina Glaciers in Switzerland, it reaches its best flows as the hot summer sun melts icy, silty water into the valleys below. The result is a combination of torrential volume, beauty, and variety. The last two featured sections are in Austria.

The upper two runs, the Giarsun and Ardez canyons in Switzerland, are mostly tight technical kayak runs with plenty of boulders added to the mix. It is easy to see how stub-nosed kayaks became popular here as a safeguard against pinning. Rafting companies now take commercial customers down the Giarsun in increasing numbers. Runs are possible even farther upstream, almost to the international resort town of Saint-Moritz. However, hydroelectric projects along the Inn dewater or otherwise make some stretches unrunnable. The scenery on this part of the Inn, the Engadine Valley, is fabulous. Engadine means "Garden of the Inn" in Romansch, one of four Swiss languages and the one spoken in this area.

The traditional Giarsun Canyon put-in at the bridge at Guarda is no longer allowed, probably due to limited parking. Boaters can now access the run upstream between Lavin and Susch, which adds a scenic but relatively flat warm-up paddle. The action begins as the river drops almost immediately into a gorge with the tough entry rapids Pruessen-Schleuder ("Prussian Slingshot"), reportedly named for a rough time experienced by a paddler from northern Germany. Technical moves and eddy-hopping are the order of the day here as kayakers set up for tricky rapids and some good drops. The last difficult rapid is Staircase. Just downstream is the take-out, on the right just upstream of a stone bridge at Ardez.

Next is the Ardez Gorge which has consistent action, with big drops from beginning to end. It is significantly more demanding than the upstream Giarsun Canyon. Put in at the take-out for the Giarsun Canyon run. The first set of big rapids is the most difficult. Although a tough double-drop rapid called Bob Bahn has been run, it is better judgment to carry around to eliminate the possibility of entering the third drop, the Bockschlitz, just below. The Bockschlitz holds a deadly wood-choked sieve which has claimed many lives. Nearly all portage the entire series on the left. The river from here sets a good pace with consistent rapids, huge boulders, and some big drops. About 550 yards (500 meters) below Bockschlitz is a 6$\frac{1}{2}$-foot (2 m) drop with a big hydraulic named Himmelssprung (Jump to Heaven). As the name implies, a normal boof will not do the job here. It is sometimes portaged right. After here the tempo slows somewhat. Downstream, river runners encounter one of the world's strangest river hazards. Giving new meaning to terms like "combat position" and "bombproof roll," the Swiss Army maintains a target range above the river complete with push-button traffic signals for passing boaters. The penalty for carelessly running a red light is apparently to be like a floating target at an amusement park. The return of the road to the river marks the take-out, but hard-boaters will want to check out the ender hole below the second rapid after the road returns before calling it quits.

Scuol (also known as Schuls) Canyon is the next run and is very popular with both rafts and kayaks. The run begins above Scuol at the spot where the road meets the river, also the take-out for the Ardez Gorge. Much of the run is visible from the road and consists of a series of holes, ledges, and eddies with plenty of play spots for kayakers and action for rafters. The last rapid, Schulser Eck ("Schulser Edge," also known as Against the Wall), is undercut and may require scouting and some good moves to avoid a flip. Take out just below the rapid and below Lischana bridge, downstream of Scuol. A path leads to the parking area. Don't miss the take-out—the downstream Prudella Dam was the site of a multiple drowning in 1994 when a raft crew paddled over the dam.

On the Austrian side of the border, Landeck is a big gathering area for boaters who often take over the campgrounds in town near the river. The stretch from Tosens to Landeck gets much use from boaters in all types of craft. Although this area is often dewa-

Inn River (Austria, Switzerland)

tered, high flows on hot summer days make this some of the best paddling in the area. At this point the riverbed is big, and flows can be quite powerful. Intermediate access points at Ried, Prutz, and Nesselgarten allow boaters to pick and choose which sections look inviting and allow them to skip the most difficult section, the Inn Shoot. Put in near the bridge on the main road just upstream from Tosens. The stretch provides nice scenery and a few challenging rapids mostly near the upper part of the run in Tosens and again near the town of Ried. Beware of two weirs in the rapids near Ried. The river eases until near Fliess where it enters the Inn Shoot, a very difficult boulder-laden stretch that should be carefully scouted from the road before committing. From Nesselgarten to Landeck is the Landeck Gorge, a solid Class 4 stretch in a limestone canyon the locals call Hohes Gericht (High Court of Justice). It is much tougher at higher flows when boaters may well feel they are on trial. Take out just above the confluence with the Sanna.

The Imst Gorge from Imst to Haiming is one of the most popular in Europe, providing recreation to boaters for decades. All types of craft negotiate the easy big-water rapids including large commercial paddle rafts. Whitish glacial runoff from the numerous tributaries collects to swell the Inn to such enormous proportions here that paddling from one bank to the other is an undertaking. The put-in and take-out are well marked in each town. The rapids in this section are mostly enormous waves with some big holes situated on bends or below tributaries. The silt-laden cross-flow of the Oetz on the right partway down creates interesting hydraulics at higher flows. With the exception of a gravel works on the left bank, the scenery is classic. The village of Roppen, with its covered wooden bridge and multicolored streamers waving from the spires of its medieval steeple, could be cut from a postcard. The put-in at Imst and take-out in Haiming are

Europe, Day One

You never know what boating might be like on the other side of the world. We were told that the Alps had runnable rivers, and we knew the names of a few and some basic information. We rented a car in Zurich and drove all day to Imst on the Inn River in Austria.

Imst is a little medieval village of a few thousand people set beneath impressive mountains. Like visitors for hundreds of years past we made our way to the town center which was decorated, as is customary in the Alps, with a water well and a bulletin board. The news was good. The wildwater world championship races began that day on the Sanna River just upstream in Landeck. The town map clearly marked a "Rafting Launch Site" for the Imst-to-Haiming run on the Inn, and for good measure Sting was in town for a concert at the outdoor park.

The put-in was teeming with commercial groups and odd-looking German rafts with rudders. Some U.S. servicemen were getting ready to be guided down the river. After a big-water run in our inflatable kayaks, we beat a path to Landeck and watched as racers paddled strange-looking ultralight kayaks straight downriver for the fastest time. That night in Imst as we finished dinner at an outdoor cafe the concert began. The familiar songs could be heard everywhere as if Sting were singing for the whole town, but the locals here do not complain much. The music echoed off the mountains and mixed with the chimes of the ancient church steeples as we walked the town's twisted streets and planned our next trip on the Oetz.

—Martha Kendall

well used and marked. Several commercial rafting companies and a kayak shop are also located in Haiming. Hard-boaters can continue a few kilometers to the town of Silz where a huge surfing wave, an artificial play hole, a beach with volleyball, a paddle shop, and a Mexican restaurant await. Below here the Inn is flat, wide, and uninteresting to the whitewater boater.

Saane River ➤

GSTAAD TO CHATEAU D'OEX
Difficulty: Class 3+
Length: 9 miles (14.4 km)

Season: April to early August
Character: Swiss Alps river followed by road

The Saane is a quaint float that crosses the Swiss-language line beginning in the German-speaking resort of Gstaad and ending near the French-speaking medieval village of Chateaux d'Oex. The Saane (not to be confused with the Sanne, a tributary of the Inn) drains an area of the Swiss Alps east of Lac Leman (Lake Geneva) with peaks over 10,000 feet (3,050 m). Although a road and railroad follow the river, neither are apparent and the river is quite intimate.

Put in on the right bank near the campground downstream of Gstaad. Although Gstaad is a ritzy ski resort, the surrounding area is largely agricultural. The Swiss prefer organic fertilizer, and the nearby farms lend a pungent odor to the area at times. The river flows north for the first 3 miles, providing an easy warm-up with a steady gradient as the rich forests nearly cover the river. As the river turns right and to the west it passes a military communication base and a few ski lifts. It then drops into a gorge with several Class 3 rapids. The setting here is almost mystical, with curious limestone rock formations draped with moss and springs pouring from the canyon walls. Downstream a second, smaller gorge signals the most difficult rapid on the run. The rapid is directly beneath the towering bridge to Gerignoz, but the bridge is more apparent from the downstream view. It can be scouted on the right. The canyons open up, and it is a scenic easy float to Chateau d'Oex where river runners can take out by the bridge above the campground.

The run can be extended downstream to a poorly marked take-out at Les Moulins. This stretch requires running or portaging an old dam at a gravel plant. Boaters may continue farther down to Rossiniere through a difficult and very narrow gorge scoutable from the highway bridge near Les Moulins.

Simme River ➤

BOLTIGEN TO ERLENBACH
Difficulty: Class 3
Length: 8 miles (12.8 km)

Season: April to early September
Character: Swiss Alps river followed by road and railroad

The Simme flows through the beautiful Simmental valley, just east of the Saane. The two rivers have their similarities, although the Simme drains an area with a slightly higher elevation and has a somewhat longer season. A railroad follows the Simme, making for a convenient hourly shuttle between Erlenbach and Boltigen.

Put in at the first covered bridge downstream of Boltigen on the left near a lumberyard. Much of the river may be scouted from the road or train, until it moves away from the road as it approaches Erlenbach. The river starts easily, though near the top there is an old weir which provides some nice waves, especially at higher flows. The Simme has a constant gradient, with the best whitewater near the Heidanweidli bridge where fairly constant Class 3 rapids keep rafters on their toes and kayakers paddling from playspot to playspot. The water is a whitish green glacial flow. Above the river is a gentle canopy created by a mixture of trees including larch, maple, white birch, and oak. The biggest obstacles encountered are tree branches reaching out over the river.

Swiss Military

The Swiss have a strict gun-control law. All males eighteen and older are issued a gun, one case of bullets, and orders for call-up in the event of invasion. The result is similar to a nuclear deterrent. For hundreds of years the country has maintained peace and unquestioned sovereignty by taking advantage of its impassable terrain, hidden defenses, and eternal readiness. Be careful here! The stump you sit on for lunch may be a remote-controlled machine gun—really. Still, the oxymoron of a benign military omnipresence has its comical aspects. On the Ardez Gorge of the Inn, boaters must press a button-operated traffic signal before paddling under a rifle range. A paddle down the Saane takes boaters past a strange military communications facility. On the Hinterrhein, river runners launch just downstream of an artillery range. While camping on what must be a strategic mountain pass above the Simme we found ourselves surrounded by Swiss soldiers on maneuvers. One armed soldier was stationed as a lookout atop the playground slide, perhaps to observe our dinner. He occasionally looked into his binoculars for playground invaders. It has been some 600 years since the Swiss fought their last war.

—Dan Dunlap

Birdwatchers may spot hawks, herons, ducks, and swallows along the river, although they might not be as entertaining as the occupants at the chicken farm on the upper reach on the left. The take-out is at the backwater of the hydroelectric plant at Erlenbach. The plant often dewaters the river below, but at higher flows it is possible to continue to the reservoir just upstream of Wimms.

◄ Aare River

THUN TO BERN
Difficulty: Class 2
Length: 12 miles (19.2 km)

Season: April to October
Character: Mild, popular float

The Aare, the outflow from Lake Thun (also known as Thuner See), is a broad and beautiful river which serves as a popular relaxing playfloat for the boaters near the Swiss capital of Bern. Although a superhighway follows the length of this river on the right, it was thoughtfully screened by broad stands of trees so as to be unnoticeable from the river. The result is a wide, vividly blue river with forgiving rapids and a countryside feel.

Though essentially an urban river, the Aare provides a series of landscapes, and the many nooks and crannies along its shores are a haven for birdlife. Expect to see other boaters on the river entertaining themselves with swims and water fights. If there is any doubt that this is a civilized run, the river goes by several nice restaurants, most of which will not turn boaters away.

Put in near the Gasthaus Bellevue in Thun, and take out in Bern.

◄ Vorderrhein (Upper Rhine) River

ILINZ TO REICHENAU
Difficulty: Class 3
Length: 12 miles (19.2 km)

Season: April through October
Character: Deep, scenic gorge with train shuttle

Known as the Grand Canyon of Switzerland and also the Flims Gorge, the Vorderrhein (Upper Rhine) is one of the great river runs of Europe, one of the best-known rivers in the world. In this reach, it bisects the giant Flims land slip (the Flimser Schlucht), creating the Grand Canyon as it etches its way through a gorge of white limestone. The river continues east, and downstream of its confluence with the Hinterrhein at Reichenau becomes the Rhein. It then begins its long journey northward.

This may well be Europe's premier run. Although not to the scale of the Grand Canyon of the Colorado, it is a similar study in the graceful persistence of erosion. Throughout the gorge there are bleached cliff walls, pinnacles, crags, and side canyons as well as beautiful mountains and lush green Rhine forest. The waters are big and suitable for both inflatables and hard boats, with consistent rapids and frequent playholes. This is one of only two major whitewater runs in Europe not followed by a road. The railroad that follows the river operates as a boater-friendly shuttle, a function that more than justifies its intrusion.

Most river runners board the train at Elan where the railway will transport both them and their gear to the put-in. The train is equipped to accommodate sightseers, and the ride is an excellent opportunity to scout much of the river and to take photos. The pass is good for the whole day, so cheapskates can start the river early and run it twice or use shortened routes at interim stations in Versam or Trin.

Boaters can carry to the put-in on the right bank. The run begins with some interesting rapids and a weir that should be scouted on the right. About 2½ miles (4 km) downstream of the put-in the river enters the limestone gorge, and the sights and the whitewater intensify as rocks and channels force boaters to choose routes. Just downstream of the confluence of the Carrerabach on the right is the most difficult rapid, the Black Hole. Landslides can change the rapid, and it is best to inquire locally as to its condition and the possibility of exposed metal stakes near the top. After the Black Hole the rapids ease down to Versam station. Aside from avoiding a dangerous undercut rock on the right just below the Rabiusa confluence, it is an easy float to the take-out on the right at Reichenau upstream of the Hinterrhein confluence.

The Vorderrhein is also popular with anglers, so be courteous and avoid confrontation. Boaters seeking more of a challenge can try runs upstream or elsewhere in the immediate area. Another possibility is the Upper Hinterrhein, a fine, relatively easy paddle from Hinterrhein to Splugen. Put in on the Upper Hinterrhein downstream of the Swiss Army artillery range.

Reuss River ➤

In the heart of the Swiss Alps is the Goddard Pass, originally a mule track and later a crucial mountain route for trade and troops. It now holds a major superhighway and tunnel between Switzerland and Italy. Here the Reuss begins its journey north from the border into Switzerland as its glacial torrent cuts an unrunnable gorge from Andermatt to Goschenen. From Goschenen downstream the Reuss offers some fine runnable whitewater as it picks up volume from several glacial side streams and passes through the Goddard Valley (Class 5) and the more open Uri Valley (Class 3–). Ask locally for river access directions.

Most boaters take out where the whitewater ends at Attinghausen, though it is possible to continue downstream to where the river flows into the Urner See, part of Lake Luzern (Lucerne). Below the outflow of Lake Luzern, at the picturesque town of Luzern, the Reuss becomes a meandering large river. Canoeists from Zurich and surrounding areas take advantage of the Class 2 run here from Bremgarten to Genenstorf. Rodeo competitions are popular in Bremgarden.

GODDARD VALLEY, GOSCHENEN TO AMSTEG
Difficulty: Class 5
Length: 9 miles (14.4 km)

URI VALLEY, AMSTEG TO ATTINGHAUSEN
Difficulty: Class 3–
Length: 7 miles (11.2 km)

Season: April through October
Character: Alpine run near superhighway

Germany

GRIESENSCHLUCHT TO GRAINAU
Difficulty: Class 4
Length: 4 miles (6.4 km)

Season: April through July
and after rains
Character: Popular,
technical Bavarian river

◁ Loisach River

The Loisach is Germany's most popular and famous whitewater river, located south of Munich between the resort towns of Ehrwald, Austria, and Garmisch-Partenkirchen in Germany. The Loisach is just a creek compared to the big-water runs in Austria and Switzerland, but its inclusion within Germany's borders assures its reputation among the country's devoted paddlers. This area of Bavaria is best known for great skiing, and the headwaters of the Loisach are in the spectacular mountains above the resort town of Ehrwald. These include the Zugspitz, Germany's highest mountain.

The Loisach is a fine technical run in an intimate setting and the site of regular whitewater competitions. In the over sixty years that it has been recreationally paddled, virtually every rock along its length has been given a name. An unobtrusive highway follows the river on the left and crosses to the right at a bridge about halfway down.

Put in near the border of Germany and Austria at a bridge in Griesenschlucht, or skip the initial flat section by driving about a mile (1.6 km) north from the border to a parking lot near the river. Just downstream of the parking lot the river passes under a footbridge and drops into a narrow gorge shaded by the rich forests. The sights and sounds of civilization disappear, and river runners must focus on the action as one technical drop follows another in a series of rock gardens, turns, and chutes. The width of the river keeps boaters on their toes and allows few route choices. First-timers may want to scout some of the tougher sections including Staircase, just downstream of where the river passes under the highway. Take out on river right just after the second footbridge near a parking area, or continue all the way to Garmisch-Partenkirchen. Because of the size of the streambed, only small craft are appropriate.

There are other popular, good-quality nearby runs, including the Isar in the next drainage to the east. The best section of the Isar is a 7-mile (11.2 km) Class 3 section upstream of Schernitz. The road is closed to private traffic, so you will have to take the taxi service that departs regularly and serves to regulate river traffic. The weir near the Karwendlebach confluence upstream of the take-out is a recommended portage.

Austria

Inn River (see Switzerland, page 228)

Oetz River ➤

The full name is the Oetztalerache, but call it the Oetz—everyone else does. The head-waters of this tributary of the Inn are glaciers hovering above the river at over 11,000 feet (3,355 m). In the heat of the summer the icy, silty-white waters tumble down this glacial side valley, joining the Inn just upstream of Haiming. Most of the runs described here are quite demanding, and throughout its length the Oetz is steep and almost barren of eddies. The flows vary considerably depending on the time of day—lower flows in the morning, higher flows later in the afternoon. The river can be dangerous, especially at higher flows. Reportedly there are even little memorial crosses placed at one river access point. This is not a good place to learn to paddle.

The upper run begins at Solden Gorge and is the domain of expert kayakers. Al-though Solden Gorge has been rafted, local laws now forbid private rafting on the Oetz, and the upper section is closed to all rafting. Commercial rafting is allowed on the lower section, but a guard is stationed at the put-in to ensure that private rafters stay off the river. Although less appropriate, inflatable kayaks are legal.

The upper reach is actually two runs, sometimes called the Solden Gorge run and the middle run (Langenfeld to Umhausen). A reasonable put-in for the run is down-stream from Solden at a bridge near the sewage treatment plant. It is possible to put in upstream, but this entails running the Soelden-Katarakt (Solden Cataract), a tough Class 5 rapid just downstream of the Wutenbach confluence. The rapid has a razor-thin line through a river-wide stopper and has earned a bad reputation. Although the river eases in sections, it is always moving, especially in the late afternoon as glacial melt arrives, raising the water level. The most difficult section downstream of the Solden Cataract is the Mad Mile about a third of a way down. The river remains relentless to Bruggen where it eases as it passes through a gravel plant.

The middle run between Langenfeld and Umhausen is an even more difficult sec-tion, as the Oetz here is filled with Class 5 rapids and worse. This stretch is usually avoided, as the obstructions, holes, and drops are much more intense than those upstream. It is considered unrunnable at any but the lowest flows, usually coming in mornings in the late fall.

The lower section, from Oetz to the Inn River and on to Haiming, is more straight-forward and has few obstructions. Much of the run can be scouted from nearby roads and bridges. Still, the gradient and the rapids are constant, and the silty-white water holds few eddies. A swimmer will have difficulty getting ashore with gear.

The put-in is at the wooden foot bridge upstream of the town of Oetz. Maps avail-able here provide all the information for the run, if you read German. A police guard is usually on duty to assure that you comply with regulations. Be especially wary of the

SOLDEN TO UMHAUSEN
Difficulty: Class 5p
Length: 14 miles (22.4 km)

OETZ TO INN CONFLUENCE
Difficulty: Class 4
Length: 8 miles (12.8 km)

Season: April through
October
Character: Swift and cold
glacier-fed river

deadly concrete weir about two-thirds of the way downstream to the Inn confluence. Not that it's easy to miss; warning is provided by a skull-and-crossbones sign on a wooden bridge just upstream. First-time boaters should scout the weir (by car or by foot) to confirm a safe exit and portage route on the right. Below the weir the action continues to the Inn confluence. Once on the Inn, it's relaxation time. The take-out at Haiming is the same as for the Imst Gorge run on the Inn, described in the chapter on Switzerland.

◁ Salza River

WILDALPEN TO ERZHALDEN
Difficulty: Class 3
Length: 9 miles (14.4 km)

ERZHALDEN TO PALFAU (GORGE RUN)
Difficulty: Class 3+
Length: 4 miles (6.4 km)

PALFAU (ALSO KNOWN AS PADDLER) TO ENNS RIVER
Difficulty: Class 4–
Length: 3 miles (4.8 km)

Season: April through October
Character: Picturesque Austrian Alps classic

The Salza is one of the finest rivers in the eastern Alps and has long served as a center of paddling activity. Surrounded by the Austrian Alps with peaks over 7,000 feet (2,135 m), the Salza runs clear and cold, flowing due west through a pristine area with forest reserves on both sides of the river. The water is usually transparent green and flows through lush mixed forests past an occasional farm or guest house. The river supplies the drinking water for nearby Vienna to the east as well as recreation to fishermen, canoeists, kayakers, and rafters in the area.

Most of the river running is centered around the resort village of Wildalpen. The flow is mostly snowmelt until June, after which it is mostly rain-fed and best after heavy rains. Some boaters continue to run the river at low flows into October. Downstream of Wildalpen there is good camping.

The featured sections are: Wildalpen to Erzhalden, with the biggest rapids at Campground and Lawinenshwall, followed by the towns of Petrus and Erzhalden; Erzhalden to Palfau (also known as Paddler), known as the gorge run; and Palfau to the Enns River. Any or all sections can be combined. The uppermost available put-in depends on flows, with the first run only available at higher flows. The rapids get a bit tougher below Wildalpen, and good surf waves can be found from Wildalpen all the way to Palfau at high flows. Beware of undercuts in the gorge run and fallen trees in the upper reaches.

Nearby is historical Mariazell where the procession of Austro-Hungarian kings were crowned and noble marriages are still performed. The Erzberg ("ore mountain") is an opencast mining site which has now been declared a World Heritage site.

Also worthy of mention is the Soca in Slovenia (known in Italy as the Isonzo), another legendary whitewater river in the eastern Alps. The Soca area was hotly contested between Austria and Italy in World War I, and between the wars a young Tony Prijon pioneered river running here. Now part of a national park, the Soca features some beautiful turquoise water and whitewater runs from Class 3 to Class 5.

Corsica

Some quarter-billion years ago, geological forces thrust upward the granite mass that now is Corsica. Subsequent plate movements added sedimentary rock to the eastern side of the island, and much more recent glaciation and erosion, as well as the stabilization of the Mediterranean Sea, left an island only about twice the area of Long Island featuring rugged mountainous terrain in excess of 9,000 feet (2,745 m).

Corsica is set between France and Italy, both geographically and culturally. The Corsican language sounds more Italian than French, and Italians are their main trading partners. Yet France has governed the island for most of the last 200 years. French rule came at the same time as the rise of the island's preeminent native son, Napoleon Bonaparte. Napoleon's family was considered too friendly with the French and apparently proved it by moving to France when he was nine; however, his rugged character is considered typically Corsican.

French domination is not popular, though the Corsicans probably could not survive without French help. Graffiti is everywhere, and political unrest is curiously institutionalized. Bombings occasionally take place and, though they are usually intended to be symbolic and rarely target humans, a blast in 1998 killed the island's top French administrator. Agriculture on the island is marginal due to poor soil, leaving tourism as the main industry.

In that vein, whitewater boating lends a small hand to the Corsicans. From late March to early May, the steep river valleys fill with sparkling clear runoff; great, waterfall-laden runs emerge, and kayakers, mostly from Europe, perform a ritual pilgrimage of ferrying their kayaks to the island. Most of these runs are tough and dangerous and claim lives nearly every year. However, Corsica does have some fine easier whitewater and even some pleasant floats where it is possible to savor the fine scenery and local color.

Tavignano River ➤

The Tavignano drains Corsica's 8,000-foot (2,440 m) central mountains and then carves a scenic path through bedrock. The put-in is at the high mountain town of Corte where the Restonica joins the Tavignano. Although there may be some good boating upstream, there is no developed access. Below Corte the river is a mellow Class 3 through some fine rural scenery. Just upstream of the Vecchio confluence the river enters a small gorge with some interesting rapids and constrictions, although overall the river is relatively easy for the first 16 miles to Pont de Peidicorte.

The most popular part of the Tavignano is downstream of Pont de Peidicorte to near the village of Falio where the rapids kick up to Class 4. The action here is continuous, with few eddies. The area is a meeting ground for boaters on the island.

To the north is the Golo, a river which offers waterfall runs in its upper reaches and stretches of easier paddling all the way to the sea.

CORTE TO VECCHIO CONFLUENCE
Difficulty: Class 3
Length: 16 miles (25.6 km)

VECCHIO CONFLUENCE TO BELOW PONT DE PEIDECORTE
Difficulty: Class 4
Length: 11 miles (17.6 km)

Season: Early March through May, also often runnable in October and November
Character: Popular; relatively large drainage for Corsica

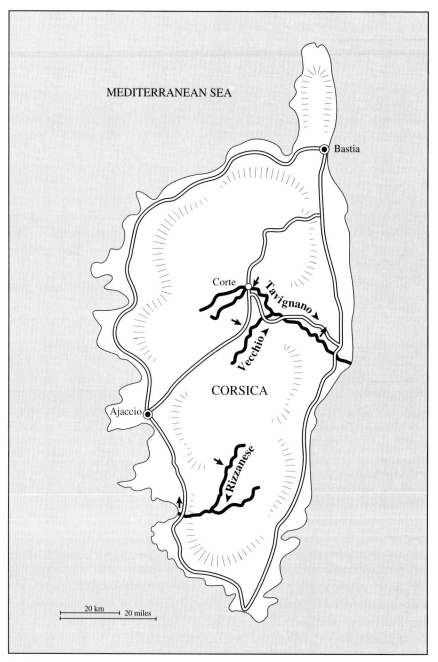

Corsica

Vecchio River ➤

This tributary of the Tavignano is a steep-creek Corsican classic where paddlers come to test their skills. The upper 5 miles (8 km) are a Class 5+ with numerous portages and usually run only at lowest flows. This is one of the toughest runs on the island, and bailing out partway down is no cause for shame. Some boaters take more than one day to complete the run. Boaters should scout the lower part of this run from near the highway bridge and the upper part from the railway.

The upper run features several big falls and big ledges, with some bumpy landings at low flows. A little over halfway down, boaters portage around a 43-foot (13 m) waterfall, putting in for a difficult stretch that continues all the way to the N193 road bridge.

The middle section is a bit easier, but still solid Class 5. Scouting and portaging are a bit less arduous, making this a good warm-up for the tougher runs on the island. The action eases somewhat in the lower part of this section.

The lower section is easy by comparison and is often combined with the lower gorge of the Tavignano.

Rizzanese River ➤

The Rizzanese is another Corsican freefall masterpiece. It is farther south than the Tavignano or the Vecchio and flows to the southwest. Its drainage is a little lower, making the season a little shorter. The upper run features probably the best-known drop on Corsica, the 30-foot Big Falls. Farther downstream is an easier middle run that is often combined with the upper run. Below this is an easier float that can be paddled to the Mediterranean.

Put in for the upper run at Zoza at the D120 Bridge. After a short section of good warm-up rapids, the action becomes more challenging. The bedrock gorge begins to constrict the drops, and boaters must scout and consider portaging two 15-foot (4.5 m) drops. After a few more drops the river pours over a small drop, followed by the 30-foot (9 m) Big Falls as the river pours into a deep pool in the sheer-walled gorge below. The small drop must be run cleanly to make the favored route on the extreme right of the big drop. The rapids below ease but include a few big drops which should not be taken lightly. The hydraulics beneath the falls on this run can be quite powerful, and one of the drops below the big falls has proven fatal. There is no substitute for thorough scouting, throw-line stations, and good judgment. Take out on the footpath near D194 or continue on to the middle run for 5 miles (8 km) of Class 3 water to the D69 bridge.

Those into an easy float with some great landscape can paddle the lower run for 9 miles (14.4 km) from the D69 bridge to the sea. Some even paddle along the shore to Propriano Harbor to take out.

Top experts wanting to take on one of the toughest and most dangerous runs in Corsica can check the stretch above Zoza. Not only are the drops in this reach near the edge of navigability, scouting and portaging them is also tough.

Other major waterfall rivers in southern Corsica include the Taravo, just to the north of the Rizzanese, and the Prunelli, even farther north. Draining to the east is the Travo, a smaller, very popular run with a slightly shorter season.

CANAGLIO TO ROAD BRIDGE (UPPER RUN)
Difficulty: Class 5+p
Length: 5 miles (8 km)

ROAD BRIDGE TO NOCETA ROAD BRIDGE (MIDDLE RUN)
Difficulty: Class 5
Length: 5 miles (8 km)

NOCETA ROAD BRIDGE TO TAVIGNANO CONFLUENCE
Difficulty: Class 4
Length: 3 miles (4.8 km)

Season: Late March to late May
Character: Prime, steep Corsican river

D120 BRIDGE IN ZOZA TO D194 (UPPER RUN)
Difficulty: Class 5p
Length: 4 miles (6.4 km)

D194 TO D69 BRIDGE (MIDDLE RUN)
Difficulty: Class 3
Length: 5 miles (8 km)

D69 BRIDGE TO THE MEDITERRANEAN SEA (LOWER RUN)
Difficulty: Class 2–
Length: 8 miles (12.8 km)

Season: Mid-March to early May
Character: Waterfall classic

Norway

*W*ith the highest peaks in Europe north of the Alps, and over two-thirds of the country covered with mountains, glaciers, rivers, and lakes, it's no surprise that Norway should have good whitewater. Yet, for the most part, it is neither a popular tourist destination nor well known to travelers. Norway is still probably best known as the land of the Vikings, and it is unlikely these able seamen spent much time shooting rapids. River running didn't really generate much interest here until the 1970s. The boating community is small but growing, and the country has an active whitewater society, with student clubs in the larger cities.

Most of the popular whitewater in Norway is south of Trondheim in the southern part of the country. The season is generally from May to September, with peak flows in mid-May to mid-June. Most of the rivers are fueled with dependably cold snowmelt. Camping is generally much less restrictive than in other parts of Europe, although few of these rivers support multi-day trips. Scandinavians traditionally think of outdoor recreation as an inalienable right, and access across private land is usually allowed under a tradition sometimes known as the "Everyman Rule." As anywhere, this blessing will only last as long as property owners' rights are respected. Fishing is also a respected ritual, and conflicts with anglers are not unknown, especially during salmon runs, so be courteous.

Traveling in Norway isn't cheap, even compared to traveling in the Alps. The availability of free camping helps the financially challenged river runner, and in the end most consider a trip here worth the cost.

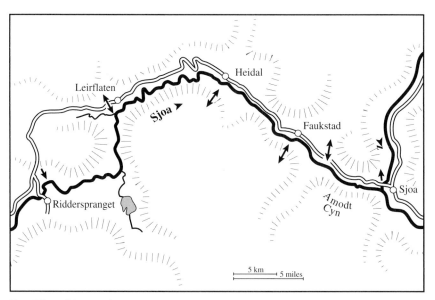

Sjoa River (Norway)

Scandinavia holds many other whitewater possibilities which get little attention. Some multi-day trips can be found in Sweden, and there are good free-flowing whitewater rivers near the Swedish-Finnish border.

Sjoa River ➢

The Sjoa (SHOO-a) is likely Norway's most popular river, garnering the attention of river runners from Norway and elsewhere. Located about 185 miles (300 km) northwest of Oslo and about 40 miles (64 km) northwest of Lillehammer, the Sjoa has a little something for everyone, its big water providing a full spectrum of whitewater difficulty. The Sjoa also runs through some great wilderness scenery and varying terrain. The river drains from scenic Gjende Lake for most of the run and then tumbles through the beautiful Heidal Valley.

According to the locals, the name derives from the sound of the big rapids. Whatever the derivation, the Sjoa means big water. The river maintains good flows even after the snowmelt ends as upstream rains usually take up the slack. Although it courses through some major canyons, winter ice floes clear the riverbed of most obstructions. The challenge for boaters is the power of the flows and the intense hydraulics.

The Sjoa is a mixture of easier whitewater in open scenic valleys and big-water rapids in the canyons. The scenery in the canyons is also impressive, with imposing black escarpments and some fine side waterfalls. The river is of interest to kayakers of all abilities, and rafting trips are popular on the second and third runs.

The river is generally divided into five sections: Ridderspranget to Leirflaten; Leirflaten to Heidal (also known as the Asengjuvet or the upper raft run); Heidal to Faukstad (the lower raft run); Faukstad to Amodt Canyon; and Amodt Canyon to the Lagen River.

The first section from Ridderspranget to Leirflaten has several portages and accordingly gets less use. The put-in requires a ⅔-mile (1 km) carry to launch downstream of a towering waterfall. The action starts with some tough but runnable rapids and eases before an even more difficult reach with several big ledges and a mandatory portage.

The second section, Leirflaten to Heidal, is popular with both kayaks and rafts as the river gushes through the Great Sjoa Canyon. The overall gradient here is 60 fpm (12 mpk). Paddlers should assess conditions before launching. This stretch is more difficult at high flows, and access out of the canyon is tough. From here down a major road follows the river on the left. The canyon lives up to its name, with steep walls, side streams, and waterfalls providing the visuals.

The put-in for the third section from Heidal to Faukstad is on river left above the bridge in Heidal. Known as the lower raft run, this stretch has a respectable gradient of 40 fpm and occasionally passes through small canyons. Although the action is fairly continuous with few eddies, it is a bit easier here than the upstream runs with only a few big rapids. The first big rapid is The Gut, about 3 miles below the Heidal bridge. Here the canyon walls narrow, and boaters must slalom through a long progression of waves and holes with few good eddies. This stretch has only two significant midstream rocks. Boaters may want to check flows by spotting one of these about ⅔ mile (1 km) below Heidal. If the water is going over the rock, paddlers are in for a very high-water run.

RIDDERSPRANGET TO LEIRFLATEN
Difficulty: Class 4p
Length: 10 miles (16 km)

LEIRFLATEN TO HEIDAL (ASENGJUVET OR UPPER RAFT RUN)
Difficulty: Class 4
Length: 7 miles (11.2 km)

HEIDAL TO FAUKSTAD (LOWER RAFT RUN)
Difficulty: Class 3+
Length: 8 miles (12.8 km)

FAUKSTAD TO AMODT CANYON
Difficulty: Class 2
Length: 3 miles (4.8 km)

AMODT CANYON TO GUDBRANDSDALS-LAGEN (LAGEN) CONFLUENCE
Difficulty: Class 5
Length: 3 miles (4.8 km)

Season: May through September
Character: Scenic, popular, many options

The run from Faukstad to Amodt Canyon is an easy float but gets less use, as the scenery is not as impressive as on the other stretches.

The fifth section, Amodt Canyon to the Lagen River, is another story altogether. Numerous big-water rapids appear and become even more difficult below the Amotsfallene bridge. Some take out at the bridge; others continue through Vaskemaskina ("The Washing Machine"), a tough rapid with a 180-degree twist decorated with some big holes, and on to the site of the National Kayak Arena. This natural course has some good play rapids. From here the river tumbles into the 2-mile (3.2 km) Amodt Canyon. The canyon is definitely for experts only and usually run just at low to medium flows. Even at low flows the action can be continuous, with four tight, big drops and several undercuts. The river is powerful here, and it's a good idea to foot-scout the entire run from river level before launching. Take out at the Gudbrandsdalen-lagen (also known as Lagen) confluence. There is good camping just upstream of Leirflaten.

◄ Jori River

BRIDGE AT NED REINDOL TO NEAR DOMBAS
Difficulty: Class 4+
Length: 8 miles (12.8 km)

Season: May through July
Character: Isolated, picturesque

The Jori (YOUR-ee) pounds through an isolated gorge in the Svartdalen, Norwegian for "Black Valley." The river lies between the more popular Sjoa River to the south and the Driva River to the north. Most consider the Jori to be worth the expedition style boating it demands. Some refer to it as the jewel of Norway.

The gorge offers tough, continuous rapids, big waves at high flows, sharp turns, a few holes, and few eddies. The scenery is great, but there is little time to enjoy it as the narrow streambed and steep gradient give the run the feel of a water slide. As the Grona River enters on the left, it marks the beginning of an easier section, although if it is adding significantly to the flow the action will continue to the take-out. The take-out just upstream of E69 Road has been made easier since the removal of the unrunnable ruins of a dam. Just below the bridge the river tumbles into a Class 5 rapid. Downstream the Jori joins the Lagen near Dombas.

◄ Driva River

MELEM TO ISHOL
Difficulty: Class 3+
Length: 11 miles (17.6 km)

ISHOL TO LIAHJELL
Difficulty: Class 4+
Length: 9 miles (14.4 km)

Season: May through September
Character: Picturesque, northernmost of the Norwegian rivers in this book

The Driva Basin and Driva River are accessed by traveling the main road and the train line upstream along the Lagen River northward over a mountain pass. The best boating on this pool-and-drop river begins where the Driva leaves the highway and railroad.

The upper run from Melem to Ishol flows through a scenic, open valley, with short rapids occasionally dropping into short gorges. The river can be tough at high flows, especially where the river narrows. There are a couple of big ledges which should be scouted and/or portaged. Be sure to scout the take-out to avoid the narrow constriction at the bridge at Ishol.

The lower run from Ishol to Liahjell includes the impressive Graura Canyon, a very challenging pool-and-drop stretch with big drops and stoppers. It is even more difficult at high flows when it has much the same feel and level of difficulty as the Amodt Canyon on the Sjoa. Climbing out is very tough, so it's a good idea to be comfortable with water levels and your abilities before committing to this stretch. The most difficult rapid is just above Storfallet. Boaters can carry to the right on first drop, but the next drop lacks a portage route and must be run at most flows.

Dagali River ➤

Also called the Degalifallene or the Numedalslagen, the Dagali is due west of Oslo, the southernmost of the Norwegian rivers covered here. The Dagali is a big-volume run, especially in May and June when the upper run above Breidset is much tougher and is usually avoided. The run reportedly holds several tough holes.

In the lower stretch near the village of Dagali, the river is much tamer. Watch out for a waterfall near Hallen. Camping is available near the take-out.

ORSJOREN TO BREIDSET
Difficulty: Class 4+
Length: 5 miles (8 km)

BREIDSET TO DAGALI
Difficulty: Class 3+
Length: 5 miles (8 km)

Season: May through September
Character: Big-volume, picturesque

Britain

LOCH INSH TO FOCHABERS
Difficulty: Class 2+
Length: 62 miles (99.2 km)

Season: April through
October
Character: Popular, good
road access, relatively
mild

◁ Spey River (Scotland)

The Spey is the largest and best known of several runnable Scottish rivers. Its name derives from the Gaelic term *speidh*, meaning "speed," a reference no doubt mindful of the fact that the Spey flows faster than most rivers in Scotland. The Spey courses north between the Monadhliath and Cairngorm ranges in Scotland, draining some of the tallest mountains in the British Isles at over 4,000 feet (1,220 m). The river provides some 62 miles (99.2 km) of good paddling from Loch Insh to its outlet on the North Sea, but the atmosphere is even better than the paddling. The Spey offers some of the best scenery anywhere as it cuts a swath through the Aviemore region of the northeast Highlands.

The Aviemore region is some of the best recreational real estate in the British Isles. Though it won't compete with the great resorts of the Alps, the largest ski area in Britain is set near its headwaters, and the best salmon fishing in the isles is found along its banks. For those so inclined, this is the domain of the world's finest malt whisky distilleries. Tandhu Distillery is on the banks at the town of Knockando, and is part of a tour that includes an alliteration of fabled names such as Glenfiddich, Glenlivet, and Glen Grant. Boaters are reminded that tasting and boating (or driving) don't mix.

Although the main north-south road in Scotland, the A-9, follows the river for the first 15 miles (24 km) and other roads and walking trails are usually nearby, access to the Spey is restricted to only eighteen designated access/egress points. Still, boaters generally have their pick of numerous reaches to run. Boating begins as far up as the heavily wooded Loch Insh and continues downstream past numerous old bridges and curious sights along the way, including ancient standing stones and stone pillars. During fishing season (February to September), access agreements limit paddling downstream of the Delefure Burn to Tuesday, Thursday, and Friday from 10 A.M. to 5 P.M. and all day Sunday. The largest rapid, Knockando, is a designated whitewater area and open from 10 A.M. to 10 P.M. all year. These restrictions are in consideration of anglers and are not typical of Scotland.

If you're in the area, you may want to consider the runnable tributaries of the Spey including the Aeon, the Dulmaian, and the more challenging Feshie. Other popular and scenic whitewater rivers in Scotland are the Teith, the Awe, and the Lochy. A very popular float is the River Tay, near Perth, about 60 miles (96 km) from Scotland's biggest cities, Glasgow and Edinburgh.

A recommended local guide is the *Guide to Scottish Rivers*, published by the Scottish Canoe Association in Edinburgh, which gives details of agreements governing access to most rivers in Scotland.

Tryweryn River (Wales) ➤

Llyn (Lake) Celyn to town of Bala
Difficulty: Class 3
Length: 5½ miles (8.8 km)

Season: April through October
Character: Dam-controlled, popular, with slalom course

No river in the British Isles is more of a training ground for paddlers than the Tryweryn, located near Snowdonia National Park in northern Wales. Flowing out of the Cambria Mountains at over 3,000 feet (915 m), the flow is dam-controlled as part of the flood-control system for the downstream Dee. Releases occur throughout the season, and the dam will not release during heavy rains or when the reservoir is too low. Although the riverbed is narrow with tight turns and small eddies, it supports plenty of good playspots.

The Tryweryn is emphatically promoted for paddlers. Commercial whitewater rafting is available, and hard-boat devotees make much use of the slalom course just below the dam on the Graveyard Rapid and another downstream, ending at Scaffold Bridge Rapid (site of a new bridge). A fee is required for boating, and the proceeds are used to maintain the courses and other facilities along the river. Rapids in the upper reaches include the Graveyard, Fedwrgog Falls, Dog Leg, Scaffold Bridge, and Chapel Falls. This is the site of the national whitewater center and of various world competitions. On weekends the course teems with eager boaters from various paddling clubs, unless it is closed for competitions.

Below Tyn y Cornel Bridge the river eases to Class 2, and from here to the town of Bala the river gets less use, with access restricted outside the winter months. Two good-sized rapids near the bottom of this stretch have names that hearken back to the Industrial Age—Bala Mill Falls and Factory Pool. Bala Mill Falls is a 6-foot drop onto a rock slab; landing upright is recommended here.

Downstream, the Dee has several good whitewater sections, but access problems limit use of the best stretches to a few weekends a year.

Farther to the south in Devon, England, the River Dart gets lots of use. The Dart has an upper, a middle, and a lower run. The middle run, sometimes called the Loop, is the most popular, providing 3 miles (4.8 km) of Class 3 whitewater from Newbridge to Holmbridge. Paddling the Dart and some other rivers requires reservations well in advance, obtained through the British Canoe Union.

ASIA

*T*he largest continent, Asia is endowed with an astonishing geographic and cultural diversity. The rivers covered here are spread across the face of the continent from Turkey to Japan, a span of some 8,000 miles.

The landscape of Asia is overshadowed by the Himalayan Mountains. Some 180 million years ago what is now India broke off from the supercontinent Gondwanaland and began a northward collision course with the mainland of Asia. The actual collision occurred fairly recently, within the last 65 million years, creating the world's tallest and most rugged mountain range with peaks over 29,000 feet (8,845 m). Asia features other lesser mountain ranges as well. The rivers described in this book generally drain peaks between 10,000 and 16,000 feet (4,880 m).

The most dramatic river-running in Asia, and arguably anywhere, is in the

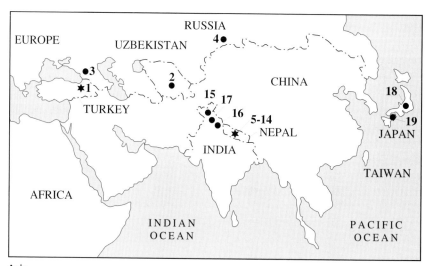

Asia

Himalayan region that includes India and Nepal. Nepal is the focus of most of the exploration and activity in the Himalayas.

Tightly controlled communist regimes in Russia and China have kept their rivers out of the reach of Western explorers until recently. Craving diversion from a regimented life, some hardy and innovative Russian boaters explored many of the country's most difficult runs using inflated boats and equipment fashioned from leftovers. The opening of the former republics of the Soviet Union to the West and "paddle diplomacy," symbolized in Project RAFT, provide information and access for many of these fine rivers.

China probably has some river-running potential, but it is still little explored. The Chinese themselves do not run whitewater recreationally, and visiting boaters are often frustrated with severe access restrictions, governmental payoffs, and lack of infrastructure.

Other areas we have covered include Turkey and Japan. Turkey and parts of the former Soviet Union straddle the elusive boundary between Asia and Europe but are included here in the section on Asia. Almost all of the good whitewater of the former Soviet Union is in Asia. Along the Pacific Rim the Japanese have a local subculture of enthusiastic kayaking clubs and some commercial rafting companies.

Turkey

Coruh River ➤

Turkey prides itself as being where East meets West. It is where Asia and the Middle East meet Europe. Istanbul, the capital, straddles the Bosphorus and can genuinely claim to be one city in two continents.

Turkey's history goes back to pre-recorded time. Mesopotamia ("the land between two rivers") was between the Tigris and the Euphrates rivers (or the Murat and Firat Nehri in Turkish), which flow out of eastern Turkey. The armies of Alexander the Great, of Islam, and the Crusades have all swept through this land. Marco Polo traveled through Turkey when exploring the Silk Road, passing Erzerum and Mount Ararat, and journeyed north through Bayburt to the Black Sea on his return.

Less than 10 percent of Turkey is level, and most of it is well over a mile in elevation. The Coruh is set in the rugged northeast corner of the country and drains an area south of the Black Sea where it follows a course in an interior valley, paralleling the southeast shore; it then turns north and empties into the Black Sea near Batumi. Alexander the Great bypassed this rugged region, and the Roman Empire only ruled it as a vassal state for three years.

Bayburt, one of the put-ins for trips down the Coruh, boasts the largest fortress in Turkey. This sixth-century castle now sits on the hill above the modern town and bears witness to a bygone age when Bayburt was a major center of commerce. From Bayburt to Ispir the river is flat, only aspiring to Class 2–3 as it nears Ispir, while being more remote, with no road intruding till Maden some 12½ miles (20 km) upstream of Ispir. In this stretch the river swings through 180 degrees and flows along the Kacgar Mountains looking for a way to break through to the Black Sea.

Though Bayburt is sometimes used as the put-in, most trips, hungry for the rapids,

BAYBURT TO ISPIR
Difficulty: Class 2
Length: 62 miles (100 km)

ISPIR TO YUSUFELI
Difficulty: Class 4 (Class 5 in high water)
Length: 60 miles (95 km)

YUSUFELI TO ARTVIN
Difficulty: Class 4 (Class 5 in high water)
Length: 43 miles (70 km)

Season: May through August
Character: Remote, exotic, varied, multi-day

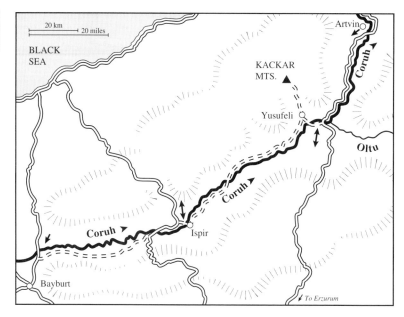

Coruh River (Turkey)

start a short way upstream of the little village of Ispir. From an old castle above Ispir, now converted into a mosque, it is possible to gain a glimpse of the river as it enters a narrow gorge full of whitewater. Though the gorge opens out after some 6 miles (10 km), the whitewater remains.

Many of the rapids on the Coruh have been named, but because of their frequency and the fact that they have been labeled by independent groups, the names are inconsistent. Much time can be spent working out whether a particular rapid is "Minister's" and whether it is the same rapid as "The Stud." In 1991 the Minister of Tourism joined a whitewater festival rafting down the river and took a lengthy swim at the rapid that now bears his name. This rapid is one of a set of rapids which, at high water, almost merge into each other and will impress even the world-weary expert.

After this opening assault, the river eases and at normal rates of river running it still provides one or two major rapids and an almost endless stream of Class 3 rapids each day, until reaching Yusufeli. On this stretch of the river you'll see castles perched on the rocks above the river, and others if you know where to look. These make great off-river excursions, though to reach the castle at Tekkale ("Single Castle") you'll need a little local knowledge and stout nerves to ascend the loose rock. A simpler and safer plan is to take a taxi to Dortkilesi ("Four Churches") and explore the ancient and unexpectedly large tenth-century Armenian church.

Irrigation canals pinch water off the river at regular intervals and contour the river-banks for several kilometers before delivering the water to the fields. Rice is spreading upstream as improved strains are developed, and paddies are gradually replacing the wheat fields. Cherry orchards and other fruits are also grown along the river, giving way to olive groves where the ground is level but the water scarce.

The Bahal River, a Class 3 trip from Sarigol down and a Class 5 kayak run upstream of Sarigol, joins the Coruh at Yusufeli. Even if you decide not to run the river, this valley

Coruh River, Turkey. *(© Cam McLeary/Adrift Expeditions)*

Coruh River, Turkey. *(Alternatif Turizm)*

is well worth exploring, though the bus ride to Altiparmak, the roadhead, takes half a day. The alpine meadows and wooded hills make for a pleasant change from the stark brown banks of the Coruh. Lepidopterists and ornithologists often visit these high-altitude pastures looking for butterflies and the rare red hawk and other birds. Brown bears still inhabit the region but are rare now. The weather on the Black Sea side of these mountains is very different; rain two days out of three is the norm. (Along this coast there are many small kayak-sized streams that never seem to run out of water.)

From Yusufeli the valley narrows, and although the road becomes more intrusive, the rapids increase in size and frequency. About 5 miles (8 km) below Yusufeli the Oltu

New Horizons for Paddlers with Disabilities

A year after coming up with the idea, we were on the Coruh. We had three weeks. For the first ten days, we paddled the river. Maggie, with her confused-vision balance problems and walking difficulties from being avalanched in the Alps, surfed a wave and grinned. Steve, totally blind since birth, paddled a single kayak down various rapids with no problem till Frank got distracted and stopped talking. Dave Tuttle, T9 paralyzed from falling out of a tree, tried the double kayak, the duckie, and then settled for strapping himself to a frame to enable him to row the raft. Keith, despite his spina bifida need for a wheelchair, fitted into any boat that was spare. Donald only seventy-two years young, was there telling us again (and again) about the last time he was here. Bob, with polio in both legs and already a veteran of the Coruh from a previous year, just enjoyed being back on the river. Ross was always improvising improvements for everyone. Alan and Jon, full of the boundless energy of youth, could always be counted on to lend a hand, either in camp or on the river. Andy and I just guided things.

Just as we were getting tired and people were wanting a rest or something extra, Project RAFT turned up. So it was back to Erzerum, with us holding up the marching bands, the parade, and the opening ceremony with our sticks and wheelchairs. Then it was down to the banks of the Coruh again and the competition. In the orienteering event we came in thirteenth out of the thirty-two teams entered and were one of the only five teams to get all the checkpoints. (We had an advantage: I had run the river over twenty times and had had some input into the design of the course. We didn't cheat; we collected all the checkpoints properly.)

(continued next page)

River joins the Coruh. About 6 miles (10 km) upstream of this confluence the Tortum Cayeli joins the Oltu.

An earthquake flattened the Oltu area in the winter of 1982–83. Seismic instability has not prevented the planning of dams on the Coruh. The 1993 Project RAFT event on the Coruh led to the stretch from Ispir to Yusufeli being declared a national park and thus out of reach of the dammers. However, dams are still planned on the river and if built will flood the river from Artvin to the Oltu-Coruh confluence and above Bayburt.

Below the confluence more rapids await the paddler, along with the Coruh's greatest challenge. Take care, as the river is now hemmed in by steep banks and rock cliffs; it is easy to career down the river, arrive above a rapid, and be committed to running it as the portage would be almost impossible (especially with laden rafts). The Coruh's largest rapid, known as King Kong—or Lava East, House Rock, or Aslam, depending on whose name you select—is one such rapid and is usually portaged in high water. Another problem on this lower stretch is rock falls. New rapids or alterations to existing rapids can confuse the regular runner. By Zeytinlik the river is slowing and the rapids less frequent. The last 12½ miles (20 km) to Artvin are flat.

Flows on the Coruh can vary dramatically. The highest water and biggest action are in May, but these flows may overwhelm some boaters. By mid-July, levels and difficulty drop dramatically, but the river may be a bit bony. The best flows are usually in mid-June, which coincides with the Kafkasor festival at Artvin: bullfighting and wrestling, along with folk dancing and exhibitions of local handicrafts. Take a tent and stay the night. The bullfighting is nothing like Spanish bullfighting; it is bull against bull, and the wrestling is Karakucak wrestling, similar to the wrestling of Edirne but without the olive oil.

We competed in the slalom event, though in the kayak event we used double topolinos as opposed to single kayaks, and using a raft with a rowing frame and oars was a severe disadvantage. At the end of our raft run we were arguing: we should have done better, we had not trained, we had no one person calling the shots, we were not a cohesive team. We came in last. When the recriminations subsided into a tactful silence, I remarked to Dave, one-time Scottish down-river champion, that his competitive spirit had returned. "Never went away," came his reply with a grin. We had a lot of grins over the three weeks.

For me personally, the highlight was the rescue event. This event was a major challenge for us; we had to paddle down the river, pick up a swimmer, pass through a gate, flip the raft, paddle the upturned raft through another gate, right the raft, and then paddle the raft to the bank, clip it to a rope, and all grab the finish pole. The kayak paddler had to paddle down through the same gates and perform an Eskimo roll before sprinting to the finish. Bob, our kayak paddler, made it to the finish line, where he had to drag his boat up the bank on his hands and knees—he had forgotten his sticks. The raft run went to plan, though we had a somewhat imaginative interpretation of the rules. We came in second-to-last but were the crowd's winners. The Californian team, the actual winners of the event, gave us their medals as a recognition of "the inspiration and example to all of us." As one hard-bitten competitor said to me as we carried everyone back to their sticks and wheelchairs, "That was amazing, it even jerked a tear from me."

—Dave Manby

Uzbekistan

Yangi-Bazar to highway bridge near Brich Mulla
Difficulty: Class 5
Length: 60 miles (96 km)

Season: Mid–July through September (too high in late spring and early summer)
Character: Remote, high elevation, dry region of snowmelt

◄ Chatkal River

Originating in the Tien Shen Mountains, whose highest summit is Pobeda Peak at 24,378 feet (7,439 m), the Chatkal has attracted river runners in the Soviet Union for decades. Located in Uzbekistan, a former republic of the Soviet Union, the Chaktal has been compared to the Bio-Bio in Chile in terms of spectacular scenery and whitewater. Flows are generally too high during late spring and early summer, as snowmelt swells the river. Runnable flows usually come after levels drop in late summer, after peak snowmelt. The Tien Shen Mountains Range, a series of rocky snow-covered peaks, is the setting for several nature reserves, including the Chatkal Biosphere Reserve, which holds more than 1,000 species of flowering plants and a vast diversity of birds and mammals. The locals are mostly Muslim, of Turko-Mongol extraction. Downstream, the Chatkal meets the Syrdarja River near the capital of Kaskent as it makes its way to the Aral Sea.

The featured trip begins at Yangi-Bazar, a village nearly a mile in elevation, in a dry area with sparse vegetation. The put-in point is about a mile downstream of the confluence of the Sandalash and Chatkal rivers.

The Sandalash itself is an exotic but very difficult expert run. Expert boaters undertaking the Sandalash can certainly continue on the Chatkal to extend the adventure. A put-in is usually accessed by helicopter, and the canyons can only be accessed by river.

The water of the Chatkal, especially in the upper reaches, is a clear, beautiful turquoise. The river is usually big-volume farther downstream, passing through several beautiful bedrock canyons, each filled with tough rapids. Boaters often elect to portage some of the toughest drops.

After the take-out, the Chatkal enters the Charvak Reservoir. The waters of the Chatkal originally flowed to the Aral Sea (a basin lake with no outflow), but like most other rivers draining to this great lake it has been diverted. The shoreline of the Aral Sea has receded some 50 miles (80 km), leaving much of the lake bed a wasteland.

If whitewater boating has an evolutionary scheme, the former Soviet Union is surely its Galapagos Islands. Stifled by the communist system and largely unaware of the whitewater equipment and techniques developed elsewhere, groups of Soviet boaters nonetheless set forth to conquer some of the world's toughest rivers.

When Jib Ellison and company first came to Russia to explore the Katun River in 1987, they must have felt like Darwin discovering strangely evolved animals on a small, remote island. Donning drysuits originally designed to repel nerve gas and sporting homemade flotation vests sewn from anything that floated, the Soviets were a sight to behold. However, the flotilla of watercraft they mustered was the real eye-popper. The Soviets had developed a bizarrely configured fleet of inflatables, hand-fabricated from materials largely purloined from such sources as shut-down aircraft factories, lashed together by birch poles felled at the put-in. The standard craft were catamarans, similar to North American catarafts but usually manned by four paddlers riding the tubes like riders on horses. The ploht was a larger version steered by oar sweeps at either end. The bublik (Russian for doughnut or bagel) was the most novel concoction, consisting of two large innertubes bottom-weighted and standing upright, held together by timbers. Paddlers were positioned in the center of each innertube above a weighted bottom facing in opposite directions. Because the tubes were bottom weighted, the whole contraption was self-righting. For cheap thrills the boat could be rolled from a hillside, paddlers and all, down into the river. So equipped, they had done first descents on several Class 5 and 6 rivers, feats rivaling anything being run elsewhere.

Reports of the Russian accomplishments spread like news of Sputnik in the West. For a time, some felt that the Russians were ahead of the rest of the world. On closer inspection, however, the boats were shown to be flimsy and no more maneuverable than conventional craft. The flotation vests were only effective for a few minutes, and the safety and rescue techniques employed were often ill-conceived and reckless. The fatality rates for Soviet boaters were unacceptably high by Western standards, and memorials can be found along the banks of many of the tougher rapids in Siberia and the Caucasus.

Slalom racing was also part of "paddle diplomacy" in the late 1980s, mostly due to the efforts of U.S. team coach Bill Endicott. Inclusion of the slalom in the Barcelona Olympics in 1992 brought official recognition and support from Goskomsport, the all-powerful Soviet sports monolith. Soviets began competing as a team in international events. The subsequent demise of the Soviet sports machine hamstrung most competitors, but they hope one day to host a World Cup event at Minsk, Belarus, the site of the only artificial course in the former Soviet Union.

—Dan Dunlap

The Russians Are Coming!

Russia

ARKHYZ TO DOWN AHKRYZ
Difficulty: Class 3+
Length: 6 miles (9.6 km)

Season: May through September
Character: Mountainous area, road follows river

◄ Bol'shoy Zelenchuk River

The Zelenchuk drains the glaciers and high peaks of the north slope of the Caucasus in southwestern Russia. Bol'shoy is Russian for "big" or "great." The run is the 6 miles (9.6 km) between two villages with the same name, Arkhyz and Down Ahkryz. Down is the Russian designation for "downstream."

The Zelenchuk begins at the confluence of the Arkhyz and Pysh rivers, and much of it drains from Sofiyski Glacier. Though partly glacial in origin, the waters of the Zelenchuk are transparent blue and quite cold. Most of the rapids are of the rock-garden variety, with frequent drops and holes. At high flows, beware of undercuts.

Much of the surrounding country is mountains covered with wild pine forests. A road follows the river on the left.

The Caucasus is often considered part of Europe, and the locals are a mix of peoples of several republics. The area has been populated since antiquity. Temples dating back to the ninth century can be visited near the take-out at the bridge at Down Arkhyz.

Another nearby run is a five-day Class 5 journey on the Big Laba River in the next drainage to the west through a less-populated wilderness area.

UST KOKSA TO CHEMAL
Difficulty: Class 3+
Length: 100 miles (160 km) or more

Season: June through August
Character: Mountainous, popular

◄ Katun River

When Jib Ellison organized the first Project RAFT trip to the Katun in 1987, it was a chance for East to meet West. Heretofore the river had been the exclusive domain of the Soviet boaters and their strange homemade craft.

The Katun is deep in Siberia, set high in the Altai Mountains, and originates in the slopes of 14,783-foot (4,509 m) Mount Belukha. This is one of the more remote areas in the world, situated close to the Mongolian border. The surrounding forests, including conifers, birches, and aspen, are part of the largest forests in the world. Bear, lynx, and musk deer may be sighted near the river. The mountains support goats, mountain sheep, and the rare and elusive snow leopard. The locals have retained much of their pre-Soviet culture and often don colorful ethnic dress.

A popular put-in is at Ust Koksa. Some run the river from farther upstream, but access is difficult. The rapids on the Katun have been compared to the big wave-train rapids on the Grand Canyon of the Colorado. Notable features include a 5-mile-long (8 km) canyon known as Akkeem Breech. Near the Argut confluence on the right, local river runners have assembled and maintain an informal whitewater exhibit. As the Chuya enters on the right, a road from Mongolia follows the Katun downstream on the right and then crosses to the left but is rarely visible from the river. The Argut and the Chuya are also runnable. Downstream the Katun goes back into another canyon which gradually opens up as villages and civilization appear. Boaters can take out at various points in this area.

Chuya River, Russia. *(© Doc Loomis)*

Katun River, Siberia, Russia. *(BioBio Expeditions Worldwide)*

Like many other rivers, the Katun is threatened by development of a massive dam project. At present the project has been shelved. Other highly regarded and difficult runs can be found on the Chulishman and Bashkhaus, tributaries of the Biya on the next drainage to the east of the Katun.

The Chuya Rally

Berkeley radicals may scribble May Day slogans on the walls of abandoned buildings, but in the former Soviet Union, commitment is a little deeper. Everyone does his part, and for the large and fanatical river-running community this means a pilgrimage to the Chuya River, a tributary of the Katun in the Altai Mountains of central Siberia. Many attend the annual whitewater rally there.

The 12th annual Chuya Rally, held in 1989, was very different from its predecessors. It included over 200 Western river runners and journalists organized by Project RAFT, the brainchild of northern California river runner Jib Ellison.

But May Day is not necessarily the best time to run rivers in Siberia. I figured this out when our plane broke through the clouds to the sight of newly fallen Siberian snow. And we still had to drive up into the mountains. Over the next week, the Siberian winter refused to relinquish its grip. While the Chuya River had thawed, its side creeks had not. Stories circulated of previous rallies where the ice had to be broken to get the boats in the river.

But spirits soared. After all, this was probably the greatest assembly of whitewater river runners in history, so the energy and human interaction kept everyone warm. Equally amazing was the exposure and sharing between the Soviet and Western whitewater communities, which had developed in complete isolation from each other. Manufacturing facilities have been unavailable in Russia for whitewater equipment. Their rafts, paddles, frames, oars, and lifejackets were handmade from metal, wood, fabric, and foam straps. Oars and frames were often cut and carved at put-in. Instead of our oval rafts, the descendants of military assault inflatables, the Soviets developed handmade two- and four-person cataraft paddle boats and large sweep-oar boats called plohts. Their fragile kayaks were used mostly on flatwater.

What the Soviets lacked in sophisticated whitewater equipment technology, they made up for in their desire to run gnarl. Their river runners make the American lunatic fringe seem tame by comparison. But the approach was costing them about fifty whitewater deaths a year.

On the morning we broke camp after the rally was over, it was cold with a steady fall of rain and snow. Vehicles were stuck in the mud as the Western participants huddled by the campfires nibbling on what little food was still in camp. I thought of Napoleon and his Grand Army on their disastrous retreat from Moscow. But by afternoon we were in comfortable Russian buses heading for home.

Two worlds met—and got along just fine.

—Jim Cassady

Nepal

$\mathcal{F}$or decades Nepal has held a magnetic attraction for counterculture types fascinated by the mystical Nepalese and their world almost untouched by the West, its rich tapestry of history and traditions, colorful temples and festivals. Many others come here to walk, or as they say "trek," up and down some of the most splendid terrain on the globe. As great as trekking can be, it is hard work, and getting lost is always a possibility. Fortunately, there is a better way to enjoy the best of Nepal, by paddling its splendid rivers.

One hopes that heaven is filled with rivers like these, remote, seemingly endless Class 3–4 journeys, filled with big, usually warm and clear-blue water, lined with broad, white sand beaches, surrounded by natural beauty and otherworldly cultures all set beneath the world's highest mountains. If not, perhaps the heavenly authorities will provide cheap transportation for river runners to return and get their fill. Many of the trips are extended odysseys with little or no road access for days on end. The climate is comfortable and the wildlife and scenery fascinating. There is little threat from the natives, insects, or animals. If all that is still not enough, boaters are warmly welcomed here. In fact, returning the many whistles and waves from children and interacting with villagers who come to your camp to stare in wonderment is a river-running skill in itself. Although there are less expensive places to travel to, once you are in Nepal, prices are cheap.

Boating in Nepal is limited by the monsoon season, during which most rivers are too high to run. The monsoons usually start in July and end in mid-September. High, runnable flows occur after the monsoons and continue in October and November. A few venture out in the winter, but temperatures can be cold. Good boating resumes for a second season in the spring.

Nepal's topography is ideal for whitewater. The land rises from sea level to the top of the world at over 29,000 feet (8,845 m) in the space of only 100 miles. Most trips to Nepal begin at Kathmandu, Nepal's largest city, which sits at an elevation of 4,500 feet (1,373 m) in the central valley between the Himalayas and the much smaller Mahabharat Range nearer the ocean. River runners should keep in mind that the monsoon floods regularly alter rapids and can even change the character of rivers. Any information given here should be checked locally, if possible, to ensure that it is current.

The drainages of Nepal are generally divided into three river systems. The eastern rivers drain into the Sun Kosi and the central rivers drain into the Trisuli, while the western rivers drain into the Karnali. Kathmandu is situated between the eastern and central rivers. All of western Nepal is much less developed and often called the "wild west." The latitude of Nepal is roughly the same as that of Florida. We feature ten rivers in Nepal, with five from the eastern drainage, four from the central drainage, and one from the western drainage.

Religion plays a central role in Nepalese culture, as can be readily seen along the country's rivers. Along the Kali Gandaki and the Marsyandi rivers near the Annapurna Range, more than 30 ethnic groups have created a kaleidoscope of exotic customs and beliefs. The Kali Gandaki headwaters are believed to be the birthplace of the goddess Kali, and boaters may see pilgrims trekking to its source. There are temples which mark every confluence, reflecting the spiritual significance of each river. Cremations take place along the holy rivers, and boaters coming across the charred remains of such ceremonies should accord the area respect.

While many of the rivers are multi-day adventures, it is often possible to run them without carrying overnight gear by utilizing lodges along the rivers for eating and sleeping. Most river runners prefer to take advantage of the great beach campgrounds and visit and villages along the river.

The remoteness of this land can be a little disconcerting to travelers. Virtually no building in Nepal has an address, even in the capital of Kathmandu. There are no ATM machines. The country further expresses its independence by offsetting its clocks an additional fifteen minutes from the rest of the world.

There are no car rentals, a fact readily understood in light of the unnerving anarchy on the country's roadways. This limits shuttle options. Public buses travel just about anywhere and will carry gear for a nominal extra charge. However, anyone who has spent 15 hours (and all night) on top of the Night Coach shuttle from the take-out of the Sun Kosi back to Kathmandu will neither forget nor wish to repeat the experience. Qualified outfitters are relatively inexpensive and probably a good bet for transportation, even for boaters who usually do their own thing. Many are willing to help out with shuttles for a reasonable price. Some Nepal veterans take advantage of cheap domestic airfares for long jaunts and ship their boats by bus.

Bhutan, to the east of Nepal, is also rich in whitewater. The rivers of Bhutan are generally more difficult than those of Nepal but more pristine.

A Tale of Two Kayaks—as Told to Peter Knowles

Don Weeden described how, on a kayak trip down the Sun Kosi in 1980 and cruising some way behind the rest of the group, he came to the confluence with the Dudh Kosi.

Don looked with amazement, because there on the beach at the confluence were two villagers washing and polishing two fiberglass kayaks. He landed alongside the men and, after the usual friendly greetings, he asked them what they were doing (Don has worked in Nepal and so speaks the language). The villagers explained that some years previously two men in strange clothes had come down the Dudh Kosi and landed on this same beach. The villagers had given them tea, and although these strange men spoke very little Nepali they managed to communicate something about a helicopter. A little while later, the helicopter arrived and the Nepalese pilot explained that he had come to collect the men, and he sternly commanded the villagers "to take very special care of these wonderful boats, because these important men will return someday and their lives will depend on it."

The villagers proudly said that ever since they had been looking after the boats, washing and polishing them every two weeks and keeping them in their houses out of the sun and the rain. Don realized that these were the two remaining "Everest" kayaks that Mike Jones and Mick Hopkinson had used on their famous descent of the Dudh Kosi. Don explained to the villagers that sadly one of the men (Mike Jones) had since died, kayaking on another river, so they would not be coming back. The villagers were saddened, but Don suggested that he take the boats off their hands. They agreed, and he gave them some money for taking such good care of the boats. Don towed the boats down to where the rafting group was camped and in due course the kayaks were transported back to Kathmandu.

—from White Water Nepal by Peter Knowles and David Allardice

Special thanks to Dave Allerdice of Ultimate Descents and Peter Knowles for sharing information on Nepal.

Sun Kosi ➤

The Sun Kosi means "River of Gold" in the local dialect. It rates as one of the world's great multi-day trips for both rafts and kayaks. The Sun Kosi is filled with surprisingly warm, big-water rapids in pool-drop configuration, with most of the rapids appearing near the mouth of side streams. The directions are fairly simple: just put in at Dolalghat, and take out at the next road access at Chatra, 170 miles (272 km) downstream.

The Sun Kosi has its share of flatwater, but it never becomes boring. Although the corridor is lightly inhabited with only a few villages, locals are rarely far away and can usually be seen on the banks fishing or working. Youngsters whistles and cries of "Namaste" and "Hello" greet boaters along nearly all reaches of the river. Terraced rice paddies and huts climb to the top of the steep hillsides along the river, somehow complementing the area's natural beauty. The river also offers plenty of white sand beaches, forests, birds, monkeys, and other wildlife. For much of this run the streambed travels back and forth along a geological fault line past an array of remarkable rock formations along its banks. The watershed for the Sun Kosi includes most of eastern Nepal and some of the highest mountains of the Himalayas. It makes its way generally eastward, eventually emptying into the Ganges in India.

The put-in is upstream of the bridge at Dolalghat where the Indrawati and the Bhote Kosi meet to form the Sun Kosi proper. It is also possible to put in upstream of Dolaghat on the Bhote Kosi as the road follows the river. The elevation for the put-in is around 2,500 feet (763 m). Typical flows at the put-in might be 3,000 cfs (84.9 cumecs) and will multiply by some eight- to tenfold at the take-out at Chatra. Conveniently, the difficulty of the rapids tends to increase along the length of the trip, although the most difficult rapid is the Class 4 Hakapur, about halfway down, between the confluences of the Likha Kosi and the Dudh Kosi, both on the left. Downstream of the Dudh Kosi are several significant rapids, including Jaws and Rhino Rock. Then the rapids become almost contin-

DOLALGHAT TO CHATRA
Difficulty: Class 4
Length: 170 miles (272 km)

Season: October through December, March through May
Character: Big-water, multi-day classic

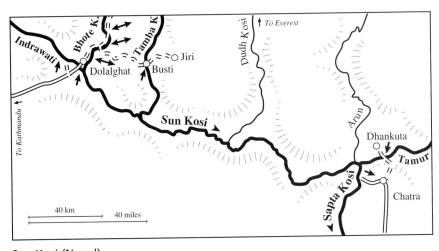

Sun Kosi (Nepal)

Hakapur II, Sun Kosi, Nepal. *(© David Allardice/Ultimate Descents)*

uous, and the river plunges into the exhilarating Jungle Corridor, featuring No Quiche and El Wasto as well as some great waterfall scenery. The last major rapid, Big Dipper, is somewhat of a postscript, announcing the end of the Sun Kosi proper. Not far below Big Dipper, the Sun Kosi is joined by the Arun and the Tamur to form the Sapta Kosi (meaning "Seven Rivers"). Take out just below the irrigation canal at Chatra and be sure to hug the left bank. Here the Sapta Kosi pours out onto the lowland flat plain called the Terai and broadens from about 200 feet (61 m) to ½ mile (0.8 km) wide. Although the Arun is one of Nepal's largest rivers and cuts through the Himalayas, draining some of the northern slope of the range, it has poor access and is rarely run.

People

It was the people and their way of living that, for me, made everything so different and often special. As we passed down the river, no matter how many days from a road, there were people; fishing, washing, waving, burning their dead, crapping, smoking, or just sitting.

Gathered around the fire at night, while relaxing and chatting, a subgroup of locals sometimes formed and would start beating a drum, chanting, dancing, and singing, but never in any competitive way, just in a graceful wandering manner for their own and our entertainment. Pleasures are natural, values so different, living rudimentary and conditions harsh; and yet the people appear so happy that by the end of your river trip you question all your Western beliefs.

—by Mark Baker, from White Water Nepal

With more time on the river, things are more relaxed, relationships progress at a more natural pace, and memories become firmly entrenched for a lifetime. Long after the white water has blurred into one long, white-knuckled thrill ride, the memories of a moonrise over the river and the friends you inevitably make will remain. After spending the better part of their adult lives on different rivers, most hard-core river people can still distinctly remember the long expeditions they've been on: it's a much more involving and enveloping experience than a short two- or three-day-trip. River trips are much more than gravity-powered roller-coaster rides; they're journeys traversed on very special highways. For many people they become a way of life.

—*Lonely Planet Nepal*

Journeys

Indrawati River ➤

A tributary of the Sun Kosi, the Indrawati is a pleasant float, particularly popular with novice boaters. This is the closest major river to Kathmandu, and it gets plenty of use. Most trips on the Sun Kosi begin at the Indrawati confluence at Dolalghat. The Indrawati is a shallow river with a steady gradient of about 30 fpm (5.79 mpk), running eastward through small settlements and subsistence agriculture. The river is somewhat braided above the Jhayanri Khola confluence.

SIPAGHAT TO DOLALGHAT
Difficulty: Class 2
Length: 12 miles (19.2 km)

Season: September through May
Character: Mild, near Kathmandu, flows into the Sun Kosi

Bhote Kosi ➤

The Bhote Kosi translates as "River from Tibet," and the name accurately describes the river's origins. The Bhote Kosi is actually the upstream section of the Sun Kosi, reached by following the road from Kathmandu to Dolalghat, the confluence of the Indrawati and the Sun Kosi, and following the Sun Kosi upstream. Although the Sun Kosi gets a little more difficult farther downstream, the Bhote Kosi is more difficult—in fact much more difficult—the farther one starts upstream. The scenery on the Bhote Kosi is inspiring. There are several gorges and a narrow river valley in the upper reaches. A diversion at Lamosangu takes much of the flow but returns it to the river a short distance downstream. Below here the river resembles the easier sections of the Sun Kosi, with clear blue waters, white sand beaches, and a wooded valley.

The river is often divided into five sections. The first begins at the Kodari bridge and is reserved for intrepid hairball kayakers only, taking out at the Lartza bridge. The second section down to where the road meets the river near the distance marker "km95" is only slightly easier. The third section down to the dam above Lamosangu drops another class; the take-out is at the dam. The next section begins at the Khadichour Bridge and receives a lot of attention from boaters of all skill levels and all types of craft. From Khadambas to Dolalghat is a nice scenic, relaxing float. Downstream of here is the 170-mile (272 km) Sun Kosi odyssey, the first river covered in this chapter.

KODARI BRIDGE TO LARTZA BRIDGE
Difficulty: Class 5+
Length: 4 miles (6.4 km)

LARTZA BRIDGE TO WHERE THE ROAD MEETS THE RIVER (95 KM)
Difficulty: Class 5
Length: 8 miles (12.8 km)

WHERE THE ROAD MEETS THE RIVER (95 KM) TO DAM ABOVE LAMOSANGA
Difficulty: Class 4
Length: 11 miles (17.6 km)

KHADICHOUR BRIDGE TO KHADAMBAS
Difficulty: Class 3
Length: 6 miles (9.6 km)

KHADAMBAS TO DOLALGHAT
Difficulty: Class 2
Length: 7 miles (11.2 km)

Season: November through May
Character: Many options, road follows river

BUSTI TO SUN KOSI CONFLUENCE
Difficulty: Class 5
Length: 26 miles (41.6 km)

SUN KOSI CONFLUENCE TO CHATRA
Difficulty: Class 4
Length: 130 miles (211 km)

Season: November, April, May
Character: A more difficult tributary of the Sun Kosi

DOBHAN TO MULGHAT (UPPER REACH, WITH TREK ACCESS)
Difficulty: Class 4
Length: 50 miles (80 km)

MULGHAT TO CHATRA ON SAPTA KOSI (LOWER REACH, WITH ROAD ACCESS)
Difficulty: Class 4
Length: 25 miles (40 km)

Season: October through April
Character: Remote, near-wilderness river

◄ Tamba Kosi

The Tamba Kosi, another tributary of the Sun Kosi, has its headwaters in Tibet. This is a difficult run that experts can use as a good alternate start for the Sun Kosi. The action is often continuous and the long rapids do not make for a good place to swim. Most kayakers take this on at low water and suffer through some portages. There is road access to the put-in at Busti Bridge and trail access to the take-out where the river meets the Sun Kosi.

◄ Tamur River

The Tamur is a remote tributary of the Sun Kosi with plenty of whitewater, great scenery, and fine camping in a secluded setting. Much of the flow is snowmelt, with Kanchenjunga, the world's third highest peak, part of the drainage. The remoteness of this river gives boaters a chance to experience the diverse languages, customs, and castes of the traditional Nepalese who live along the river.

There is no vehicle access to the put-in on the upper reach, so boaters have their choice of flying to the Taplejung airstrip and hiking about two hours to the put-in at Dobhan or trekking for three days from Basantapur. Boaters can hire porters at very reasonable rates to carry equipment for the trek. The journey is one of Nepal's finest, with views of some of the world's highest mountains. The best vehicle access allows running the lower reach from the bridge at Mulghat, although both reaches are usually run as one stretch.

The whitewater in the upper reach begins almost immediately with dozens of steep, technical Class 3 to 4 rapids and virtual nonstop action to the Kabeli confluence about 7 miles (11 km) downstream on the left. The rapids ease somewhat, and the river is flat be-

Himalayan Hospitality

As a child I remember making the long journey to visit my grandparents in northern Alabama. As we drove through the early evenings, I was mesmerized by the soft glow radiating from country farmhouses and wondered why we couldn't just stop there for a home-cooked meal and a sound sleep. My mother, noting my prepubescent communist tendencies, dutifully informed me of the dangers of strangers and the rules of the road. It seemed a limited view. Upon arrival in Nepal, I was immediately affected by the openness and kind-hearted generosity of the people. I found my soul's home in this exotic land and culture. During my years of schlopping kayaks deep into the high mountains, we would most often migrate toward that glowing farmhouse perched up on a knoll with a stellar view. All we did was ask, and most times we were fed a most delicious "didi special" and given a spot to sleep for the night. Just as I thought it could/should be. But the key is to always give, in some special way, more than you take. We are the ambassadors for the Western world, and often the only ones that the local people have ever met. And you know the eggs are fresh when the chicken lays them on your jacket while you're sleeping!

—Arlene Burns

tween Nawakhola and Teliyakhola. This section has excellent beaches and wildlife set in a series of jungle gorges. The last several days are filled with whitewater as the gradient steepens to the interim access point at Mulghat. Below Mulghat, consistent Class 4 rapids continue to the confluence with the Sun Kosi. At one point as many as forty or fifty rapids follow in quick succession. The last canyon is an impressive sheer rock gorge before the river cascades into the Sun Kosi. As the Sun Kosi, Arun, and Tamur rivers meet, they form the Sapta Kosi. The take-out is the same as for the Sun Kosi run, just below the irrigation canal at Chatra.

Trisuli River ➢

The Trisuli is the main river in central Nepal and quite popular with kayakers and commercial rafters alike due to its excellent scenery, good intermediate whitewater, and big volume, as well as its proximity to Kathmandu, Nepal's largest city. Access is made easier by the main road running west of Kathmandu which follows the river for a while. The various access points allow river runners to choose trips as short as a half day or as long as a week, and to pick and choose among several impressive gorges.

The Trisuli adds substantially to its volume as it flows to the lowland plain. At the end of this run the inflow of the Marsyandi, Seti Khola, and the Kali Gandaki swell it to enormous proportions. After the confluence with the Kali Gandaki the river is called the Narayani. Although recommended flows on the river range to 10,000 cfs (283 cumecs), the monsoon flows on the lower range have reached 900,000 cfs (25,470 cumecs).

Access is good. The main road follows the river generally from Baireni to the take-out, encompassing the lower three-quarters of the run. Another road follows from the put-in down to Devighat. The two roads combine to provide river access nearly the entire length.

The name Trisuli means "three springs" and reportedly derives from a legend that its headwaters high in the Himalayas at Gosainkund were formed by Hindu god Shiva piercing the ground with a trident.

BETRAWATI TO NARAYANGHAT
Difficulty: Class 3+
Length: 88 miles (140.8 km)

Season: October through December, March through May
Character: Popular, scenic river with many options

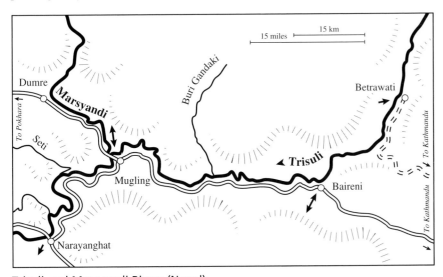

Trisuli and Marsyandi Rivers (Nepal)

Sightseers and wildlife buffs can follow the river onto the lowland plains and by the Royal Chitwan National Park, an area teeming with exotic and rare animals. Camping in the park is restricted to certain areas.

BHOTE ODAR TO BIMALNAGAR
Difficulty: Class 4
Length: 17 miles (27.2 km)

Season: November to December, March through April
Character: Tributary of the Trisuli; good whitewater, camping, and road access for rafts and kayaks

◁ Marsyandi River

The Marsyandi drains the east side of the Annapurnas. The name means "Raging River" in the local dialect, and it combines dramatic mountain scenery, azure blue water, fine camping, and consistent rapids. Boaters usually put in at Bhote Odar, but the more difficult upstream stretches above have been kayaked. The road that follows much of the river is very poor above Bhote Odar and often impassable for normal vehicles at certain times of the year.

The put-in near Bhote Odar is at the Bel Ghari Bazar bridge, and the take-out is at a suspension bridge at Bimalnagar. Downstream from here a dam diverts the stream flow, and the river below the take-out is not recommended for boating. The overall gradient of this run is 30 fpm (5.79 mpk), with the steepest reach above the Bhote Odar at some 75 fpm (14 mpk).

Marsyandi River, Nepal. *(Whit Deschner)*

Seti River ➤

The full name of the river is the Seti Khola, but it usually goes by the name Seti, meaning "white." The waters of the Seti, however, are usually clear, blue, and warm. The river holds some good intermediate whitewater and passes through some fine Nepalese mountain scenery.

Below Damauli and the confluence with the Nardi Chola, at mile 14 (22.4 km), the river enters an exotic, lushly vegetated reach known as the jungle corridor. This section has easier whitewater and is home to a range of wildlife and birds. The jungle corridor continues to the confluence with the Trisuli where boaters can take out on the other side of the larger river or continue down the Trisuli for another 14 miles (22.4 km) to Narayanghat.

The Seti is boatable above the described put-in at Bhimad where there is a hydro project and the large city of Pokhara along the river. This section has some deep canyons, and the rapids are more difficult. These obstacles are more easily dealt with than the fact that the river flows underground for a distance upstream of the put-in. River runners should make sure of a safe entry point below this underground passage before embarking.

BHIMAD TO THE TRISULI
CONFLUENCE
Difficulty: Class 3
Length: 35 miles (56 km)

Season: October through April
Character: Small-volume intermediate run; tributary of the Trisuli

Kali Gandaki River ➤

The Kali Gandaki begins in the mountains along the Tibetan border and then flows southward, cutting a notch between the high peaks of the Dhaulagiri and Annapurna ranges, forming what is probably the second deepest gorge in the world from Kalopani to Tatopani. River running sometimes starts at Baglung where a new access road has been constructed, but most boaters put in downstream near the Modi Khola River. The upper run is laced with big rapids, and features some outstanding scenery and ample camping along the river as it passes through a series of small gorges. Waterfalls and hot springs punctuate the scenery along the way. Although there are many bridges crossing the river, there are few villages or people to be found. Most villages are on terraces high above the river. This is one of the best areas for trekking in Nepal, with a temple at Rudra Beni and an abandoned palace at Ranighat, 9 miles (14 km) downstream of the town of Ridi, among the attractions.

Below Ridi the rapids are much easier as the river passes through a valley and near several villages. This surrounding area then takes on a more isolated look, with wildlife such as monkeys and birds. As yet the villagers in this area see so few boaters that they welcome them with open arms.

The take-out is at Narayanghat on the Trisuli, although an upstream take-out at Devghat may also be possible. Boaters can continue even farther downstream to the Chitwan National Park for more exotic jungle wildlife.

Upstream on the Modi Khola is a small, technical run favored by kayakers. The 10 miles from Birethanti down to the Kali Gandaki is solid Class 4–5 boating. The river follows the road most of the way. It is even possible to put in farther upstream at Landrung, trekking to the put-in by following the Modi Khola upstream toward the Annapurna Range.

MODI KHOLA TO RIDI
Difficulty: Class 4
Length: 57 miles (91.2 km)

RIDI TO NARAYANGHAT ON THE TRISULI RIVER
Difficulty: Class 2
Length: 80 miles (128 km)

Season: October through December, March through May
Character: Large, isolated tributary of the Trisuli

SAULI TO CHISAPANI
Difficulty: Class 4
Length: 113 miles
  (180.8 km)

Season: October through
  December, March
  through May
Character: Isolated western
  Nepal river accessed by
  trek

◁ Karnali River

The Karnali is the longest and largest river in Nepal and, in many respects, the most spectacular. Its headwaters are high in Tibet near Holy Mount Kailash. The river traces a turquoise-blue path through the more isolated western end of Nepal, through a mostly untouched and unpopulated series of canyons and stretches of jungle only recently opened to foreigners. The big-volume whitewater and the narrow, challenging canyons together create tremendous hydraulics and pressure waves. The canyons reveal some striking geology, including impressive sedimentary and aggregate rock formations. Unspoiled jungle terrain provides the opportunity to see the animals of the Himalayan foothills—even monkeys and leopards—in their natural habitat. The camping is unsurpassed, with ample, broad sand beaches.

Part of the Karnali's charm is its remoteness. The price tag is the effort of a two-day trek of about 15 miles (24 k) from Surkhet to Sauli. Porters can be hired in Surkhet. The trek is not easy, but it's usually enjoyable, and the locals are excited to get a rare glimpse of Westerners. Those interested can extend the run upstream by putting in at Simikot after an even longer trek or optional remote fly-in. This makes an expedition of almost 250 miles (400 k).

From Sauli to Chisapani the run is big-volume with an overall gradient of 10 fpm (1.9 mpk). Nearly all of the whitewater is in the upper reaches above the Seti confluence as the river passes through five separate canyons. Major rapids include Sweetness and Light, Jailhouse Rock, Inversion, God's House (A.K.A. Captivity), Juicer, and Flip and Strip. God's House, a little over halfway to the Seti confluence, is the most difficult and rates a Class 5– at some flows, when the rapid becomes a river-wide hole.

Below the Seti confluence, the rapids ease and dramatic cliffs dominate the scenery. Civilization gradually reappears though wildlife and jungle scenery are big attractions downstream. Take out at the impressive suspension bridge at Chisapani.

Downstream, the Karnali splits and forms a distributary, the Geruwa. Both the Geruwa and the Karnali then flow through the Royal Bardiya Wildlife Preserve and National Park before finally emptying into the Ganges. Royal Bardiya offers hundreds of species of birds as well as big cats such as tigers, rhinos, elephants, crocodiles, pytho, and even fresh-water dolphins. Although it is possible to float through the park, the river channels can be confusing, and camping is prohibited.

Karnali River, Nepal. (© Dave Allardice/Ultimate Descents)

India

$\mathcal{A}$lthough they don't receive the attention of the rivers in Nepal, the rivers of Himalayan Mountains in Pakistan, India, and Tibet hold some outstanding glacier-and-snowmelt-fed whitewater in an equally exotic setting. We have included three rivers in India.

River running and travel in Tibet are tightly controlled by the Chinese government. It is hoped that whitewater exploration, particularly on the Great Bend of the Tsangpo, will take place in the near future.

Zanskar River ➤

Set high in the Indian Himalayas and the Tibetan plateau, the Zanskar River flows through an area sometimes described as more like ancient Tibet than Tibet itself: the Zanskar and Ladakh region of Kashmir. This northernmost area in India remains exotic largely because it is so inaccessible. Padam, the capital of Zanskar, is linked to the outside world by mountain passes over 14,000 feet (4,270 m), possibly the highest vehicle-accessible passes in the world. The passes may be open only two months out of the year, and single-lane, one-direction caravans may block traffic in the other direction for days.

The Zanskaris maintain the religious-ritual-and-monastery-centered lifestyle that has been displaced in Chinese-occupied Tibet. They are ethnic Tibetans and are among the most hardy and colorfully dressed of all Himalayan people. The Zanskari women wear enormous turquoise-encrusted headdresses. The area is an ancient Buddhist kingdom and two monarchs ostensibly reign here, but their power is essentially ceremonial; one resides near the put-in at Padam.

The Zanskar cuts a path northward directly through the jagged Zanskar Range, a subrange of the Himalayas. Glaciers feed the river, and the elevations of this run are impressive. The put-in for the upper run is about 11,000 feet (3,355 m), and the take-out at the confluence of the Zanskar and Indus rivers is about 9,000 feet (2,745 m). The river forms a twisted and oxbowed path through gorges, with the mountains next to the river rising to over 18,000 feet (5,490 m). Because the area sits in a rain shadow far north of the sweep of the monsoons, it is much drier than the river corridors of Nepal. The hills hold groves of willows and high mountain grasses, and the villages are quaint, almost medieval in appearance and function.

Most trips on the Zanskar begin at Padam, although kayakers looking for adventure can put in even farther upstream on the Tsarap for a longer run with Class 5 whitewater. Four miles below Padam, the Doda River empties into the Tsarap, forming the Zanskar. Downstream of here the valley gradually closes in as the river enters the canyon. In several areas it is squeezed as narrow as 13 feet (4 m). Most of the rapids are easy Class 2 rapids, with a few big rapids up to Class 4 in the canyons; however, at really big water, the rapids become formidable and continuous. The take-out is on the Indus just downstream of the mouth of the Zanskar at the town of Nimu. If one continues upstream on the Indus from the Zanskar confluence, there is the sacred Buddhist city of Leh, the cap-

PADAM ON THE TSARAP RIVER TO NIMU ON THE INDUS RIVER (JUST DOWNSTREAM OF CONFLUENCE)
Difficulty: Class 4
Length: 90 miles (144 km)

Season: April through October
Character: High, dry, and remote region; mostly flatwater with a few big rapids

ital of Ladakh. River runners can also continue down the Indus to the Khalsi, and short river trips are possible on the Indus near Leh. River runners taking on the Zanskar or other rivers of this region should be prepared for turns of cold weather and the lack of driftwood or other fuel for campfires.

A word of caution: The area around Zanskar is generally Buddhist. Most of Kashmir is Muslim. The Muslims tend to resist dominance by the Hindu-controlled Indian government. This has led to incidents of armed violence in Kashmir over the last few decades. River runners are still considered a novelty, and as yet the tensions have not interfered with river trips. Boaters should nonetheless be aware and sensitive to the possibilities of problems generated by ethnic factionalism.

TEHRI, ON THE BHAGIRATHI RIVER, TO THE ALAKNANDA CONFLUENCE
Difficulty: Class 4–
Length: 24 miles (38.4 km)

ALAKNANDA CONFLUENCE TO RISHIKESH
Difficulty: Class 4–
Length: 36 miles (57.6 km)

(continued on following page)

◁ Upper Ganges River

The Ganges upstream of Rishikesh is the mecca of river running on the Indian subcontinent. It flows from some of the highest mountain peaks of the world at over 25,000 feet (7,625 m), with much of the flow being snowmelt. This is the sacred river in the Hindu religion, and the Upper Ganges enjoys reverence as well as great popularity due to its "spiritual cleansing value." It is locally known as the Uttar Ganga.

A popular section is the 20-mile (32 km) stretch through the canyon, ending at Rishikesh, that is usually run in one- or two-day trips. Ask locally for access information. At Rishikesh, the Ganges abruptly and dramatically leaves the canyon and opens

The Great Bend of the Tsangpo

The ultimate river-running challenge waits at the bottom of the deepest canyon on the planet. This is the Great Bend of the Tsangpo, as it is called in Tibet. For eons it has cut a course through the eastern Himalayas, roaring through the heart of the great mountain range. It emerges in India as the Brahmaputra, one of the major rivers in India. At its deepest point in the upper canyon, the river passes between the 25,000-foot (7,625 m) Namcha Barwa and the 24,000-foot (7,320 m) Gyala Peri, just downstream of the Tibetan town of Gyala. Here the river elevation is about 10,000 feet (3050 m), leaving canyon walls and mountainsides climbing about 3 vertical miles (4.8 km) above the river on either side. The most difficult stretch is the 40 miles (64 km) from Gyala to where the Po Tsangpo enters from the left and the river drops nearly 5,000 feet (1,525 m) to about 5,100 feet (1,555 m). After another 80 miles (128 km) of spectacular gorge, the river rejoins "civilization." In this lower gorge, the river cuts between the Namche Barwa and the 22,000-foot (6,710 m) Nanchen Kangri. The elevation of the river here is only about 3,000 feet (915 m).

In October 1998, an attempt to run this most difficult stretch resulted in tragedy as American kayaker Doug Gordon was swept into a series of massive reversals and drowned. The Great Bend of the Tsangpo remains the last and the greatest unconquered canyon on the globe, although the downstream sections into India have been run commercially. With Tibet opening its doors to foreign visitors, it is likely that attempts will be made on this incredible run. Its difficulty can hardly be overstated. Flows are usually in excess of 50,000 cfs (1,415 cumecs), and the gradient in the 22-mile (35.2 km) section just before the Po Tsangpo enters exceeds 100 fpm (19.3 mpk). It is likely that the first descent, even with state-of-the-art equipment and support, will be as daring and dangerous as Powell's expedition down the Grand Canyon of Colorado in 1869.

up onto the plains where it becomes the lifeblood of much of India's civilization, agriculture, and trade.

If you are looking for a wilderness expedition, then put in upstream on the Bhagirathi at Tehri and float the 24 miles (38.4 km) to the confluence with the Alaknanda. This is the headwaters of the Ganges and the site of Devaprayag, a most sacred place in the Hindu religion. It is 36 miles (57.6 km) from here to the lower take-out at Rishikesh. Upstream runs can be found on the Alaknanda as far upstream as Rudraprayag. This area is popular and has good road access, but the road tends to detract from the wilderness feel of the area.

Beas River ➤

Located about 200 miles (320 km) northwest of the Upper Ganges in the Himachal Pradesh, the Beas has its headwaters in Himalayan peaks above 21,000 feet (6,402 m). Most of the river running begins at the mountain resort town of Manali. A hot spring/spa is just above the river on the left at Manali. A road follows the river in this area.

The first 5 miles (8 km) downstream of Manali is a difficult, experts-only run. The Beas here is relatively small and makes a steep, difficult descent. The rapids ease to Class 4 to Katrin. Over the next 15 miles (25 km) the river is more manageable for intermediates as it goes into the Kulu Valley and on to Bajura. From here the river drops into a very difficult cataract sometimes called the Larji Gorge. Here, difficult rapids combine with much larger volume to make a much more challenging run than the upstream stretches. A tributary empties into the river from the left at Larji in the lower gorge. The river then opens up into the lower valley and is impounded behind a small dam at Pondoh.

Although the Beas drainage is in a partial rain shadow and somewhat dry, it does not completely escape the monsoon rains. High flows usually make the river unrunnable during the monsoon season of July through mid-September. The winter months of December through March are generally too cold, and in June the intense heat drives boaters from the river. The latitude of the Beas is about 31° north, equivalent to the lower Southern states in the United States.

Season: Mid-September through May (nippy December through February)
Character: Sacred Hindu river draining from high mountains with good road access

MANALI TO KATRIN
Difficulty: Class 5
Length: 10 miles (16 km)

KATRIN TO KULU
Difficulty: Class 3
Length: 10 miles (16 km)

KULU TO BAJURA
Difficulty: Class 3
Length: 7 miles (11 km)

BAJURA TO MANDI (LARJI GORGE)
Difficulty: Class 5
Length: 30 miles (50 km)

Season: Best in mid-September through November, April through May
Character: Snowmelt from Himalayas with road close to river

Japan

The islands of Japan were formed by eons of volcanic activity that continues to this day. Nearly all of Japan is mountainous, with the highest peaks about 10,000 feet (3,030 m), although sacred Mount Fuji towers some 3,000 feet (909 m) higher.

The Japanese word for river is *gawa*, and Japan boasts some 30,000 streams and rivers, fed by heavy rainfall and considerable snowmelt. River running, however, is limited: most of the rivers are small and short, unable to support extended trips. Major reconstruction and industrialization after World War II resulted in significant deforestation, and the hydroelectric and flood-control projects proliferated. Today there are dams on every major river in Japan. Japan is also densely populated and developed (a population about half that of the United States shares an area smaller and more mountainous than Montana). Nonetheless, the Japanese enjoy one of the highest standards of living in the world.

Although the Japanese traditionally had little reason to navigate their rivers, today they are taking up river running in increasing numbers. The sport is still in its infancy here, but a subculture is developing, with paddling schools and many river-running clubs. Most good whitewater runs are short, and the lack of river exploration possibilities puts the focus on kayaking races and rodeo contests. Some rivers are rafted commercially, and most trips are half-day adventures. There are many good, although mostly short, whitewater runs and most are easily accessible by the highly developed mass-transit system. Equipment, technique, and even paddling heroes are, for the present, mostly imported.

Ratings and logistical information from Japan are hard to come by. The information here has only been verified in a few instances. River runners without competent guides should check locally for information before undertaking any of these runs.

A river use dilemma could be in the offing if the Japanese embrace paddling with the same fervor and in the same numbers as they do other originally Western pastimes, such as golf and baseball. At present, few of Japan's millions of golfers can afford to set foot on the islands' precious golf courses, and most bide their time on crowded driving ranges. With some 28 million inhabitants in the greater Tokyo area and the Tone-gawa being the probable paddling destination of choice, demand may again outpace the island's limited supply of resources.

◁ Nagara-gawa

GUJO-HACHIMAN TO MINO-SHI (CITY)
Difficulty: Class 3–, easier at bottom
Length: 20 miles (32 km)

Season: April through September
Character: Free-flowing, popular with hard boats and inflatables

Located north of Nagoya, the Nagara-gawa flows out of the mountains of Gifu Prefecture in Central Japan through a narrow basalt canyon for half of its 102-mile (165 km) length. The headwaters are at over 5,000 feet elevation. In its lower reaches the river flows between dike walls across the low-lying plain and into Ise Bay. The Nagara-gawa supports one of the richest and cleanest aquatic ecosystems in Japan and is a famous fishery for satsuku (spring salmon) and ayu (sweetfish). It is one of the few places in Japan where the art of fishing with cormorants, tethered by the neck, is still practiced, and a 1¼-mile (2 km) section is designated as reserved for the Emperor's table. The area is popular with tourists, and the river culture, supported by fishing and crafts, thrives along its banks.

Until recently the Nagara-gawa remained the last major free-flowing stream in Japan. With the construction of the Nagara River Estuary Dam in the lower reaches, over the opposition of a number of diverse groups (including river runners, anglers, and environmentalists), this status was lost.

Although the construction of the dam is a loss in many respects, it will not destroy some of Japan's best whitewater which is farther upstream. Boaters can put in at Gujo-Hachiman and run to Minami-Mura, a half-day run popular in all craft including commercial rafts. When flows are lower, boaters put in downstream at Fukado. Upstream of Gujo-Hachiman the river is usually too bony for boating. Many take out at Konna, although some continue down to Suhara. From here it is mostly flatter water down to Mino, although the toughest rapid on the river is found on this stretch. Downstream from the whitewater section is a kayak school near Seki-Shi.

As on most rivers in Japan, anglers take their fishing seriously and conflicts can develop between anglers and boaters. Ayu (sweetfish) fishing season is from June to September, concurrent with some of the best paddling, and the ayu tend to gather in rapids as do anglers with their long poles. At present paddlers try to target windows for paddling right before and right after the season. As the popularity of river running grows, it is hoped that an agreement can be reached to open the river for each sort for specified hours or specified days during the season.

Another river to the east, the Hida-gawa, is a dam-controlled river that gets some use and has more difficult whitewater.

Yoshino-gawa (Shikoku) ➤

The Yoshino-gawa is probably the most popular whitewater river in Japan. Its headwaters are on Mount Ishizuchi. The best whitewater is where the river runs through the Oboke and Koboke gorges; the names reportedly translate as "a narrow, dangerous place to walk" and "a wide, dangerous place to walk." The rapids are generally pool-and-drop, and good, dependable hydroelectric releases can be expected from the Sameura Dam upstream. Heavy rains can raise the flow, making the run more challenging. Fishing for Ayu is popular here from June to September, making conflicts with anglers a problem.

To run the Oboke and Koboke gorges, put in near the Oboke train station and take out near the Awa-Kawaguchi train station. This is also near where the Iyo-gawa highway (Route 319) meets Route 32. Kayakers sometimes enjoy good playspots near the put-in. Route 32 and the railroad follow the river through the run. The sections of the river upstream and downstream are easier but get less use.

The island of Shikoku is southwest of Osaka and is usually reached via a toll bridge on the north end of the island.

ROUTE 32 BRIDGE TO IKEDA
Difficulty: Class 4–
Length: 25 miles (40 km), 8 miles (12.8 km) in Oboke and Koboke gorges

Season: April through October (kayaks year round)
Character: Dam-controlled, popular

*O*ther runs in Japan worthy of description here include the Sai-gawa, the Tone-gawa, the Kitayama-gawa, and the Kushiro-gawa (Hokkaido).

The Sai-gawa is located northwest of Tokyo and drains the highest mountain ranges in Japan at over 10,000 feet (3,300 m). The run offers easy Class 2 rapids, ideal for beginners in training, usually from April to October. Paddlers put in at Akashina-machi for a 5-mile (8 km) run. Downstream the river flows past the resort area of Nagano, site of the 1998 Winter Olympics. One of Japan's foremost canoe and kayak schools, which goes by the English name "Sunday Planning," is operated here.

The Tone-gawa is located northwest of metropolitan Tokyo about an hour and a half by car (traffic permitting) or an hour by the so-called "Shinkansen" high-speed train. Partly due to its location, the river's popularity is outpacing that of most other rivers in Japan.

The Tone-gawa begins in the high ranges of the Japanese Alps in Gumma Prefecture, near Mount Tanigawa and Mount Hotaka. The drainage includes the Houdaigi, Okutone, and Tenjin daira ski areas, and snowmelt provides most of the water, sometimes year round. Nagano Prefecture is to the west. The river races south from the mountains and is impounded behind Fujiwara Dam which diverts water to Tokyo for drinking. Near the river is Minakami Hot Springs, and a gauge for the middle section can be found on the right upstream of the Minakami hanging bridge, near a park.

The Tone-gawa offers three runs, the first of which is a Class 5 run beginning just downstream of Fujiwara Dam, which controls flows. A shorter Class 4+ reach is next, followed by a Class 3+ stretch ending at Goken (Gokeri). The river runs from April to October and is rafted commercially. The two lower runs are more popular than the difficult upstream run.

The Kitayama-gawa is located south of Osaka in a relatively isolated part of Japan on the Kii Peninsula in the southern part of the Kinki area. The most popular stretch, run by kayakers and rafted commercially, is a Class 3− reach from Otonori to Komatsu through a scenic canyon. Boatable dam-releases for the commercial rafts allow others to paddle. Downstream the Kitayama flows into the Kumano where it eases and is popular with beginners. Jet boats roam the river downstream of Tado.

Located on the eastern part of the northern island of Hokkaido, the Kushiro-gawa is a popular touring river. The best whitewater is near the top of the run, downstream of Kutcharoko Lake, but before the river leaves the high mountains. In the river's lower reaches it flows through a scenic marshlands area to the Pacific Ocean.

More whitewater action on the north island of Hokkaido can be found on the Toyohira-gawa or the Mukawa-gawa near Sapporo.

China

Richard Flasher

Covering the topic of whitewater in China in a few pages is a challenge. The country is enormous, larger than the continental United States, and while Americans have explored relatively few miles of Chinese rivers to date, there are already numerous tales worth telling. Add to this the dramatic changes looming on the horizon in China that might inspire rapid development of outdoor recreation, and the topic grows even larger. The following is a mere summarization or generalization, if you will, in hopes that anyone truly intrigued about whitewater boating in China will make use of the available materials to expand their knowledge.

Within the past ten years Americans have explored most of the major drainages in China, along with a few small ones. Five are born in the highlands of Tibet: the Brahmaputra, the Salween, the Yangtze, the Mekong, and the Yellow. The mountains bordering Korea in the northeast feed the sixth major drainage, the Songhua, which looks more promising for canoes than rafts. The successes gained in exploration haven't come easily: disappointment, expense, failure, and death—glorious or otherwise—have been a large part of American-led whitewater exploration in China.

The Chinese do not have a tradition of river running. When they first received inquiries from foreigners about river explorations, they likened them to mountain-climbing expeditions, and proceeded to charge accordingly. The dream of being the first American to run the mighty Yangtze led to a bidding war between competing American groups and some Japanese interests. The Chinese asked for a permit fee of one million U.S. dollars for the privilege, with a few amenities thrown in. Unfortunately, the idea of their river being "stolen" by foreigners prompted two very bold but poorly equipped groups of Chinese nationals to vow to win the race down the Yangtze. Their boldness and tenacity ultimately carried the day, though at a cost of perhaps as many as a dozen lives. Mutual of Omaha televised their version of the race, which included some frightening footage of a Chinese craft making the only successful run of Tiger's Leap Gorge. Richard Bangs offers his version of the story in *Riding the Dragon's Back*, and Michael McRae yet another saga in *Outside* magazine, May 1987.

These high permit fees and other inflated costs of doing business in China slowed and limited the development of whitewater recreation by Americans. Three established U.S.–based international whitewater outfitters—Sobek, Steve Curry, and Ken Warren—all gave it a shot in China, but ended up folding their tents in pretty short order.

The tradition in China is to bargain for goods and services. People unfamiliar with this practice often find it culturally difficult to do and, regardless, are no match for a seasoned Chinese negotiator. The Chinese government has effectively controlled foreign-led whitewater boating to date by asserting that the only way to gain access to China's backcountry is through a state-licensed tourism company or official sponsor; however, things are not always as they seem, even in China.

I had come to believe that recent economic developments in China may have created a good opportunity to test their contention, so in October 1996, I entered China with one raft, two co-conspirators, and every intention of calling their bluff. We had, in good faith, negotiated what we thought was a reasonable offer with a state-licensed tourism company prior to our arrival. Not surprisingly, they wanted to up the ante once we had arrived. We bargained long into the night, and the next morning they drove us to our launch place in an area officially closed to foreign visitors. They dropped us off at dusk with our gear, and sped off as soon as we'd promised that we wouldn't reveal who had brought us there should we be "caught." We launched our raft before the moon came up and floated a short way downstream to a place with no visible motor access: an auspicious start.

We ended up thoroughly enjoying our six-day exploratory river trip, camping out and visiting with the friendly inhabitants on a scenic stretch of the Yellow River which featured Class 3 whitewater, waterfalls, Tibetan herdsmen, and ancient Buddhist temples that can only be reached from the water. We were able to raft the entire 80-mile section we'd hoped to, and negotiated directly with Chinese citizens for motorboat, truck, and jeep rides back to the airport for about one-seventh the fee that we paid to the tourism company. Recent economic changes in China have enabled a few citizens to own vehicles, and while their driving skills are a bit raw and the comfort level in the vehicles questionable, the price was right for us. For the record, the likely consequence of getting "caught" would have been a fine (negotiable amounts, bargain gingerly), although a Taiwanese group was reportedly thwarted and deported before they were able to launch their river trip about two years ago. Many areas in China are still listed as closed to foreigners, for reasons mostly innocuous.

Predicting the future in China is a vocation best suited to people who don't mind seeing themselves made fools of, often in remarkably short order; the reader has thus been advised. An apt metaphor for the complex ebb and flow of power in China would be a whitewater river, where a calm surface may hide powerful currents churning below, and where turbulent rapids that appear formidable may also obscure the strength and direction beneath the waves. Pushing this metaphor even further, imagine yourself staring at a frightening rapid for the first time, trying to find a navigable line through the chaotic maelstrom. The longer you look, the worse it gets, and just when you have resigned yourself to an arduous portage, other boaters appear, and you watch them glide through the cataract without undue effort. The rapid now looks altogether different, more intriguing than intimidating, and undeniably boatable. So, too, is China; often overwhelming and complex, then suddenly becoming clear and straightforward.

It is possible, now that the mainland government has taken full control of Hong Kong, that the rapid growth of contacts and opportunities for Chinese business people will occur, and coupled with the recent appearance of both leisure time and disposable income we may see a sudden growth in the domestic recreation industry in China. As more entrepreneurs venture abroad, they will encounter commercial and recreational boating and stores full of colorful, tempting products. There already is at least one out-

Once we even acted like barnyard animals in a shack in rural China that doubled as a restaurant in an effort to communicate that my good friend, Joe Dengler, was a vegetarian and couldn't eat flesh.

—*Beth Rypins*

fitter on the Wujiang River in Guangdong province running half-day rafting trips for domestic tourists.

There are several very good reasons that all previous rafting trips in China have been conducted through state-licensed agencies and tourism companies. Communication may be the biggest; if you cannot speak and read some Mandarin, you'll find it almost impossible to manage in China. In the countryside, you won't even find signs written in Pinyan, Mandarin words written in sound-alike Roman letters. Useful local maps available in China bookstores are typically written only in Mandarin characters, as well as all of the road signs. Unfortunately, Mandarin and English have nothing in common, and while visitors who memorize and recite a few phrases will surely draw complements, in reality it takes most students years to learn to speak the language passably. There are some people with adequate English working in tourism companies in China, and while they may have little experience outdoors, they try hard to accommodate your wishes. Another reason that tourism companies were always hired was that they were among the few organizations with access to motor vehicles; there are no automobile rental agencies in China for foreigners. A third very good reason is the practice of reserving the best seats on airplanes, trains, and other facilities for clients of tourism companies. There is a tradition in China by which foreigners are charged two to five times the local price that local people pay for admission to a museum, a seat on a train, or a bowl of soup. Tourism companies are accustomed to charging foreigners by the day, even when the goods and services they provide are negligible. Anyone interested in exploring China's hinterlands on their own should be forewarned that there is a costly learning curve that is unavoidable; consider it an initiation fee that may begin to yield benefits only the second time around.

All river trips have certain elements in common; what is unique about a river trip in China is the people that you meet. The peasants and villagers in the countryside are worlds apart in terms of their life experience and familiarity with modern Western society, and yet they do not act intimidated by the odd physical appearance of Westerners or humbled by their apparent wealth. The Chinese seem to find plenty of amusement in Westerners, and enjoy seeing the strange and colorful accoutrements with which we travel. On the other hand, they don't seem to mind our propensity to photograph everything that we see, even though a weathered goat herder's wife asked us, "Why are you photograph me? I am not beautiful." We told her we want our friends back home to see what the real people in China look like; I'm not sure she was convinced. With all of this said and done, I can heartily recommend boating in China, with a few conditions. If you want to take daredevil risks, go to New Zealand instead, a place with modern medical facilities, good transportation, and very limited legal liability laws, so you won't become a burden on local taxpayers. If you want to see abundant wildlife and pristine forests, better head for Alaska or Canada. But if you want to meet an astounding variety of resilient cultures and religious groups whose experiences and expectations in life are so profoundly different than yours that you are sure to come away with a respect and admiration for people who must struggle every day for things that we take for granted, try boating in China. Don't overlook the added bonus of getting to eat out Chinese food every night!

Taiwan

Richard Flasher

*T*aiwan is a mountainous, subtropical island the size of Switzerland with one famous whitewater river and numerous other boatable streams. According to local legend, a Taiwanese businessman vacationing in Canada took a commercial rafting trip, and upon his return home set about establishing operations on the Hsiukuluan (shoo-koo-LAHN) River on Taiwan's rugged east coast. About a dozen companies now offer daily trips in the summertime, covering the 14-mile section from Juisui to the Pacific Ocean in about four hours. Fed by the rain runoff from a 13,000-foot peak (3,939 m), the river is probably boatable year-round. Enjoying a steady gradient and occasional, short Class 2 rapids, the river winds a scenic course through the Coastal Mountain Range and among huge white marble boulders. The water temperature is typically tepid, and the water relatively unpolluted. Visitors wishing to sign up for a commercial rafting excursion should have no trouble getting connected through any tourist hotel in Hualien, a popular east coast city close to Taroko Gorge and the Hsiukuluan.

One common feature of Taiwan's whitewater rivers is that they change without notice. Most of the exposed rock is fractured shale, and the torrential downpours of big typhoons can radically alter a streambed in a very few minutes. The Liwu River that runs through the east coast's top scenic attraction, Taroko Gorge, drops at over 100 fpm through a white marble gorge. A big typhoon in 1990 caused so much erosion that the pristine Class 5 stream became overnight a silty Class 3+ sluice. The river is still in recovery.

There is a nascent whitewater boating community in Taiwan, mostly based in Taipei. Distances in Taiwan are short and it is not difficult to get around, though few people in the countryside will understand English. Boaters should feel safe and welcome, and, once out of Taipei, should find whitewater exploring a pleasant task indeed. Getting in touch with local boaters is not a simple matter as of this writing; however, the National Tourism Bureau in Taipei should soon be able to help put interested parties in touch with each other. Boaters interested in the pursuit of more serious whitewater will need some local help, unless you can read Mandarin and speak Taiwanese.

A popular west-coast river with unsanctioned commercial rafting is the Laonung, near Luikeui, not far from Kaohsiung. If you are in the area during the summer months, you may want to give it a try. It has similar whitewater to the Hsiukuluanbe, but not as clean or scenic. I enjoyed a west-coast raft run down the Peikang (bay-GHAN) from Hwaisun Forest to the town of Kuohshing (gwo-SHEEN). The scenery is excellent, and more of a pool-and-drop stream than the typical broken-ledge, gravel-bar rapids. Watch out for the broken dam about halfway down the run; opt for a short portage on the right through the papaya plantation if concrete-and-rebar-encrusted drops make you nervous.

Taiwan has sixty-one peaks over 10,000 feet, and its frequent year-round rainfall makes numerous short whitewater runs possible. Road access can be a problem, as typhoon rains often cause rock slides to block the backcountry access roads; carry a shovel. Rental cars are available, and if you can overcome the frightening driving you see in the cities, you'll find it much saner in the countryside.

AUSTRALASIA

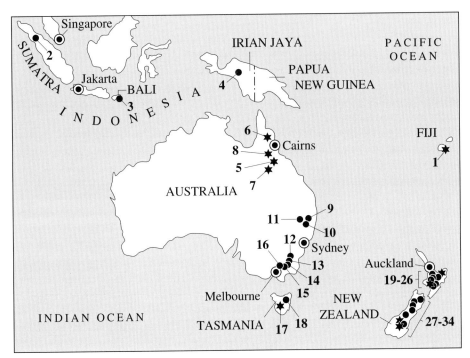

1 Navua River (see page 278)
2 Alas River
3 Ayung River
4 Baliem River
5 Tully River (see page 286)
6 Barron River (see page 286)
7 Herbert River (see page 286)
8 North Johnstone River
   (see page 286)
9 Nymboida River, including the
   Mann and Clarence Rivers
10 Clarence River
11 Gwydir River
12 Murrumbidgee River
13 Murray River
14 Snowy River
15 Mitchell River
16 Thomson River
17 Franklin River (see page 298)
18 South Esk River
19 Motu River (see page 303)
20 Wairoa River
21 Kaituna River
22 Rangitaiki River
23 Tongariro River
24 Ngaruroro River
25 Rangitikei River
26 Wanganui River (see page 308)
27 Shotover River (see page 310)
28 Kawarau River (see page 310)
29 Buller River
30 Clarence River
31 Karamea River
32 Rangitata River
33 Taieri River
34 Landsborough River
   (see page 315)

Fiji

◄ Navua River

Formed of ancient volcanoes and coral, Fiji is a large group of islands almost directly north of New Zealand. The Fiji group offers clear blue water, sunny beaches, world-class diving, and sea kayaking. It also has the best small-island whitewater in the South Pacific.

According to his log, Captain William Bligh may have had the first contact with Fijian paddlers. He and his small, weaponless crew visited the island in a small boat in 1789 after being banished by mutineers from the Bounty. Having no choice but to sail directly through what were then known as the Cannibal Islands, they soon found themselves pursued by two large war canoes paddled by enthusiastic, decidedly unfriendly, and, one might imagine, hungry natives. The Fijians were paddling a drua, a speedy, seaworthy craft that clearly outclassed the Bounty's launch. Bligh's first gambit was to sneak through a passage in a nearby reef, but he found himself becalmed. His men were obliged to resort to oars as the canoes closed. Bligh's prayers for a miracle were answered when an abrupt thunderstorm brought high seas and low visibility. When the squall cleared, only one canoe remained and a fair breeze allowed Bligh to raise sail. They held the Fijians at a distance until sunset when the pursuers turned back. Bligh sailed 2,500 miles (4,000 km) to Timor, claiming justice and cinematic immortality.

The native Fijians of today have changed their menu and are among the most amiable and generous people on Earth. Keep this in mind and act accordingly. The natives retain ownership of 83 percent of the land and most of the rivers. If you are not on a commercial trip, you will need permission to run the rivers. They may offer to share a bowl of a mild intoxicant called kava, an honor not to be taken lightly.

Most of the whitewater is on the main island of Viti Levu, about 80 miles (128 km) in diameter. Viti Levu is a land of sharply defined, mountainous landscapes, ancient volcanoes, and rock outcroppings. Paddling is the easiest way to explore and enjoy the

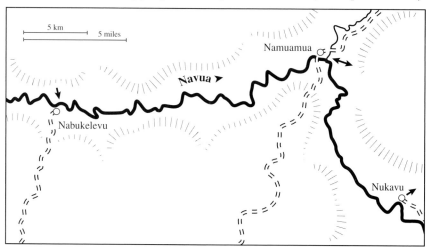

Navua River (Fiji)

rugged interior of the main island, away from the mainland tourist activities. The rainy season is November through March. Nearly constant rains fall on the southeastern side of the island, and they support good river running, pioneered by a few locals. There is some limited commercial rafting for tourists who usually hail from Australia, New Zealand, or Japan.

The Navua drains a large portion of the southeast of Viti Levu. The best whitewater starts immediately at the top of the upper gorge. The canyon opens and the rapids ease before the village of Namuamua. The river then leaves the village and most of the rapids behind and enters another beautiful canyon with dramatic scenery. The gorges are often shrouded in mist and have been likened to a Chinese painting set against Fiji's serrated mountains. Motorized boats work their way between Nukavu and Namuamua on the lower run.

Other runs on the island worth considering include Wainikoroiluva, a tributary that meets the Navua at the village of Namuamua and has a fine Class 2 run. On the north side of the island, the Wailoa is a one-day Class 3 float. On the island's drier northwest side is the Ba River. Here commercial outfitters take guests to the headwaters of the river for an easy whitewater float through narrow gorges and native villages. Exotic birds are part of the attraction.

Navua River, Magic Waterfalls, Fiji.
(Discover Fiji Tours)

Bamboo raft, HMS *Bilibili* downriver, Navua River, Fiji. *(Discover Fiji Tours)*

Indonesia

*E*xtending 3,000 miles (4,800 km) across two oceans and consisting of 7,000 islands, Indonesia is the largest archipelago nation in the world. Situated on the Equator, it holds vast stretches of rainforests, exceeded only by the Amazon, and perhaps the most intensely diverse flora and fauna on Earth. Ancient land bridges to both Asia and Australia allowed passage of exotic animals to the islands; Indonesia is home to rhinoceros, tiger, kangaroo, elephant, several species of monkeys and apes, at least forty-seven species of marsupials, and a dazzling array of tropical birds. More than 430 bird species are unique to Indonesia, including five different birds of paradise. A view of the bizarre and spectacular rhinoceros hornbill is a treat for birdwatchers. The islands are also the home of some of the most oversized creatures on the planet, such as the 8-foot (2.5 m) Komodo dragon lizard which hunts and kills deer. Here one can find the flying fox, a bat with a 5-foot (1.5 m) wingspan, and the ratflesia, the world's largest flower with a diameter of 3 feet.

Formerly the Dutch East Indies, Indonesia gained its independence from the Netherlands in 1945. Its population is diverse and extremely dense in some areas. The island of Java is probably the most densely populated island in the world, with 107,000,000 people sharing a space the size of New York state. Fortunately, most of the river running is on other, less-populated islands. Indonesia is the eastern fringe of the Islamic Crescent and is mostly Muslim. However, most Balinese are Hindu. The Melanesian natives of Irian Jaya have been courted by Catholic missionaries, but the warlike and cannibalistic Melanesian past is not at all forgotten.

Indonesia is mountainous, as it sits on the juncture of the Pacific and Australian tectonic plates. The terrain, combined with the massive amounts of rain it receives, make the Indonesian archipelago ideal for wild and exotic big-water river trips.

◁ Alas River (Sumatra)

With Bali in the center of the archipelago and Irian Jaya on the eastern flank, Sumatra is the major island on the western flank of Indonesia. This lightly populated island has been cleared of much of its lowland rainforests. However, large areas of forest remain in the highlands, and mountain parks protect significant numbers of Indonesia's large mammals including the Asian elephant, silver leaf monkey, Thomas leaf monkey, longtail malaque, orangutan, Koloss gibbon, Sumatran tiger, and possibly the near-extinct Javan rhinoceros. The island has two rainy seasons, the first from mid-September to December, and the second from March to early June. The Alas River drains the mountains of northwest Sumatra, flowing south in the interior of the island before emptying into the Indian Ocean.

Most of the river's watershed is in the Gunung Leuser National Park, and much of the attraction of the Alas River is the opportunity to view the spectacular wildlife. The area is the home of much of the world's remaining population of orangutans. The best wildlife viewing is on the lower-gorge section where the warm, big-volume water and

SERIKIL TO GELOMBANG
Difficulty: Class 3+
Length: 5 miles (5 km), half-day run

MIDDLE GURAH TO PINTU ALAS
Difficulty: Class 2–
Length: 12 miles (19.2 km), one-and-a-half-day run

PINTU ALAS TO GELOMBANG (LOWER GORGE)
Difficulty: Class 2+
Length: 34 miles (55 km), three-day run

Season: All year
Character: Exotic tropical river

mild current allow boaters to keep a lookout for orangutans, gibbons, monkeys, and elephants. Hornbills abound.

Access to the lower section is at the village of Muara Situlan. The common first-night camp is at Serakut on the left. The second night is usually spent at Soraya Camp on the right. From here downstream to Gelombang motorized tow boats are used.

Boaters sometimes run the section above Scrikil, putting in at Agusan, but this is an experts-only run and flows can be skimpy in the dry season.

The future of the Alas is uncertain. Clear-cutting and exploitation of other resources threaten the river habitat. However, efforts sponsored by the European Union to preserve the Leuser ecosystem may offer salvation. Severe economic and political disruption visiting the area in 1998 may also affect the island's future.

Ayung River (Bali) ➢

Just east of the island of Java is the volcanic island of Bali. Bali's rich tropical landscape, innumerable temples, splendid beaches, relaxed, beautiful natives, and spicy food draw more and more visitors to the island. Traffic and smog have made an appearance, but even the traffic seems to have its own pleasant rhythm. Life remains simple for the friendly Balians, and few travelers leave disappointed.

The Ayung, also called the Yeh Ayung, is found in south-central Bali, just west of the village of Ubud. The Ayung has gained distinction as a half-day diversion to other commercial tourist activities. To say the trip is popular is an understatement. It is reported that commercial outfitters take more than 50,000 visitors a year down the river. Most are thrill-seeking Japanese and Australian tourists.

Fed by the plentiful rains, the river drops from Bali's volcanic hills and flows through a narrow gorge in the rice fields of the Ayung Valley over technical, rocky, pool-and-drop rapids. Although close to civilization, the tropical forests of the Ayung Gorge provide a sense of solitude. The best flows are during the rainy season from November through April when the waterfalls along the river are running and add to the scenery. Rafting companies, however, run the river even during the low flows of the dry season. The put-in and the take-out are both just off main roads that follow the river, and each require a short hike. The take-out can be found near the Amandari Hotel.

AYUNG GORGE, WEST OF UBUD
Difficulty: Class 3–
Length: 6 miles (9.6 km)

Season: Year-round; best November through April
Character: Tight, isolated gorge in developed area; sometimes a low-water run

Baliem River (Irian Jaya) ➢

"On earth your river may dry out. But in heaven it is always good."
—*Dani proverb*

Irian Jaya means "victorious hot land," but with 200 inches of rain a year, it is doubtful Irian Jaya's rivers will ever dry out. This largest and least developed of Indonesia's provinces is the last great wilderness of the Asian Pacific and one of the wildest, most isolated frontiers on Earth. It is a world of rainforests, spectacular wildlife, and tribesmen only recently removed from the Stone Age. Sitting atop the juncture of the Australian and Pacific tectonic plates, Irian Jaya juts upward with spectacular mountains reaching heights of 16,000 feet (4,880 m), the setting of the spectacular oxymoron "tropical glaciers."

WANUGGI TO THE END OF THE
MOUNTAINS
Difficulty: Class 3+, first 30 miles (48 km); Class 1+, 15 miles (24 km) to Kurima; Class 5+ through the lower gorge
Length: 100 miles (160 km)

Season: All year; usually too high during January–March monsoons; best March through April
Character: Remote, tropical rainforest

But to say this island is wild is an understatement. The native Melanesians lived in a state of almost constant warfare for centuries. The Asmat tribe, inhabiting the swampland at the bottom of the Baliem River, may have been the last people on Earth to abandon cannibalism, as late as the 1970s. One notable victim of a paddling mishap was American oil heir Michael Rockefeller, who vanished in 1961 on an anthropological expedition. His craft capsized in an area inhabited by the Asmat, and he was never seen again. Times have changed, however, and modern travelers should not fear dinner reservations.

Modern extractive culture exacts a dear cost here, which can be seen near the summit of Puncak Jaya, the highest peak in Southeast Asia. Here the massive Grasberg open pit mine operates below its glaciers. The project, run by New Orleans–based Freeport McMoRan and its president, former University of Texas football star Jim Bob Moffet, systematically removes much of the mountain, unearthing the world's single largest gold reserve and third largest copper reserve. Massive tunnels move ore slurry mixed with the abundant rains from 13,000 feet (3,965 m) to 5,000 feet (1,525 m) and recoup hydro-

Notes from an Early Descent of the Baliem River

Your first rule of business will be to obtain a Surat Jalan, a must for travel in the Baliem Valley. This will be your walking paper or travel permit for land travel. Something that also proved invaluable for our group was a letter that Ken Ratin (one of our guides) provided, written by the management of a hotel that Ken worked for as a river guide. It contained words written in both English and Indonesian that said: "This group of explorers are on an expedition from the United States and are authorized by our government to explore the Wamena and Baliem rivers in Irian Jaya. The government of the United States requests that you assist them in any way possible and thanks you for your help. Signed _____." It will also help if such a letter contains a colored letterhead, embossing or a seal, and colored ink in the signature. Sounds crazy, but without it we would not have been allowed access to the river.

At the Wamena Market you can take some great pictures of men wearing kotekas *(penis gourds), ladies covered with mud (grieving the loss of a loved one), and colorful fruits and vegetables on display for sale. A picture of a Dani local sporting his koteka will cost you anywhere from 500 to 1,000 Rupiah (Rp). Be sure to settle the price first before taking a picture. The traditionally dressed ones want cash for every shutter click, but all are pleasant and friendly.*

The village of Pumo is the site of a 300-year-old mummy, about Rp 3,000 ($1.50 U.S.) to look at and photograph, named "Agat Mo Make," a great warrior and ancestor. They smoked him in a fetal position, complete with his koteka in place. The skin is shrunk up tight against its bones and black from being regularly treated with pig grease and soot. Three hundred years is a long time to be greased up and carried in and out of the hut. . . .

The ladies of the village have several fingers missing on each hand. When a family member dies, it is customary for the women to cut off a digit with a small stone axe. Most of the older ones are missing fingers, but the young ladies have stopped maiming themselves. Like headhunting, it's a good tradition to quit practicing.

—*John Volkman*

electric power at the bottom. The mining process creates acidic tailings at the rate of 120,000 tons per day, all of which will eventually and perpetually produce acid rain. The Grasberg mine has been called the largest non-accidental, peacetime, ecological disaster created by man. Seventy-five percent of the gold will be used for jewelry. Considered a land of opportunity, outsiders from Indonesia and abroad are coming to the islands to reap its treasures.

The Baliem River has its source near Puncak Jaya in the Maoke Mountains, flowing southwest through the expansive, mile-high Baliem Valley. The put-in point for the upper run is near the village of Wanuggi, downstream of an unrunnable section of the river that goes underground near the village of Kuyuwhei and comes out more than a mile downstream as a beautiful 400-foot (122 m) waterfall. The upper run offers nicely spaced rapids ranging up to Class 3+. Most rapids wash out at high water.

The middle section runs through the mile-high central valley, through potato fields that cover the banks and ridges much like the vineyards of Italy. The central valley is the home of the Dani tribe, subject of the classic anthropological film *Dead Birds*. Although the tribe was often at war, crude weapons worked to keep casualties to a minimum. The town of Wamena provides airport access to the valley at this point.

The village of Kurima is found as the river leaves the valley and begins its drop into the lower gorge. From here it cuts through a deep cataract with a gradient of about 100 fpm (19.3 mpk). While this section of the river has been run, the sections downstream drop even more steeply and remain to be explored. The river then passes through the swampy lowlands inhabited by the Asmat Tribe.

Torrential rains cause the river to be generally too high to run from January through March. Even at other times, rains can swell the river and boaters should be prepared.

Australia

*A*bout 150 million years ago, forces from deep inside the Earth began to break up the supercontinent of Gondwana, a conglomeration of what is today Australia, India, Arabia, Africa, and South America. Australia and Antarctica moved together toward their present locations, parting ways 65 million years ago.

Little tectonic activity and a stable land mass have paved the path for erosion as the prime force in forming present-day Australia. Ancient highlands to the west have been leveled into vast plains. What is now the outback was a massive inland sea that has left sedimentary beds over a mile deep. Erosion has also rounded and lowered the younger mountain ranges on the east coast, where nearly all of Australia's whitewater is found.

Australia remains the driest continent (after Antarctica). Its largest lake, Lake Eyre (3,600 square miles), is usually bone dry. Its Great Barrier Reef, formed of the skeletons of small animals, is almost half as long as its longest river system (the Murray-Darling at 2,300 miles, 3,680 km). Its tallest mountain, Mount Kosciusko, is only 7,310 feet (2,215 m).

Australia's original settlers were probably its first boaters. It is believed that the ancestors of the modern aborigines migrated from Southeast Asia more than 40,000 years ago, clinging to primitive rafts and walking over a partial land bridge. The aborigines lived undisturbed and in relative harmony with the environment as the world's oldest undisplaced culture until European settlement began some 200 years ago. This new intrusion has had a profound effect on the land, bringing plants and animals that find few natural enemies and often thrive to the point of calamity.

Many Australians trace their roots to hapless occupants of the colonial prisons built by the English after the loss of the American Colonies. The new Australians are modern, hardworking people who rarely lose their quick wit. A good-natured rivalry stands between the various regions. A Queenslander takes pride in the unregulated "wild west" character of the north, while his or her southern neighbors deride Brisbane as a "cow town." Victorians call the Murray River that forms the border with New South Wales the Indi, a name at which boaters from New South Wales would scoff.

The Cairns Area

Traveling north in Australia takes one closer to the equator. Cairns (pronounced "cans"), in the northeast corner of the continent, is a tropical enclave that has grown from sleepy, quaint beginnings to a major resort area. Best known as a jumping-off spot to the extraordinary diving, fishing, and sightseeing of the Great Barrier Reef, Cairns is also a whitewater haven. Hidden in the mountainous rainforests nearby are several excellent river-running opportunities, some available year round and most during the rainy season from November through April.

Paddlers should also be cautious. A number of venomous snakes live in Queensland, including the tiapan. Saltwater crocodiles ("salties") range as far as 25 miles (40 km) inland and account for several deaths every year. Scuba diving, bungee jumping, and sky diving are popular in the area for those who still cannot get enough.

Tully River (Queensland) ➤

The Tully, Australia's most popular river, is a wild, raucous, warm-water ride through dense and beautiful jungle. This is tourist territory, and the bulk of the 51,000 boaters a year are the guests of the two private rafting companies that purchase raftable flows from the Water Resources Commission. Experienced private boaters, including the local paddling clubs, benefit from the releases and join in the fun.

The bed of the Tully consists of volcanic rocks and is tough on boats and kayaks. With some two dozen technical rapids, even experienced boaters can get caught up in the tricky rock gardens. Keep an eye peeled for the next horizon line through the jungle mist. Some routes are narrow, requiring rafters to tube-stand to get through. Heavy traffic will find boats lined up to run some rapids.

Put in near the parking lot at the Kareeya Power Station west of the town of Tully. The station draws water from upstream Koombooloomba Dam. A wake-up call to boaters is Alarm Clock, directly around the first bend, followed by Double Waterfall. A series of rapids called The Theater is where all the drama takes place, culminating in Full Stop (Class 4) where less nimble boaters can find themselves slamming into a rock wall. Staircase (Class 4) leads boaters to Ponytail Falls, a stream entering from high cliffs on the left. Farther downstream boaters can usually run a cheat route on the extreme left of Cardstone Weir. From this point the rapids slacken, with only one Class 3 rapid to the take-out. Little camping is possible in the upper section, but the river is usually run in one day. There is some primitive camping downstream of the take-out. A road follows the river, providing access at several points.

Farther downstream the river flows into a mangrove-filled estuary near the mouth of the Tully on the Coral Sea. This is a haven for a fascinating array of birds, but beware of crocodiles.

Barron River (Queensland) ➤

The Barron offers a short whitewater run only a few miles from Cairns in the scenic Barron Gorge National Park. Commercial outfitters on the Barron, like those on the Tully, purchase boatable flows from the local dam authority. The outfitters dominate this less-demanding half-day stretch. But anyone who shows up with a boat at the right time is free to frolic in the rapids and enjoy the scenery.

To get to the put-in follow the signs to the Barron Gorge Hydro-Electric Station, off the Captain Cook Highway north of Cairns. Access the river at a bridge near the station.

The only significant rapids are the Boulders (Class 3) and Washing Machine (Class 3). Downstream of the take-out at the Kamerunga Bridge, the river enters the Barron River Estuary for a 6¼-mile (10 km) flatwater float rich in birdlife and, fortunately, only a few crocodiles.

KAREEYA POWER STATION TO TULLY RIVER BRIDGE
Difficulty: Class 4; Class 2 for the last 5 miles (8 km)
Length: 11 miles (17.6 km)

Season: All year
Character: Dam-release through tropical rainforest

BARRON FALLS POWER STATION TO KAMERUNGA BRIDGE
Difficulty: Class 3
Length: 3 miles (4.8 km)

Season: All year
Character: Short run in gorge near Cairns

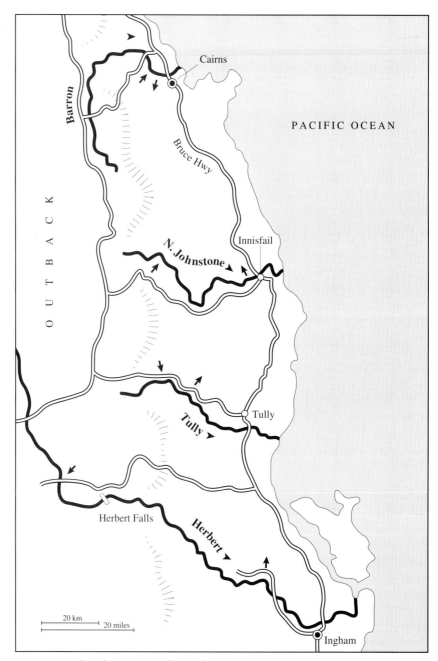

Barron, North Johnstone, Tully, and Herbert Rivers (Queensland, Australia)

Herbert River (Queensland) ➤

CASHMERE-GLENEAGLES TO
UPSTREAM OF ABERGOWRIE
Difficulty: Class 4p
Length: 60 miles (96 km)

Season: All year, but often
too high in rainy season
Character: Wilderness run
going from dry outback
to lush coastal area

Just south of the Tully is the Herbert, the southernmost of the tropical Cairns-area rivers. The Herbert flows through Herbert River Falls National Park, an area slightly drier than the drainages to the north. In the upper reaches, the lush tropical vegetation is confined to the river's banks, and the landscape away from the river is drier. As the river nears the wetter coastal area, the vegetation is more profuse and tropical. The Herbert provides a beautiful multi-day wilderness trip for those who can handle challenging rapids, as well as a portage or two. The dramatic granite formations of the Herbert generate some long technical rapids as well as stained and bleached outcroppings overhead. Some fine sandy beaches can be found along the river, but boaters who don't plan ahead may find themselves sleeping on a granite mattress.

The run starts off easy as the river meanders through several tree hazards until small ledges begin to appear. The highlight of the trip is the main gorge, announced by a set of drops leading to the spectacular Herbert Falls at about mile 15 (24 km). The two drops combine for a 200-foot (61 m) vertical drop requiring a tough portage on the left; be sure to bring ropes. Good camping is available here with sandy shoals and flat rocks. About a mile (1.6 km) below Herbert Falls are two additional cascading drops, each about 30 feet (9 m) and portaged on the left. From here downstream are good ledge rapids and a few possible portages. Blencoe Creek enters from the left, with poor road access, at around mile 22 (35 km). Power lines mark this area. Good camping and Blencoe Falls make this a popular stop. Colorful rock walls several hundred feet high follow the river from the top of the gorge all the way to Yaminie Creek, entering on the left side at mile 40 (64 km).

After Blencoe Creek, the gorge begins to open and the rapids ease. Yaminie Creek is another popular stop, with a tough but worthwhile side hike to Yamanie Falls. It's an easy paddle from here to the take-out upstream of Abergowrie. Boaters may also continue over easy water to the Bruce Highway and Ingham.

North Johnstone River (Queensland) ➤

THERESA CREEK TO BRUCE
HIGHWAY BRIDGE NORTH
OF INNISFAIL
Difficulty: Class 5–
Length: 50 miles (80 km)

Season: All year
Character: Wilderness river
in tropical rainforest

Just north of the Tully is the North Johnstone, a classic multi-day adventure with some very challenging rapids. The North Johnstone is for serious boaters willing to fly to the put-in, run countless Class 5– rapids in a remote area where a boat or helicopter is the only way out, scrounge for campsites in thick rainforest, and deal with the possibility of wildly fluctuating flows in a narrow, rocky streambed. Being alert and traveling light are essential.

This river corridor is the remaining portion of a vast rainforest area and is one of the last undisturbed wilderness runs in Australia. The area became a World Heritage site in 1988 and is part of the Palmerstone National Park. The forest holds large cicadia palms, which grow 2 feet (0.6 m) every 100 years, the indigenous hardwood Johnstone pine, and an indigenous ginger tree. The wildlife is exotic, if sometimes unsettling, with water dragons, pythons, and the palm-sized bird spider, named for its prey.

Boaters can arrange a helicopter shuttle in Cairns to either of the two main landing spots at Theresa Creek or the Beatrice River, both of which enter on the right. Most boaters begin at Theresa Creek, about 15 miles (24 km) upstream of the Beatrice River confluence. Using upstream road access from the Palmerstone Highway onto the Beatrice River is also possible. Nine miles (14.4 km) farther downstream, about a mile below

Douglas Creek, is Crawfords Lookout trail which provides access for those willing to undertake a tough hike, stinging nettles, and rope-ladder access to the river.

Tough rapids below Theresa Creek include Black Ass Falls, the Berlin Wall, and Snake Falls. Going can be slow, and this section may take a full day. Downstream is Mine Shaft (a narrow slot between two large boulders) and a mandatory portage at Stairway to Heaven, a 150-foot (46 m) waterfall near an ancient aboriginal burial ground. The next major feature is Mordor Gorge, a ⅔-mile-long (1 km) jigsaw puzzle of basalt boulders with a very slippery scout. At the entrance to the gorge is Pete's Arch, a natural tunnel formed by two basalt boulders. Below this is Junction Rapid and the confluence with the Beatrice River.

Downstream of the Beatrice the rapids are mostly Class 4, including Mushroom, Rooster Tail, Lookout, and Champagne Falls. These continue to the World Heritage boundary and flatwater about midway between Douglas Creek and the take-out. Keep an eye out for saltwater crocodiles in the flatwater as the river gradually returns to civilization. The Nurada Tea Plantation may provide private access in this area, and there are other possible access points several miles upstream of the Bruce Highway bridge.

East-Central Australia

Moving south in Australia, away from the equator, brings cooler and drier terrain. The area between Sydney and Brisbane where the Nymboida, Clarence, and Gwydir rivers flow is semitropical. Though not supporting the lush rainforest of the Cairns area, it is greener and wetter here than farther south towards Melbourne. Rainfall east of the Great Dividing Range is more plentiful than to the west.

◁ Nymboida River, including the Mann and Clarence Rivers (New South Wales)

PLATYPUS FLAT TO LITTLE
NYMBOIDA RIVER
CONFLUENCE
Difficulty: Class 4+
Length: 14 miles (22.4 km)

LITTLE NYMBOIDA CONFLUENCE TO
POLLACKS BRIDGE
Difficulty: Class 3
Length: 12 miles (19.2 km)

POLLACKS BRIDGE TO
JACKADGERY (RARELY RUN)
Difficulty: Class 3
Length: 45 miles (72 km)

JACKADGERY TO LILYDALE BRIDGE
(THE LOOP)
Difficulty: Class 3
Length: 50 miles (80 km)

Season: All year except
after long dry periods
Character: Many options,
most sections wild

The Nymboida River is a major tributary of the Clarence, draining the east slope of the Great Dividing Range between Brisbane and Sydney. The Nymboida flows north, parallel to the east coast. The Nymboida takes the name of the Mann River, although the Mann is much smaller, as the two join just upstream of Jackadgery. It then joins the Clarence and turns back south for another fine boating run, discussed below. Locals call the combined section from Jackadgery to Lilydale on the Clarence "The Loop," and it is as close as it gets to the river runner's impossible dream of a circular river, sans shuttle, providing 50 miles (80 km) of fine paddling for the effort of only a 7½-mile (12 km)shuttle. The entire stretch of the Nymboida, Mann, and Clarence rivers described here traverses thickly forested country with excellent scenery and good wildlife viewing including wallabies, kangaroos, wild horses, turtles, snakes, and eels. Birdwatchers may see kingfishers, eagles, budgerigars, and parakeets.

The upper Nymboida provides some challenging whitewater for experienced boaters. The section from Platypus Flat to the Little Nymboida River confluence has several 6- to 8-foot (1.8 to 2.5 m) drops and at least three that are often portaged. The bigger rapids include Lucifer's Leap, Rock Bar, and Waterfall, which lurks just below a rock garden called Cod Hole. Downstream are more tough rapids, including Blockup Gorge where the river almost disappears beneath big boulders at most flows. Other rapids in this stretch include Devil's Cauldron, S-Bend, Gutter, Mushroom, and Slippery Dip. Boaters can usually take out where the Little Nymboida River enters on the right. In wet weather use the better access downstream at Pollacks Bridge near the town of Nymboida. Camping is better in the upper reaches but still available at low water levels throughout the run.

The whitewater slackens, and the rapids between the Little Nymboida confluence and Jackadgery are Class 2 and 3 with pleasing scenery throughout. About 3½ miles (5.6 km) below Pollacks Bridge is the Nymboida Power Station Weir where much of the water is diverted for hydropower, much to the dismay of conservationists who are concerned that the reduced flows will threaten the river. Be ready for the possibility of skimpy flows downstream of the weir as well as the ruins of an old bridge just below the weir. The water is returned into Goolang Creek, and the releases there make the creek popular with kayakers.

A rapid at Cunglebung Creek just inside the Ramorine State Forest is sometimes portaged by less-experienced boaters in this otherwise easy section. Downstream the Mann River enters on the left, and the river from this point is known as the Mann River. Almost immediately downstream of the confluence is Junction Falls which is scouted on the left. About 5 miles (8 km) below the confluence with the Mann River is New Zealand Falls. Boaters may wish to scout and/or portage on the right.

To do The Loop, put in at Jackadgery. This will give you 50 miles (80 km) of fine Class 3 water when combined with the Clarence, and you will end up within 7½ miles of the put-in. The Loop is popular not just for its logistical efficiency, but for the beauty of the surroundings. The road stays near for the first three-quarters of the way down to the Clarence, which is 26 miles (41.6 km) below Jackadgery. The section from the Clarence confluence to Lilydale, discussed below, is often run separately. Boaters wishing to undertake the entire trip from Platypus Flat to Lilydale can treat themselves to about 121 miles (193.6 km) of fine Aussie river running.

Clarence River (New South Wales) ➤

The Clarence combines a large drainage, a scenic backdrop, and easier rapids, for some of the most enjoyable whitewater boating in Australia.

This section can be run separately or as part of The Loop, described in the previous essay. Although much of the run is easy Class 2 water through farming country, the run does feature the spectacular Clarence River Gorge (Class 3). Heed the warning not to park cars near the bridge—it's subject to flooding. Fluctuating flows can be serious here. Don't let your vehicle turn into someone else's surf wave. Brush and trees are a factor in the slower sections.

The confluence with the Mann River is about 1½ miles (2.4 km) downstream of the put-in. The Clarence River Gorge begins about 2 miles (3.2 km) downstream of the confluence with the Mann River. The highlight of the gorge is Clarence Falls (3), known to locals as Rainbow Falls, where the river drops over a massive granite outcropping. Boaters can portage the falls over the downstream end of the outcropping or scout for a runnable route. Most paddlers consider the falls an excellent place to spend some time exploring the imposing rock formations and fine swimming holes on either side of the river.

CARNHAM BRIDGE TO LILYDALE
Difficulty: Class 2, except for the Clarence River Gorge (Class 3)
Length: 25 miles (40 km)

Season: All year
Character: Isolated, scenic area

For the next 2 miles (3.2 km) the river flows between dramatic rock walls and over nonstop rapids, including one big runnable drop. The river then opens up to easy Class 2 rapids.

◁ Gwydir River (New South Wales)

COPETON DAM TO HORSE
    STEALERS GULLY, OR
    DOWNSTREAM TO KEERA
Difficulty: Class 4+
Length: 7 miles (11.2 km),
    18 miles (28.8 km) to
    Keera

Season: All year, though
    most usage is from
    November to March
Character: Dry west-slope
    country downstream
    from dam

On the west side of the Great Dividing Range from the Nymboida/Clarence river system is a challenging dam-release run through rugged dry terrain. This is the Gwydir River below the Copeton Dam, the whitewater hub on the west side of the mountains. The main season here is from November to February or later in wet years, but in dry years releases can be rare. However, heavy rains can bring boaters out anytime if the dam is releasing irrigation flows.

On the Gwydir below Copeton Dam the fine scenery is forgotten in the face of the unrelenting whitewater, some 7 miles (11.2 km) of it down to Horse Stealers Gully. Among the numerous rapids, the biggest drop, Sapphire Falls, possibly also known as Dead End Falls, is often portaged.

Boaters may choose between two put-ins below the dam: one, a long, narrow road to the river which may require a high-clearance vehicle; the second, a Department of Resources road off of Inverell Road which may be gated. After the big rapids, most take out at Horse Stealers Gully, as the additional reach to Keera is flat and brushy.

Boaters can also take advantage of the scenic and challenging Uralla Gorge (Class 4–) above the reservoir when flows permit.

Southeastern Australia

The highest mountains on the continent are found in the southern portion of the Great Dividing Range in southeastern Australia. Although at 6,000+ feet (1,830+ m) the peaks are not to the scale of great mountains elsewhere on the globe, they support some good river running and are located within driving range of Australia's largest cities, Sydney and Melbourne, as well as the national capital, Canberra. The rainfall is less seasonal than north in the Cairns area where the rainy season is limited to the summer from November to April.

Although we have included the most popular runs, one that deserves mention is the Mitta-Mitta, a southern tributary of the Murray. Sadly, the best reaches of the Mitta-Mitta were drowned under the backwater of the Dartmouth Dam. Good boating still can be found on the Mitta-Mitta upstream on the scenic Class 4 section from Bundarrah River confluence to the Hinnomunjie Bridge near Omeo, when flows allow.

◁ Murrumbidgee River (New South Wales)

LAKE BURRINJUCK TO
    CHILDOWLAH
Difficulty: Class 3
Length: 8 miles (12.8 km)

(continued on following page)

No rivalry is more celebrated in Australia than that between its two major cities, Sydney and Melbourne. When Australia gained independence, feelings were such that neither city was willing to let the other be the new nation's capital. In 1908, a site found between the cities was accepted as a compromise. American architect Walter Barley, whose name graces the lake near the center of town, planned and designed the city. Canberra has a generally young population that appreciates the foresight of the founding fathers to establish the seat of government near good whitewater.

Like the Murray and Snowy rivers, the Murrumbidgee has headwaters in Kosciusko National Park. The section described here begins at Burrinjuck Reservoir as the river leaves the wetter mountainous area and heads west into progressively drier climates. The Burrinjuck Dam is an irrigation dam, and controlled releases are variable. Good Class 3+ rapids just below the dam are followed by easier whitewater as the river widens down to Chowdilla. The rapids range from technical to big-water depending on flows, but for the last few years construction to augment the dam has made access difficult and flows unpredictable. The scenery is untouched bush until a couple of miles (3.2 km) above Chowdilla, which is grazing country. At Chowdilla is Chowdilla Rapid, a long, technical boulder garden. Whereas the recreational area at Burrinjuck has a developed campground, downstream there is only primitive camping.

The take-out at Childowlah and the put-in below the reservoir are approached from the north on long connecting roads off the Hume Highway, making for a fairly long shuttle.

Boaters may also continue downstream for about 3 miles (4.8 km) of more leisurely rapids followed by flatwater. At Bundarlo, the river canyon begins to open up about 9 miles (14.4 km) from Childowlah as it continues its course westward and eventually into the desert.

Upstream from Lake Burrinjuck are several runnable sections, including the scenic Red Rocks Gorge section along Canberra's southern outskirts. The run features the beautiful but difficult Red Rocks Chasm. Runnable flows are less dependable upstream of Burrinjuck Reservoir.

Season: October through April, when dam is releasing
Character: Downstream dam-regulated run

Murray River (New South Wales, Victoria) ➤

Beneath Australia's highest point, Mount Kosciusko, 7,300 feet (2,228 m), in the southern Snowy Mountains is the Murray Gates section of the Murray River. This is the upper reach of the continent's most important waterway which drains most of the west slope of the Great Dividing Range. It ultimately flows westward on its long trek into the dry country, marking along its way the boundary between Victoria and New South Wales. The good-natured rivalry across these waters is such that even its name is in dispute. Victorians commonly refer to the section above the confluence with the Swampy Plain River as the "Indi," a name scorned by boaters from New South Wales. Neither dispute that this is the most challenging whitewater run in southeastern Australia.

This is also the most rugged mountain country in mainland Australia. For the first 4½ miles (7.2 km) the river pours through a large, cliff-lined canyon with prominent rock formations forming the major Class 4 rapids. Scouting is difficult and eddies are scarce. Flows fluctuate widely with rains. When the Biggara Dam gauge is below 1.0 m the river is pool-and-drop; however, above 2.0 m the rapids come in quick succession, and boat-eating holes await the less fortunate. Major rapids include The Wall, Headbanger, South African Swim, and The Thing.

Put in at the bottom of a short dirt road off of Alpine Way south of Khancoban at Tom Groggin. The take-out is north of Khancoban, turning left on Biggara Road. At

GATES OF THE MURRAY, TOM GROGGIN TO COLEMANS BEND
Difficulty: Class 4
Length: 15 miles (24 km)

Season: Mid-September through April (except after long dry periods)
Character: Good whitewater in rugged mountain area

mile 4½ (7.2 km) where Hermit Creek enters on the left, the action tapers off, and the river eases to a scenic Class 2+ for the remaining 10½ miles (16.8 km). A trail (track) runs along the left bank of the river, rising far above the bank in the gorge. Most paddlers usually run the river in one day, but commercial groups sometimes camp at Surveyor's Creek on the left and then continue to the Indi Bridge or Bringenbrong Bridge the next day. Finding campsites or tracks in the dense foliage can be tricky.

The Murray is also a good place to watch wildlife. Sharp-eyed boaters stand a good chance of encountering platypus. These strange monotremes, seemingly assembled from nature's spare parts, are more likely to be seen at low flows. Wallabies are common here, too. These hopping marsupials look identical to kangaroo, except that they are smaller. In the summer, multitudes of cicadas provide a near-deafening rhythmic call.

Winner of the World Food Contest

New paddling food is a bonus for boating around the world. Don't miss the biltong (beef jerky) in South African or the ice cream in Italy. Stay away from the "completo" in Chile, unless you like a cold hot dog covered with a mound of yellowish mayonnaise. As a Yankee, I can survive on peanut butter. The rough Australian equivalent is Vegamite (or Marmite in New Zealand), a truly foul yeast extract that I only learned to appreciate on a cold day in Tasmania. Europeans rely on Nutella, a sticky sweet spread sure to make dentists wealthy.

However, one favorite recipe came from Australia. I arrived at Khancoban at near dark during a brief interlude in the storms that had swollen the Murray Gates to almost unrunnable levels. This area is as close as it gets to "mountain redneck" down under. I found the only possibility for food, a bar called the Pickled Parrot, filled with ill-tempered fishermen hunkered down from the storms. Although the kitchen was closing, the bartender sensed that I hadn't eaten since morning. She asked if the kitchen would stay open. In no position to push things, I ordered what had to be the easiest dish to prepare, a "hamburger with the lot." She paused, shook her head, and walked away. After a long wait and a few beers, the crowd didn't seem any friendlier. I was rewarded when the following appeared before me:

½ pound hamburger
cheese
lettuce
tomato
1 fried egg
3 strips bacon
1 slice pineapple (ring)
3 pickled beets
fried onions
sesame-seed bun
margarine (apparently for health reasons)

The meal stuck to my ribs like an anchor throughout the wild high-water paddle on the Murray Gates the next day.

—Dan Dunlap

Snowy River (Victoria) ➢

DEDDICK RIVER TO BUCHAN RIVER
Difficulty: Class 3
Length: 50 miles (80 km)

Season: October through
April (except after dry
periods)
Character: Multi-day,
wilderness

Australians are left to reconcile tradition in a land where Christmas falls at the beginning of summer. An Australian Christmas carol even has Santa hitching large, white kangaroos to his sleigh to deliver presents "in the raging sun."

While a white Christmas down under is an oxymoron, paddling clubs in Sydney and Melbourne like to go on multi-day wilderness trips on the Snowy in Snowy River National Park. The snow is long gone, but a little rain can help bring the flows up. The only thing white is the beach, but who cares? Boaters get by with fine campsites and impressive scenery, all in a remote, secluded setting. Although it is possible to extend this run both above and below the described run, the 50 miles (80 km) between the Deddick and Buchan rivers provide the best combination of camping, landscape, and warm whitewater.

While the Murray River flows to the south and west of Australia's highest peak, Mount Kosciusko, the Snowy begins to the northeast of Mount Kosciusko in New South Wales and flows south into Victoria to the coastline at Marlow. Other long runs are upstream but have flow and access problems. The put-in for this run is at McKillops Bridge on a road between Buchan–Jindabyne Road, and the Bonang Highway. The take-out is approximately 2½ miles (4 km) east of Buchan just above the junction of the Snowy and Buchan rivers.

From the Deddick River to the Buchan River, the Snowy passes through four different gorges. The first is a small gorge approximately 4 miles (6.4 km) below the put-in and provides some Class 2 and 3 whitewater. Good camping can be found along the sand beaches for approximately the next 5 miles (8 km). At this point, the river walls begin to narrow drastically as boaters enter the Tulloch Ard Gorge, the most dramatic section of the river. Class 3 rapids continue for the next 5 to 6 miles (8 to 9.6 km) and include A Frame at the beginning of the gorge where two large boulders, if exposed, appear to block the entire river, forcing boaters to the left. This is followed by a double-drop rapid

The Man from Snowy River

The former owner of the sheep station across from the put-in was Jack Reilly, believed to be the "Man from Snowy River" immortalized in Banjo Paterson's 1895 ballad. He is interred along the track above the left bank, a path used by celebrants on horseback every March for the Man from Snowy River Festival. Paterson, who also penned "Waltzing Matilda," wrote of an unheralded horseman's ride to capture a runaway renegade horse in a poem close to the heart of all Australians:

"I think we ought to let him come," he said.
"I want he'll be with us when he's wanted at the end.
For both his horse and he are mountain bred.
He hails from Snowy River, up by Kosciusko's side.
Where the hills are twice as steep and twice as rough:
Where a horse's hooves strike firelight from the flint stones every stride.
The man that holds his own is good enough.
And the Snowy River riders on the mountains make their home,
Where the river runs those giant hills between;
I have seen full many a horseman since
I first commenced to roam, but nowhere yet such a horseman have I seen."

known as George's Mistake (Class 3), followed by Washing Machine (Class 3) and Gentle Annie (Class 3+). Good camping can be found downstream of Gentle Annie on the right bank. Mountain Creek enters on the left at mile 28 (44.8 km) below Tulloch Ard Gorge.

After several miles of easier water, the river enters a third gorge that is also quite scenic and has some Class 3 action. Poor four-wheel-drive access can be found at Jackson's Crossing on the right between the third gorge and where Roger River enters on the left at mile 40 (64 km). The rest of the trip to Buchan is Class 1 and 2.

Much of the water from the Snowy River drainage is diverted by the massive Snowy Mountain hydroelectric scheme. The system includes seven power stations (two of which are underground), sixteen major dams, and more than 85 miles (136 km) of trans-mountain tunnels that divert much of the Snowy's water to the Murray River and the drier west slope.

◁ Mitchell River (Victoria)

TABBERABBERA TO GLENALADLE
BRIDGE
Difficulty: Class 3 (mostly
flatwater)
Length: 20 miles (32 km)

Season: October through
April (except after dry
periods)
Character: Wilderness run
with fluctuating flows

Located a 45-minute drive northwest of Bairnsdale, the Mitchell River National Park covers an area of about 47 square miles (122 sq. km) along the banks and towering red cliffs of the Mitchell River. Upstream of this run the river goes by its aboriginal name, Wonnangaha.

The first recorded descent of the Mitchell River was by explorer Alfred Howitt who explored this section in an aboriginal bark canoe accompanied by natives in 1825. What he saw is little changed today. The river flows through a broad rainforest valley with numerous campsites, easy access, and several side hikes. A walking track named for the river follows alongside for about 10 miles (16 km) from Angus Veil to the Den of Nargun. The forest includes a mix of varieties of eucalyptus and ferns. Wallabies and koalas dwell here, as does the laughing kookaburra bird.

Put in at Tabberabbera near the mouth of the Wentworth River on the left. Although much of the Mitchell is flatwater, especially at low flows, it does have enough rapids to make the float interesting. The first rapid, Slalom (Class 3), is at the site of what was to be the Howitt Dam, part of a defunct irrigation hydroscheme. The most dramatic and spectacular rapid is Amphitheater (Class 3+), which sits under a spectacular 90-foot-high (28 m) silt-stone cliff. The third major rapid is at the Den of Nargun, beneath a smaller cliff. Farther down on the left is an old stone weir completed in 1893 despite recurrent flooding problems affecting its foundations. The weir was never operated and now lies in ruins. The final rapid, appropriately called Final Fling, is just above the take-out at the first bridge after the canyon opens up.

A short side hike to the Den of Nargun is worthwhile. This is the site of an aboriginal legend since adapted to an Aussie child's tale. Here an enchanted waterfall veils a den filled with fragile stalactites. The story tells of a creature of stone called the "nargun" who preys upon those who stray too close to the den. The den is best observed from a safe distance.

Thomson River (Victoria) ➢

The Thomson has fine intermediate whitewater, good scenery, and surprising solitude only two hours from Melbourne. The river drains the Gippsland hills, and the run described here is below the Thomson Dam, an irrigation project that provides year-round minimum flows of approximately 500 cfs (14 cumecs). After heavy rains, flows from Deep Creek, on the left about a third of the way down, and other side creeks provide bigger water.

The run from Bruntons Bridge to Cowwarr Weir is sometimes broken into two days. Although camping is scarce in the upper reaches, two fine beach campgrounds on the left at mile 7 (11.2 km) provide obvious layover spots. The rapids in this stretch are classic pool-and-drop and are consistent throughout the length of the river, although the last four rapids near the end are much larger than those upstream. Long pools announce the bigger drops, including Triple Stage, marked by a small island before the first of three drops, and Boulder, a straightforward drop near the end. A gauging station on river left marks the end of the whitewater and the beginning of a 1½-mile (2.4 km) paddle to the take-out.

Although the area has a long history of mining and agricultural demands, this run is relatively untouched. Only one or two tracks (trails) on the right lead out of the canyon, and they are almost impossible to find with the imposing vegetation—as eucalyptus, ferns, and blackberry bushes grow down to the riverbed. Parrots, scarlet rosellas, and white cockatoos are common. Iguanas, known locally as water dragons, are frequently seen basking along the banks, some up to 3 feet (1 m) long.

To reach the take-out, turn north just east of Toongabbie toward Heyfield. Follow this road about 20 miles (32 km), then turn left at the sign to Cowwarr Weir. The reservoir keeper requests that boaters check in. To reach the put-in, take the right turn when exiting Cowwarr Weir, following the signs to Erica; turn right to Bruntons Bridge.

An additional Class 2 run of 6 miles (9.6 km) from just below the dam to either Coopers Bridge or Bruntons Bridge is also possible and is popular with leisurely floaters.

Bruntons Bridge was built in 1888 as part of the main supply line to the nearby ghost town of Walhalla. For those interested in abandoned mining towns, the bridge and Walhalla itself are worth the time to take a look.

BRUNTONS BRIDGE TO COWWARR WEIR
Difficulty: Class 3
Length: 18 miles (28.8 km)

Season: October through April
Character: Scenic near-wilderness canyon, dam-release

Tasmania

In contrast to the mainland, Tasmania's landscape, particularly in the west and southwest, is one of rugged, glacier-carved mountains and temperate rainforest. The island gets plenty of rain from the Indian Ocean but the weather is cooler and more severe than on the mainland. The aboriginal Tasmanians traveled to and from the continent on foot until rising ocean levels created an island more than 10,000 years ago. The aborigines wore only grease and charcoal (something to think about during a cold storm on the Franklin River). With the coming of white settlers, the few remaining aborigines were banished to outlying areas. Today, most Tasmanians still consider themselves cut from a different cloth from those of the "north island," as they call the mainland.

Lyell Highway Bridge on the
Collingwood River to
Gordon River confluence

Difficulty: Class 5p
Length: 50 miles (80 km)
on the Franklin, plus 20
miles (32 km) on the
Gordon River and
another 25 miles (40 km)
on the bay to Strahan

Season: October through
April (except after
extended dry periods; be
prepared for cold
weather and rain during
any season)
Character: Difficult, multi-
day trip with widely
fluctuating water levels

◁ Franklin River

Virtually untouched by humans, the Franklin River takes a wild and striking course, beginning in central Tasmania's Cheyne Range and steadily building until it becomes a major river in its lower reaches before reaching the Indian Ocean. Southwestern Tasmania, called Transylvania until 1830, is perhaps the most rugged and inaccessible pocket on the island. An expedition on the Franklin is one of the only ways to enjoy the pristine beauty of this corridor; it is one of the world's great trips. Rescued from dam proposals in a well-publicized preservation campaign in the 1980s, the free-flowing Franklin stands as a globally recognized monument to river conservation.

The political battle to preserve the Franklin was fought between those led by Dr. Bob Brown, a river-running pioneer on the Franklin, and a pro-development government, whose leader publicly referred to the Franklin as a "leech-filled ditch." Running as a Green Independent, Brown and his allies controlled the balance of power in the parliament in 1989 and toppled the pro-development government. Unlike the Gordon River, the beauty of which was largely flooded by the Scott's Peak Dam, the Franklin and its entire watershed are now protected by the Franklin, Lower Gordon Wild Rivers National Park.

This beauty was little comfort to the area's first explorers, who were more worried about their escape from Maquarie Harbor, one of Australia's most inhumane prisons. These included James Goodwin and Ton Connely, who paddled a Huon pine canoe up the Gordon and to the lower reaches of the Franklin in 1828. Like their fellow prisoners, they were brought to the island primarily to harvest and mill the ancient Huon pine, a native tree that lives up to two thousand years. Logging felled more than 90 percent of the Franklin's Huon pines from 1900 to 1950.

Official European exploration began in 1840, when surveyor James Calder came upon the river and named it for Tasmania's governor, John Franklin. Two years later, Calder led an expedition with the governor and his wife, Lady Jane Franklin, to the lower reaches of the river where the Jane River now bears her name.

Modern river-running exploration dates to the 1950s when Henry Crocker and John Dean successfully descended the river in 1958 after two failed attempts. Others soon began running the daunting rapids in small, gear-laden rafts.

Today, running the Franklin is still a challenge. Paddlers must be prepared to wrestle with nature. Weather fronts change quickly, and rainstorms and cold weather are common. River levels can fluctuate up to 30 feet (9 m) overnight. Light, self-bailing paddle boats are recommended for their ability to handle the tough whitewater, carry gear, and facilitate getting around several difficult rapids in the upper half of the river, which are almost always portaged. Self-contained kayak trips are also possible and make portages easier and faster than the times mentioned here. The overall gradient is 20 fpm (3.9 mpk) and 50 fpm (9.7 mpk) in the Great Ravine. Although highway access to the put-in is easy, taking out usually requires ferry service to Straugh.

The rewards of running the Franklin are abundant. The air in Tasmania is the cleanest in the world, as monitored by the U.N. Station in nearby Cape Grim in the 1980s. Tannins from button grass upstream turn the water the color of a forgotten cola drink diluted with melted ice, giving the river an unforgettable appearance. Huge granite and shale formations tower above the river, changing to limestones in the lower reaches. Side-stream waterfalls are abundant, including the spectacular Blush Rock Falls. Stands of ancient Huon pines were spared, as most of the river corridor was inaccessible to loggers; they still dominate the lush vegetation of ferns and tea plants. Side hikes include a vigorous day hike to Frenchman's Cap. Sharp-eyed boaters may spot platypus, cormorants, cockatoos, rosellas, martins, ground parrots, and even glowworms. Leeches lurk on tea plants waiting for the chance to attach to something warm-blooded.

Put in on the bridge over the Collingwood River on the Lyell Highway. Flows are usually skimpy for the first 3 miles (4.8 km) on the Collingwood, and rocks and fallen trees can make the going here slow.

The Franklin joins on the left at mile 3 (4.8 km). Downstream on the right is Angel Rain Cavern where a dramatic overhang provides a cozy campground. Downstream of here at about mile 5½ (8.8 km) is Log Jam where an enormous Huon pine blocks the entire river. This is a mandatory portage except at very high flows when some boaters take a risky route over the top. The Loddon River joins from the left at mile 6 (9.6 km). The first big rapid is Nasty Notch where a midstream boulder creates an ugly keeper, often portaged.

At about mile 12½ (20 km), a series of Class 3 rapids lead to Descension Gorge, a calm-water float between spectacular sheer walls, just upstream of Irenabyss, a large pool whose name means "Chasm of Peace" in Greek. This was the proposed site of the first dam. Good camping can be found here, along with the trailhead to Frenchman's Cap. From this point the river circles Frenchman's Cap counterclockwise in a long, peaceful reach featuring Blush Rock Falls, visible on the right.

Haunted Port Arthur

Tasmania is a beautiful and an eerie place. Its aborigines got by for thousands of years, somehow wearing only grease and charcoal. European settlers, who called the island Transylvania, didn't appreciate the aborigines. After years of slaughter and cruelty the settlers declared martial law in 1828 and formed a "Black Line," a human chain that moved for weeks throughout the island to flush out every remaining native. The total aboriginal population was ultimately reduced to fewer than 200.

Tasmania's first river explorers were not necessarily natives. Some were inmates escaping Tasmania's prisons, the largest and cruelest in the British Empire. Some chose almost certain death ascending the lower reaches of the Franklin River over brutal incarceration and frequent whipping at places such as Port Arthur. If there is a haunted pocket in the world, it is Port Arthur. The empty buildings seem filled with the suffering of the ghosts of the convicts, most of whom were guilty only of petty crimes.

After spending a week running the Franklin River, I drove to Port Arthur. I spent some time in the tiny Broad Arrow coffee shop, where the staff there fed me and did their best to make me feel at home. Photos on the wall with strange, unexplained shapes purport to show the presence of ghosts in the nearby buildings. Such nice people, I thought, living in such a strange place.

Five months later I read the bad news. A deranged Australian, Martin Bryant, had entered the coffee shop and began shooting workers and tourists systematically. Many of the workers I had met were doubtlessly among the first of thirty-five victims in what became the worst mass murder in Australian history.

—Dan Dunlap

On completing the half circle around Frenchman's Cap, the river turns south toward the Great Ravine, where the biggest rapids are found. The first is Churn, with multiple drops up to 10 feet (3 m) through a gauntlet of house-sized boulders. Portage over a high trail on the left, or at low flows over rocks on the right. Less than a mile (1.6 km) downstream is Coruscades, a less severe but somewhat longer version of Churn, also usually portaged on the left. Boaters often relaunch partway down the rapid. A good campsite is adjacent to the portage route. Carefully assess river levels here in preparation for Thunderush, where easy entrance rapids lead directly to a 12-foot (4 m) waterfall followed by a gauntlet of rocks and waves. There is an easy portage route on the left at low to moderate flows. At higher flows the only alternative is to catch a small eddy upstream on the right and begin an exhausting, rope-assisted portage up and over the cliff, putting in below the rapid and only a stone's throw from where you started. The whole process takes about six hours with rafts and gear. Some elect to camp one or more days upstream waiting for water levels to drop.

A short float below Thunderush is Cauldron, a witch's concoction of undercut rocks, sieves, and blocked routes. A roped walkway marks the beginning of a three-hour portage with gear-laden rafts on the left. The alternative at low to moderate flows is a blood-pressure-elevating portage on the right over a huge flat boulder that is inundated

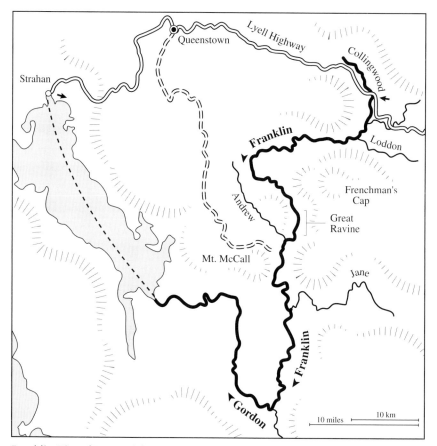

Franklin River (Tasmania)

at higher flows. The rock is nearly completely undercut, and much of the river flows under it. Boaters must be careful to catch an eddy at the upstream edge and carry across. The real excitement begins on lowering the boats to relaunch into the foaming torrent below, sometimes called the Wild Thing. A sieve on the left of the rock took the life of a river guide in 1982, a tragedy that inspired native Tasmanian Richard Flanagan's fine novel *Death of a River Guide*. Miss the eddy above the rock, and you will be swept into the same sieve.

At about mile 28 (44.8 km) the Andrews River enters on the right and downstream about a mile is Mount McCall Sway Bridge, the site of the second proposed dam. A near-vertical 20-minute rope-assisted climb on the right leads to an emergency road access.

Downstream of here the river begins to open up, and at about mile 37 (59.2 km) the Jane River enters on the left. It is worth the time to stop and explore Kutikina Cave at about mile 42 (67.2 km). This section of the Franklin features impressive limestone formations.

At about mile 46 (73.6 km) is Big Fall, a 6-foot (1.8 m) drop with a deceptively powerful and potentially dangerous hydraulic. Below this point the river is usually navigable by motorboat. At about mile 50 (80 km) the Gordon River enters. This is the site of the third proposed dam.

From here, it is 20 miles (32 km) on the Gordon River and then another 25 miles (40 km) across the bay to Strahan and civilization. Make arrangements in advance for ferry service, possibly from Butler Island.

South Esk River ➤

Though they are neighbors on the same island, it is unlikely two runs in this book have less in common than the Franklin River and the Cataract Gorge section of the South Esk. The South Esk is short and dam-controlled; the Franklin is long and free-flowing. Cataract Gorge is located in the middle of Launceston, Tasmania's second largest city, in an urban park filled with imported trees; the Franklin is in the middle of a mostly impassable wilderness of native forests. Scouting on the Esk is a self-guided stroll over bridges and along park paths with the option of an elevated view from a chairlift; the Franklin has only a few tough trails, and the portages are the stuff of legend. The Esk can easily be run twice a day; for most, the Franklin is run once in a lifetime. The Esk run is a symbol of cooperation between river runners and hydroelectric interests; the Franklin is a monument to their irreconcilable differences.

Still, the two runs have one thing in common. Neither is for the faint of heart. Scouting the Gorge from the various pathways and lookouts is both a pleasure and a necessity. There are two low overhead dams, many undercut rocks, and a series of boulder mazes. The gradient is up to 100 fpm (19.3 mpk). The difficulty varies greatly with water levels, and at high levels it can be extremely dangerous.

Calling ahead to confirm recreational releases is a good idea. A local rafting company pays for the releases, and availability of commercial rafting service and flows depends on the company. Recently, one operator left, but a new operator planned to take over the run. In addition to releases, the downwash of great rains on the east coast and western tiers can last for months and usually provides several days' warning of really big whitewater action.

CATARACT GORGE, TREVALLYN
DAM TO TAMAR RIVER
Difficulty: Class 4+
Length: 3 miles (4.8 km)

Season: November through April, with dam-releases and natural flow over much of the winter months
Character: Dam-controlled, tight canyon adjacent to a city

Put in right below the Trevallyn Dam. A few nice Class 3 rapids provide a good warm-up at the top. The difficult action begins above Duck Reach, just below a concrete weir with a nasty diagonal stopper. Above Duck Reach is a ledge drop followed by a difficult undercut route and more Class 4 rapids. The Rooster Tail marks the beginning of another long, difficult boulder garden below the old Duck Reach power station; a chicken route or portage on the right is usually available. The river then divides around a large island. The high-water route to the left leads to a difficult rock garden, but this is easier than the route on the right. Top Corner is next and can be scouted upstream from the suspension bridge. Scout carefully and beware of the stopper at the concrete weir near the bottom. The river then pauses in the lower of two basins, where one may take out in the park. The chairlift crosses the river at the lower basin and the river flows into Final Fling (Class 4). It is an easy paddle to the take-out just downstream of the Kings Bridge in the center of Launceston. From here the South Esk joins the Tamar River, a wide tidal river that meanders north to the ocean.

The Cataract Gorge itself is a splendid urban park in a class with the Capilano in Vancouver as among the most scenic urban whitewater areas to be found. The park is populated by peacocks and wallabies and furnished with imported redwood, maple, spruce, and fern trees, ornate multicolored pavilions, and Victorian gardens. The chairlift is claimed to be the world's longest single-span lift. Duck Reach Powerhouse, the remains of which can be seen midway on the run, was the first hydroelectric project as well as the first municipally funded project of any significance on the Australian continent.

New Zealand

*I*solation and tectonic uplift have combined to form the unique natural playground of New Zealand. Along with Australia, India, Arabia, and South America, what is now New Zealand journeyed across the Earth's surface as part of the supercontinent Gondwana. Some 70 million years ago it separated and eventually drifted to its present position in the Pacific, where it sits alone atop the subduction zone of the Indo-Australian and Australian plates. The Taupo Volcanic Zone on the North Island and the Southern Alpine Fault on the South Island evidence the volatility of this region, and earthquake slides and faults along the rivers form some of the rapids. The mountains of the South Island are more substantial, formed by a hard rock core. The North Island mountains are formed of softer rock and are more prone to erosion.

The two islands of New Zealand hold incredible geographical, geological, and climatic diversity for a combined area only the size of Colorado. Nearly all the rivers in the north are rain fed. The extreme south of the South Island is a coastline rich in fjords and mountains covered in glacial ice, giving birth to some of the world's best whitewater rivers.

Throughout the islands, isolation and the lack of large predators resulted in unique flora and fauna. Three-quarters of the flowering plants are unique to the islands. The native birdlife is especially diverse. New Zealand was recently the home of the colossal moa, hunted to extinction with the coming of early man. Other indigenous birds remain, including the mischievous kea and the disheveled, nocturnal kiwi, a name now adopted by the locals. The only native mammals are bats.

Aside from the remnants of mining from the gold rush era and some overzealous hydro projects, the rivers are pristine, running through lightly developed country, and are blessed with rains, snowmelt, and glacier flows.

Before Europeans came to New Zealand, the islands were home of the Maori, a Polynesian people whose legacy was marked with a rich folklore, tradition, and battles among themselves as well as with the European invaders. Most rivers and geological features still bear names from Maori folklore, a source of both interest and confusion to outsiders.

New Zealand looks to tourism as its second most important industry after agriculture. Blessed with rugged terrain and dramatic scenery, the recreation industry generates income while giving impetus to preserve much of the country's natural beauty.

Although generally reserved, the Kiwis are known for taking risks in recreational sports and encouraging others to do the same. Perhaps because of limited liability and a national medical system that foots the bill, invention of adventure sports is a national industry. This is the birthplace of jet-boating and bungee jumping, and a hotbed of such undertakings as BASE jumping, abseiling, spelunking, and cave tubing. Newspapers here sometimes speak of a "right to adventure."

The attitude of "pushing the envelope" thrives in the boating community. New Zealand's paddlers have taken on the plethora of tough kayaking runs, and some of the toughest rivers are run by commercial rafting companies. Where else would paying customers be given a chance to run a 20-foot (6 m) waterfall? In the words of Kiwi writer/river runner Graham Charles, if Kiwis aren't pushing the envelope, they're "licking the stamps."

This attitude has caused problems as well. A spate of incidents involving three drownings and one serious injury on the Shotover River in 1994 and 1995 generated criticism of the multi-million-dollar Queenstown rafting industry. Whether these incidents were preventable is debatable, but the result was a temporary drop in commercial patronage and a reexamination of safety measures. Since then new owners have taken over the major companies in the area, and the rafting industry has come under regulation. The Maritime Safety Authority of New Zealand has established strict safety regulations for commercial rafting and ensures that customers are well-informed.

North Island

DOWNSTREAM OF MOTU
   FALLS TO COAST HIGHWAY
   (ROUTE 35)
Difficulty: Class 4–
Length: 55 miles (88 km)

Season: September
   through May
Character: Rugged
   wilderness, good
   camping, highly
   fluctuating flow

◁ Motu River

Located in the rugged wilderness area in the northeast corner of the North Island, the Motu is one of New Zealand's wildest rivers. Motu means "cut off" or "isolated" in the Maori tongue, and the river has changed very little with the coming of the Europeans. This is a remote river in rugged terrain, and those running the river will find help hard to come by. Thick virgin forests of silver beech, ferns, and native palm come down to river's edge and make hiking out unrealistic.

The Motu was first paddled by four local lads in a wooden boat in 1919. Their planned three-day adventure turned into a ten-day struggle with rapids, tough terrain, and near starvation. The river remains much the same today. In the 1970s it was saved from a hydroelectric project and was designated as New Zealand's first wild and scenic river. The free-flowing Motu is known as the multi-day paddling classic of the North Island.

Christmas Down Under

A whisper of breeze had picked up off the ocean, and the temperature was at last slipping out of the 80s, where it had been all day. There was muffled surf, and laughter coming from a nearby barbecue. The scene was a perfectly laid-back summer evening—was until Santa Claus roared into the midst of the barbecuers on a reindeerless Honda three-wheeler. As he came to a stop, kids materialized from nowhere and were upon him like a swarm of ants on a grasshopper.

It's a shame, but even in New Zealand, Christmas has become the same manufactured madness that it has in the States, only that in New Zealand the holiday comes in summer, which makes the occasion all the more demented.

The three-wheeling Santa attempted a "Ho-ho-ho," but with a winter suit on, Santa's famous quote sounded more like the mournful cries of a person locked in a sauna.

"Let's forget Christmas," my companion, Carol Haslett, said.

The next morning we were on the way to do the Motu River.

—Whit Deschner

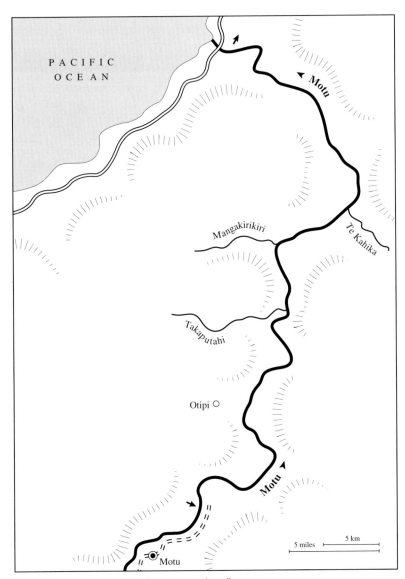

Motu River (North Island, New Zealand)

Although the flow is modest near the put-in, the volume grows by the time it completes its journey through the Raukumara range. The mountains don't catch much snow, so big rains can change water levels dramatically and flash floods have trapped boaters in the canyon for days. Plenty of good campsites are available, except in the gorges; however, they are rarely obvious and finding them can be a trick.

The put-in is downstream of Motu Falls. The road follows the river here, allowing several choices. The river soon leaves all signs of civilization, and Waitangarua Stream then enters on the right. At about mile 18 (28.8 km) is the Upper Gorge, just upstream of Otipi where there is poor road access. When flows are low, putting in downstream is an option. The most common downstream put-in is at the four-wheel-drive access at Otipi at about mile 20 (32 km).

The Upper Gorge is long with few good campsites, so camping upstream (around Kirk's Clearing) or downstream (around Takaputahi River) is recommended. The rapids here are short and technical, and not as challenging as those in the Lower Gorge. They include Bullivant's Cascade and Mother Slot, both long, narrow cataracts. Keep an eye out for log hazards, especially at Mother Slot.

Downstream of Otipi is Te Paku Gorge and then the Lower Gorge. The Te Paku Gorge is a short stretch with little whitewater, located upstream of where Mangakirikiri Stream enters on the left. The Lower Gorge is 3 miles (4. 8 km) long from Karamu Stream to Te Kahika Stream, with some big, long rapids including The Hump, Double Staircase, and Helicopter. Near the Te Kahika Stream confluence on the right is a popular campsite. Wild goats may be seen in the cliffs along the lower reaches. The last 18 miles (28.8 km) of easy water is sometimes shared with jet boats.

◄ Wairoa River

Bridge below McLaren Falls and Dam to power station (SH29)
Difficulty: Class 5–
Length: 3 miles (4.8 km)

Season: September through May
Character: Dam-controlled, low-volume, steep

The mere fact that this steep, technical stretch of river is a popular commercial run typifies a lot of stereotypes about New Zealand river running. While the run is only 3 miles (4.8 km) long, it drops at about 80 fpm (15.4 mpk) and many of the drops lack a clear upstream view. Lack of familiarity with the drops can easily be overcome by running the river more than once a day. The steepest drops include Mother's Nightmare, Double Trouble, Waterfall, and Roller Coaster. Waterfall comes complete with a rope to assist swimmers to climb to safety from the hydraulic. Roller Coaster has a rope-assisted scout and requires a tricky move to reach the portage route. A sneak route is also available.

The Wairoa meanders from the Kaimai Range. There are scheduled releases of around 400 cfs (11 cumecs) from 10 A.M. to 4 P.M. for about twenty-six days a year, a schedule agreed to in order to appease opposition to the upstream dam. Heavy rains still occasionally trigger big-water flows. The popularity of the Wairoa is partly due to the fact that it's only a two-hour drive from Auckland. Before the dam was built and diverted much of the flow to Auckland, the Wairoa enjoyed notoriety as the most popular commercial run in New Zealand.

Downstream the river meets the ocean near the city of Tauranga.

◄ Kaituna River

Kaituna River Bridge to just above Trout Pool Falls
Difficulty: Class 5
Length: Less than 1 mile (1.6 km)

Season: September through May
Character: Short waterfall run in deep gorge

The Okere Falls run on the Kaituna is the latest rage for New Zealand's adrenaline junkies. Once the exclusive domain of daredevil kayakers, things changed dramatically here in 1992 when the thought of sending rafts filled with paying customers down this waterfall-laden run finally was too tempting for outfitters to resist. This "new" discovery of the '90s is now the most popular run on the North Island, taking much of the usage of the nearby Rangitaiki River (see below). Rarely is the thrill of adventure sports better depicted than in the photos of rafting customers plunging over 20-foot (6 m) Okere Falls.

The principal outlet of Lake Rotorua, the Kaituna passes downstream through Lake Rotoiti. The outflow of Lake Rotoiti is controlled by a dam which regulates flows for this run. The Rotorua area is popular with tourists. This is a land of geysers and is the historical center of New Zealand's Maori culture.

Kaituna Falls, Kaituna River, New Zealand. *(© Dave Allardice/Ultimate Descents)*

The put-in is below the Kaituna River Bridge in a lush canyon. A slalom course is set up here. Paddling to the left of the remains of a cement power plant leads boaters to Okere Falls and a decent hydraulic in the pool below. Tutea's Falls follows and leads to a series of drops over Hinemoa's Steps where kayakers will find plenty of great play action, especially near the take-out. Nearly all take out before Trout Pool Falls, a dangerous rapid with a total vertical drop of about 20 feet (6 m), probably best left to the fish for which it is named.

About 8 miles (12.8 km) upstream of Murupara to about 2 miles (3.2 km) upstream of Murupara
Difficulty: Class 3+$_4$
Length: 6 miles (9.6 km)

Season: September though May
Character: Popular, heavily forested

◁ Rangitaiki River

Located southeast of the major tourist center of Rotorua, the Rangitaiki was, until recently, the most popular river trip on the North Island. The newly promoted run on the Okere Falls section of the Kaituna, described above, has taken the honors as the prime tourist run in the Rotorua area.

The upper dam-controlled run cuts through New Zealand's largest pine plantation forest. Ferns and pampas grass line the banks. The river drains the Ahimanawa range with a relatively constant gradient of about 50 fpm (9.7 mpk) on the edge of the Kaingaroa Plateau. This is a good place to learn to paddle or to try your hand at the nearby slalom course. Floating rocks made of pumice (aerated lava) sometimes break off upstream pumice fields and join boaters in the river. Jeff's Joy (Class 4), the biggest rapid on the run, is near the beginning. Just upstream of Jeff's Joy is Fantail Falls, another rapid that causes a lot of trouble. The rest is a fairly constant Class 2 and 3. The put-in and take-out are hard to find, so it's best to inquire locally at Murupara.

Downstream of Murupara the river is not well suited for river running, but downstream of Aniwhenua Falls is a Class 2 run of about 5 miles (8 km) that is popular with novices. The river meets the ocean at the Bay of Plenty.

Poutu Intake to Blue Pool
Difficulty: Class 3+
Length: 8 miles (12.8 km)

Season: September through May
Character: Dam-controlled, many rapids, volcanic area

◁ Tongariro River

This is a scenic, isolated run draining the volcanoes and glaciers of the North Island. Its headwaters are on Mount Ruapehu, at 9,166 feet (2,797 m) the highest peak on the North Island. Mount Ruapehu most recently erupted in 1995 and 1996. The eruptions washed much ash down the river to Lake Taupo and still give the river a gray-green tinge in very high water, but did not alter the rapids much. The Tongariro is dam-controlled, with continuous whitewater throughout its length as it flows north to Lake Taupo near Turangi.

This run is just east of Route 1, and volcanoes Ngauruhoe and Tongariro can be seen from the river looking west. Some sixty-five rapids are spread along this run; some say there are even more if you can keep count. The gradient is a relatively steady 80 fpm (15.4 mpk). Releases are fairly constant at 560 cfs (16 cumecs), and the rapids are mostly shallow boulder gardens at these flows, but rains bring out the best in this run.

The put-in is off of Access Road 10 (Kaimanawa Road) just downstream of where the upstream diversions reenter the river below Waikaro Falls. Take out at Blue Pool or continue down to Red Hut Bridge.

Above the Waikaro Falls is an old run that has been dewatered due to diversions. Farther upstream are two similar rain-driven runs off Access Roads 13 (Tree Trunk Gorge Road) and 14 (Rangipo Dam). When running either of these sections, it is imperative that you scout the take-out in advance and not paddle past it. Both runs end just above unrunnable and unsurvivable cataracts, and, as one Kiwi lamented, "then you would die and that would be sad."

Boaters here have a good chance of spotting the blue duck of Whio, an endangered native bird that favors pristine mountain streams. If fishing is your thing, the area is famous for rainbow and brown trout. They were originally brought to New Zealand from the United States and Europe in the early 1900s and thrived in the ideal habitat.

If you're in the Taupo area, it's worth joining the camera-clicking crowds at Huka Falls on the Waikato River. Few river runners can look at this big-water drop and not imagine paddling down the rock-lined entrance chute and over the lip into the massive pool below. Huka has been run many times in kayaks on the far left and once, unsuccessfully (though not fatally), by raft. This doesn't mean you should try. It has taken the life of at least one kayaker and may be illegal. A better choice is downstream at Nagaawapurua, where the Fulljames Front Wave makes for what may be the most popular surf spot on any river in New Zealand.

Ngaruroro River ➢

Ngaruroro means the "forgotten" river in the language of the Maoris. For those looking for rugged wilderness, the Ngaruroro is one of the best. This rain-fed run drains the 6,000-foot (1,830 m) Kaweka mountains between the Mohaka and Rangitikei rivers. It flows eastward and eventually empties into Hawke Bay near Napier.

The upper run requires a fly-in to an airstrip at Boyd Hut near the headwaters. Lower water may involve putting in downstream. The river is rarely large enough for most rafts; inflatable kayaks and small rafts are usually used. Trips last from two to five days, with great scenery and relatively easy whitewater. The lower gorge run from Kuripapango and the Napier–Taihape Road to Whanawhana Road and Otaumuri Stream has challenging whitewater set in wild and remote country. Although kayaks can hurry through in a day, most take their time and enjoy the good camping along the way. The water quality is outstanding, with huge trout sometimes visible in the deep, clear pools.

On the lower gorge run, after a relatively mild stretch, the Ngaruroro enters a 5-mile-long (8 km) gorge where most of the big pool-and-drop action is. The toughest rapid is a tight squeeze and drop called the Barricade near the bottom. After leaving the gorge, the whitewater eases again. About two-thirds of the way down, the Taruarau River enters on the right. The last 5 miles (8 km) before Otaumuri Stream enters on the left is open, flat, and braided. Take out where Whanawhana Road and Otaumuri Stream meet. Below here is a long, easy drift down to the next good access at the Fernhill Bridge.

Another good alternative to the Ngaruroro is the Mohaka River, to the north. The best whitewater (Class 4+) is the 9-mile (14.4 km) section from Te Hoe Station to Willow Flat, featuring some unusual geology and good rapids in a limestone canyon. Farther upstream between Mangatanguru Stream and McVickers (near the Taupo-Napier highway bridge) is a lovely, 28-mile (44.8 km), Class 3 wilderness run featuring Mangatainoka Hot Springs.

Boyd Hut to Kuripapango
(upper run)
Difficulty: Class 2+
Length: 30 miles (48 km)

Kuripapango to Otaumuri
Stream (lower gorge run)
Difficulty: Class 4–
Length: 24 miles (38.4 km)

Season: September
through May
Character: Isolated,
wilderness run

Rangitikei River ➢

The headwaters of the Rangitikei River are in the 5,000- to 6,000-foot (1,525 to 1,830 m) Kaimanawa Mountains near the middle of the North Island. The river courses southward, carving through gorges and providing great scenery and a range of rapids and playspots for paddlers of various abilities. Because of the large drainage, big rains can cause flows to surge wildly.

The first stretch, from the Springvale bridge, is an easy 8 miles (12.8 km) down to the Mangaohane bridge. The popular whitewater gorge section is from Mangaohane bridge to east of Pukeokahu, where there is access and good facilities for a fee at River Valley Lodge. The gradient is about 60 fpm (11.6 mpk), with the steepest stretch and the best rapids during the last half of the whitewater gorge run, including The Gates, Max's Drop, Fulcrum, and Foamy. The river downstream from this run remains in a very

Springvale bridge to
Mangaohane bridge
Difficulty: Class 2
Length: 8 miles (12.8 km)

Mangaohane bridge to east
of Pukeokahu (whitewater
gorge section)
Difficulty: Class 4+
Length: 8 miles (12.8 km)

(continued on following page)

EAST OF PUKEOKAHU TO TARATA
(MOKAI ROAD BRIDGE)
(SCENIC GORGE SECTION)
Difficulty: Class 2+
Length: 9 miles (14.4 km)

TARATA (MOKAI ROAD BRIDGE)
TO OMATANE
Difficulty: Class 2
Length: 7 miles (11.2 km)

OMATANE TO MANGAWEKA
Difficulty: Class 2–
Length: 15 miles (24 km)

Season: September
through May (flows year-
round)
Character: Many options,
large river by end

scenic gorge with plenty of side falls, sheer sandstone cliffs, and easier rapids. The take-out for this (third) section is at Tarata upstream of the Mokai Road bridge.

Downstream there is a type of additional river access at Mokai Road bridge. The access is via a specially designed lift associated with the "High Time" bungee site and operated by a local outfitter. It's another 7 miles (11.2 km) downstream from Tarata to access at Omatane. The river opens up here, and it's a further 15 miles (24 km) down to Mangaweka. Access is also possible via the Toe Toe Road near Utiku and the confluence with the Hautapu River that enters on the right; from here to Mangaweka it is 10 miles (16 km), with civilization never far away. Jet boats roam this last section.

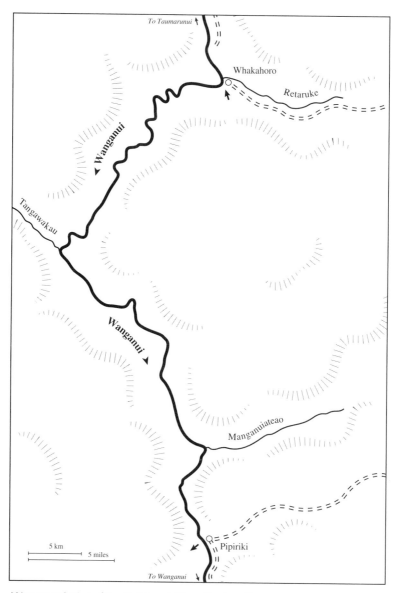

Wanganui River (North Island, New Zealand)

Upstream on the Rangitikei is yet another remote six-day reach called the Headwaters section, requiring a helicopter fly-in from Tiahape to the put-in near the Mangamaire River confluence. The take-out is at the Springvale bridge (on the Napier–Taihape Road), which is also the put-in for the first featured run. A small drainage area limits the Headwaters section to small rafts and kayaks only.

In the next drainage south of the Rangitikei is the Mangahao River, which draws hordes of boaters to its Class 4 rapids two days a year for the spring and fall dam-releases. If you're around for the release, it's one of the best runs on the North Island.

Wanganui River ➢

The Wanganui is a classic multi-day wilderness trip, considered by some to be among the best canoe trips in the world. It has a large drainage area on the western part of the North Island and runs through rugged mountain country, although the mountains only reach to around 2,500 feet (763 m). The run is historical as well as scenic, with pre-European artifacts common. This river has its own subculture, complete with books and newsletters. Although the scenery is excellent, the water is often muddy.

The put-in is where the Retaruke River enters the Wanganui on the left, although boaters can add about 20 miles (32 km) by putting in upstream at the Te Maire Bridge. The Manganuiateao River confluence on the left marks the beginning of an 8-mile (12.8 km) gorge. The best rapids are near the end, although they are only Class 2. Although the volume is big, it's an easy float downstream.

The river can be run both upstream and downstream from the featured stretch, but boaters will find fewer rapids. The total distance from Taumarunui to Wanganui is 140 miles (224 km).

WHAKAHORO TO PIPIRIKI
Difficulty: Class 2–
Length: 54 miles (86.4 km)

Season: September through May
Character: Mild, big-volume, away from civilization

South Island

Shotover River ➢

Affectionately called the "Shotty" by the locals, the Shotover is one of New Zealand's most dramatic rivers and the most heavily used on the South Island. It pours through a deep bedrock canyon filled with memories of the gold rush of the 1860s, when the river corridor was considered one of the richest in the world. The gorge is now sometimes called the Grand Canyon of New Zealand. The river features tough rapids, a run through a narrow mining tunnel, and a legendary shuttle road that might be considered the crux of the run by some. What more could you ask for? Apparently not much. The Shotover receives more commercial use than any other river in New Zealand.

Upstream of the described runs is a heavily braided section called The Branches. By the time the river reaches Strohles Flat, about 4 miles (6.4 km) farther downstream, and the put-in for the first of the featured runs, the riverbed narrows. Sandy Bluff is about a mile (1.6 km) downstream from Strohles Flat. It's a relatively easy 7-mile (11.2 km) run down to Skippers Bridge, the next access, as the river flows through a deep wilderness canyon.

STROHLES FLAT TO SKIPPERS BRIDGE (UPPER RUN)
Difficulty: Class 2+
Length: 7 miles (11.2 km)

SKIPPERS BRIDGE TO DEEP CREEK (MIDDLE RUN)
Difficulty: Class 2–
Length: 4 miles (6.4 km)

DEEP CREEK TO ARTHURS POINT (LOWER RUN)
Difficulty: Class 4+
Length: 9 miles (14.4 km)

Season: November through March or after rains
Character: Deep gorge near popular resort area

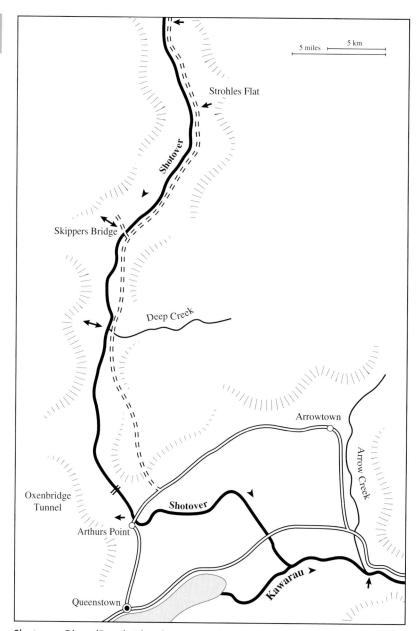

Shotover River (South Island, New Zealand)

Skippers Bridge is a popular platform for bungee jumping. The road follows far above the river on the left.

The rapids remain easy to the next access at Deep Creek. The best whitewater is downstream of Deep Creek as the road leaves the river canyon, not to return until Arthurs Point. Kayakers can find good action throughout this stretch. The major rapids are caused by huge stone slabs clogging the narrow streambed. The biggest are toward the end of the run. A stretch called Mother includes Shark's Fin, Anvil, Toilet, and Pinball rapids. At high flows this stretch is considerably more challenging, and the consequences of a swim are unpleasant to contemplate.

Just after the last major set of rapids including Jaws and Sequel, much of the river flows through the 557-foot (170 m) Oxenbridge Tunnel, a narrow drift just large enough for a kayak or raft. The product of three years of backbreaking toil by the Oxenbridge brothers, the tunnel is a much longer, narrower version of the same mining scheme used at Tunnel Chute rapid on the Middle Fork of California's American River. The concept is simple: divert the river through a ridge, and the dry streambed around the ridge is easy pickings for gold nuggets and dust. Apparently no one bothered to tell the Oxenbridge brothers that the riverbed had been worked previously during a particularly nasty winter, when the river froze in its upper reaches. One of the brothers took his life in disappointment, but the other later struck it rich farther upstream.

The Oxenbridge Tunnel cannot be run if flows are too high to accommodate your craft, so it's best to inquire locally to see if commercial companies are running it. If flows are accommodating, keep your craft straight and aim for the proverbial light at the end of the tunnel. At the exit the river tumbles down the outflow of the tunnel called Cascade. A dangerous weir to the left side, called the Toaster, has been modified to make it safe for boating, but is still best to avoid. Downstream from here, jet-boat use is heavy. Overall, the gradient on the Shotover ranges from 20 fpm (3.9 mpk) near the beginning to 80 fpm (15.5 mpk) near the end. At high flows, the river's original roundabout route to the left, sometimes called Mother-in-Law, is available.

The shuttle and access to put-ins for all three runs is on Skippers Canyon Road, a working monument to gold-rush-era tenacity and skills, and a memorial to the laborers who constructed it. The standard practice of New Zealand's rental car companies is to present customers with a map showing Skippers Canyon Road and to exact a written pledge not to drive it for fear that the vehicle will be damaged. The take-out is at the Cavell Bridge at Arthurs Point, just north of Queenstown. Below Arthurs Point, the Shotover winds down to meet the Kawarau River downstream of Queenstown.

Kawarau River ➢

The Kawarau River is the outflow of Lake Wakatipu, which usually supports big-volume flows in the range of 3,000 to 20,000 cfs (85 to 566 cumecs). The river starts about 5 miles (8 km) east of Queenstown and flows eastward. The uppermost 10-mile (16 km) run from the lake down to the confluences of the Arrow and Shotover rivers on the left is easy and seldom paddled. Downstream of the Arrow confluence, the Kawarau goes through a section called the Upper Kawarau Gorge. This is a popular half-day, 4-mile (6.4 km) run. Commercial boogie-board and rafting trips are popular here as well. Rapids include Smith Falls, with a big hole on the right, and Twin Bridges, where bungee jumpers often join in the fun. Below Twin Bridges is a section called Do Little, Do Nothing where kayakers can find good playspots. Lastly is the toughest drop, Chinese Dogleg, just upstream of the take-out.

The 14 miles (22.4 km) from Chinese Dogleg down to Natural Bridge and the beginning of the Roaring Meg section holds some easy water, but is interrupted by serious megarapids including the Nevis Bluff, a man-made maelstrom that was not run in its entirety at normal flows until 1990. Farther downstream, below the confluence of the Nevis River, are tough rapids named Citroen and Retrospect. The latter name is from a state-

ARROW RIVER TO BELOW CHINESE
DOGLEG
Difficulty: Class 4
Length: 4 miles (6.4 km)

NATURAL BRIDGE TO UPSTREAM
OF CLYDE RESERVOIR
(ROARING MEG SECTION)
Difficulty: Class 3
Length: 5 miles (8 km)

Season: November through
March
Character: Big-volume,
great play waves, several
sections

ment after the first descent to the effect that "In retrospect, it would have been better not to run it."

Below the unrunnable sieve called Natural Bridge is the Class 3 Roaring Meg section, named for the Roaring Meg River that enters from the left shortly below the put-in. This is a popular half-day commercial rafting trip and a good play section for kayaks. After about 5 miles (8 km) of big-water hydraulics, eddy lines, boils, and the biggest drop, Man Eater, the river empties into Clyde Reservoir.

◄ Buller River

LAKE ROTOITI TO IRON BRIDGE
DOWNSTREAM OF LYELL
Difficulty: Class 2 to 4
Length: 70 miles (112 km),
several half-day trips
popular

Season: October through
April
Character: Big-volume,
road close, many choices

The rivers of the west coast of New Zealand's South Island are still being prospected for whitewater gems, but a few, such as the Landsborough, Buller, and Karamea rivers, are already well known. The Buller drains a big, heavily forested drainage surrounded by mountains reaching over 6,000 feet (1,830 m). The area is wide open with plenty of options for paddlers of all skill levels. The Maori name is Kawatiri, believed to mean "fast and swift." The Buller is one of the last major free-flowing river systems in the country.

The Buller was first explored by Europeans in 1846 when an ill-prepared group under Thomas Brunner spent over three months in the gorge battling starvation. Today, the main road follows the river, allowing for a wide choice of runs. The river is now considered a popular, non-technical river, and its big-water waves and forgiving rapids make it a favorite with kayakers.

Boaters can put in as far upstream as the Buller Bridge at the Lake Rotoiti outlet for Class 3 rapids and take their choice of several access points down to Harley Rock Bridge (at Route 63), about 4.3 miles (7 km) downstream. One of the most popular stretches is through a very short upper canyon between the Gowan Bridge (at Route 6) and the Raits Road Bridge (at Route 6) or continuing on to the Owen River or Doctor's Creek confluences. Additional common access points are at the Mangles River confluence and at O'Sullivans bridge (at Route 65) below Murchison to below Ariki Falls. O'Sullivans Rapid near O'Sullivans Bridge is a popular kayak surfing rapid. Ariki Falls, set on an active earthquake fault, is considered the most challenging rapid on the Buller at Class 4+. The float down to the Iron Bridge just downstream of Lyell is also popular.

Downstream of the Iron Bridge, the lower Buller flows through an open, scenic valley as the whitewater fades. Eventually, the river empties into the ocean at Westport.

Many of the Buller's tributaries offer good paddling, including the Mangles, Matakitaki, Matiri, and Maruia rivers. Others include the Gowen, Owen, Inangahua, and Waitahu rivers. The Gowen, located between Lake Rotoroa and the Buller River, is the most popular of the Buller's tributaries.

◄ Clarence River

ACHERON BRIDGE TO CLARENCE
RIVER BRIDGE, JUST UPSTREAM
OF CLARENCE
Difficulty: Class 3
Length: 125 miles (200 km)

Season: October through
April
Character: Isolated, multi-
day

The Clarence, set in the northeastern corner of the South Island, offers the longest wilderness river trip in the Australasian region. It has become a classic, multi-day trip with fine scenery in a remote area and some decent whitewater in sections. A trip down the Clarence usually takes at least four days, as the river corridor provides some good camping. Temperatures can be severe on both extremes, making springtime the best boating season.

The described section passes between parallel Kaikoura mountain ranges, each topping 8,000 feet (2,440 m) in elevation. The river makes its way through a series of gorges and valleys, with the best Class 3 whitewater in Top Gorge in the upper reaches and in Sawtooth Gorge in the lower reaches. The vegetation in the upper reaches is somewhat barren, with mostly tussocks and grasses. The landscape gets more lush in the lower reaches. Braiding and upstream winds can make for tough going for rafts near the bottom.

The put-in is reached by going northeast of Hanmer Springs. The run ends where the river opens up just upstream of the town of Clarence and the ocean. The gradient averages 15 fpm (2.9 mpk).

Karamea River ➢

The Karamea begins at the foot of Mount Kendall in the 5,000-foot (1,525 m) to 6,000-foot (1,830 m) Tasman Mountains in the northwest corner of the South Island, and flows through Karamea National Park. This is a remote run that makes a great two- to three-day trip, although one-day runs are also possible. Some even extend the trip a couple of days by hiking to the put-in and having gear dropped by helicopter. The scenery throughout the area is inspiring, as are the rapids, many of which are the result of earthquake slides.

HELICOPTER FLY-IN POINT (KARAMEA BEND HUT OR VENUS CREEK HUT) TO CIVILIZATION UPSTREAM OF KARAMEA
Difficulty: Class 4+
Length: 24 miles (38.4 km) from Karamea Bend Hut, 38 miles (60.8 km) from Venus Creek Hut

Season: October through April
Character: Isolated, helicopter access necessary

Karamea River, New Zealand. *(© Dave Allardice/Ultimate Descents)*

The fly-in on the Karamea is worth the cost and effort. The river offers a fine wilderness setting, dramatic mountain scenery, boulder-strewn rapids, and fine cliff-lined gorges. Don't worry if flows seem skimpy at the top; the volume grows considerably in the downstream reaches. A trail follows the river on the right its whole length.

Logistical discussions about the Karamea and other fly-in rivers in New Zealand are usually couched in terms of "huts." Each hut is a spartan structure with a helicopter pad its most important amenity. Venus Creek Hut is the uppermost hut commonly used as a put-in, although launching farther upstream is possible. The next hut downstream is Crow Hut, followed by Karamea Bend Hut near the site of the first earthquake dam and the Leslie River confluence on the right. Most commercial rafting groups launch here. The whitewater to this point is mostly Class 3. However, downstream at Roaring Lion Hut, where the river of the same name enters on the right, a second big earthquake dam creates a suspiciously large lake; this leads to Class 4+ Roaring Lion Rapids, which are often portaged at no small effort. Farther down is Grey's Hut, located near a section of big rapids, the toughest drops being Growler and Holy Shit.

The river opens up about 5 miles (8 km) from the town of Karamea and the ocean. The overall gradient is 35 fpm (6.8 mpk). As with many other rivers in New Zealand, insect repellent and coverage are a good idea during sandfly season.

◄ Rangitata River

RANGITATA GORGE TO KLONDYKE DIVERSION DAM
Difficulty: Class 5–
Length: 8 miles (12.8 km)

KLONDYKE DIVERSION DAM TO PEEL FOREST
Difficulty: Class 2
Length: 7 miles (11.2 km)

Season: October through April
Character: In rain shadow, gorge through mountains in a sea of flatness

The Rangitata River flows east from the center of the South Island and drains glaciers on the eastern slope of the 9,000-foot (2,745 m) peaks of the Southern Alps. After flowing through an upper valley with characteristic highly braided channels, the otherwise unremarkable river cuts a wild course through a mountain of stubborn bedrock before opening up again and flowing onto the Canterbury Plain. Conveniently located between Christchurch and Queenstown, the Rangitata is developing a reputation as holding some of the most exciting commercially run whitewater on the island. Downstream is a popular but mellow float.

Put in for the Rangitata Gorge run from a gated trail where the gravel road that leads upstream around the gorge returns to the river. Along with some big rapids, this run often carries big-volume flows, especially if rains or warm temperatures cause glacial flows to surge. The biggest rapids include Glacier and Pencil Sharpener, followed closely by Tsunami at the entrance to the gorge. Rooster Tail is next, often considered the crux of the run. Just downstream is The Pinch, a series of the largest rapids; the entry is called Mouse Trap, the main drop Hell's Gate, and the exit rapid The Slot.

Right after leaving the gorge, a diversion dam diverts some of the water to the left for irrigation needs on the Canterbury Plain. This is the take-out for the gorge run. Downstream of the diversion dam the rapids ease, and boats can put in for a popular Class 2 float down to Peel Forest.

◄ Taieri River

PAERAU TO PATEAROA ROAD BRIDGE (UPPER GORGE RUN)
Difficulty: Class 4
Length: 12 miles 19.2 km)

(continued on following page)

Not all South Island rivers have lofty glacial beginnings. The Taieri drains a large low-lying area that includes the Great Moss Swamp on the southeastern part of the South Island. The headwaters are without any high peaks, and the entire drainage area is less than

3,000 feet (915 m) in elevation. As the drainage is dependent on rains, it is often too low to run by late summer.

The Taieri cuts through three dramatic gorges, each of which holds good rapids. The gradient is 50 fpm (9.7 mpk) in the upper gorge; 25 fpm (4.8 mpk) in the middle gorge; and 30 fpm (5.8 mpk) in the lower gorge . The upper gorge is remote, with warm water and technical rapids. Between the upper and middle gorges is a long swampy area. The middle gorge is on the top side of the Rock and Pillar Range, with the road and railroad sometimes near.

In the lower gorge section, from Sutton Stream to Outram, railroad tracks follow the river most of the way, and the Taieri Gorge Excursion Train is often available as a shuttle. Downstream of Mullocky Creek, the railroad tracks leave the river. The biggest whitewater is in the first several miles of the lower gorge, with rapids including Castle Hill (also known as Pump House), Hole in the Wall, and Boxcar, which is often considered the toughest. After Lee Stream enters on the right, it is an easy float down to Outram. Below Outram the river opens up into flat farmland. Jet boats use the last 7 miles (11.2 km) from where the challenging whitewater ends downstream to Outram. This run is near the city of Dunedin.

The origin of the river's name is unclear. It is apparently drawn either from the Maori words for "shining river" or "to smash, pound up, or pulp." The interpretation probably depends on whether you're having a good day or a bad day.

Landsborough River ➢

The Landsborough River is a wild, untouched run tumbling beneath glaciers and snow-covered peaks alongside silver beech and totara forests. It is considered one of the great wilderness runs of the world. The river drains 9,000-foot (2,745+ m) glacial peaks at its

KOKONGA TO NEAR HYDE
(MIDDLE GORGE RUN)
Difficulty: Class 3–
Length: 9 miles (14.4 km)

SUTTON STREAM TO OUTRAM
BRIDGE (LOWER GORGE RUN)
Difficulty: Class 3+
Length: 25 miles (40 km)

Season: October through March
Character: Long river with many different sections

HINDS FLAT TO HAAST HIGHWAY
AND HAAST RIVER
Difficulty: Class 4+
Length: 30 miles (48 km)

Season: November through March
Character: Alpine wilderness, helicopter fly-in necessary

Landsborough River (South Island, New Zealand)

headwaters in Mount Cook National Park and then makes its way south along the west slope of the Southern Alps. Named after Scottish explorer William Landsborough, it was known to the Maori as Otoatahi. Its upper reaches are part of the Hooker-Landsborough Wilderness, and the nearest roads are 30 miles (48 km) from the put-in. Reaching the put-in involves a dramatic fly-in into the high mountains. The whitewater is demanding, with gradients up to 125 fpm (24 mpk), averaging 50 fpm (9.7 mpk). A radio is recommended in the event of an emergency in this remote area. The possibility of flow surges due to upstream rains or heat-induced glacier melt should not be taken lightly, so check the forecasts before committing.

A common put-in is at Hinds Flat, near where the Dechen Glacier approaches the river from the west. It is also possible to launch about 4 miles (6.4 km) farther downstream at Kea Flat. Another 4 miles (6.4 km) downstream of Hinds Flat is another popular access point, Toe Toe Flat. About 4 miles (6.4 km) farther downstream is Fraser Hut, a popular overnight spot.

The best rapids begin about 2 miles (3.2 km) downstream of Fraser Hut in Upper Gates and Lower Gates gorges, and all can be portaged if necessary. They include Hunt's Hole, Squeeze, and the most difficult, Hellfire, a collection of boulders and sieves. Near the bottom is Surprise Corner, followed by Billy the Maori. The river shortly enters Lower Gates Gorge, with easier whitewater. Below Lower Gates Gorge the river opens up into Landsborough Valley, and the Clarke River enters on the right. This is about 9 miles (14.4 km) downstream of the Upper Gates Gorge entrance. From here, it is an easy float down to the main highway and civilization. In this last section the river is heavily braided.

Afterword

Our Role in Conserving and Restoring Whitewater Rivers

Rich Bowers

*I*n most guidebooks and river anthologies, the conservation section focuses on threats to the river's well-being—for good reason, as every river in every country (whitewater or not) seems to be under some form of threat or danger, usually on a continuous and ever-changing basis.

You have read about these threats in *World Whitewater*, as it is impossible to understand a river's individual personality without a good grasp of the issues surrounding it (especially one you may never have seen or paddled). But hearing about threats is not enough. Boaters and other river users need to fully comprehend the economic, political, biological, and increasingly recreational relationships that link rivers the world over. More importantly, it is crucial that boaters come to understand the changing role they play in rivers today, and their new-found and very real ability—and responsibility—to change the course of rivers for future generations.

This may sound slightly grandiose, especially for those who do not care to understand whitewater boating or who perceive all outdoor recreation as elitist sports . . . as only fun . . . as risk . . . or all too often as merely a dangerous waste of time. But for those who understand the sport, who consider it a lifestyle and a passion, there is a real opportunity to change how rivers are understood, treated, developed, or conserved.

This opportunity has been created by changes in economic values and dependency; the growing number of participants in outdoor and river recreation (in combination with visibly diminished resources); and the creation of coalitions. From a more global perspective, recreational change comes also from an improving standard of living and the simultaneous and growing disparity between those who can enjoy this standard, and those who cannot.

However, it is not enough to just recognize this opportunity. Paddlers must understand it, embrace it, and run with it, as this position may prove to have only a short window of opportunity in the historical flow of rivers.

For each of us who spend time on rivers, paddling, fishing, or just living alongside the water, there is an intimate relationship and understanding. Outdoor users, especially whitewater boaters, are an important part of this, spending time weekly, often daily on rivers—and not just one river, but paddling rivers everywhere and in all corners of the globe. This knowledge, this understanding of the link between recreation, water quality, beauty, and all the other advantages that our rivers provide, will be critical information if we expect to play a part in how others view our river resources.

The goal of this book is more than just to broaden your knowledge of rivers, or to help plan for new runs and river trips. While each of these is important, the real goal is to empower those who love rivers to share this knowledge and understanding with others.

Today, individuals, local communities, and global corporations all understand that rivers mean money, power, and life. In the future, I hope everyone will also appreciate the beauty of surfing a wave, running through wilderness, traveling to unknown places, or just watching water flow over rock. But it will be up to those with experience to lead the way, and what better leaders than those who understand and enjoy whitewater, representing some of the world's wildest, most dramatic, and most beautiful rivers!

Changes in Economic Values and Dependency

Throughout history, our relationship and economic dependency with rivers has been driven by the need for safety, drinking water, transportation, irrigation, and power.

Today, this relationship continues. Just look at the headlines, and you can see that, even with the tremendous growth in technology, the changing of borders, and the changing of governments and major powers, the role of rivers as boundaries continues. Recent political tensions between Israel and Jordan, Turkey and her neighbors, and many other countries document this issue on an almost daily basis.

But new trends are also developing that will change the way we look at rivers. In developed countries, such as those in Europe, North America, and Asia, most of the rivers that can produce economically viable hydropower have already been developed (see McCully, *Silenced Rivers*), and changes in power reserves and environmental laws have made almost all future small-dam construction uneconomical. This trend has caused two reactions. First, it has virtually eliminated the threat of new dams for hydropower in the United States, although dams for other needs, like water supply, threaten many rivers including whitewater runs from California's Mokelumne (the just-defeated Devils Nose Project) to Tennessee's Emory-Obed system. And second, it has sent the power developers off in search of new sites that will produce larger profits and are unprotected by strong and enforceable environmental regulations.

Changing Economics for Dams

Since whitewater and power production both seek rivers with speed and gradient, no form of development has been more detrimental to whitewater rivers than hydropower dams.

While the first dams may have been built for irrigation in Mesopotamia over 8,000 years ago, it wasn't until the recent beginning of the industrial revolution that large-scale dam building began in earnest, with the motivation of obtaining cheap and dependable power. In 1832, the first water turbine was developed, and in 1882, fifty years later, the world's first hydro plant began producing power in Appleton, Wisconsin. By 1900, Britain had almost as many large dams as the rest of the world put together, and dam building in the United States was also in full swing. Today, there are over 40,000 large dams on the world's rivers, all but 5,000 of them built since 1950, and another 800,000 small dams. But just as important as the need for power, the era of dams also began with individuals and companies who saw an opportunity to conquer nature, to prove the ingenuity of man, and to make big profits.

Many of these dams are now considered historic sites, and dam proponents claim these to be monuments to human engineering. And in many ways, they are. If you have the opportunity to walk through these dams, you cannot help but be impressed that human labor was able to create them. Many were built by pouring, building, and shaping the dams and powerhouses by hand.

However, if you love rivers, it is impossible not to realize (after a century of evidence) the true cost of technology on the aesthetic, chemical, recreational, and biological aspects of rivers, and on the impacts that these dams have had on the fish, wildlife, and humans that depend on them. When looking at these marvels of engineering, it is equally impossible not to look away from the dam and wonder what canyons, rapids, and rivers exist under the impoundment. Or why some dams, with energy conservation techniques and new renewable energy sources, cannot be removed and the natural river restored.

Today, the power of economics is changing once again with the deregulation of the power industry in the United States and just completed in Chile. What this will mean for rivers and recreation is not yet clear. But deregulation (for homes and businesses, the ability to buy power at the best price from numerous and often remote suppliers) was never conceived to conserve or restore rivers. It is simply and purely an economic issue. As consumers, we may save money on our electrical bills, and we may even eliminate some small uneconomical dams, but deregulation will produce larger, better-consolidated, and more powerful energy companies—companies with the resources and technology to operate on a global scale, and who, in the long term, will destroy even more rivers.

Dams in underdeveloped countries pose a serious threat to some of the world's greatest whitewater rivers, including the Reventazon, Pacuare, and others in Costa Rica, the Pangue Dam on the Bio-Bio in Chile, and on one of the world's last great unexplored regions, the Yangtze in China. These rivers are threatened because of the need to develop more power, but even more so because the need to conquer nature, to prove the ingenuity of man, and to make big profits, still exists.

Growing Participation in Outdoor and River Recreation

Recreation is becoming ever more important in rural areas, where even small numbers of boaters can make a big difference to the local economy. Maryland's Upper Youghiogheny supports a modest amount of both private and commercial boaters, bringing an estimated $2 million into Garrett County and nearby communities. The National Kayak Center on the St. Louis River in Minnesota has generated approximately $1.25 million from 1986 to 1993. On the Russell Fork, straddling the border between Virginia and Kentucky, four weekends of whitewater each October and about a thousand boaters total have created a strong relationship between recreationists and local businesses. In fact, whitewater is so important in this area that the U.S. Army Corps of Engineers is proposing to build a new dam on the Levisa Fork (upstream of the whitewater run) which includes increased storage for additional whitewater releases. Unfortunately, the Corps forgot to ask boating organizations if they wanted a dam and the destruction of another 11 miles of free-flowing waterway, and many groups are now actively opposing this proposal.

As with most issues, there is both an upside and a downside to increased recreation. While more users may provide a stronger constituency for rivers, this is little solace to someone who finds his favorite stream suddenly overrun by hordes of others. This growing problem is causing increased friction on many rivers. It can be seen between anglers and boaters on Connecticut's Housatonic River and Maine's Rapid River, between local landowners and recreational users on the West Branch of the Chattooga in South Carolina and almost every river in Great Britain, and even between commercial and noncommercial boaters on the Grand Canyon's Colorado River and the Gauley River in West Virginia.

As standards of living increase in many areas of the globe, and as the world shrinks through travel and better communications, undeveloped countries are also seeing increased recreation. In many third world countries, the economic benefits of recreation are less visible, and the differences between perceptions, cultures, and affluence are even greater. But even here, recreation economics can supply yet another weapon to save rivers. For instance, whitewater and tourism played an active part in halting, at least temporarily, ENDESAS construction of hydropower dams on Chile's Futaleufu, and each played a part in saving the Franklin River in southwestern Tasmania.

And changes are also taking place even within recreation. For years, recreation on rivers had been limited to upstream use on lakes and impoundments, primarily fishing, swimming, wading, and powerboating and sailboating. This emphasis has often been used by developers and recreationists alike as yet another reason for damming rivers. In the United States, this has resulted in the development of an estimated 2,100 man-made lakes and reservoirs owned or managed just by the federal government, and more than 400,000 square kilometers have been inundated by reservoirs worldwide. More recently, however, recreationists, agencies, and local communities have increased the attention given to downstream river recreation including whitewater, fishing, hiking, and climbing. This change within recreation has also revamped the economic worth of free-flowing rivers, and has brought a new balance between the need to protect lake levels and the need to return natural flow to rivers.

Perhaps the greatest example of how recreation can revise economics can be seen in the United States through the stronger terms being required for both recreation and conservation at existing private hydropower dams. In the last few years, individual boaters, whitewater clubs, and others have succeeded in demonstrating the importance of whitewater economics, and in doing so have improved river flows on multiple sections of the Deerfield River in Massachusetts, the Pemigewasset in New Hampshire, on the Black and Beaver rivers in New York, the St. Louis River in Minnesota, Little Quinessec Falls on Wisconsin's Menominee River, the Kern River in California, the Coosa in Alabama, and on other whitewater rivers. Perhaps more importantly, these same groups have opened up many sections of rivers that have been dewatered and off-limits for almost a century, rivers such as the Tallulah in Georgia, the Nisqually in Washington state, and on the Middle Fork Feather in California—rivers so new to recreation that they appear in no guidebooks to date.

Recreation and Conservation: The Need for Coalitions

Unfortunately, the ability to legally intervene in hydro licenses is restricted to the United States, and even here it does not offer a solution to improving recreation on rivers affected by irrigation, flood control, or water supply.

But what the dam license renewal process does offer is a very important example, not just of how to improve recreation, but also of how boaters and other outdoor recreationists can make a real difference in river conservation everywhere.

Because whitewater often needs the same style of river that power developers seek (usually wild and moving downhill), paddlers in the United States were some of the first to recognize how license terms for dams could protect rivers, and how a federal license could be leveraged to protect and restore flows beneficial to boaters, anglers, and the river environment. But boaters were also aware that this process was long, technical, and highly legalistic, and that, by themselves, they had no chance to beat power brokers at their own game. So early in the late 1980s boaters began to look for others to help them out.

Organized coalitions began to form, including conservation organizations, state and federal agencies, and, more and more often, local river communities and landowners. Coalitions allowed small groups and individuals to pool resources, to speak in unity about rivers, and to learn to respect each other's needs and wants. Combining resources and a vision for rivers proved a valuable tool in offsetting the limited argument for more power at any cost, and promoted a more diversified image of rivers to the public.

Today, groups such as the national Hydropower Reform Coalition and the California Hydropower Reform Coalition have effectively merged river recreation and conservation efforts and dramatically improved rivers. In 1997 the Deerfield agreement, one of the largest river relicensing settlements ever completed, provided flow to previously dewatered segments (flatwater and whitewater alike) of the Deerfield River in Massachusetts, created a $100,000 river enhancement fund, and installed conservation restrictions on over 18,000 acres of riverside land. On other rivers, recreation and conservation coalitions produced similar victories for public access, better water quality, and improved fish passage.

These coalitions have also begun to change how the public views dams, and have been successful in demonstrating that a dam whose value has diminished or whose environmental costs have become too high can be removed. Over the last two years in the United States, these coalitions have made significant progress in eventually removing the Elwha and Glines Canyon dams in Washington state, the Condit Dam on Washington's White Salmon River, Edwards Dam on Maine's lower Penobscot, and the Newport Dam on Vermont's Clyde River (which collapsed under high spring run-off).

While other countries do not have limited license terms for dams, the use of coalitions can still help save rivers, and boaters should continue to support these efforts. The issues affecting all outdoor recreationists (enjoyment, access, safety, and liability) create a perfect reason for climbers, hikers, bikers, anglers and others to work in unison. Outdoor recreation's reliance on natural resources provides a great reason to link with conservation groups and those who live along rivers. These coalitions have already been formed at home, but the opportunity exists to expand these coalitions and to create worldwide efforts to improve rivers. Combining resources and a vision for rivers is the only way we can truly be effective in offsetting the political and financial resources available to large development companies and multinational corporations.

What Does the Future Hold?

Like the course of a wild river, the future is totally unpredictable. But we can look at lessons already learned—upcoming issues and trends—and make an educated guess at where we should (or should not) be standing when the river starts running. This is especially true of those nations and communities where river development is just now beginning.

If we can band together, put aside the polarization that often follows river efforts (including the ridiculous, worldwide, and often continuous bickering between boaters and anglers), and build a strong economic argument for conservation and recreation, we may have a chance to offset future destruction and restore those rivers degraded in the past.

And future coalitions will need to be far broader than just river conservation and recreation groups. If we are to avoid having rivers return to providing only water, transportation, power, and survival, we will need to find a way to tackle large problems like population control and global and sustainable power. For these issues, we need coalitions that include governments and even those large companies we may oppose today.

For those who are interested in paddling a favorite river, this may seem an impossible and perhaps unnecessary level of commitment. But boaters can get this moving within our own sport, and along the rivers and streams we paddle. We can start by building coalitions among our friends and others who enjoy rivers. Boaters know who these people are; we see them every day!

Rich Bowers is the Executive Director for American Whitewater, a national recreation and river conservation organization representing over 6,000 individual whitewater boaters and 100 affiliated clubs in the United States. Organized in 1957, American Whitewater's mission is to conserve and restore America's whitewater resources and to enhance opportunities to enjoy them safely. Prior to being elected Executive Director, Rich had been American Whitewater's Conservation and Hydropower Program Director since 1992.

Resources

Books

Alaska Geographic Society. *The Stikine River.* Edmonds, WA: Alaska Geographic Society, 1979.

Appalachian Whitewater, vols. 1–3. Birmingham, AL: Menasha Ridge Press, 1987.

Barrow, Pope. *Nationwide Whitewater Inventory: A Geographic Information System for Whitewater Rivers in the United States.* American Whitewater, 1992.

Bolling, David M. *How to Save a River: A Handbook for Citizen Action.* Washington, DC: Island Press, 1994.

Bowermaster, Jon. "The Colca Plunge." *Summit Magazine,* fall 1994.

Callan, Kevin. *Up the Creek: A Paddler's Guide to Ontario.* Erin, ON: Boston Mills Press, 1996.

Cassady, Jim, Bill Cross, and Fryar Calhoun. *Western Whitewater: From the Rockies to the Pacific: A River Guide for Raft, Kayak, and Canoe.* Berkeley, CA: North Fork Press, 1994 (available from Pacific River Supply).

Charles, Graham. *New Zealand Whitewater.* Nelson, New Zealand: Craig Potton Publishing, 1996.

Davidson, Paul, Ward Eister, and Dirk Davidson. *Wildwater West Virginia,* vols. 1 and 2. Hillsborough, NC: Menasha Ridge Press, 1985.

Dawson, Simon. *Corsica White Water.* Oxford, UK: T. Storry, Pound House, Woodeaton.

Echeverria, John D., Pope Barrow, and Richard Roos-Collins. *Rivers at Risk: The Concerned Citizen's Guide to Hydropower.* Washington, DC: Island Press, 1989.

Embick, Andrew. *Fast and Cold: A Guide to Alaska Whitewater.* Valdez, AK: Valdez Alpine Books, 1994.

Fisher, Richard D. *Copper Canyon.* Tucson, AZ: Sunracer Publications, 1994.

———. *Earth's Mystical Grand Canyons.* Tucson, AZ: Sunracer Publications, 1995.

Flakstad, Nils, and Leif Ongstad. *Whitewater Canoeing: Guide to Southern Norway.* Norway: Norges Kajakk- og Kanoforbund, 1987.

Foss, John. *The Whitewater Rivers of Chile.* Boulder, CO: Blue Sky Press, 1998.

Fox, Alan. *Run River Run.* London: Diadem Books, 1990.

Gavrilov, Vladimir. "Rivers of an Unknown Land: The Best Whitewater in the Former Soviet Union." Rocklin, CA; unpublished.

Great American Rivers Flip Maps. Birmingham, AL: Menasha Ridge Press, 1989.

Hargreaves, Jim. *Ottawa River Whitewater.* Quebec: Cascades Press, 1998.

Harrington, Richard. *River Rafting in Canada.* Edmonds, WA: Alaska Northwest Publishing, 1987.

Hartling, Neil. *Nahanni: River of Gold . . . River of Dreams.* Hyde Park, ON: Canadian Recreational Canoeing Association, 1993.

Hass, Josef. *Gems of the High Alps.* Konstanz, Germany: Rosgarten Verlag/Sudkurier, 1990.

Hibbard, Andrew. *Honduras: A Whitewater River Guide.* Ventura, CA: 1996.

Holbek, Lars. *The Rivers of Chile.* Silver Spring, MD: American Whitewater, 1992.

Jettmar, Karen. *The Alaska River Guide: Canoeing, Kayaking, and Rafting in the Last Frontier.* Anchorage, Alaska: Northwest Books, 1993.

Jowett, Peter. *Nahanni: The River Guide.* Calgary, AB: Rocky Mountain Books, 1993.

Kane, Joe. "Roaring through the Colca Canyon." *National Geographic Magazine,* Jan. 1993.

———. *Running the Amazon.* New York: Vintage Books, 1990.

Kennon, Tom. *Ozark Whitewater: A Paddler's Guide to the Mountain Streams of Arkansas and Missouri.* Birmingham, AL: Menasha Ridge Press, 1989.

Knowles, Peter. *White Water Europe,* 2 vols. Surrey, UK: Rivers Publishing, 1996.

————, and Dave Allardice. *White Water Nepal: A Rivers Guidebook for Rafting and Kayaking.* Birmingham, AL: Menasha Ridge Press, 1997.

Mayfield, Michael W., and Rafael E. Gallo. *The Rivers of Costa Rica: A Canoeing, Kayaking, and Rafting Guide.* Birmingham, AL: Menasha Ridge Press, 1988.

McCully, Patrick. *Silenced Rivers: The Ecology and Politics of Large Dams.* Atlantic Highlands, NJ: Zed Books, 1996.

McLaughlin, Chris and Yvonne. *The Rivers and Lakes of Victoria, New South Wales, Queensland,* 3 vols. Hampton, Australia; Macstyle, 1989–91.

McRae, Micahel. "Wilderness Rafting Siberian Style." *National Geographic,* Nov. 1997.

Nealy, William. *Whitewater Home Companion: Southeastern Rivers,* vols. 1 and 2. Birmingham, AL: Dolly Ridge Press, 1981.

Paddle about Tasmania, Australia. Tasmanian Canoe Association, 1984.

Palzer, Bob, and Jody Palzer. *Whitewater, Quietwater: A Guide to the Rivers of Wisconsin, Upper Michigan, and N.E. Minnesota.* Lake Mills, WI: Rural Life Press, 1973.

Pratt-Johnson, Betty. *Whitewater Trips for Kayakers, Canoeists, and Rafters in British Columbia: Greater Vancouver through Whistler, Okanagan, and Thompson River Regions.* Seattle: Pacific Search Press, 1986.

Rivers, Trails, and Conservation Assistance Program. *River Renewal, Restoring Rivers through Hydropower Dam Relicensing.* National Park Service and American Rivers, May 1996.

Robbins, Tom. "An Adventure in Meat." In *Paths Less Traveled.* New York: Macmillan, 1988.

Robey, Tom. *Gringo's Guide to Mexican Whitewater.* Albuquerque, NM: Heritage Associates, 1992.

Smith, Stuart. *Canadian Rockies Whitewater,* 2 vols. Jasper, AB: Headwaters Press, 1996.

Upper Delaware Council. *Visitor Information Map and Guide for Touring the Upper Delaware Scenic and Recreational River, New York and Pennsylvania: A Map and Guide with Information on Recreation, Safety, Restaurants, Accommodations, and More.* Narrowsburg, NY: Upper Delaware Council, 1998.

Walbridge, Charles, and Wayne A. Sundmacher Sr. *Whitewater Rescue Manual: New Techniques for Canoeists, Kayakers, and Rafters.* Camden, ME: Ragged Mountain Press, 1995.

Wright, Richard, and Rochelle Wright. *Canoe Routes: British Columbia.* Surrey, BC: Antonson, 1977.

River Conservation Organizations

AMERICAN RIVERS, INC.
1025 Vermont Avenue, NW
Suite 720
Washington, DC 20005
202-347-7550
800-296-6900
www.amrivers.org

AMERICAN WHITEWATER (AWA)
P.O. Box 636
Margaretville, NY 12455
914-586-2355
Fax 914-586-3050
E-mail: RichB@amwhitewater.org
www.awa.org

FRIENDS OF THE RIVER
916 20th Street
Sacramento, CA 95814
916-442-3155

INTERNATIONAL RIVERS NETWORK
1847 Berkeley Way
Berkeley, CA 94703
510-848-1155

RIVER NETWORK
P.O. Box 8787
Portland, OR 97207
503-241-3506

Other Sources

MAP LINK
30 S. La Patera Lane #5
Santa Barbara, CA 93117
805-692-6777
800-962-1394

PACIFIC RIVER SUPPLY
3675 San Pablo Dam Road
El Sobrante, CA 94803
510-223-3675

Index

Photo Sources

Adrift/River Journeys
Worldwide
P.O. Box 310
Queenstown, New Zealand
64 (0)3 442-5458
fax 64 (0)3 443-5950
E-mail: raft@adrift.co.nz
http://www.adrift.co.nz

Adventure World
Freizeit Aktiv AG
Postfach [P.O. Box] 645
CH-3800 Interlaken
Switzerland
0041 (0)33 826 77 11
fax 0041 (0)33 826 77 15
E-mail: adventure.world@
 spectraweb.ch
http://www.adventureworld.
 com

Alaska Vistas
P.O. Box 2245
Wrangell, AK 99929
907-874-2429
fax 907-874-3006
E-mail: info@alaskavistas.com
http://www.alaskavistas.com

Alternatif Turizm Ltd.
fax 90-252-413-32-08
E-mail: alternatif@
 superonline.com
http://www.alternatifraft.com

Aventuras Naturales
E-mail: avenat@sol.racsa.co.cr
http://www.toenjoynature.com
U.S.A.:
 SJO 745
 P.O. Box 025216
 Miami, FL 33102-5216
 fax 506-253-6934
Costa Rica:
 P.O. Box 10736-1000
 San Jose, Costa Rica
 506-225-3939/224-0505
 fax 506-253-6934

Bio Bio Expeditions Worldwide
P.O. Box 2028
Truckee, CA 96160
800-2GO-RAFT (246-7238)
fax 916-582-6865
E-mail: H2Omarc@aol.com;
 LarsAlvarez@compuserve.
 com
http://www.bbxrafting.com

Discover Fiji Tours
P.O. Box 171
Navua, Fiji Islands
679-450-180
fax 011-679-450-540

Earth River Expeditions
180 Towpath Rd.
Accord, NY 12404

Madawaska Kanu Centre
Summer:
 Box 635
 Barry's Bay, Ontario
 Canada K0J 1B0
 613-756-3620
 fax: 613-234-4097
Winter:
 39 First Ave.
 Ottawa, Ontario
 Canada K1S 2G1
 613-594-KANU
E-mail: whitewater@
 owl-mkc.ca
http://fox.nstn.ca:80/~owlmkc

Pacific River Supply
3675 San Pablo Dam Road
El Sobrante, CA 94803
510-223-3675
fax 800-551-6067;
 510-223-3346

River Run Paddling Centre
P.O. Box 179
Beachburg, Ontario
Canada K0J 1C0
800-267-8504; 613-646-2501
fax 613-646-2958
E-mail: riverrun@renc.igs.net
http://www.riverrunners.com

Russell Fork Expeditions, Inc.
P.O. Box 37
Shady Valley, TN 37688
1-800-THE-FORK
fax 423-739-9421
E-mail: thefork@preferred.com

Safaris Corobici, S.A.
Aptdo. 99-5700
Cañas, Guanacaste
Costa Rica
fax and ph. 506-669-1091
E-mail: Safaris@sol.racsa.co.cr
http://www.nicoya.com

Veraventuras
Santos Degollado #81 int. 8
C.P. 91000
Xalapa Veracruz
Mexico
28-18-9579
fax 28-18-9680
E-mail: veraventuras@
 yahoo.com
http://www.dpc.com.mx/
 Veraventuras

Whitewater Challengers, Inc.
P.O. Box 8
White Haven, PA 18661
fax 570-443-9727

The Wilderness Echo Company
6529 Telegraph Ave.
Oakland, CA 94609-1113
800-652-ECHO (3246);
 510-652-1600
fax 510-652-3987
E-mail: echo@echotrips.com
http://www.echotrips.com